Rodale's Pest & Disease Problem Solver

A Chemical-Free Guide to Keeping Your Garden Healthy

Linda Gilkeson
Pam Peirce
Miranda Smith

Rodale Press, Inc.
Emmaus, Pennsylvania

OUR MISSION

We publish books that empower people's lives.

RODALE BOOKS

If you have any questions or comments concerning
this book, please write to:

Rodale Press, Inc.
Book Readers' Service
33 East Minor Street
Emmaus, PA 18098

Lansdowne Publishing Staff:
Managing Director: Jane Curry
Publishing Manager: Deborah Nixon
Production Manager: Sally Stokes
Editor/Project Coordinator: Jenny Coren
Layouts: Sylvie Abecassis

Rodale Press Staff:
Managing Editor, Garden Books: Ellen Phillips
Senior Associate Editor: Nancy J. Ondra
Associate Editors: Deborah L. Martin, Jean M. A. Nick
Copy Editor: Sarah Dunn
Vice President and Editorial Director,
    Home and Garden: Margaret Lydic Balitas
Copy Director, Home and Garden: Dolores Plikaitis
Art Director, Home and Garden: Michael Mandarano

Library of Congress Cataloging-in-Publication Data

Gilkeson, Linda A.
    Rodale's pest and disease problem solver: a
chemical–free guide to keeping your garden healthy
/ Linda Gilkeson, Pam Peirce, Miranda Smith.
        p.   cm.
    Includes bibliographical references and index.
    ISBN 0–87596–705–1 (hardcover: alk. paper)
    1. Garden pests—Control—Handbooks, manuals,
etc.   2. Plant diseases—Handbooks, manuals, etc.
4. Plants, Protection of—Handbooks, manuals, etc.
I. Peirce, Pam. II. Smith, Miranda, III. Title.
SB974.G54   1996
635'.04996—dc20   95–30429

Distributed in the book trade by St. Martin's Press

2 4 6 8 10 9 7 5 3   hardcover

Contents

How To Use This Book   **6**

WHAT'S MY PROBLEM?

A plant-by-plant guide to common problems arranged by symptom, with descriptions of the symptom, possible causes, and prevention and cures for each.

Plants A to Z
Vegetables   **8**
Herbs   **60**
Fruits and Nuts   **68**
Annuals   **104**
Perennials   **126**
Bulbs   **157**
Trees, Shrubs, and Vines   **168**
Lawns   **237**

WHAT GARDEN PEST OR DISEASE IS THAT?

A field guide to more than 100 pests, diseases, and disorders, with descriptions, plants attacked, and prevention and controls for each.

All About Pests   **242**
Pests A to Z   **244**

All About Diseases   **299**
Diseases A to Z   **300**

Disorders: When is A Disease Not A Disease?   **334**
Disorders A to Z   **335**

THE HEALTHY GARDEN

A guide to planting and maintaining a healthy garden using organic techniques.

Building Healthy Soil   342
Buying Healthy Plants   345
Preventing Pests and Diseases   347
Controlling Pests and Diseases   353

WHERE'S THAT PEST OR DISEASE?

A regional guide to the most troublesome pests and diseases.

Where's That Pest?   364
Where's That Disease?   366

USDA Plant Hardiness Zone Map   368
Recommended Reading   369
Resources   370
Photography Credits   371
About the Authors   372
Index   373

HOW TO USE THIS BOOK

R odale's Pest and Disease Problem Solver is the most effective tool you can use to keep pests and diseases from ruining your beautiful garden. By using the quick reference features and up-to-date solutions in this book, you will be able to identify dozens of common pests, diseases, and disorders (such as nutrient deficiencies) and learn how to keep them from damaging your plants. It's easy, because Rodale's Pest and Disease Problem Solver is so simple to use.

First, look up the plant under attack in "What's My Problem?" starting on page 8. In this section, you'll find over 100 vegetables, herbs, fruits and nuts, flowers, trees and shrubs, and even lawns, with their most common problems, possible causes, and prevention and control strategies. Skim through the symptoms under your plant until you find the one that matches your problem. Jot down the possible causes. Then turn to "Where's That Pest or Disease?" beginning on page 364 to see which problems are most likely to strike in your area.

Next, look up each pest, disease, or disorder in "What Garden Pest or Disease Is That?" on page 242. This section is a field guide to more than 100 of the worst pests, diseases, and disorders in the United States. For each entry, you'll find a color photo, description, plants most likely to be attacked, and prevention or control advice. The descriptions are easy

to understand—no plowing through tons of technical jargon—and the organic controls are up-to-the-minute. You won't find any dangerous, toxic, or outdated controls recommended in Rodale's Pest and Disease Problem Solver.

It's important to remember that problem-free plants start with a healthy garden. You'll learn how to keep your plants thriving and trouble-free in "The Healthy Garden" on page 342. From building great soil to buying healthy plants, you'll find the basics of good organic gardening. You'll learn more about preventing problems through practices like companion planting. And you'll find everything you need to choose and use all the best controls, including beneficial insects, traps and barriers, biocontrols, and sprays and dusts.

Special features make Rodale's Pest and Disease Problem Solver even more useful. Each plant entry in the "What's My Problem?" section features an "At-a-Glance" box with plant descriptions and growing guidelines. Resistant cultivars are listed whenever they're available, so you can by-pass problems from the beginning. "Resources" on page 370 tells you where to go to get plants and organic controls. And throughout the book, color photos make it supereasy to identify a problem and apply the right control.

Say goodbye to problems—and hello to Rodale's Pest and Disease Problem Solver.

What's My Problem?

A plant-by-plant guide to common problems arranged by symptom, with descriptions of the symptom, possible causes, and prevention and cures for each.

VEGETABLES

Most Common Vegetable Pests

Symptom: Leaves curled, puckered, and
           sticky
Cause: **Aphids**

Aphids are $\frac{1}{16}$–$\frac{3}{8}$-inch-long, pear-shaped
insects, usually found in clusters on growing
tips and undersides of leaves. Most species drip
a sticky honeydew onto leaves as they feed.
Wash aphids from plants with a strong stream
of water, repeating every few days as necessary,
or spray insecticidal soap, neem, or pyrethrins.

Symptom: Seedlings and transplants cut off
           or girdled at soil level
Cause: **Cutworms**

During the day, search for fat, greasy-looking,
gray caterpillars hiding in the soil around the
base of damaged plants, or go out at night
with a flashlight to catch feeding cutworms.
Where infestations are severe, drench soil with
neem or a solution of parasitic nematodes, or
sprinkle a bran bait mixed with *Bacillus
thuringiensis* var. *kurstaki* (BTK) on the soil

before planting. Spray plants with neem to
control climbing cutworms. Planting later also
avoids the main generation of cutworms. To
prevent problems, always use cutworm collars
around transplants and seedlings.

Symptom: Holes in leaves; slime trails
           present
Cause: **Slugs**

Maintain permanent walkways of clover, sod, or
stone mulches to harbor natural predators.
Edge garden beds with copper flashing or
screening, first making sure you remove all slugs
from the enclosed area. Set out slug traps
(boards, grapefruit rinds, or commercial traps),
check daily, and destroy accumulated slugs. For
light infestations, spread a wide band of cinders,
wood ashes, or diatomaceous earth around
plants, renewing after each rain. Protect small
plants with floating row covers, well secured at
the edges, until they are well grown.

Symptom: Large holes in leaves or leaves
           skeletonized
Cause: **Japanese beetles**

Look for blue-green beetles, $\frac{1}{2}$ inch long, with
bronze wingcovers. Go out early in the
morning and knock them from the plants into
a bucket of soapy water or onto a ground
sheet, and destroy them. In light infestations,
handpick or vacuum up beetles. Protect plants
with screens or floating row covers, particularly in midsummer when beetle numbers are
at their highest.

Symptom: Light yellow speckles on leaves
Cause: **Spider mites**

Tiny ($\frac{1}{50}$ inch long) mites may be visible on fine
webs on the undersides of leaves. Spider mites

are most damaging in hot, dry weather and where natural enemies have been destroyed by sulfur or other pesticides. For light infestations, spray foliage with water or insecticidal soap. For heavy infestations, which cause leaf edges to curl, turn brown, and dry up, spray neem or summer oil. Release predatory mites such as *Metaseiulus occidentalis* or other species adapted to the local climate. Plan to spray lime sulfur in late winter.

Symptom: Puckered and scarred foliage, pods, or fruit
Cause: **Tarnished plant bugs**

Plant bug feeding injury causes pits, scars, and distortions of plant tissue. Pods are misshapen and fruit may be "catfaced." In heavy infestations losses occur because flowers drop without fruiting. These ¼-inch-long, agile bugs are difficult to control with sprays because they flee so quickly. Control weeds around garden beds to reduce host plants. For heavy infestations, spray pyrethrins or summer oil on plants that tolerate it. Cover small plants with floating row covers to prevent bugs from reaching plants.

Most Common Vegetable Diseases

Symptom: Plants wilt in midday sun
Cause: **Root knot nematodes**

Suspect these microscopic worms if you find hard, irregular galls on the roots of affected plants. Pull and destroy severely stunted plants, and give remaining plants the best of care because they may still produce a small crop. Dig in chitosan (a natural polymer derived from the chitin components of crab and shrimp shells), or drench soil with neem. In warm regions, soil solarization suppresses nematodes in the top layer of soil. In some soils, digging in green manure crops also suppresses nematodes. Practice a 3- to 5-year rotation with crops that aren't susceptible (such as corn and onions). Grow resistant cultivars where they are available.

Symptom: Grayish, fuzzy growth on leaves and pods
Cause: **Botrytis**

Once established on a plant, botrytis spreads rapidly. On leaves, stems, and fruit, the first signs of botrytis are tiny, water-soaked spots that enlarge, become light brown, and crack open, producing gray mold. Botrytis enters plants through wounds, bruises, and dying tissue. For controls see "Botrytis Blight" on page 305.

Symptom: Reddish brown or black pustules on leaf undersides and pods
Cause: **Rust (several fungal species)**

To prevent rust, grow resistant or tolerant cultivars. For controls see "Rust" on page 327.

Symptoms: Yellow lesions on upper leaf surfaces; purple to gray mold on leaf undersides
Cause: **Downy mildew**

Downy mildew is most serious in humid regions. Older leaves are usually infected first. For controls see "Downy Mildew" on page 312.

Symptom: White powdery coating on leaves
Cause: **Powdery mildew**

These infections weaken host plants. Minimize problems by spacing plants evenly to allow for good air circulation. For controls see "Powdery Mildew" on page 323.

ARTICHOKES
Cynara scolymus

ARTICHOKES AT A GLANCE

Botanical Name: *Cynara scolymus*
Height: To 6 feet
Spread: To 6 feet
Shade Tolerance: Full sun
Hardiness: Perennial in Zones 7–11
Preferred Soil: Fertile, moist, high
   in organic matter

Most Common Artichoke Pests

Symptom: Black, green, or yellowish insects on foliage
Cause: **Aphids**

Inspect undersides of leaves and inside buds for developing aphid colonies. Aphids don't usually harm artichokes, but they may spread viral diseases. To limit aphid problems, maintain healthy plants, but do not over-fertilize with nitrogen. If aphids show up anyway, knock them off plants with a strong stream of water; repeat frequently as needed. Plant pollen and nectar plants to attract native predators and parasites. Release purchases aphid midges, lacewings, or parasitic wasps. Control severe infestations with sprays of insecticidal soap, neem, homemade garlic sprays, or, as a last resort, pyrethrins. Repeat as needed for control.

Symptom: Holes bored in buds and stalks
Cause: **Artichoke plume moths**

Watch for brown moths with plumed wings about 1 inch across flying around plants at night. Female moths lay eggs on the undersides of leaves and on stems below buds. Larvae are ½–1-inch-long, yellowish caterpillars that feed on leaves in the center of the plant. They move to the buds and burrow through the scales into the artichoke heart. Handpick moths and eggs when you see them. Cut and destroy infested buds and stalks. Spray *Bacillus thuringiensis* var. *kurstaki* (BTK) or a solution of parasitic nematodes into the centers of plants as soon as you see caterpillars boring into young leaves. Clean up old artichoke leaves and nearby thistles in the fall and burn them to eliminate overwintering places for pests.

Most Common Artichoke Diseases

Symptoms: Leaves crinkled and mottled; plants stunted
Cause: **Mottled crinkle virus**

This virus may be spread by a soil organism. Dig and destroy infected plants, taking as much surrounding soil as possible.

Artichokes (Cynara scolymus)

ASPARAGUS

Asparagus officinalis

> ### ASPARAGUS AT A GLANCE
>
> **Botanical Name:** *Asparagus officinalis*
> **Height:** To 6 feet
> **Spread:** To 2 feet
> **Shade Tolerance:** Full sun in summer
> **Hardiness:** Perennial in Zones 2–8
> **Preferred Soil:** Fertile, deep, moist, well-
> drained, high in organic matter, neutral
> to slightly acidic

Most Common Asparagus Pests

Symptom: Brown scars on spears
Cause: **Asparagus miners**

If spears have brown scars or are girdled at the soil line, the ⅛-inch-long, white maggots of the asparagus miner are the cause. Destroy any spears with miners. Burn old stalks in fall to eliminate overwintering pupae inside stems.

Symptom: Spears distorted, with brown
             blemishes
Cause: **Asparagus beetles**

These beetles are easy to see in the foliage. For controls see "Asparagus Beetle" on page 247.

Symptom: Fronds stripped of leaves
Cause: **Beet armyworms
             (asparagus fern caterpillars)**

Look for caterpillars up to 1½ inches long and handpick them or spray *Bacillus thuringiensis* var. *kurstaki* (BTK) or neem. For severe infestations, cover beds in early spring with floating row covers for the harvesting period.

Symptom: Spears chewed at soil level
Cause: **Cutworms**

Severed spears or spears with bites out of them at the soil line that topple over were probably attacked by cutworms. For controls see "Cutworms" on page 258.

Symptom: Foliage dull silvery-gray
Cause: **Onion thrips**

Thrips are minute, quick insects that pierce and suck plant cells. They are almost impossible to see, but the damage gives plants a characteristic silvery, streaked appearance. If the infestation is severe, spray neem or pyrethrins.

Symptom: Plants stunted
Cause: **Asparagus aphids**

Asparagus aphids are small, pear-shaped, dusty green insects that suck the sap from stems and leaves. For controls see "Aphids" on page 244.

Asparagus (Asparagus officinalis)

Most Common Asparagus Diseases

Symptom: Elongated, reddish, powdery blisters on stems and leaves
Cause: **Rust (*Puccinia asparagi*)**

Look for reddish brown streaks or spots on stems and leaves that turn black in fall. Moderately infected plants are usually stunted. Prevent this common problem by planting resistant cultivars, such as 'California 500', 'Jersey Giant', and 'Jersey King'. For controls see "Rust" on page 327.

Symptoms: Weak spears in spring; large lesions at or slightly below the soil line
Cause: **Fusarium wilt (*Fusarium oxysporum*; *F. moniliforme*)**

Prevent problems by choosing tolerant or resistant cultivars, such as 'Jersey Giant' and 'Martha Washington'. For controls see "Fusarium Wilt" on page 315.

Symptoms: Water-soaked areas on stems; areas dry to a lighter color; cottony growth at base of stems
Cause: **White rot (*Sclerotinia* spp.)**

White rot spreads rapidly under warm, high-humidity conditions. Dig out infected plants, being careful to remove the top 2 inches of soil where fungal resting bodies may have dropped.

Most Common Asparagus Disorders

Symptom: Spears small
Cause: **Low soil fertility**

Asparagus is a heavy feeder. At fall clean-up each year, cover the asparagus beds with 2–3 inches of finished compost before mulching.

BEANS
Phaseolus spp.

BEANS AT A GLANCE

Botanical Name: *Phaseolus* spp.
Height: Bush, 1½–2½ feet; pole, to 7 feet or more
Spread: About 1½ feet
Shade Tolerance: Full sun
Hardiness: Killed by frost
Preferred Soil: Moderately fertile, moist, well-drained, high in organic matter

Most Common Bean Pests

Symptom: Tiny, warty bumps on pods
Cause: **Stink bugs**

These rarely cause much damage, and damaged beans are edible. For light infestations, shake plants over trays of soapy water to catch stink bugs. For heavy infestations, spray pyrethrins.

Symptom: Round holes drilled in seeds
Cause: **Bean weevils**

To kill weevil larvae in beans to be used for food, freeze dried beans for a week or heat at 125°F for half an hour. Protect beans for seed by mixing 1 tablespoon of diatomaceous earth with each quart of seed.

Symptom: Young leaves distorted and turning yellow
Cause: **Tarnished plant bugs**

Feeding by plant bugs withers and distorts leaves, but the bugs may not be visible in light infestations. Plants can sustain some leaf damage without harm. For controls see "Tarnished Plant Bug" on page 291.

Symptom: Leaves withered and turning
yellow

Causes: **Bean aphids; pea aphids**

Look for clusters of these tiny, black or green insects on shoots and undersides of leaves. Knock aphids off plants with a strong stream of water; repeat frequently as needed. Attract native predators and parasites by planting pollen and nectar plants. Release purchased aphid midges, lacewings, or parasitic wasps. Spray insecticidal soap, neem, homemade garlic sprays, or, as a last resort, pyrethrins. Repeat as needed for control.

Symptom: Leaves with pale speckles

Cause: **Spider mites**

Look for fine webbing on undersides of leaves. Tiny (less than ⅟₅₀ inch long) mites may be visible on the webbing. Outbreaks can be sudden and severe in hot, dry conditions. For controls see "Spider Mites" on page 286.

Symptom: Leaves skeletonized

Cause: **Mexican bean beetles**

Look for yellowish brown beetles with black spots and yellow, spiny larvae. To prevent problems plant resistant cultivars such as 'Wade' and 'Logan' snap beans and 'Black Valentine' lima beans. For controls see "Mexican Bean Beetle" on page 273.

Symptom: Large holes in leaves

Causes: **Bean leaf beetles; caterpillars**

Most damage from beetles and caterpillars is limited and can be controlled by handpicking the culprits. Caterpillars leave crumbly castings behind where they feed. If numerous, spray *Bacillus thuringiensis* var. *kurstaki* (BTK) or neem. For leaf beetles, spray pyrethrins.

Beans (*Phaseolus vulgaris*)

Most Common Bean Diseases

Symptoms: Water-soaked, bordered lesions;
reddish color between veins
of leaves

Cause: **Halo blight**
(*Pseudomonas phaseolicola*)

Halo blight can be carried on the seed; the plants collapse when pods begin to develop. When older plants are infected, greasy or watery spots develop on pods, leaves, or stems. The halo around the spots is usually pale yellow on leaves and stems but can be a brown or red color on pods. Avoid overhead sprinkling. Destroy infected plants. Use 4-year rotations.

Symptom: Reddish brown or black
pustules on leaf undersides
and pods

Cause: **Rust (*Uromyces* spp.)**

Minimize problems with this disease by growing tolerant cultivars, such as 'Roma' and 'Sungold'. For controls see "Rust" on page 327.

Symptom: Grayish, fuzzy growth on leaves and pods

Cause: **Botrytis (*Botrytis cinerea*)**

Prevent problems by thinning plants to allow for good air circulation. Once established on a plant, botrytis spreads rapidly. On leaves, stems, and fruit, the first signs of infection are tiny, water-soaked spots that enlarge, become light brown, and crack open, producing gray mold. For controls see "Botrytis Blight" on page 305.

Symptoms: Dark streaks on leaves; sunken spots on pods

Cause: **Anthracnose (*Colletotrichum lindemuthianum*)**

Look for anthracnose-tolerant cultivars, such as 'Dorabel', 'Marbel', and 'Rocdor'. Preventive tactics include cleaning up garden debris, crop rotation, wide plant spacing to increase air movement, keeping leaves dry while watering, and not working in the garden when plants are wet. On smaller plants, prune off and destroy all infected growth at the first sign of infection. Copper fungicides control these fungi if applied before the disease takes hold, but should be used only as a last resort.

Symptoms: Leaves mottled, puckered, or curled; rough spots on pods

Cause: **Bean mosaic**

Prevent virus problems by keeping beans growing vigorously. To control the spread of mosaic virus, avoid touching plants when they're wet. Control sucking insects, which spread viral diseases, and use floating row covers when possible. Remove and destroy infected plants immediately. Mosaic-tolerant cultivars, such as 'Goldcrop', 'Provider', 'Roma Z', and 'Sungold', can produce a crop even when infected with this disease.

BEETS
Beta vulgaris (Crassa group)

BEETS AT A GLANCE

Botanical Name: *Beta vulgaris* (Crassa group)
Height: 8 inches
Spread: 6–8 inches
Shade Tolerance: Full sun; tolerate partial shade
Hardiness: Tolerate light frost
Preferred Soil: Fertile, moist, well-drained, high in organic matter

Most Common Beet Pests

Symptom: Curving mines in leaves

Cause: **Beet leafminers**

Leafminer fly larvae tunnel between the upper and lower surfaces of the leaf. Handpick and destroy all damaged leaves to reduce the next generation of leafminers. For heavy infestations, spray plants with neem. Protect plants with floating row covers from seeding until harvest.

Symptom: Large holes chewed in leaves

Causes: **Beet armyworms; garden webworms**

Damage to leaves has little effect on the size of roots unless more than half of the leaf area is eaten. Handpick caterpillars, which are on the leaves and in rolled sections of leaf edges or knock them from plants into a pail of soapy water. For heavy infestations, spray *Bacillus thuringiensis* var. *kurstaki* (BTK), neem, or pyrethrins when larvae are very small.

Most Common Beet Diseases

Symptoms: Stunted growth; leaves curl downward; gray or purple fuzz on leaf undersides

Cause: **Downy mildew (*Peronospora farinosa* f. sp. *betae*)**

Downy mildew symptoms often first appear on the oldest leaves. For controls see "Downy Mildew" on page 312.

Symptom: Tiny, cinnamon-colored spots on leaves

Cause: **Rust (*Uromyces betae*)**

Prevent problems by spacing plants widely to allow for good air circulation. For controls see "Rust" on page 327.

Symptom: Leaves stunted and distorted

Cause: **Curly top**

Leafhoppers can spread this virus as they feed on your plants. For controls see "Curly Top or Beet Leaf Curl Virus" on page 310.

BROCCOLI
Brassica oleracea (Botrytis group)

BROCCOLI AT A GLANCE

Botanical Name: *Brassica oleracea* (Botrytis group)
Height: To 2 feet
Spread: To 2½ feet
Shade Tolerance: Full sun; tolerate partial shade
Hardiness: Tolerate light frost
Preferred Soil: Fertile, moist, well-drained, high in organic matter

Most Common Broccoli Pests
Same pests as cabbage. See "Cabbage" on page 16.

Most Common Broccoli Diseases
Same diseases as cabbage. See "Cabbage" on page 16.

Beets (Beta vulgaris, Crassa group)

Broccoli (Brassica oleracea, Botrytis group)

BRUSSELS SPROUTS
Brassica oleracea
(Gemmifera group)

BRUSSELS SPROUTS AT A GLANCE

Botanical Name: *Brassica oleracea*
(Gemmifera group)
Height: To 2½ feet
Spread: 1–1½ feet
Shade Tolerance: Full sun; tolerate
partial shade
Hardiness: Tolerate light frost
Preferred Soil: Fertile, moist, well-drained,
high in organic matter

Most Common Brussels Sprouts Pests
Same pests as cabbage. See "Cabbage."

Most Common Brussels Sprouts Diseases
Same diseases as cabbage. See "Cabbage."

Brussels sprouts (Brassica oleracea, Gemmifera group)

CABBAGE
Brassica oleracea
(Capitata group)

CABBAGE AT A GLANCE

Botanical Name: *Brassica oleracea*
(Capitata group)
Height: 1–1½ feet
Spread: To 3 feet
Shade Tolerance: Full sun; tolerates
partial shade
Hardiness: Tolerates light frost
Preferred Soil: Fertile, moist, well-
drained, high in organic matter

Most Common Cabbage Pests

Symptom: Light-colored, distorted patches
on leaves
Cause: **Cabbage aphids**

Look for colonies of tiny, powdery gray insects on undersides of affected cabbage leaves. Their feeding causes foliage distortion and they excrete a sweet, sticky honeydew. This allows sooty mold to grow. For controls see "Aphids" on page 244.

Symptom: Silvery brown streaks on leaves
Cause: **Thrips**

Thrips are almost too small (and too quick) to see. If damage is severe, spray with insecticidal soap or neem, especially on undersides of leaves, or dust diatomaceous earth at the base of each plant and on undersides of leaves. Plant resistant cultivars such as 'Albion', 'Galaxy', 'Hilton', 'Multikeeper', 'Struckton', and 'Super Red'.

Symptom: Large, ragged holes chewed
in leaves

Causes: **Imported cabbageworms;
cabbage loopers**

Look for crumbly, green castings on the
leaves, which show caterpillars are present.
For light infestations, handpick caterpillars.
For heavy infestations, spray every 7–10 days
with *Bacillus thuringiensis* var. *kurstaki* (BTK) or
neem. Prevent damage by covering small
plants with floating row covers from the
seedling stage onward. Try red cultivars, which
seem to be less attacked.

Symptom: Many small, round holes
in leaves

Cause: **Flea beetles**

Look for small, swift, jumping insects. These
are most damaging in early spring and may kill
seedlings. Larger plants usually outgrow the
damage. For control see "Flea Beetles" on
page 262.

Symptom: Plants wilt in midday sun

Cause: **Cabbage maggots**

The first sign of injury is usually plants that
wilt in the midday heat. Pull an affected plant
and look for tunnels and rotting in roots. You
may also see the tiny, white maggots in the
damaged root. For controls see "Cabbage
Maggot" on page 250.

Most Common Cabbage Diseases

Symptom: Plants wilt in midday sun

Cause: **Root knot nematodes**

Suspect nematodes if you find hard, pea-size,
irregular galls on the roots of plants. Most
roots have strings of swellings. Feeding also

'Eureka' cabbage (<u>Brassica oleracea</u>*, Capitata group)*

causes plants to wilt and stunts growth.
Remove and destroy infected plants. For
further controls see "Nematodes, Root Knot"
on page 322.

Symptom: Bottom leaves or tops of heads
covered with white mold

Cause: **White rot *(Sclerotinia
sclerotiorum)***

The fungal spores that cause this disease
overwinter in the soil. The fungal spores that
cause this disease overwinter in the soil.
White rot spreads rapidly under warm, high-
humidity conditions. Dig out infected plants,
being careful to remove the top 2 inches of
soil where fungi may have dropped.

Symptom: Outside leaves of heads dry
and brown

Cause: **Head rot *(Rhizoctonia solani)***

The organism that causes this disease is
present in all garden soils, so prevention is

the only course. Choose a garden site with well-drained soil and regularly pick up dropped leaves and other plant debris to keep the garden clean. Destroy infected plants.

Symptoms: Leaves with wedge-shaped brown areas on margins; plant growth slows
Cause: **Black rot (*Xanthomonas campestris*)**

Prevent problems by choosing a resistant cabbage cultivar, such as 'Bravo'. Black rot spreads quickly in warm, wet weather. This disease may kill or severely stunt young plants; older plants may be defoliated. For controls see "Bacterial Spot" on page 303.

Symptoms: Swelling on roots; plants stunted; leaves droopy
Cause: **Club root (*Plasmodiophora brassicae*)**

This fungus stimulates root cells to grow abnormally large, creating galls that are swollen and usually tapered at both ends. Minimize club root problems by choosing a well-drained planting site and by rotating your crops. Remove all infected plants, including weeds, immediately. The soil surrounding the roots should also be removed.

Symptoms: Dark cankers at stem bases; round, brown spots on leaves
Cause: **Blackleg (*Phoma lingam*)**

Blackleg fungi overwinter in plant debris or on infected seed. Dip self-saved cabbage-family seeds in a 10 percent solution of laundry bleach before planting. Rotate crops, leaving 3–4 years between planting in the same soil.

Symptom: Brown spots with concentric circles on lower leaves
Cause: **Alternaria leaf spot (*Alternaria brassicae*)**

Alternaria is favored by high humidity and overwinters in the seed and in plant debris. Plant cabbage-family plants in well-drained soil and space them so air can freely circulate around them. Destroy infected plants.

Symptoms: Yellow lesions on upper sides of leaves; white mold on leaf undersides
Cause: **Downy mildew (*Peronospora parasitica*)**

Wet weather promotes the rapid spread of this fungus; cabbage seedlings are most susceptible to severe injury from downy mildew. Infected heads may have dark patches on the leaves. To prevent outbreaks, space plants to encourage air circulation, and water early in the day. Choose resistant or tolerant cultivars when possible. Clean up all debris in fall to remove overwintering spores. In greenhouses and other enclosed spaces, keep ventilation high. Remove and destroy infected tissues.

Symptom: White, powdery growth on leaves
Cause: **Powdery mildew (*Erysiphe cruciferarum*)**

Powdery white or gray spots are usually the first symptoms you will notice. The spots enlarge quickly, covering the entire leaf, flower, or shoot. Infected tissues become pale, then turn brown and shrivel. Pick off and destroy infected plant tissues. To prevent problems, space plants widely to allow for good air circulation. For further controls see "Powdery Mildew" on page 323.

Symptoms: Leaves yellow; plant growth
             slows
Cause: **Yellows (*Fusarium oxysporum*
             f. *conglutinans*)**

To prevent problems, grow resistant cabbage cultivars, such as 'Bravo' and 'Super Red 83'. Healthy plants are the best defense against this fungus. Potassium deficiency and nematode damage make plants more susceptible to yellows, as does excess nitrogen. Keeping soil temperatures cool with light-reflecting mulch may help limit infection in hot climates. Remove infected plants, taking the roots and surrounding soil.

Most Common Cabbage Disorders

Symptom: Brown tips on leaves
Cause: **Tip burn**

Tip burn on leaves can be caused by calcium deficiency or by extremely high temperatures. Keep soil moisture constant and provide adequate calcium with compost applications or side-dressing with bonemeal. Spray liquid seaweed, diluted as recommended on the bottle, on seedlings if tip burn has been a problem in the past.

Symptoms: Leaves corky; stem hollow or
             water-soaked
Cause: **Boron deficiency**

Cabbage-family crops require slightly higher levels of boron than do most other garden crops. If you see symptoms of boron deficiency, apply liquid seaweed, diluted as recommended on the bottle, to the soil around roots.

CARROTS
Daucus carota var. *sativus*

CARROTS AT A GLANCE

Botanical Name: *Daucus carota* var. *sativus*
Height To 14 inches
Spread: To 10 inches
Shade Tolerance: Full sun
Hardiness: Tolerate light frost
Preferred Soil: Fertile, moist, well-drained,
     high in organic matter; best if rock-free,
     sandy loam

Most Common Carrot Pests

Symptom: Tunnels bored in roots
Causes: **Carrot rust flies; carrot weevils**

If the tunnels are in the lower part of the root and are filled with rusty brown castings, the problem is carrot rust flies. The pearly white maggots may be in the tunnels. Weevils feed in crowns, lower stems, and the top part of the root. Sprays are ineffective once roots are infested. Drenching soil with parasitic nematodes may give some control. For control next season, rotate crops and cover beds with floating row covers from seeding to harvest.

Symptom: Small, round holes drilled
             in roots
Cause: **Wireworms**

If slender, brown, leathery larvae are found in the roots, wireworms are the problem. Undamaged parts are edible, but damaged roots won't keep in storage. For controls see "Wireworms" on page 298.

Most Common Carrot Diseases

Symptom: Pale, wilted leaves
Cause: **Root knot nematodes**

Suspect nematodes if the roots are distorted with forks, galls, and tufts of side roots. Practice at least a 2-year rotation with plants that aren't susceptible (such as onions, radishes, and lettuce). For other controls see "Nematodes, Root Knot" on page 322.

Symptom: Crown and roots rot
Cause: **Black rot (*Alternaria radicina*)**

Black rot invades and weakens the crown. When infected carrots are stored, they develop a white mold. The fungus is spread primarily through seeds or water. It can overwinter on plant debris or in the soil. To prevent this disease, use 3- to 4-year rotations. Water with drip irrigation or through furrows rather than overhead sprinklers. Remove all carrot residue from the garden in autumn. Remove and destroy infected plants.

'All Seasons' carrots (*Daucus carota* var. *sativus*)

Symptom: Tops weaken
Cause: **Leaf blight (*Alternaria dauci*)**

You may also notice dark, yellow-bordered spots on the leaves. Prevent problems by growing resistant cultivars, such as 'Cheyenne' and 'Huron'. Use 3- to 4-year rotations. Use drip irrigation to avoid wetting the leaves when watering. Remove and destroy infected plants.

Symptom: Pale spots on leaves that
               brown and die, leaving a pale
               halo
Cause: **Leaf spot (*Septoria apiicola;*
               Cercospora carotae;
               Xanthomonas carotae)**

Leaf spots may merge to cover whole leaves. For controls see "Bacterial Spot" on page 303 and "Septoria Leaf Spot" on page 328.

Symptoms: Young leaves pale and bushy;
               roots covered with many hair-
               like roots
Cause: **Aster yellows**

Carrots affected with yellows may have a bitter taste. Floating row covers, used as long as possible into the season, provide a good barrier against leafhoppers, which spread this disease. However, once the covers are removed, infections can occur. Remove and destroy infected plants, including trees, to avoid spread. Eliminate weeds such as asters, chicory, dandelions, and thistle.

CAULIFLOWER

Brassica oleracea (Botrytis group)

Most Common Cauliflower Pests
Same pests as cabbage. See "Cabbage" on page 16.

Most Common Cauliflower Diseases
Same diseases as cabbage. See "Cabbage" on page 16.

Cauliflower (<u>Brassica oleracea</u>, Botrytis group)

CELERY

Apium graveolens

Most Common Celery Pests

Symptom: Distorted leaves with a
sticky coating
Cause: **Aphids**

Look for colonies of small, green aphids on leaves and stalks. Spray a strong stream of water into crowns every few days, or spray insecticidal soap, neem, or pyrethrins. Cover plants with floating row covers from planting until harvest.

Symptom: Scooped-out holes in stalks
Cause: **Slugs**

Slugs are most damaging in spring, when the weather is moist and plants are small. For controls see "Slugs and Snails" on page 283.

Symptom: Large holes chewed in leaves
Cause: **Caterpillars**

Caterpillars of several species of butterflies and moths feed on celery. They leave behind

Celery (Apium graveolens)

dark green pellets of excrement where they feed and usually do little damage. Handpick a few caterpillars or leave them to become butterflies. If more than half of the foliage has been eaten, spray *Bacillus thuringiensis* var. *kurstaki* (BTK) or neem.

Most Common Celery Diseases

Symptoms: Plants wilt suddenly; crown and stalks rot
Cause: **Pink rot**
         (*Sclerotinia sclerotiorum*)

As pink rot progresses, infected stems become covered with a white mold that contains fungal resting bodies. These spores can remain viable in the soil for many years. Remove and destroy infected plants at the first sign of the fungus. Rotate crops carefully, leaving 4 years between carrot-family crops on the same soil.

Symptoms: Leaves are mottled; plant is stunted
Causes: **Celery mosaic; cucumber mosaic**

Insects can spread viruses as they feed on your plants. For controls see "Mosaic" on page 319.

Symptom: Stalks rot and smell foul
Cause: **Bacterial soft rot**
         (*Erwinia carotovora*)

These bacteria can enter celery through wounds, so handle the roots carefully at harvest time. Infected plant tissues give off a foul odor and the area is slimy. For controls see "Bacterial Soft Rot" on page 302.

Symptom: Spots on leaves
Cause: **Leaf spot (*Cercospora apii*;**
         ***Septoria apiicola*)**

Leaf spot damage ranges from simply cosmetic to seriously damaging. For controls see "Bacterial Spot" on page 303 and "Septoria Leaf Spot" on page 328.

Most Common Celery Disorders

Symptoms: Water-soaked tips on young leaves; center stalks and leaves darken and rot
Cause: **Black heart**

Celery requires high levels of calcium as well as high soil moisture. Black heart develops when these requirements aren't met. If black heart begins to develop, spray leaves with liquid seaweed and side-dress with a sprinkling of bonemeal down the row. Irrigate well for the rest of the season. When soil is tested, check to determine if potassium levels are too high in relation to calcium. If so, amend with bonemeal in beds where calcium-lovers are to grow.

CHARD

Beta vulgaris (Cicla group)

CORN

Zea mays

SWISS CHARD AT A GLANCE

Botanical Name: *Beta vulgaris* (Cicla group)
Height: To 1½ feet
Spread: To 1½ feet
Shade Tolerance: Full sun; tolerates partial shade
Hardiness: Tolerates light frost
Preferred Soil: Fertile, moist, well-drained, high in organic matter

SWEET CORN AT A GLANCE

Botanical Name: *Zea mays* var. *rugosa*
Height: 4–7 feet
Spread: 1½ feet
Shade Tolerance: Full sun
Hardiness: Killed by frost
Preferred Soil: Fertile, moist, well-drained, high in organic matter

POPCORN AT A GLANCE

Botanical Name: *Zea mays* var. *praecox*
Height: 3½–7 feet
Spread: 1½ feet
Shade Tolerance: Full sun
Hardiness: Killed by light frost
Preferred Soil: Fertile, moist, well-drained, high in organic matter

Most Common Chard Pests

Same pests as beets. See "Beets" on page 14.

Most Common Chard Diseases

Same diseases as beets. See "Beets" on page 14.

Most Common Corn Pests

Symptom: Silks and kernels in ears chewed
Causes: **Corn earworms; European corn borers**

Both caterpillars produce crumbly excrement, and both are usually visible on the ear when the husks are pulled back. Check all maturing ears and dig out any caterpillars in the tip or at the base before they cause further damage. The undamaged part of the ear is edible. Where caterpillars infest ears every year, treat the tips of each ear, inside the husk, as soon as the silks start to dry with *Bacillus thuringiensis* var. *kurstaki* (BTK)—sprays or

Rhubarb chard (<u>Beta vulgaris</u>, Cicla group)

granular form—a solution of parasitic nematodes, or 20 drops of mineral oil. Plant resistant cultivars such as 'Northern Super Sweet', 'Tri-Sweet', and others with tight husks and good tip cover.

Symptom: Silks chewed away
Cause: **Earwigs**

If only the silks are gone and there are no signs of caterpillars, suspect earwigs. These ¾-inch-long, brown, elongated insects with pincers on the tail may also drop out of the husks. Although often beneficial because they eat aphids and other pests, earwigs also chew blossoms and corn silk. They rarely cause severe damage. Where numbers are very high, place traps (lengths of old hose, hollow bamboo tubes, or rolled-up newspaper) among plants. Once a day, shake earwigs from traps into soapy water.

Corn (Zea mays) in the field

Symptom: Stunted, wilted plants
Cause: **Corn rootworms**

Look for slender, white larvae with brown heads among the roots of affected plants. Lightly infested plants and late-season corn may survive to produce a crop. Applying parasitic nematodes to soil may suppress rootworms sufficiently in moist soil. Cultivate the soil after harvest to destroy larvae. Rotate crops next year; rotation is very effective against northern corn rootworms.

Symptom: Shotholes chewed in
             leaf whorls
Cause: **European corn borers**

Look for gray or beige caterpillars with brown spots feeding on leaves early in the season or boring into stalks and ears later in the season. For controls see "European Corn Borer" on page 260.

Symptom: Stalks break easily
Causes: **Stalk borers; southwestern
             corn borers**

Look for borer entry holes in stalks and cut open broken stalks to look for caterpillars and sawdust inside. Pull and shred infested plants. After harvest, shred and compost stalks and plow under crop debris deeply. Control nearby giant ragweed and other large-stalked weeds, which host stalk borers. Plant resistant cultivars that resist wind breakage such as 'Polar Super Sweet' and 'Milk N' Honey'.

Symptom: Seeds fail to come up
Causes: **Wireworms; seedcorn maggots**

Dig up seeds to diagnose the problem. If ¼-inch-long, white larvae are feeding in the seed, the problem is seedcorn maggots.

If narrow, brown, leathery larvae are present, the problem is wireworms. If seeds have rotted but no larvae seem to be present, soil may have been too cold at planting. Replant, using 2–3 times more seed than required to ensure that sufficient plants survive. Planting late, when soil is quite warm, will also help avoid some wireworms, which burrow deeper in summer. Apply parasitic nematodes to the soil to control larvae.

Symptom: Plants turn yellow and wilt in midday sun
Cause: **Corn root aphids**

Look on the roots for colonies of $\frac{1}{12}$-inch-long, yellowish to greenish insects covered with white fluff. Ants place root aphids on corn and tend them, so you need to control the ants. Use boric acid baits, and search for and destroy nearby ant nests in the soil. Before planting next year, cultivate deeply to break up ant nests.

Symptoms: Husks torn; kernels picked from cobs
Causes: **Birds; other animals**

To prevent further bird damage, tie small paper bags over each ear at least a week before cobs are ready to pick. If birds are a common problem, choose cultivars with upright ears that discourage perching and those with good husk cover. Resistant cultivars include 'Earlivee', 'Flavorvee', and 'Flavor King'.

Symptom: Leaves skeletonized
Cause: **Japanese beetles**

These voracious pests are a common garden problem in many areas. For controls see "Japanese Beetle" on page 268.

Symptom: Base of stalks girdled
Cause: **Southwestern corn borers**

Corn borers attack stalks and roots as well as ears. This weakens stems and causes them to break easily. There are two or more generations per year. For controls see "Southwestern Corn Borer" on page 284.

Most Common Corn Diseases

Symptom: Spots on leaves
Causes: **Leaf spot diseases, including northern corn leaf blight (*Helminthosporium turcicum*), southern corn leaf blight (*Helminthosporium maydis*), yellow leaf blight (*Phyllosticta maydis*), anthracnose (*Colletotrichum graminicola*), and bacterial leaf spot (*Pseudomonas albo-precipitans*)**

You can prevent some leaf spot diseases by planting resistant cultivars. 'Apache', for instance, is resistant to both northern and southern leaf blight. For leaf blight controls see "Bacterial Spot" on page 303 and "Anthracnose" on page 300.

Symptoms: Pale green to yellow streaks on young leaves; plant wilts; growth is stunted
Cause: **Bacterial wilt (*Erwinia stewartii*)**

Wilt diseases can be mystifying because the first symptoms may be subtle. Young plants are most susceptible and usually die if infected during their first month of growth. On older plants, leaf streaks soon turn brown and the stalks may have hollows or brown areas. Flea beetles and cucumber beetles spread this disease as they feed. Prevent infections by planting disease-free corn seed. Control insects as much as possible; if the winter has been warm, use floating row covers to protect your plants for the first month. Minimize problems by choosing disease-tolerant cultivars, such as 'Lancelot', 'Miracle', 'Silver Queen', or 'Tuxedo'. For other flea beetle controls see "Flea Beetles" on page 262.

Symptom:	Oval, cinnamon-brown pustules on both leaf surfaces
Causes:	**Common rust (*Puccinia sorghi*); southern rust (*Puccinia polysora*)**

Minimize problems by planting tolerant cultivars, such as 'Lancelot' and 'Tecumseh'. You can make plants more resistant: Avoid amendments high in nitrogen, and prune, space, and water carefully to increase air circulation and keep leaves dry. Pick off and destroy infected leaves. Sulfur spray, used when spots first appear, kills new spores.

Symptoms:	Fleshy galls on ears, leaves, and stem; black spores inside gall membrane
Cause:	**Corn smut (*Ustilago maydis*)**

Smut infections remain fairly localized in the host, forming new spores that are released to cause successive infections during the season. The membrane surrounding the gall splits and releases masses of black spores. If corn smut has been a problem in your garden, practice 3- to 4-year rotations and regularly check plants for fleshy white galls during the growing season. If you see a gall, pick it off immediately; do not let the spores mature. Look for resistant cultivars, such as 'Merit' and 'Viking'. For more controls see "Smut" on page 329.

Symptoms:	Tassels distorted and too numerous; plants with excessive tillers and ear shoots
Cause:	**Crazy top (*Sclerophthora macrospora*)**

Crazy top only strikes plants that are smaller than about 6 inches in height when their soil is flooded or waterlogged for at least 24 hours. This disease remains in the soil for many years. Plant in well-drained soil or raised beds and destroy infected plants.

Symptoms:	Leaves mottled; plants with distorted or stunted growth
Cause:	**Virus**

Insects can spread viruses as they feed on your plants. For controls see "Mosaic" on page 319.

Most Common Corn Disorders

Symptom:	Plants have a purple coloration
Causes:	**Cultivar characteristic; phosphorus deficiency**

Some corn cultivars naturally have a purple tint to their leaves. However, other cultivars turn purplish when deprived of adequate phosphorus. Cool soils intensify the effect. Avoid problems or treat symptoms by spraying foliage with liquid seaweed or compost tea every week until midsummer.

Symptoms:	Areas of undeveloped kernels on ears; bare cobs
Cause:	**Poor pollination**

Plant corn in a block rather than in a long row to ensure effective wind pollination. Insects feeding on silks can prevent pollination, as can dry conditions. Control insects that feed on silks, and keep soil moist.

CUCUMBERS
Cucumis sativus

CUCUMBERS AT A GLANCE

Botanical Name: *Cucumis sativus*
Height: To 1½ feet
Spread: To 5 feet
Shade Tolerance: Full sun
Hardiness: Killed by frost
Preferred Soil: Fertile, moist, well-drained, high in organic matter

Most Common Cucumber Pests
See also "Squash and Pumpkins" on page 51.

Symptom:	Holes chewed in leaves
Cause:	**Cucumber beetles, spotted or striped**

If you see elongated, greenish yellow beetles with stripes or spots feeding on leaves, the problem is cucumber beetles. Although their feeding causes little direct damage, they spread bacterial wilt and mosaic diseases. For controls see "Cucumber Beetle, Spotted" on page 256 and "Cucumber Beetle, Striped" on page 257. Choose resistant cultivars such as 'Stono' and 'Niagara', which are tolerant of bacterial wilt and mosaic.

Symptoms:	Blossoms chewed; holes bored in fruit
Cause:	**Pickleworm**

Use squash as a trap crop to attract pickleworms away from cucumber. Grow resistant cucumber cultivars such as 'Ashley', 'Colorado', 'Princess', and 'Slicemaster'. For more controls see "Squash and Pumpkins" on page 51.

Most Common Cucumber Diseases
See also "Melons" on page 34 and "Squash and Pumpkins" on page 51.

Symptoms:	Angular spots on leaves; bacterial slime oozes from leaf undersides
Cause:	**Angular leaf spot** (***Pseudomonas lachrymans***)

Angular leaf spot can also produce small, brown, angular spots on fruit. For controls see "Bacterial Spot" on page 303.

Symptoms:	Plants wilt when soil is moist; death follows
Cause:	**Bacterial wilt** (***Erwinia tracheiphila***)

Cucumber beetles spread this disease as they feed on your plants. For controls see "Bacterial Wilt" on page 303.

Symptoms:	Angular spots on leaves; scab-like lesions on fruit and stems
Cause:	**Scab** (***Cladosporium cucumerinum***)

Grow tolerant or resistant cultivars, such as 'Green Spear', 'Pioneer', and 'Sweet Slice'. For controls see "Scab" on page 328.

Symptoms:	Yellow lesions on upper leaf surfaces; purple to gray mold on leaf undersides
Cause:	**Downy mildew** (***Pseudoperonospora cubensis***)

Minimize damage by planting tolerant cultivars, such as 'Comet II', 'Fanfare', 'Supersett', and 'Sweet Slice'. For controls see "Downy Mildew" on page 312.

Symptom: White, powdery coating
on leaves

Cause: **Powdery mildew (*Sphaerotheca
fuligenea; Erysiphe cichoracearum*)**

Prevent problems by growing tolerant or resistant cultivars, such as 'Bush Baby', 'Supersett', and 'Sweet Slice'. For controls see "Powdery Mildew" on page 323.

Symptoms: Brown or dead spots on leaves;
sunken spots on fruit with pink
ooze in center

Cause: **Anthracnose (*Colletotrichum
lagenarium*)**

Look for tolerant cultivars, such as 'Bush Baby', 'Supersett', and 'Turbo'. For controls see "Anthracnose" on page 300.

Symptom: Mottled, stunted, or distorted
leaves

Cause: **Mosaic**

Insects can spread viruses as they feed on your plants. For controls see "Mosaic" on page 319.

'Park Fanfare' cucumber (<u>Cucumis sativus</u>)

EGGPLANT

*Solanum melongena
var. esculentum*

Most Common Eggplant Pests
See also "Tomatoes" on page 55.

Symptom: Large holes chewed in leaves
Cause: **Colorado potato beetles**

Eggplant is a favorite of potato beetles, which may completely defoliate plants. For controls see "Colorado Potato Beetle" on page 254.

Symptom: Many small, round holes in
leaves
Cause: **Flea beetles**

Adults are tiny, active black, brown, or bronze beetles, 1/10 inch long. They have enlarged hind legs and jump like fleas when they are disturbed. The larvae live in the soil and are thin, white, legless grubs with brown heads. Flea beetles do little lasting damage to older cucumber plants, but seedlings may be destroyed by heavy infestations. Cover plants with floating row covers until blossoms open. If beetles are damaging, spray pyrethrins.

Most Common Eggplant Diseases

Symptoms: Gray to brown spots on leaves
and stems; pale, sunken areas
on fruit
Cause: **Phomopsis blight**
(***Phomopsis vexans***)

Seedborne phomopsis blight kills seedlings
rapidly. The disease can also overwinter in
plant residue and travel with splashing water
onto new plants. Fruit spots are quite large
and often look like targets. Shiny, black
fruiting bodies are visible on fruit and leaf
spots. Use a 4-year rotation and practice good
fall sanitation. Choose resistant cultivars, such
as 'Florida Market'. Copper, sprayed at the
first sign of symptoms, and again 10–14 days
later, can control the disease.

Symptom: Small (½ inch long), sunken
spots on fruit and leaves
Cause: **Anthracnose**
(***Colletotrichum* spp.**)

Reduce the chances of anthracnose damage
by spacing plants evenly to allow for good air
circulation. Preventive tactics include cleaning
up garden debris, rotating crops, keeping
leaves dry while watering, and not working in
the garden when plants are wet. Prune off and
destroy all infected growth at the first sign of
infection. Copper fungicides control these
fungi if applied before the disease takes hold.

Symptoms: Dark leathery spots on leaves;
sunken rotting spots on fruit
Cause: **Alternaria blight**
(***Alternaria solani***)

This fungus can spread through wind, rain,
and contaminated tools; flea beetles may also
spread it as they feed. Mulch plants, and feed

Eggplant (<u>Solanum melongena</u> var. <u>esculentum</u>)

and water regularly, since stressed plants are
more susceptible. Practice 3- to 4-year
rotations and clean up all debris in fall. At the
first sign of infection, spray with copper,
repeating at 7- to 10-day intervals. Destroy
severely infected plants.

Symptoms: Crown and base of stem rots;
whole plant dies
Cause: **Southern blight**
(***Sclerotium rolfsii***)

Southern blight overwinters in the soil. To
avoid this disease, rotate crops, leaving 4 years
between planting on the same soil.

Symptoms: Leaves mottled and malformed; young fruits mottled
Causes: **Tobacco mosaic; cucumber
mosiac**

Minimize the damage caused by viruses by
growing tolerant cultivars, such as 'Dusky' and
'Vernal'. Prevent viruses by keeping plants
growing vigorously. Do not touch wet plants.
Try to control sucking insects, and use floating
row covers when possible. Remove and destroy
virus-infected plants immediately.

GARLIC
Allium sativum

GARLIC AT A GLANCE

Botanical Name: *Allium sativum*
Height: 10–15 inches
Spread: 6–8 inches
Shade Tolerance: Full sun; tolerates partial shade
Hardiness: Perennial in Zones 3–11
Preferred Soil: Fertile, moist, well-drained, high in organic matter

---

Most Common Garlic Pests
Same pests as onions. See "Onions" on page 38.

Most Common Garlic Diseases
See also "Onions" on page 38.

Symptom: Water-soaked spots or brown mold on leaves
Cause: **Purple blotch (Alternaria porri)**

Purple blotch attacks when the weather is wet. Leaf spots turn brown, sometimes with a dark margin and yellow border. Well-drained soil and good air circulation protect your plants. Spray affected plants with sulfur to keep the disease from spreading.

Symptoms: Leaves yellow and wilt; bottom of bulb rots in the garden or in storage
Causes: **Fusarium wilt; fusarium bottom rot**

Choose a well-drained planting site. For controls see "Fusarium Wilt" on page 315.

Symptom: Brown to black rotting tissue at neck
Cause: **Botrytis neck rot**

This fungal disease usually appears near harvest or in storage. For controls see "Botrytis Blight" on page 305.

Most Common Garlic Disorders

Symptom: Plants don't come up in spring, or first leaves die in early spring
Cause: **Frost damage**

A winter mulch can help to minimize this damage. Choose late blooming cultivars whenever possible.

Symptom: Thick necks that do not dry down during curing
Cause: **Potassium deficiency**

If your soil tests low in potassium, apply greensand to the area before planting. Water with a liquid seaweed dilution every 2–4 weeks during the growing season.

Garlic (Allium sativum)

KALE

Brassica oleracea (Acephala group)

KALE AT A GLANCE

Botanical Name: *Brassica oleracea*
(Acephala group)
Height: To 2 feet
Spread: To 1½ feet
Shade Tolerance: Full sun; tolerate partial
shade
Hardiness: Tolerate light frost
Preferred Soil: Fertile, moist, well-drained,
high in organic matter

Most Common Kale Pests

Same pests as cabbage. See "Cabbage" on
page 16.

Most Common Kale Diseases

Same diseases as cabbage. See "Cabbage" on
page 16.

Kale (<u>Brassica oleracea</u>, Acephala group)

LEEKS

Allium ampeloprasum

LEEKS AT A GLANCE

Botanical Name: *Allium ampeloprasum*
Height: To 18 inches
Spread: To 12 inches
Shade Tolerance: Full sun
Hardiness: Tolerate light frost
Preferred Soil: Fertile, moist, well-drained,
high in organic matter

Most Common Leek Pests

Same pests as onions. See "Onions" on page 38.

Most Common Leek Diseases

Symptom:	Bright orange pustules form between the veins of the leaf
Cause:	**Rust**

Choose a sunny,well-drained planting site. For
controls see "Rust" on page 327.

Leeks (<u>Allium ampeloprasum</u>)

LETTUCE

Lactuca sativa

LETTUCE AT A GLANCE

Botanical Name: *Lactuca sativa*
Height: 6–12 inches
Spread: 6–12 inches
Shade Tolerance: Full sun (partial shade in warm weather)
Hardiness: Tolerates light frost
Preferred Soil: Fertile, moist, well-drained, high in organic matter

Most Common Lettuce Pests

Symptom: Curled, distorted patches on leaves
Cause: **Aphids**

Aphids are the problem if you see colonies of green, pink, or yellow pear-shaped insects on the leaves or inside heads. Several species of aphids feed on lettuce and can spread viral diseases; some species feed deep inside the head, out of reach of predatory insects or sprays. Wash aphids from plants with a strong stream of water, or spray insecticidal soap, pyrethrins, or neem. Where aphids are a persistent problem in head lettuce, grow looseleaf cultivars to make it easier to control aphids.

Symptom: Silvery streaks on leaves
Cause: **Thrips**

These tiny insects are almost too small and too quick to see. If damage is severe, spray with insecticidal soap or neem, especially on undersides of leaves. Dust diatomaceous earth around the base of plants.

Symptom: Large holes chewed in leaves
Causes: **Armyworms; loopers; other caterpillars**

Many different species of caterpillars may attack lettuce. Even if they are hard to see, you can tell caterpillars are at work if you find green pellets of excrement between the leaves. If there are only a few, handpick caterpillars. For heavy infestations, spray *Bacillus thuringiensis* var. *kurstaki* (BTK) or neem frequently. Where caterpillars are always a problem, cover the next planting of lettuce with floating row covers as soon as you sow the seeds, and keep them on until harvest.

Symptom: Holes in leaves, slime trails present
Cause: **Slugs or snails**

Lettuce's soft leaves are prime targets for slugs and snails. For controls see "Slugs and Snails" on page 283.

Most Common Lettuce Diseases

Symptom: Plants stunted
Cause: **Root knot nematodes**

Look for hard, pea-size, irregular galls on the roots of affected plants. For controls see "Nematodes, Root Knot" on page 322.

Symptom: Dark, slimy rot starting at base of plant
Cause: **Rhizoctonia bottom rot (*Rhizoctonia solani*)**

Bottom rot moves quickly up the plant, killing tissues as it goes. Dead tissues dry and turn papery. The organism that causes this disease is in almost all soils. Wet weather promotes it. Prevent problems by planting in well-drained, high-fertility soils or raised beds. Grow a resistant cultivar, such as 'Canasta'. Do not transplant sickly plants. Remove and destroy any plants with bottom rot.

Symptoms: Clearing or yellowing of tissues next to major veins; leaves ruffled

Cause: **Big vein (viroid organism)**

The big vein organism is carried by a soilborne fungus, *Olpidium brassicae*, and attacks most frequently when temperatures are 42°–65°F. This soil-dwelling fungus survives without a host for as long as 10 years. Strong, vigorous plants rarely contract the disease. Plant in well-drained, compost-amended soils. If big vein appears, dig out and destroy the plant, taking the soil around the roots.

Symptom: Wet rotting on bottom of plant

Cause: **Sclerotinia drop (*Sclerotinia sclerotiorum*)**

The wet rot that develops spreads to the roots and up into the center of the head. Black resting bodies are visible in the white mold that develops in humid conditions. Sclerotinia also infects tomatoes, cabbage, and celery. Wet conditions favor it. Plant lettuce in well-drained, fertile soil. Destroy infected plants.

Symptoms: Plant is stunted and yellowish; roots are malformed and have corky lesions

Cause: **Corky root (*Pyrenochaeta lycopersici*)**

Corky root also infects tomatoes. Check for root symptoms on sickly plants. Dig out infected plants, taking the surrounding soil, and apply compost. Rotate with plants that

'Imperial' lettuce (*Lactuca sativa*)

aren't susceptible such as corn, squash-family plants, or cabbages. Prevent corky root problems by planting a resistant cultivar, such as 'Saguaro'.

Symptoms: Pale or yellowish spots on leaves; white mold on leaf undersides

Cause: **Downy mildew (*Bremia lactucae*)**

Minimize damage from this disease by planting a tolerant cultivar, such as 'Nancy'. For controls see "Downy Mildew" on page 312.

Symptom: White, powdery coating on leaves

Cause: **Powdery mildew (*Erysiphe* spp.)**

Symptoms usually appear on the oldest leaves first. Infected tissues look dusty white, then turn brown and shrivel. Powdery mildew infections are unsightly and weaken host plants. For controls see "Powdery Mildew" on page 323.

Symptoms: Rotting on lower leaves and
stem; gray mold on
affected areas

Cause: **Botrytis gray mold**
(*Botrytis cinerea*)

Spacing plants evenly to allow for good air
circulation can minimize problems with this
fungus. For controls see "Botrytis Blight" on
page 305.

Symptom: Young leaves stunted, curled,
or twisted

Cause: **Aster yellows**
(mycoplasma-like organism)

Leafhoppers can spread this disease as they
feed on your plants. For controls see "Yellows"
on page 333.

Symptom: Plants are stunted with
mottled or yellowish,
distorted leaves

Causes: **Lettuce mosaic;**
cucumber mosaic

Prevent problems by growing resistant cultivars, such as 'Montella' and 'Saguaro'. For
controls see "Mosaic" on page 319.

Most Common Lettuce Disorders

Symptom: Leaf margins yellow, brown,
and dry

Cause: **Tip burn**

Tip burn is caused by calcium deficiencies and
generally appears when the weather is sunny
after a cool, wet spell. Amend soil to maintain
calcium levels. Spray with liquid seaweed or
compost tea every 2–4 weeks. Resistant cultivars are widely available; they include 'Grand
Rapids' and 'Montello'.

MELONS
Cucumis melo

MUSKMELON AND HONEYDEW
MELON AT A GLANCE

Botanical Name: *Cucumis melo*
Height: To 14 inches
Spread: 6–10 feet
Shade Tolerance: Full sun
Hardiness: Killed by frost
Preferred Soil: Fertile, moist, well-drained,
high in organic matter

Most Common Melon Pests

See also "Squash and Pumpkins" on page 51
and "Watermelon" on page 59.

Symptom: Holes chewed in leaves
Cause: **Cucumber beetles, spotted**
or striped

Plant resistant cultivars such as 'Hearts of
Gold'. For controls see "Cucumbers" on
page 27.

Symptom: Vines suddenly wilt and die
Cause: **Squash vine borers**

You can distinguish borer attack from a wilt
disease by looking for signs of girdling and
yellowish castings from borer holes at the base
of stems. Adults are narrow-winged moths,
with wingspans of 1–1½ inches. They have
olive brown forewings, clear hindwings, and a
red abdomen with black rings. The larvae are
white grubs with a brown head, growing up to
1 inch long. For controls see "Squash Vine
Borer" on page 289.

Most Common Melon Diseases

Symptoms: Pale brown or gray spots or streaks on leaves and stems; stems rot; infected leaves turn yellow and die.
Cause: **Gummy stem blight (*Didymella bryoniae*)**

A gummy material oozes from stem streaks. Fruit develops dark-colored, rotting areas. Use 3- to 4-year rotations and plant in well-drained, fertile soil. At the first sign of infection, prune off and destroy all infected tissues. Remove severely infected plants.

Symptom: Leaves with small dark spots with brown or white centers, sometimes haloed
Cause: **Target spot (*Corynespora cassilicola*); Cercospora leaf spot (*Cercospora citrullina*)**

Cool, humid conditions favor these diseases. Plant in well-drained soils amended with compost and use black plastic mulch with floating row covers or slitted plastic tunnels in cool climates.

Symptoms: Spots on leaves and fruit; fruit rots under spots
Causes: **Angular leaf spot (*Pseudomonas lachrymans*); alternaria blight (*Alternaria cucumerina*); anthracnose (*Colletotrichum lagenarium*); scab (*Cladosporium cucumerinum*)**

Minimize all of these problems by careful watering or drip irrigation so you don't get the leaves wet. For controls see "Bacterial Spot" on page 303, "Scab" on page 328, and "Anthracnose" on page 300.

*Honeydew melons (*Cucumis melo*)*

Symptoms: Foliage is dull green; leaves and branches wilt
Cause: **Bacterial wilt (*Erwinia tracheiphila*)**

To test melons for bacterial wilt, cut through a wilted vine and pull the cut ends away from one another. Bacterial wilt forms a sticky thread between the cut ends of the stem. The bacteria that causes wilt in squash and other cucurbit overwinters in the salivary glands of cucumber beetles. The beetles transmit the disease as they feed on your plants. To prevent bacterial wilt, control insects as much as possible or use floating row covers over plants, hand-pollinating early flowers if necessary.

Symptom: White, powdery coating on leaves
Cause: **Powdery mildew (*Sphaerotheca fuliginea*)**

As this disease progresses, the leaves turn dry and brown. To prevent or reduce powdery mildew, choose resistant cultivars such as 'Earligold' or 'Crete' cantaloupes. Plant melons in well-drained soil; space widely enough for good air circulation. Compost all plant debris after harvest. Spraying compost tea on leaves every 2–4 weeks can help prevent infection. Remove and destroy infected plant parts.

Symptoms: Yellow spots on leaves; purple or gray mold on leaf undersides
Cause: **Downy mildew**
(***Pseudoperonospora cubensis***)

Symptoms usually start on older leaves and spread to new foliage. For controls see "Downy Mildew" on page 312.

Symptoms: Leaf margins dry and brown; leaves and branches wilt; fruit rots
Cause: **Fusarium wilt**
(***Fusarium roseum***)

Prevent fusarium wilt with good cultural care, planting in well-drained soil. Choose resistant cultivars when possible; try 'Earlisweet' and 'Crete' for melons. Warm air and soil temperatures favor this disease, so mulching with light-reflective straw or hay may help in hot climates. Potassium deficiencies and nitrogen excesses also encourage fusarium problems. To reduce root injuries, control nematodes. If plants show infection, remove and destroy them, taking the roots and surrounding soil.

Symptoms: Leaves stunted, mottled, and distorted; crown of plant yellow and dry
Causes: **Cucumber mosaic; watermelon mosaic**

Aphids and cucumber beetles can spread viruses as they feed. Prevent viruses by keeping plants growing vigorously. Choose resistant cultivars and certified disease-free planting stock. Do not touch wet plants.

OKRA
Abelmoschus esculentus

OKRA AT A GLANCE

Botanical Name: *Abelmoschus esculentus*
Height: 3–8 feet
Spread: 2–4 feet
Shade Tolerance: Full sun
Hardiness: Killed by frost
Preferred Soil: Moderately fertile, moderately moist, well-drained, high in organic matter; tolerate clay and clay loam

Most Common Okra Pests

Symptom: Holes chewed in pods or leaves
Causes: **Corn earworms; other caterpillars**

If you do not see caterpillars, look for their crumbly green castings. Once inside the pod, caterpillars are protected from sprays, so start inspecting plants early in the season for eggs and caterpillars. While caterpillars are small, spray *Bacillus thuringiensis* var. *kurstaki* (BTK) or neem. For light infestations, handpicking eggs and caterpillars gives sufficient control.

Symptom: Curled, distorted leaves
Cause: **Aphids**

Aphids feed in clusters under leaves and on growing tips. Their feeding usually causes distorted leaves and branch tips. They excrete a sticky honeydew onto leaves below. Spray aphids with insecticidal soap, neem, summer oil, homemade garlic sprays, or, as a last resort, pyrethrins. For further controls see "Aphids" on page 244.

Symptom: Plants wilt in midday sun
Cause: **Root knot nematodes**

Check the roots for hard, irregular galls up to 1 inch long, which indicate a nematode infestation. For control see "Nematodes, Root Knot" on page 322. Choose resistant cultivars such as 'Annie Oakley'.

Symptom: Deformed buds and pods
Cause: **Stink bugs**

Suspect these plant bugs if flowers and pods have hard, warty dimples or drop prematurely. Where damage is slight, handpick adults, nymphs, and eggs (which are barrel-shaped, in clusters on undersides of leaves), or shake plants over trays of soapy water to catch bugs. For heavy infestations, spray insecticidal soap for nymphs and dust or spray pyrethrins to control adults.

Most Common Okra Diseases

Symptoms: Flowers and pods brown and rot; raised black spots on rotting areas
Cause: **Choanephora rot**
   (***Choanephora cucurbitarum***)

This disease also infects cucurbits, peppers, and peas. Plant in well-drained soil where air circulation is high. Foliar sprays with compost tea or sulfur may prevent infections or keep mild infections from spreading.

Symptoms: Leaves yellow, wilt, and drop; plant dies
Cause: **Fusarium wilt (*Fusarium* spp.)**

You may also notice that the insides of affected stems are discolored when you cut them open. For controls see "Fusarium Wilt" on page 315.

Symptom: White, powdery coating on leaves and pods
Cause: **Powdery mildew**
   (***Sphaerotheca fuliginea***)

Powdery mildew infections are unsightly and can also weaken host plants. The powdery white or gray spots on leaves enlarge quickly, finally covering the entire leaf. Infected tissues become pale, then turn brown and shrivel. Prevent problems by spacing plants widely to allow for good air circulation. For controls see "Powdery Mildew" on page 323.

Okra (<u>*Abelmoschus esculentus*</u>*)*

ONIONS

Allium cepa

ONIONS AT A GLANCE

Botanical Name: *Allium cepa*
Height: 12 inches
Spread: 6–8 inches
Shade Tolerance: Full sun
Hardiness: Tolerate light frost
Preferred Soil: Fertile, moist, well-drained, high in organic matter

---

Most Common Onion Pests

Symptom: Silvery leaves with browned tips
Cause: **Onion thrips**

Thrips suck juice from plant cells, which leaves silver streaks on the leaves. For controls see "Thrips" on page 293.

Symptom: Plants wilt and turn yellow
Causes: **Onion maggots; bulbflies**

Look for tunnels in the bulbs and signs of feeding damage on the roots. Small bulbs may be hollowed out. Tiny, white maggots in the tunnels are onion maggots. Bulbfly larvae are ½ inch long, grayish and wrinkled. Pesticides are ineffective once bulbs are infested by either pest, but applying parasitic nematodes to the soil may provide some control. Destroy all infected plants. Cover onions with floating row covers from planting until late July, or plant sets late to avoid the first generation of flies. Plant red cultivars such as Japanese bunching onions and cultivars with hard skins (try 'Northern Oak', 'Bingo', and 'Copper King').

Most Common Onion Diseases

Symptom: Dark green or black mold on bulb
Cause: **Smudge** (*Colletotrichum circinans*)

Smudge infects nearly full-sized bulbs and occurs when soil is excessively moist and temperatures are 75°–85°F. Destroy all infected plants. Well-drained soil and compost application helps to protect plants. Choose tolerant or resistant cultivars, such as 'Early Yellow Globe'.

Symptom: Gray-colored streaks on leaves and bulbs
Cause: **Smut** (*Urocystis cepulae*)

This fungal disease is most common on young plants growing in cool soil. For controls see "Smut" on page 329.

Symptoms: Roots and bulb have pink coloration; plants may be stunted
Cause: **Pink root** (*Pyrenochaeta terrestris*)

Members of the onion family should not be planted in soil where this disease has occurred for at least 5 years. Yearly applications of an inch of compost will introduce beneficial microorganisms that prey on it.

Symptoms: Leaf tips yellow and die; roots and bulb base rots; white mold develops
Cause: **White rot** (*Sclerotium cepivorum*)

Cool, poorly drained soil favors this disease. Soak seeds in compost tea before planting and give transplants a compost-tea root-drenching when planting. Destroy infected plants.

Symptoms: White or purple specks on
leaves; plant tops die
Causes: **Downy mildew** *(Peronospora
destructor);* **botrytis blight**

Handling plants only when they are dry can
minimize the spread of these diseases. For
controls see "Downy Mildew" on page 312 and
"Botrytis Blight" on page 305.

Symptoms: Water-soaked spots on leaves;
spots turn purple
Cause: **Purple blotch** *(Alternaria porri)*

This fungal disease thrives in wet weather. For
controls see "Garlic" on page 30.

Symptoms: Tops yellow; neck tissue rots
Cause: **Basal rot** *(Fusarium* **spp.***)*

Minimize the damage caused by this disease by
growing a tolerant cultivar, such as 'Duration'.
For controls see "Most Common Bulb
Diseases" on page 157.

Onion (<u>*Allium cepa*</u>*)*

PEANUTS
Arachis hypogaea

PEANUTS AT A GLANCE

Botanical Name: *Arachis hypogaea*
Height: To 1½ feet
Spread: To 2 feet
Shade Tolerance: Full sun
Hardiness: Killed by frost
Preferred Soil: Fertile, moist, well-drained,
  sandy or sandy loam, slightly acidic

Most Common Peanut Pests

Symptom: Plants wilt in midday sun
Cause: **Root knot nematodes**

Check the roots for hard, irregular knots and
galls, which indicate a nematode infestation.
For controls see "Nematodes, Root Knot" on
page 322.

Symptom: Puckered leaves
Cause: **Leafhoppers**

Feeding by leafhoppers causes the leaf tissue
to react with distorted puckers. Light infestations are not damaging. For heavy infestations
of leafhoppers, spray insecticidal soap, neem,
or pyrethrins.

Symptom: Holes chewed in leaves
Causes: **Corn earworms; other
  caterpillars**

Several caterpillars may feed on peanuts.
Handpick light infestations. For heavy infesta-
tions, spray *Bacillus thuringiensis* var. *kurstaki*
(BTK), neem, or pyrethrins.

Symptom: Leaves with pale speckles
Cause: **Spider mites**

If spider mites are the problem, you will see the fine webbing on undersides of leaves. For controls see "Spider Mites" on page 286.

Most Common Peanut Diseases

Symptom: White, powdery coating
                    on leaves
Cause: **Powdery mildew**
                    (*Erysiphe polygoni*)

Minimize problems by spacing plants widely to allow for good air circulation. For controls see "Powdery Mildew" on page 323.

Most Common Peanut Disorders

Symptom: Plant does not form nuts
Causes: **Compacted soil; short**
                    growing season

Peanuts form on tendrils, or "pegs," that grow from the plant's stems and burrow into the soil. Plant peanuts in loose, friable soil and hill with a loose organic mulch, such as straw. In the North, choose short-season cultivars and start plants in peat pots about 6 weeks before the frost-free date.

Peanuts (<u>Arachis hypogaea</u>)

PEAS

Pisum sativum

PEAS AT A GLANCE

Botanical Name: *Pisum sativum*
Height: Bush, to 2 feet; pole, to 6 feet
Spread: 6–8 inches
Shade Tolerance: Full sun
Hardiness: Tolerate light frost
Preferred Soil: Fertile, moist, well-drained, high in organic matter

Most Common Pea Pests
See also "Beans" on page 12.

Symptom: Superficial puckers and
                    scars on pods
Cause: **Thrips**

Thrips damage is most evident on sugar snap peas. Damaged pods are still edible since the damage is only cosmetic. If damage is unacceptable, wash thrips from plants with a strong stream of water or spray with insecticidal soap. Keep nearby weeds pulled to eliminate host plants of thrips.

Symptom: Pea seeds hollowed out
Cause: **Pea weevils**

You may see the ⅕-inch-long, cream-colored larvae in the seeds, but damage is usually noticed only after the larvae have matured and left behind holes in the seeds. This is too late to apply controls, but to reduce the problem next year, remove and destroy all crop debris after harvest to remove overwintering sites. Weevils remain in stored seeds, so do not use infested seed for planting unless it has been heat-treated. (To heat-treat seeds, place them in cold water, heat rapidly to 140°F, then remove and dry seeds.) Where weevils are a serious problem, spray pyrethrins to control adults on plants, or cover plants with floating row covers from the time you plant seed through the blossom period.

Symptoms: Silk webs inside pods; holes chewed in seeds
Cause: **Pea moths**

This is a pest in spring peas in the northeastern United States and in eastern and western Canada. Undamaged peas in a pod are edible, but you can't tell whether snap peas are infested unless they are shelled. Pick and destroy all yellowing pods and destroy crop debris when plants have finished yielding. Cultivate to destroy cocoons in the soil. Where infestations are usually severe, spray pyrethrins as soon as you see tiny entry holes in pods.

Symptom: Young foliage curled and sticky
Cause: **Pea aphids**

Pea aphids are tiny, green or black insects found in clusters on shoots and new leaves. For controls see "Aphids" on page 244.

Symptom: Winding, whitish tunnels between upper and lower leaf surfaces
Cause: **Leafminers**

The pale green maggots of leafminer flies chew mines in the leaves, but do little damage to plants unless they are small or heavily infested. Handpicking the damaged leaves usually provides sufficient control. For heavy infestations of leafminers, try spraying neem.

Cover plants with floating row covers early in the season to avoid the most damaging generations of leafminers.

Symptom: Half-circle notches in leaf edges
Cause: **Pea leaf weevils**

Suspect weevils if you see their characteristic notches cut in leaves. They may also chew on stems of seedlings. Weevils usually do not cause serious damage unless plants are small. For heavy infestations, spray plants with pyrethrins to control adults.

Symptom: Large holes chewed in leaves
Causes: **Loopers; other caterpillars**

If you do not see caterpillars, look for their crumbly green castings. Caterpillars are usually not very damaging unless present in large numbers (and then they may strip leaves). Handpick light infestations. For heavy infestations, spray *Bacillus thuringiensis* var. *kurstaki* (BTK) or neem.

Most Common Pea Diseases

Symptoms: Stem and roots rot; plants die
Cause: **Root rot**

Choosing a planting site with good drainage can minimize root rot problems. For controls see "Root Rot" on page 326.

Symptoms: Lower leaves turn yellow; growth slows
Cause: **Fusarium wilt** (*Fusarium oxysporum* f. *pisi*)

Prevent problems by planting resistant cultivars, such as 'Maestro' and 'Oregon Sugar Pod II'. For controls see "Fusarium Wilt" on page 315.

Symptom: Brown, purple, or water-soaked
              spots on leaves, stems,
              and pods
Cause: **Blight (*Ascochyta* spp.;**
              ***Pseudomonas pisi*)**

Blight diseases are favored by cool, wet weather and are carried on the seed. Soak seed in compost tea before planting. Don't touch plants when they are wet. Remove and destroy severely infected plants.

Symptoms: White, powdery coating on
              leaves; purplish mold on leaves
Cause: **Powdery mildew**
              (*Erysiphe polygoni*)

To prevent powdery mildew, grow a resistant cultivar, such as 'Knight' or 'Oregon Giant'. For controls see "Powdery Mildew" on page 323.

Symptoms: Mottled or malformed leaves
              and pods; purplish brown pods
Causes: **Viral diseases, including pea**
              enation mosaic, pea stunt, bean
              yellow mosaic, and pea streak

Grow resistant cultivars such as 'Maestro' and 'Oregon Sugar Pod II'. For controls see "Mosaic" on page 319.

Peas (Pisum sativum)

PEPPERS

Capsicum annuum var. *annuum*

PEPPERS AT A GLANCE

Botanical Name: *Capsicum annuum* var.
  annuum
Height: To 3 feet
Spread: To 1½ feet
Shade Tolerance: Full sun
Hardiness: Damaged or killed by light frost
Preferred Soil: Fertile, moist, well-drained,
  high in organic matter; not suited to
  heavy clay

Most Common Pepper Pests

Symptom: Holes bored in peppers
Causes: **Corn earworms;**
              European corn borers

You will know caterpillars are the culprits if you find them inside, but they may have already left the peppers. Caterpillars inside peppers are safe from sprays. Where corn earworms are a serious problem, sprays of *Bacillus thuringiensis* var. *kurstaki* (BTK) or neem every 3 or 4 days may provide control if applied early, while caterpillars are still feeding on leaves. This will not control corn borers because they enter peppers immediately upon hatching. Destroy damaged peppers (undamaged parts are edible) and destroy crop residues.

Symptom: Yellowing, misshapen flowers
              and peppers
Cause: **Pepper weevils**

Pepper weevils are common from southern California to Florida. Infested peppers may drop, and surviving peppers have holes and red or yellow patches. You may see the small, white larvae, up to ⅕ inch long, inside damaged peppers. Pesticides are not effective against larvae inside the peppers. Destroy all dropped and damaged buds and peppers and clean up crop debris to eliminate all overwintering sites.

Symptom: Sticky coating on leaves; leaves may be distorted

Cause: **Aphids**

Aphids are tiny, green or black insects, found mainly in clusters on undersides of old leaves and in growing tips. Their feeding can cause distorted leaves and branch tips. For controls see "Aphids" on page 244.

Symptom: Whitish, winding tunnels between upper and lower leaf surfaces

Cause: **Serpentine leafminers**

Peppers suffer little damage from leafminers unless a large area of leaf tissue is consumed. Handpick and destroy damaged leaves to reduce the next generation of leafminers. Spray neem to control larvae in leaves. Where heavy infestations are common, cover transplants with floating row covers until blossoms open to prevent adults from laying eggs on plants.

Symptom: Minute, yellow speckles on leaves

Cause: **Spider mites**

If spider mites are present, you may see fine webbing on undersides of leaves. When numerous, their feeding weakens plants, causes leaves to drop, and results in stunting. For controls see "Spider Mites" on page 286.

Symptom: Many small round holes in leaves

Cause: **Flea beetles**

Seedlings and small plants may be destroyed by heavy infestations. For controls see "Flea Beetles" on page 262.

Most Common Pepper Diseases

Symptoms: Sunken spots on leaves; water-soaked or scabby spots on fruit

Cause: **Bacterial spot (*Xanthomonas vesicatoria*)**

Prevent problems by growing resistant cultivars, such as 'Admiral' and 'Guardian'. For controls see "Bacterial Spot" on page 303.

Symptom: Large, pale-colored spots with reddish borders on leaves

Cause: **Cercospora leaf spot (*Cercospora beticola*)**

This fungus overwinters on crop residue or in seeds. High humidity in combination with cool temperatures favor it. Practice 4-year rotations and plants to facilitate good air circulation.

Symptoms: Mottled, distorted leaves, stems, and fruit; stunted growth

Causes: **Many viruses, including tobacco mosaic (TMV), potato virus X (PVX), cucumber mosaic (CMV), tobacco etch (TEV), potato virus Y (PVY), and alfalfa mosaic (AMV)**

Some cultivars can tolerate or resist some viruses. 'Admiral', 'Figaro', and 'Guardian' resist tobacco mosaic virus and potato virus Y; 'Figaro' and 'Guardian' also resist tobacco etch virus. For controls see "Mosaic" on page 319.

Symptoms: Leaves are spotted; cankers form on stems; fruit rots

Cause: **Late blight (*Phytophthora capsici*)**

Late blight damage on peppers usually begins just before blossoming. Lower leaves have large, water-soaked, irregularly shaped spots at their tips or margins. After 7–10 days, a whitish mold develops around the spots on the under-sides of leaves. Dark green, water-soaked cankers may girdle stems at the soil line. The spores of this fungus overwinter in crop debris. To control late blight, remove crop residues in the fall; rotate tomato family crops.

Bell peppers (<u>Capsicum annuum</u> var. <u>annuum</u>)

Symptoms: Leaves curled, spotted; pale spots with visible black spores on fruit

Cause: **Early blight (*Alternaria* spp.)**

Leaf spots may run together to cover whole leaves. For controls see "Early Blight" on page 313.

Symptoms: Older leaves yellow; plant wilts and may die

Cause: **Fusarium wilt; Verticillium wilt**

Symptoms usually appear on the oldest leaves first. For controls see "Fusarium Wilt" on page 315 and "Verticillium Wilt" on page 332.

Most Common Pepper Disorders

Symptom: Fruit with white or tan sunken area, generally on one side

Cause: **Sunscald**

Prevent sunscald by controlling leaf diseases that can lead to leaf drop. For controls see "Sunscald" on page 338.

Symptom: Water-soaked, dark rot at blossom end of fruit

Cause: **Blossom end rot**

Blossom end rot is a calcium deficiency symptom that can affect either green or ripe fruit. Calcium deficiency can occur even when soil tests indicate adequate calcium. High nitrogen or magnesium levels can interfere with calcium absorption. Drought can also contribute to the problem. For controls see "Blossom End Rot" on page 335.

Note

Exposure to high or steady wind lowers yields somewhat. Plant behind a windbreak or screen of tall, bushy plants.

POTATOES

Solanum tuberosum

POTATOES AT A GLANCE

Botanical Name: *Solanum tuberosum*
Height: 1½ feet
Spread: 1½ feet
Shade Tolerance: Partial shade
Hardiness: Damaged by light frost
Preferred Soil: Fertile, moist, well-drained, high in organic matter, slightly acidic

---

Most Common Potato Pests

Symptom: Large holes chewed in leaves
Cause: **Colorado potato beetles**

Moderate leaf damage from this pest has little effect on yields, but in heavy infestations, the entire plant may be defoliated. Mulch plants with deep straw, which seems to impede the movement of beetles in early spring before they have fed enough to be able to fly. Trap overwintered beetles in trenches around the potato patch lined with plastic. Cover plants with floating row covers until mid-season. For further controls see "Colorado Potato Beetle" on page 254. Choose resistant cultivars such as 'Katadin' and 'Sequoia'.

Symptom: Downward-curling, puckered leaves
Cause: **Potato aphids**

Potato aphids are ⅒-inch-long, pinkish or green insects found singly or in small clusters on undersides of leaves. For controls see "Aphids" on page 244.

Symptoms: Yellow and brown spots; brown edges on leaves
Cause: **Leafhoppers**

Early leafhopper damage starts as light green stipples, then browning starts at the tips of leaflets, spreading to the entire leaf. You may be able to see the quick, wedge-shaped insects on undersides of leaves. Severely attacked plants may die from "hopperburn" or from viruses spread by leafhoppers. If there is more than one leafhopper per ten leaves, spray insecticidal soap, pyrethrins, or neem.

Symptom: Many small, round holes in leaves
Cause: **Flea beetles**

Although leaf feeding by adult flea beetles has little effect, the larvae, which feed on tubers, are much more damaging. Plant as late as possible to avoid the most damaging generation. Cover seedlings and potato shoots with floating row covers or fine mesh until adult beetles die off. Interplant crops to shade susceptible plants. Spray pyrethrins to control adult flea beetles. Drench roots with parasitic nematodes to control larvae.

Symptom: Shoots wilt and die
Cause: **Potato tuberworm**

These are pests in California and the southern states. Look for tunnels in the leaves and stems of plants. Destroy infested plants and tubers, and carefully check all tubers for larvae before storing. Signs of larvae are holes bored in the eyes of tubers, with pinkish webbing and castings visible around the holes. Next season, plant potato pieces deeply, hill soil at least 2 inches deep over developing tubers, and mulch plants to prevent adult moths from reaching tubers to lay eggs. Rotate crops.

Symptom: Large holes chewed in leaves
Causes: **Loopers; climbing cutworms;**
              other caterpillars

Several species of caterpillars may attack potatoes. If caterpillars are not visible, look for crumbly green castings. Moderate infestations cause little damage and handpicking caterpillars is usually sufficient. If not, spray *Bacillus thuringiensis* var. *kurstaki* (BTK) or neem. Where caterpillars are always a problem, use floating row covers to keep adult moths from laying eggs on leaves.

Symptoms: Networks of fine tunnels;
              cracks on tubers
Cause: **Tuber flea beetles**

Damaged tubers are edible once the surface damage is removed; however, they won't keep in storage. Next season, plan to spray pyrethrins to control adults as soon as they appear on leaves in May. Drench roots with parasitic nematodes to control larvae. Cover plants with floating row covers until August.

*Potatoes (*Solanum tuberosum*)*

Symptom: Plants are stunted and
              turn yellow
Cause: **Root knot nematodes**

Look for small bumps or warts on the tubers and small, hard galls on other roots. Destroy infested potato plants, including all roots and undersized tubers. For controls see "Nematodes, Root Knot" on page 322.

Most Common Potato Diseases

Symptoms: Leaves curl and pucker; plants
              are stunted with low yields
Cause: **Several viruses**

Aphids can spread viruses as they feed on your plants. For controls see "Mosaic" on page 319.

Symptom: Corky spots on potato skins
Cause: **Scab (*Streptomyces scabies*)**

Trim out scab spots before cooking affected potatoes. For controls see "Scab" on page 328.

Symptom: Black patches on skin of tuber
Cause: **Scurf (*Pellicularia filamentosa*)**

This organism is actually a form of the ubiquitous fungus *Rhizoctonia solani.* On potatoes for immediate home use, peel off the superficial scurf. Do not store scurf-infected tubers. Discard infected seed potatoes.

Symptom: Leaves with gray or brown
              ringed spots
Cause: **Early blight (*Alternaria* spp.)**

Leaf spots are the first symptom of early blight. Potatos are usually affected around the time they blossom. Minimize crop damage by growing a tolerant cultivar, such as 'Butte'. For controls see "Early Blight" on page 313.

Symptoms: Water-soaked brown spots on
leaves; white mold on leaf
undersides

Cause: **Late blight**
(*Phytophthora infestans*)

Late blight fungi overwinter as fungal threads
in infected potato tubers or crop refuse. Tubers
from infected plants have brown or purplish
sunken spots on the skin and develop dry rot or
a white mold when kept in storage. To avoid
problems, plant only disease-free potatoes.
Choose cultivars such as 'Butte', 'Katahdin',
and 'Onaway' that tolerate or resist late blight
infection. Rotate tomato family crops; clean up
crop residues in the fall. For more information
see "Late Blight" on page 315.

Most Common Potato Disorders

Symptom: Sprouts don't emerge from the
soil in spring

Cause: **Many fungal and bacterial**
pathogens

Potatoes planted in extremely cold, wet soils
sometimes rot. Wait until the soil has dried
slightly and the soil temperature is at least
40°F. Let cut surfaces form a callus before
planting. Cover plants shallowly with soil for
fast emergence.

Symptom: Tubers have green patches on
skin and underlying flesh

Cause: **Light exposure**

Potatoes are stems, not roots, and develop
chlorophyll when they are exposed to light.
However, poisonous alkaloids also develop. To
prevent this, hill potatoes so that at least an
inch of soil covers all developing tubers. Cure
and store potatoes in the dark. Peel off any
green areas before cooking.

RADISHES
Raphanus sativus

RADISHES AT A GLANCE

Botanical Name: *Raphanus sativus*
Height: 6–8 inches
Spread: 6–8 inches
Shade Tolerance: Full sun; tolerate
partial shade
Hardiness: Tolerate light frost
Preferred Soil: Fertile, moist, well-drained,
high in organic matter

Most Common Radish Pests

Same pests as cabbage. See "Cabbage" on
page 16.

Most Common Radish Diseases

Symptom: Roots enlarged and misshapen

Cause: **Club root**
(*Plasmodiophora brassicae*)

Symptoms include stunted growth and
yellowed or wilted leaves. This fungus stimulates radish root cells to grow abnormally
large, creating galls that are swollen and usually
tapered at both ends. Choose a well-drained
planting site and rotate crops. Remove all
infected plants, weeds, and surrounding soil.

Symptoms: Leaves yellow, pucker;
roots are small

Cause: **Yellows (*Fusarium oxysporum***
f. *conglutinans*)

Look for tolerant or resistant cultivars such as
'Fancy Red' and 'Red Pak'. For controls see
"Fusarium Wilt" on page 315.

Symptom: Roots cracked with rough skin and dark flesh
Cause: **Downy mildew**

Downy mildew is most serious in humid regions. Prevent problems by choosing a planting site with good drainage. Space plants to encourage good air circulation, and water early in the day. Clean up all plant debris in fall to remove overwintering spores. Remove and destroy infected plants and plant parts.

Most Common Radish Disorders

Symptom: Roots split
Cause: **Overmaturity**

Radishes crack within a few days of reaching their optimum size. Heavy rains at harvest time also stimulate cracking. Make small plantings every 2 weeks so you can pick them just at their peak. If heavy rains come, pick them a little small.

Radishes (Raphanus sativus)

RHUBARB
Rheum rhabarbarum

RHUBARB AT A GLANCE

Botanical Name: *Rheum rhabarbarum*
Height: To 2½ feet
Spread: To 4 feet
Shade Tolerance: Full sun; tolerates partial shade
Hardiness: Perennial in Zones 2–7
Preferred Soil: Fertile, moist, well-drained, high in organic matter, slightly acidic

Most Common Rhubarb Pests

Symptom: Small holes or spots bored in stalks
Cause: **Rhubarb curculios**

These ½-inch-long, grayish black snout beetles pierce the stalks to suck the juice. The larvae also feed on dock, sunflower, and thistle stalks. Handpick adults and remove nearby larval host plants to reduce populations. Maintain vigorous plants, which suffer little harm from curculios.

Symptom: Large holes chewed in leaves
Causes: **Caterpillars; Japanese beetles**

Rhubarb can tolerate a heavy infestation of leaf-eating insects, so handpicking caterpillars or knocking beetles from the leaves onto a ground sheet provides sufficient control. For heavy caterpillar infestations spray *Bacillus thuringiensis* var. *kurstaki* (BTK). For more controls see "Most Common Vegetable Pests" on page 8.

Most Common Rhubarb Diseases

Symptom: Pale or brown concentric spots
             on leaves
Cause: **Ring spot**

This virus infects beans, beets, peas, squash, cucumbers, and tomatoes, as well as rhubarb. Remove all infected leaves immediately. Destroy badly infected plants.

Symptoms: Leaves yellow; stalks wilt
Cause: **Verticillium wilt**
             (*Verticillium albo-atrum*)

Prevent problems by planting in well-drained soil or raised beds. For controls see "Verticillium Wilt" on page 332.

Most Common Rhubarb Disorders

Symptom: Stalks thin and small
Cause: **Poor nutrition**

For the highest yields and healthiest plants, side-dress or mulch this heavy feeder with an inch or two of finished compost each year. In spring, spray plants with compost tea or fish emulsion.

Rhubarb (Rheum rhabarbarum)

SPINACH
Spinacia oleracea

SPINACH AT A GLANCE

Botanical Name: *Spinacia oleracea*
Height: 4–8 inches
Spread: 4–12 inches
Shade Tolerance: Full sun; tolerates partial
  shade
Hardiness: Tolerates light frost
Preferred Soil: Fertile, moist, well-drained,
  high in organic matter

Most Common Spinach Pests

Symptom: Clear or brownish blotches
             on leaves
Cause: **Leafminers**

Leafminer larvae feed between the upper and lower layers of leaves. In light infestations, pick and destroy damaged leaves to reduce the next generation of leafminers. For heavy infestations, spray neem to control larvae in leaf mines. Where infestations are usually heavy, protect the crop with floating row covers from the time you plant seeds until harvest.

Symptom: Curled, distorted leaves
Cause: **Aphids**

Aphids are tiny, green, pink, or black insects, found mainly in clusters on undersides of old leaves and in growing tips. For controls see "Aphids" on page 244. Test on several leaves before using sprays, since spinach can be sensitive to sprays. Where aphids are a common problem, grow smooth-leaved cultivars such as 'Olympia Hybrid' that are easier than crinkled leaves to wash free of aphids.

Symptom: Large, ragged holes chewed
                in leaves
Causes: **Loopers; beet armyworms**

If caterpillars are not visible, you can tell they
are present if you find crumbly green castings.
Handpick caterpillars or, if they are
numerous, spray *Bacillus thuringiensis* var.
kurstaki (BTK) or neem. Where caterpillars
are always damaging, cover plants with
floating row covers to prevent adult moths
from laying eggs on leaves.

Symptom: Many small, round holes
                in leaves
Cause: **Flea beetles**

Flea beetles mainly do cosmetic damage to
older plants, but seedlings and small plants
may be destroyed by heavy infestations. The
damage is recognizable by the small, round
holes the adults chew through the leaves.
Grow spinach under floating row covers to
prevent flea beetle damage. Flea beetles
prefer full sun; interplant spinach with taller
crops to supply shade. Spray pyrethrins to
control adult beetles if damage reaches
unacceptable levels.

Spinach (<u>Spinacia oleracea</u>)

Most Common Spinach Diseases

Symptoms: Pale yellow patches on leaves;
                gray or purple mold on
                leaf undersides
Cause: **Downy mildew
                (*Peronospora effusa*)**

Prevent problems by planting resistant culti-
vars, such as 'Melody', 'Tyee', and 'Winter
Bloomsdale'. For controls see "Downy
Mildew" on page 312.

Symptoms: Leaves mottled, curled, and
                puckered; plants stunted
Cause: **Cucumber mosaic virus**

Minimize the damage caused by this disease by
growing tolerant cultivars, such as 'Melody'
and 'Winter Bloomsdale'. For controls see
"Mosaic" on page 319.

Symptom: Pale yellow spots that turn
                orange
Cause: **Rust (*Puccinia aristidae*)**

You may also notice whitish blisters on leaf
undersides. The plants show general lack of
vigor and slow growth. Moderately infected
plants are usually stunted; seriously infected
plants die. For controls see "Rust" on page 327.

Symptoms: Leaves yellow; plants wilt
Cause: **Fusarium wilt**

This fungus thrives in warm soil, so grow
spinach when the soil is cool. Wilting when
the soil is moist is usually the first sign. Often
only one side of a plant will wilt, but as the
disease progresses, more of the plant is
affected. For controls see "Fusarium Wilt" on
page 315.

SQUASH AND PUMPKINS

Cucurbita spp.

SQUASH AND PUMPKINS AT A GLANCE

Botanical Name: *Cucurbita* spp.
Height: To 3 feet
Spread: Bush, to 4 feet; vine, to 12 feet
Shade Tolerance: Full sun
Hardiness: Damaged or killed by light frost
Preferred Soil: Fertile, moist, well-drained, high in organic matter

---

Most Common Squash Pests

Symptoms: Blossoms chewed; holes bored in fruit
Cause: **Pickleworms**

Pickleworms are a pest in the Southeast. Holes in fruit are filled with green castings and you may see pale green caterpillars inside fruit. Destroy damaged fruit and crush rolled sections of leaves, which have the pickleworm pupae inside. Spray *Bacillus thuringiensis* var. *kurstaki* (BTK) as soon as caterpillars appear on blossoms. Pupae overwinter in weeds or rolled squash leaves; brown-banded adult moths emerge in spring and lay eggs on vines. Remove and compost or till under crop debris immediately after harvest. Plant early-maturing cultivars as early as possible so squash are ready for harvest before pickleworm populations peak. Choose resistant cultivars such as 'Blue Hubbard', 'Boston Marrow', 'Buttercup', and 'Summer Crookneck'.

Symptom: Leaves yellow with sticky patches
Cause: **Whiteflies**

Turn over leaves and look for tiny, snowy white insects that fly up when disturbed. A light infestation of whiteflies does little damage, and the sticky honeydew they produce can be washed off. For controls see "Whiteflies" on page 297.

Symptom: Leaves with tiny, yellow speckles
Cause: **Spider mites**

If spider mites are present, you may see fine webbing on undersides of leaves. For controls see "Spider Mites" on page 286. Before spraying insecticidal soap, test-spray first to make sure it does not damage leaves.

Symptom: Holes chewed in leaves
Cause: **Cucumber beetles, spotted or striped**

These elongated, greenish yellow beetles with stripes or spots are found feeding on leaves. Although their feeding causes little direct damage, they spread bacterial wilt and mosaic diseases. For controls see "Cucumber Beetle, Spotted" on page 256 and "Cucumber Beetle, Striped" on page 257. Choose cultivars such as 'Blue Hubbard', 'Green Hubbard', 'Summer Crookneck', and 'Summer Straightneck', which are tolerant to bacterial wilt and mosaics.

Symptom: Vines suddenly wilt and die
Cause: **Squash vine borers**

You can distinguish borer attack from a wilt disease by looking for signs of girdling and yellowish castings from borer holes at the base of stems. For controls see "Squash Vine Borer" on page 289. Resistant cultivars are 'Butternut', 'Butternut 23', and 'Green Striped Cushaw'.

Symptoms: Pale blotches on leaves; shoots
blackened and wilted
Cause: **Squash bugs**

Look for large, oval, dark brown to black bugs
with flattened abdomens and green, reddish,
or gray powdery nymphs. For controls see
"Squash Bug" on page 288. Resistant cultivars
are 'Butternut', 'Early Golden Bush Scallop',
'Early Prolific Straightneck', 'Early Summer
Crookneck', 'Improved Green Hubbard',
'Royal Acorn', and 'Table Queen'.

Symptom: Curled, twisted leaves and shoots
Cause: **Melon aphids**

These mustard yellow to dark green aphids are
1/20 inch long and develop in crowded clusters
on undersides of leaves. For controls see
"Aphids" on page 244.

Crookneck squash (Cucurbita pepo)

Most Common Squash Diseases

Symptoms: Blossoms wilt and rot; stem end
of squash rots; white mold
develops
Cause: **Choanephora wet-rot
(Choanephora cucurbitarum)**

This disease attacks only summer squash. Use
3- to 4-year rotations and space widely enough
to promote good air circulation. Remove all
infected fruit and blossoms from the garden at
the first sign of infection its reduce the spread.

Symptoms: Irregularly shaped, pale spots on
fruit; spots turn gray, brown,
or black
Cause: **Black rot (Didymella bryoniae)**

This fungus causes a dry rot of squash flesh. In
melons, it is known as gummy stem blight. Use
3- to 4-year rotations and plant in well-
drained, fertile soil. At the first sign of infection, prune off and destroy all infected tissues.
Remove severely infected plants.

Symptoms: Leaves and fruit with mottled
spots; distorted growth patterns
Cause: **Mosaic viruses**

You can minimize damage from this disease by
planting a tolerant cultivar, such as 'Multipik'.
Aphids, which carry viruses, tend to stay away
from squash cultivars that have silver or white
markings on their leaves, such as 'Cocozelle'.
Other cultivars, such as 'Multipik', are
tolerant. Prevent viruses by keeping plants
growing vigorously. Choose resistant cultivars
and certified disease-free planting stock. Do
not touch wet plants. Try to control sucking
insects, and use floating row covers when
possible. Remove and destroy virus-infected
plants immediately.

Symptoms: White, powdery coating on leaves; plant dies

Cause: **Powdery mildew (*Erysiphe cichoracearum*)**

As the powdery mildew disease progresses, affected leaves may turn brown and dry. For controls see "Powdery Mildew" on page 323.

Symptoms: Yellow or brown spots on leaves; purple or gray mold on leaf undersides

Cause: **Downy mildew (*Pseudoperonospora cubensis*)**

Reduce crop damage by growing tolerant cultivars, such as 'Super Select' and 'Zucchini Select'. For controls see "Downy Mildew" on page 312.

Symptom: Spots on leaves and fruit

Cause: **Leaf spot**

Leaf spots may run together to cover whole leaves. See "Melons" on page 34 for descriptions and controls of common leaf spot diseases.

Most Common Squash Disorders

Symptoms: Blossom rots; tiny squash rot at blossom end

Cause: **Lack of pollination**

Pollinating insects must transfer pollen from male to female flowers. Rainy periods sometimes keep these insects home, so flowers don't get pollinated. Floating row covers left over the plants once blooming begins can also prevent pollination. Remove the covers or pollinate the flowers yourself by rubbing a male flower over several female blooms. (Male flowers are the ones with slender stems; female flowers have a tiny fruit at the base.)

SWEET POTATOES
Ipomoea batatas

SWEET POTATOES AT A GLANCE

Botanical Name: *Ipomoea batatas*
Height: To 32 inches
Spread: 5 feet or more
Shade Tolerance: Full sun
Hardiness: Damaged by soil temperatures below 50°F
Preferred Soil: Moderately fertile, deep, moist, well-drained, sandy or sandy loam; tolerate slightly acidic soils

---

Most Common Sweet Potato Pests

Symptom: Grooves chewed along upper surface of leaf veins

Cause: **Sweet potato flea beetles**

When infestations are advanced, the leaves may wilt and die. Spray pyrethrins to control adults. Remove bindweed, and don't plant dichondra near sweet potato beds because larvae develop in the roots of these plants. Where infestations are heavy, cover plants with floating row covers until June, or plant late to avoid the peak populations.

Symptom: Tunnels throughout roots

Cause: **Sweet potato weevils**

These are pests found from Texas to South Carolina. Look for ⅛-inch-long, white grubs in the tunnels and for reddish black weevils on the foliage. Destroy all crop debris, volunteer sweet potatoes, and stored roots before the next crop. Pull any nearby morning glories to eliminate alternate host plants for weevils. Start slips from certified weevil-free roots.

Most Common Sweet Potato Diseases

Symptoms: Leaves yellow and plants lose vigor; dark-colored, sunken spots on tubers
Cause: **Black rot (*Ceratostomella fimbriata*)**

Decayed areas under the spots extend only a little way into the tuber. Waterlogged soils promote this disease, and nematodes provide entry sites for it. Plant certified disease-free slips in well-drained soil or raised beds and choose a resistant cultivar, such as 'Allgold'. Use 3- to 4-year rotations. Control nematodes as directed in "Nematodes, Root Knot" on page 322. Do not store infected tubers; trim below infected tissue before cooking.

Sweet potatoes (<u>Ipomoea batatas</u>)

Symptom: Brown areas on tubers
Cause: **Scurf (*Monilochaetes infuscans*)**

This problem often doesn't appear until storage. For controls see "Potatoes" on page 45.

Symptoms: Plants pale and stunted; tubers small or distorted with small dark spots or pits
Cause: **Pox (*Streptomyces ipomoea*)**

Pox overwinters in soil and plant debris and is most prevalent when pH is too high. Use sulfur to reduce pH to at least 5.8 before planting. If pox has caused trouble in the past, reduce pH to as low as 5.3. Plant certified disease-free slips and practice 3- to 4-year rotations. Destroy infected plants.

Symptom: Corky, dark spots in tuber flesh
Cause: **Internal cork**

Internal cork is not likely to develop until the tubers have been in storage for a few weeks. To minimize damage, choose tolerant cultivars, such as 'Allgold' and 'Nemagold', and keep storage temperatures at 55°–60°F.

Symptoms: Plants stunted; leaves yellowing
Cause: **Root knot nematodes**

Minimize crop damage by growing a resistant cultivar, such as 'Nemagold'. For controls see "Nematodes, Root Knot" on page 322.

Symptom: Circular, light-colored spots on tuber skins
Cause: **Fusarium wilt (*Fusarium oxysporum*)**

Aboveground symptoms include yellow, wilted young leaves and dropped older leaves. For controls see "Fusarium Wilt" on page 315.

TOMATOES
Lycopersicon esculentum

TOMATOES AT A GLANCE

Botanical Name: *Lycopersicon esculentum*
Height: Determinate, to 3 feet
    indetermi nate, to 5 feet or more
Spread: 1½–2 feet
Shade Tolerance: Full sun
Hardiness: Damaged or killed by light frost
Preferred Soil: Moderately fertile, moist,
    well-drained, high in organic matter

Most Common Tomato Pests

Symptom: Deep holes chewed in fruit
Cause: **Tomato fruitworm**

These caterpillars have lengthwise stripes. In tomatoes, the caterpillars eat the flower buds, chew large holes in leaves and burrow into fruit. Handpick when there are only a few cater-pillars, or spray *Bacillus thuringiensis* var. *kurstaki* (BTK) or neem weekly where heavy infestations are a problem.

Symptom: Dark tunnels inside fruit
Cause: **Tomato pinworms**

This is mostly a problem in the South and in California. You may see the ⅛-inch-long, mottled worms in the tunnels and small holes bored in the stem end of ripening fruit. Plan to remove or deeply till under all crop debris, and eliminate all tomatoes in the area for at least 3 months before growing another crop. Where infestations are heavy, cover plants with floating row covers (shake plants daily to ensure that flowers are pollinated).

Symptom: Tiny white insects on
                 upper leaves
Cause: **Whiteflies**

A light infestation of whiteflies does little damage, and the sticky honeydew they produce can be washed off. For controls see "Whiteflies" on page 297. Release the parasitic wasp *Encarsia formosa* to control whiteflies in greenhouse tomatoes.

Symptom: Downward-curling or
                 puckered leaves
Cause: **Aphids**

Look for clusters of small, pink, green, or black insects on undersides of leaves. For controls see "Aphids" on page 244.

Tomatoes (<u>Lycopersicon esculentum</u>)

Symptom: Leaves eaten, leaving only stems
Cause: **Tomato hornworms**

Hornworms make large holes in foliage and fruit and leave pellets of green excrement where they feed. They are huge caterpillars (up to 4 inches long), with a "horn" on the tail end. Tomatoes can withstand light infestations without loss of yield, and handpicking the caterpillars daily is usually sufficient. In severe infestations of tomato hornworms, they also feed on stems and chew large holes in fruit. Native parasitic wasps usually control hornworms sufficiently. For other controls see "Tomato Hornworm" on page 294.

Symptom: Whitish, winding tunnels between upper and lower leaf surfaces
Cause: **Serpentine leafminers**

Tomatoes suffer little damage from leafminers unless a large area of leaf is damaged. Handpick and destroy mined leaves to reduce the next generation of leafminers. For heavy infestations, spray foliage with neem or drench soil with neem solution. Cover transplants with floating row covers until plants are well grown—as large as possible—to prevent adults from laying eggs on plants.

Symptom: Lower leaves bronzed or brown
Cause: **Tomato russet mites**

Russet mites are microscopic, only $\frac{1}{100}$ inch long, and their damage may be mistaken for a disease because the lower stems may crack. Affected leaves have a greasy sheen and eventually dry up and drop. Spray or dust with sulfur to control mites, but not too frequently because sulfur can damage plants. Where russet mites are usually a problem, apply sulfur once very early in the season.

Symptom: Small, round holes in leaves
Cause: **Flea beetles**

Flea beetles do little lasting damage to older plants, but seedlings and small plants may be destroyed by heavy infestations. If beetles are damaging, spray pyrethrins. Cover plants with floating row covers until blossoms open. For controls see "Flea Beetles" on page 262.

Most Common Tomato Diseases

Symptoms: Plants stunted; leaves yellowing
Cause: **Root knot nematodes**

Pull up a plant and look for hard knobs and swollen galls on the roots, which are caused by nematodes. For controls see "Nematodes, Root Knot" on page 322. Plant resistant cultivars such as 'Ultra Girl', 'Ultra Boy', 'Beefeater Hybrid', 'Celebrity', and 'Sweet Million'.

Symptoms: Gray areas on leaves; white mold on leaf undersides; brown spots on fruit
Cause: **Late blight** (*Phytophthora infestans*)

This fungal disease often occurs during periods of humid weather with cool nights and warm days. For controls see "Late Blight" on page 315.

Symptoms: Leaves wilt and die; small white spots with dark centers on fruit
Cause: **Bacterial canker** (*Corynebacterium michiganense*)

Stems often crack and turn brown and leaves may curl. Bacterial canker survives on seeds and for a year on plant debris. The bacteria enter plants through wounds. Destroy all infected plants. When transplanting seedlings, discard any that appear weak or sickly.

Symptoms: Plants stunted and wilted; leaflets curl down
Cause: **Bacterial wilt (*Pseudomonas solanacearum*)**

Wilted plants do not recover when watered. For controls see "Bacterial Wilt" on page 303.

Symptoms: Gray, circular spots with dark border on leaves; leaves yellow
Cause: **Septoria leaf spot (*Septoria lycopersici*)**

This fungal disease affects older leaves first. For controls see "Septoria Leaf Spot" on page 328.

Symptoms: Leaves mottled and distorted; green fruit mottled
Causes: **Tobacco mosaic virus (TMV), cucumber mosaic virus (CMV), and potato virus X (PVX)**

Aphids can spread viruses as they feed on your plants. For controls see "Mosaic" on page 319.

Symptoms: Oldest leaves turn yellow; plant wilts
Cause: **Verticillium wilt; fusarium wilt (*Fusarium oxysporum* f. *lycopersicae*)**

Grow resistant cultivars, such as 'Casa del Sol', 'Celebrity', and 'Fabulous'. For controls see "Verticillium Wilt" on page 332 and "Fusarium Wilt" on page 315.

Symptom: Sunken spots on ripe fruit
Cause: **Anthracnose (*Colletotrichum coccodes*)**

Pick fruit promptly, as overripe fruit is more susceptible to this disease. For controls see "Anthracnose" on page 300.

Symptom: Oldest leaves have dark brown spots with concentric rings
Cause: **Early blight (*Alternaria solani*)**

Minimize the damage caused by this disease by planting a resistant or tolerant cultivar, such as 'Mountain Fresh' or 'Fabulous'. For controls see "Early Blight" on page 313.

Most Common Tomato Disorders

Symptom: Fruit is scarred and malformed
Cause: **Catface**

Low light and cool temperatures during fruit set cause this disorder. Drifting herbicide spray from the highway or a neighbor's garden can cause it as well. If the cause is environmental, pick off the distorted fruit and wait for the next cluster to ripen. If herbicide drift has occurred, do your best to locate the source. If you know that herbicides are being applied nearby, cover your plants with plastic during the spraying to protect them from the spray drift. Remove affected fruit; clean new fruit should form.

Symptom: Blossom end of fruit is dark and rotted
Cause: **Blossom end rot**

This disorder can affect either green or ripe fruit. It is most likely to occur when bright, sunny days follow a cloudy, wet period. This disorder is a symptom of calcium deficiency. The blossom end of the fruit develops a dark-colored, watery spot. For controls see "Blossom End Rot" on page 335.

Note
Before planting seeds saved from home-grown tomato plants, it's wise to soak the seeds in a 10 percent bleach solution (1 part bleach to 9 parts water) for 10 minutes. This will help to control some of the seedborne diseases.

TURNIPS

Brassica rapa

TURNIPS AT A GLANCE

Botanical Name: *Brassica rapa*
Height: 8–12 inches
Spread: 8–12 inches
Shade Tolerance: Full sun; tolerate partial shade
Hardiness: Tolerate light frost
Preferred Soil: Fertile, moist, well-drained, high in organic matter

---

Most Common Turnip Pests

Same pests as cabbage. See "Cabbage" on page 16.

Turnips (*Brassica rapa*)

Most Common Turnip Diseases

Symptom: Roots black and rotted
Cause: **Black rot (Xanthomonas campestris)**

Slow growth may be the only above-ground symptom of black rot. You may also notice yellow, V-shaped spots on the edges of the leaves. Black rot spreads quickly in warm, wet weather. This disease may kill or severely stunt young plants; older plants may be defoliated. As spots age, they either become dark and greasy-looking or tan and dry. Infected tissue often drops out producing a "shothole" look. For controls see "Bacterial Spot" on page 16.

Symptoms: Spots with white or gray mold on leaf undersides; blackened roots
Cause: **Downy mildew (Peronospora parasitica)**

This fungal disease can also produce rough, cracked skin on the roots. Minimize problems by choosing a planting site with good drainage. For controls see "Downy Mildew" on page 312.

Most Common Turnip Disorders

Symptom: Small pits or water-soaked spots on roots
Cause: **Cold injury**

Late-planted turnips hold well in the soil during fall and early winter if they are adequately mulched. If left uncovered, exposed portions of the root can suffer from frost injury at temperatures of 30°F or lower. Protect roots by covering with a 6-inch layer of straw or other organic mulch.

WATERMELON

Citrullus lanatus

WATERMELON AT A GLANCE

Botanical Name: *Citrullus lanatus*
Height: To 14 inches
Spread: Trailing, 6–10 feet
Shade Tolerance: Full sun
Hardiness: Killed by frost
Preferred Soil: Fertile, moist, well-drained, high in organic matter

'Bushbaby' watermelons (Citrullus lanatus)

Most Common Watermelon Pests

See also "Squash and Pumpkins" on page 51 and "Melons" on page 34.

Symptom: Holes chewed in leaves
Cause: **Cucumber beetles, spotted or striped**

Plant resistant cultivars such as 'Crimson Sweet' and 'Sweet Princess' to avoid the main cause of damage from these beetles. Where beetles are numerous, cover small and low-growing plants with floating row covers; grow gynoecious female cultivars or hand-pollinate melons. Spray or dust plants with pyrethrins to control adults. After harvest, remove and destroy crop residues to eliminate overwintering sites.

Most Common Watermelon Diseases

Same diseases as squash and melons. See "Squash and Pumpkins" on page 51 and "Melons" on page 34.

Symptom: Brown, sunken lesions on watermelons
Cause: **Watermelon fruit blotch**

This seedborne bacterial disease can wipe out whole plantings. Drip irrigate or hand-water. Bottom-water potted seedlings. Space plants widely. Copper sprays can prevent the spread of the disease but may injure melon leaves. Mix to the lightest dilution possible, spray only in low-light conditions when temperatures are 80°F or below, and water the soil thoroughly before spraying.

HERBS

Most Common Herb Pests

Symptom: Leaves and new shoots distorted and sticky
Cause: **Aphids**

Look for clusters of 1/16–3/8-inch-long, pear-shaped insects on undersides of leaves, on new shoots, and in flower buds. Native beneficial insects usually provide sufficient control in mixed plantings. Wash honeydew and aphids from leaves with a strong stream of water, repeating as necessary. For heavy infestations, spray insecticidal soap, neem, or pyrethrins.

Symptom: Light yellow speckles on leaves
Cause: **Spider mites**

For light infestations of mites, spray foliage with water or insecticidal soap. For heavy infestations, which cause leaf edges to curl, turn brown, and dry up, spray neem or summer oil. Release predatory mites (*Metaseiulus occidentalis* or other species adapted to the local climate). Spray plants with lime sulfur in late winter.

Symptom: Young plants or seedlings cut off or girdled at soil level
Cause: **Cutworms**

During the day, search destroy the fat, greasy, gray caterpillars hiding in soil around plants, or go out at night with a flashlight to catch feeding cutworms. For severe infestations, drench soil with neem or a solution of insect parasitic nematodes before planting, or use a bran bait mixed with *Bacillus thuringiensis* var. *kurstaki* (BTK) sprinkled over the soil. Always use cutworm collars around transplants.

Most Common Herb Diseases

Symptoms: Plants wilt; leaves yellow and die
Causes: **Verticillium wilt (*Verticillium albo-atrum*); fusarium wilt**

Choosing a planting site with well-drained soil can prevent help to prevent wilt damage. For controls see "Verticillium Wilt" on page 332, and "Fusarium Wilt" on page 315.

Symptoms: Water-soaked spots on leaves; gray mold develops in humid conditions
Cause: **Botrytis**

This disease can also produce tan to gray, fuzzy mold on flowers. Once established on a plant, this fungus rapidly spreads to infect the entire plant. Plant in well-drained soil and keep air circulation high. Destroy infected plant parts to reduce the spread of the disease.

Symptom: White, powdery coating on leaves
Cause: **Powdery mildew**

Thinning crowded plantings to improve air circulation can minimize problems. For controls see "Powdery Mildew" on page 323.

Symptoms: Plants yellow and stunted; roots have swollen galls
Cause: **Nematodes, particularly root knot species**

The first symptom of root knot nematodes that you're likely to notice is a general stunting, yellowing, and wilting of the plant. If you dig up the plant, you'll see the enlarged galls (swellings) on the roots or tubers. For controls see "Nematodes, Root Knot" on page 322.

Symptom: Spots on leaves
Causes: **Various fungi and bacteria,**
             including *Pseudomonas* spp.,
             ***Xanthomonas* spp.,**
             ***Colletotrichum* spp.,**
             ***Alternaria* spp., *Septoria* spp.,**
             ***Cercospora* spp.**

Leaf spots may merge to cover whole leaves. For controls see "Bacterial Spot" on page 303, "Anthracnose" on page 300, and "Septoria Leaf Spot" on page 328.

Symptom: Tan, orange, or reddish pustules
             on leaves
Cause: **Rust (most frequently *Puccinia***
             ***menthae*)**

Rust fungi are among the easiest diseases to notice because of their brightly colored spores. The first symptoms are general lack of vigor and slow growth. The fungus then produces pustules, often on leaf undersides. Moderately infected plants are stunted, while seriously infected plants die. Keeping plants vigorous with good general care can help prevent problems. For controls see "Rust" on page 327.

Symptoms: Mottled leaf coloration; growth
             distortions
Cause: **Viruses**

Viruses cause many plant problems, including distorted growth, spots on plant tissues, stunting, yellowing, and mottled plant tissue. Plants grow slowly; stems can become brittle. Aphids and other insects can spread viruses as they feed on your plants. They can also enter through bruises and wounds. They cause the host cell to replicate them and build populations on living tissues. For controls see "Mosaic" on page 319.

BASIL
Ocimum basilicum

BASIL AT A GLANCE

Botanical Name: *Ocimum basilicum*
Height: Usually 1–3 feet
Spread: To 1½ feet
Shade Tolerance: Full sun
Hardiness: Killed by light frost
Preferred Soil: Fertile, moist, well-drained, high in organic matter

Most Common Basil Pests
Rarely troubled by pests; see "Most Common Herb Pests" on page 60.

Basil (Ocimum basilicum)

Most Common Basil Diseases

Symptom: Dark-colored, water-soaked
                  spots on leaves
Cause: **Leaf spots**

Pick off the affected leaves and stems. If plants
are severely infected, pull and destroy them.
Plant in well-drained, fertile soil once the
weather is warm. Cover seedlings with floating
row covers in cool weather. Thin or harvest
leaves so that plants are spaced widely enough
for good air circulation. Sulfur sprays kill most
of the fungi but can discolor leaves.

Symptom: Leaves curled down and
                  mottled
Cause: **Cucumber mosaic virus**

Aphids and other insects can spread viruses as
they feed on your plants. For controls see
"Mosaic" on page 319.

Chives (<u>Allium schoenoprasum</u>)

CHIVES
Allium schoenoprasum

CHIVES AT A GLANCE

Botanical Name: *Allium schoenoprasum*
Height: To 10 inches
Spread: 6–10 inches, clumps
Shade Tolerance: Full sun; tolerate partial
  shade
Hardiness: Perennial in Zones 3–11
Preferred Soil: Fertile, moist, well-drained,
  high in organic matter

Most Common Chives Pests
Not troubled by pests.

Most Common Chives Diseases

Symptoms: White or purple specks on
                  leaves; plant tops die
Causes: **Downy mildew (*Peronospora
                  destructor*); botrytis blight
                  (*Botrytis* spp.)**

These fungal diseases thrive in moist weather.
To prevent problems, plant chives in well-
drained soil. Space plants to promote good air
circulation and water early in the day. Remove
and destroy infected plant parts. For other
controls see "Downy Mildew" on page 312 and
"Botrytis Blight" on page 305.

Symptom: Gray-colored streaks on leaves
                  and bulbs
Cause: **Smut (*Urocystis cepulae*)**

Young plants growing in cool soil are most
prone to this disease. For controls see "Smut"
on page 329.

DILL

Anethum graveolens

DILL AT A GLANCE

Botanical Name: *Anethum graveolens*
Height: 3–5 feet
Spread: To 1½ feet
Shade Tolerance: Full sun
Hardiness: Tolerates light frost
Preferred Soil: Fertile, moist, well-drained, high in organic matter

Most Common Dill Pests

Symptom: Leaves and new shoots distorted and sticky
Cause: **Aphids**

Aphids are common on dill. For controls see "Aphids" on page 244.

Symptom: Foliage stripped from stems
Cause: **Parsleyworms**

Look for very large, fat, green caterpillars with black and yellow crosswise stripes. They may occasionally defoliate dill and related plants. Gently move the caterpillars to more robust carrot family plants, such as lovage, that can tolerate their feeding.

Most Common Dill Diseases

Symptoms: Yellowed, deformed leaves; slow or stunted growth
Cause: **Mosaic**

Leafhoppers and other insects can spread viruses. Prevent these by keeping your plants growing vigorously. Choose resistant cultivars and certified disease-free planting stock. Do not touch wet plants. Try to control sucking insects, and use floating row covers whenever possible. Remove and destroy virus-infected plants immediately.

Symptom: Brown or gray spots on leaves
Cause: **Various fungi and bacteria**

Good air circulation can help prevent these problems. For controls see "Bacterial Spot" on page 303 and "Septoria Leaf Spot" on page 328.

Most Common Dill Disorders

Symptom: Small plants don't form large seedheads
Cause: **Overcrowding**

To avoid crowding, space plants at least 3–4 inches apart to give them plenty of room to develop to their full potential.

Dill (Anethum graveolens)

MINTS

Mentha spp.

MINTS AT A GLANCE

Botanical Name: *Mentha* spp.
Height: To 15 inches
Spread: Indefinite; runners
Shade Tolerance: Tolerate partial shade
Hardiness: Perennial in Zones 5–11
Preferred Soil: Fertile, moist, well-drained, high in organic matter

---

Most Common Mint Pests

Symptoms: Light yellow speckles on leaves; webbing present
Cause: **Spider mites**

Look for fine webbing on undersides of leaves. For controls see "Spider Mites" on page 286.

Spearmint (<u>Mentha spicata</u>)

Most Common Mint Diseases

Symptom: Spots on leaves
Cause: **Various fungi**

Mints are normally so vigorous that a slight case of fungal leaf spot is unlikely to kill them. However, a serious infection can reduce yields. Pick off and destroy all infected leaves, and thin the plant to improve air circulation.

Symptom: Plant wilts when soil is moist
Cause: **Verticillium wilt (*Verticillium albo-atrum*)**

Verticillium wilt is one of the most common diseases of wild and cultivated plants. Infected plants wilt, even when the soil is moist, and eventually die. Verticillium fungi overwinter in plant residues and can survive on old organic matter in the soil for as long as 15 years. Plant in well-drained soil that warms quickly in the spring. Remove crop debris in the fall and compost it in piles that reach 150°–160°F for several days. Use row covers or other season-extending materials to raise the air temperature around plants; verticillium spores germinate best at temperatures of 70°–75°F.

Symptom: Tan, orange, or reddish blisters on leaves
Cause: **Rust (*Puccinia menthae*)**

To prevent the spread of rust, avoid wetting plant leaves when you water. While you can't stop rust fungi, which are airborne, from infecting your plants, you can make plants more resistant. Avoid amendments high in nitrogen, and prune, space, and water carefully to increase air circulation and keep leaves dry. Pick off and destroy infected leaves. Sulfur spray, used when spots first appear, kills new spores.

OREGANO

Origanum spp. and varieties

OREGANO AT A GLANCE

Botanical Name: *Origanum* spp. and varieties
Height: To 1½ feet
Spread: 1½ feet or more
Shade Tolerance: Full sun
Hardiness: Perennial in Zones 5–11
Preferred Soil: Moderately fertile, moderately moist, well-drained

Most Common Oregano Pests

Rarely troubled by pests. See "Most Common Herb Pests" on page 60.

Most Common Oregano Diseases

Symptom: Spots on leaves
Cause: **Various fungi**

To control leaf spots, pick off all infected foliage. Thin out or divide plants to allow better air circulation around the stems and leaves.

Golden oregano (Origanum vulgare 'Aureum')

PARSLEY

Petroselinum crispum

PARSLEY AT A GLANCE

Botanical Name: *Petroselinum crispum*
Height: 10 inches
Spread: 10–12 inches
Shade Tolerance: Full sun (partial shade in warm weather)
Hardiness: Tolerates light frost
Preferred Soil: Fertile, moist, well-drained, high in organic matter

Most Common Parsley Pests

Rarely troubled by pests. See "Most Common Herb Pests" on page 60.

Most Common Parsley Diseases

Symptom: Spots on leaves
Cause: **Leaf spot diseases (*Septoria apiicola; Cercospora carotae; Xanthomonas carotae*)**

For controls see "Bacterial Spot" on page 303 and "Septoria Leaf Spot" on page 328.

Parsley (Petroselinum crispum)

ROSEMARY

Rosmarinus officinalis

ROSEMARY AT A GLANCE

Botanical Name: *Rosmarinus officinalis*
Height: 6 inches–4 feet (cultivars vary)
Spread: 1–4 feet
Shade Tolerance: Full sun
Hardiness: Perennial in Zones 7–11
Preferred Soil: Moderately fertile, moderately moist, well-drained

---

Most Common Rosemary Pests

Rarely troubled by pests. See "Most Common Herb Pests" on page 60.

Rosemary (Rosmarinus officinalis)

Most Common Rosemary Diseases

Symptoms: Leaves yellow and drop; plant dies
Cause: **Root rot fungi**

Since root rot fungi are in all soils, prevention is more effective than control. Avoid overwatering rosemary. Plant in well-drained soil and space plants for good air circulation. Resist the temptation to plant or transplant before the soil warms up in spring.

Symptom: White, powdery growth on leaves and stems
Cause: **Powdery mildew**

Powdery mildew fungi spread quickly on rosemary. Powdery white or gray spots appear on leaves and stems. Infected parts become pale, then turn brown and shrivel. Prevent problems by planting in well-drained soil in a site with good air circulation. Spraying compost tea on leaves every 2–4 weeks can help prevent infection. Pick off and destroy infected plant parts. Sprays of baking soda or baking soda plus oil are often an effective control against powdery mildew (see "Oil Sprays" on page 361).

Most Common Rosemary Disorders

Symptom: Plant dies over the winter
Cause: **Cold injury**

Rosemary cultivars, even those promised to be hardy to Zone 6, are tender perennials. If you are trying to overwinter them outside, plant them in a sheltered spot. Deep mulches will protect the roots but, if placed too near the stem, they may hold so much moisture that the crown rots. If you live in a borderline area, it's safer to pot the plant and bring it in for the winter. Low light and dry air won't harm it at all.

SAGE

Salvia officinalis

SAGE AT A GLANCE

Botanical Name: *Salvia officinalis*
Height: 10–18 inches
Spread: 1–2 feet
Shade Tolerance: Full sun
Hardiness: Perennial in Zones 2–11
Preferred Soil: Moderately fertile,
   moderately moist, well-drained

Most Common Sage Pests

See "Most Common Herb Pests" on page 60.

Most Common Sage Diseases

Symptom: Leaves yellow; plant bushy and
         stunted
Cause: **Aster yellows
         (mycoplasma-like organism)**

Leafhoppers can spread this disease as they
feed. For controls see "Yellows" on page 333.

Symptom: Reddish spots on leaves
Cause: **Rust (*Puccinia* spp.)**

Avoid wetting plant leaves when you water. For
controls see "Rust" on page 327.

Sage (Salvia officinalis)

THYME

Thymus vulgaris

THYME AT A GLANCE

Botanical Name: *Thymus vulgaris*
Height: To 1 foot
Spread: To 2 feet
Shade Tolerance: Full sun
Hardiness: Perennial in Zones 5–11
Preferred Soil: Moderately fertile, moder-
   ately moist, well-drained

Most Common Thyme Pests

See "Most Common Herb Pests" on page 60.

Most Common Thyme Diseases

Symptom: Spots on leaves
Cause: **Leaf spots**

Control leaf spots by picking off infected
foliage. Thin out or divide crowded plantings
to allow for better air circulation.

Symptom: Reddish spots on leaves
Cause: **Rust (*Puccinia* spp.)**

Avoid wetting plant leaves when you water. For
controls see "Rust" on page 327.

Thyme (Thymus vulgaris)

FRUITS AND NUTS

Most Common Fruit and Nut Pests

Symptom: Leaves distorted and sticky
Cause: **Aphids**

Look for colonies of ⅟₁₆–⅜-inch-long, pear-shaped insects on undersides of affected leaves. Native predators usually control aphids. For heavy infestations, wash aphids from plants with a strong spray of water, or spray insecticidal soap, pyrethrins, or neem. Spray dormant oil to control overwintering eggs on twigs. Release aphid midges (*Aphidoletes aphidimyza*) in early spring or late summer.

Symptom: Tree is weak, no pests or
                      diseases obvious
Cause: **Borers**

Carefully examine the base of the trunk for sawdust and holes in the bark. Slide a fine wire into holes to kill borers, or inject a solution of parasitic nematodes into the holes.

Symptom: Irregular, deep brown scars
                      on fruit
Causes: **Oriental fruit moth; leafrollers**

Although unsightly, fruit with scars from earlier feeding by various caterpillars is still edible. However, it may not store well. If a high proportion of fruit was scarred, spray dormant oil in winter. Inspect trees carefully in spring for the first signs of caterpillars feeding to determine whether sprays of *Bacillus thuringiensis* var. *kurstaki* (BTK), neem, or pyrethrins are needed to control larvae while they are small. Cultivate soil 4 inches deep around the trees before bloom to eliminate overwintering larvae. Spray summer oil to kill eggs and larvae.

Symptom: Fruit disappears
Cause: **Birds**

Birds can strip cherry trees and small fruit bushes very quickly before the fruit is fully ripe. Prevent further depredations by covering trees or bushes with bird netting.

Symptom: Leaves pulled together by
                      fine webs
Cause: **Leafrollers**

Many different species of leafroller caterpillars feed on young foliage and fruit for a month in spring. You can find the ⅝-inch-long, greenish caterpillars inside the leaves which have been rolled up with webs to protect the pests from predators and sprays. In light infestions, handpick leaves with webbing. Where leafrollers cause serious damage, plan to spray *Bacillus thuringiensis* var. *kurstaki* (BTK) or neem early in spring, before caterpillars spin webs. Spray dormant oil on trees to reduce the number of overwintering eggs.

Symptom: Leaves skeletonized
Cause: **Japanese beetles**

These ½-inch-long, blue-green beetles with bronze wing covers are easy to see and so is the damage from their feeding, which skeletonizes leaves. In early morning, knock them from the plants into a bucket of soapy water or onto a ground sheet and destroy them. When infestations are light, handpick or vacuum up beetles.

Symptom: Leaves sticky
Cause: **Mealybugs**

If mealybugs are the problem, you will see clusters of tiny (⅟₁₀-inch long), oval, powdery white insects on twigs and on leaf undersides. Native parasites and predators usually provide sufficient control. Wash leaves with water to knock off whiteflies and mealybugs and to remove the sticky honeydew coating and black mold that may have developed. Control ants, which remove the native predators of both pests, by using sticky bands around tree trunks. For heavy infestations, spray with insecticidal soap. You can also control mealybugs by releasing Australian lady beetles (*Cryptolaemus montrouzieri*.)

Symptom: Holes chewed in leaves and fruit

Cause: **Snails**

If the culprit is not visible but slimy trails are left behind, snails may be the problem. Permanently prevent them from climbing plants by fastening copper bands around trunks. Prune low branches; if they touch the ground they give snails an alternate route to the leaves and fruit.

Symptoms: Tree grows poorly; leaves of whole branches wilt

Cause: **Scales**

Look for clusters of ¹⁄₁₀–¹⁄₅-inch reddish, purple, white, gray, yellowish, or brown bumps on bark of branches. Small red or white spots may be present on fruit. Prune out heavily infested branches and, in late winter, spray dormant oil.

Symptom: Tree grows poorly
Cause: **Nematodes**

If you see no sign of diseases, microscopic root nematodes could be the problem, especially in sandy soils. Maintain vigorous growth through regular feeding and watering and mulch with organic mulches. Turn in green manure crops to stimulate growth of soil fungi that control nematodes or dig in chitosan, a natural polymer derived from the chitin components of the shells of crabs and shrimp. Chitosan is available through mail-order and organic gardening specialty sources. Try drenching soil around the roots with neem.

Symptom: Leaves lose color and dry up
Cause: **Leafhoppers**

Leafhopper damage is first noticeable as pale green stipples along the leaf veins. Serious damage from leafhoppers is rare because native parasites and predators usually provide sufficient control. Spray neem, insecticidal soap, pyrethrins, or summer oil (on plants that tolerate it) if infestation is severe enough to cause leaves to turn yellow and drop.

Symptom: Deformed, "catfaced" fruit with corky scars

Cause: **Tarnished plant bugs**

Plant bugs rarely cause serious damage in home gardens. (The blemished fruit is still edible.) Control weeds around the plants and reduce overwintering populations of bugs by removing crop debris around the base of plants. For heavy infestations, spray pyrethrins in spring and early summer to protect fruit and blossoms from damage. To protect bees, do not spray during bloom.

Symptom: Light yellow speckles on leaves
Cause: **Spider mites**

Most species of spider mites spin fine webbing on leaf undersides. The tiny mites (under ¹⁄₅₀ inch long) may be visible crawling on the webbing. Spider mites are most damaging in hot, dry weather and where natural enemies have been destroyed by sulfur or other pesticides. For light infestations, spray foliage with water or insecticidal soap. Spray neem or summer oil for heavy infestations, which cause leaf edges to curl, turn brown, and dry up. Release predatory mites (*Metaseiulus occidentalis* or any other species adapted your local climate). Plan to spray lime-sulfur in late winter.

Most Common Fruit and Nut Diseases

Symptoms: Spots on leaves; tree loses vigor
Causes: **Leaf spot diseases (many fungi and bacteria)**

Rake up and destroy all fallen leaves, through the season and in fall. Try to identify the disease to determine if you should spray with copper, sulfur, or lime-sulfur. If you can't make a good identification, check with your state plant pathologist at the extension service.

Symptom: White, powdery growth on leaves
Cause: **Powdery mildew**

Minimize problems by choosing a site with good air circulation and by pruning to keep the tree open to light and air. For controls see "Powdery Mildew" on page 323.

Symptom: Clusters of mushrooms appear around the trunk
Cause: **Mushroom root rot (*Armillaria mellea*)**

Armillaria root rot causes a gradual dieback on large trees, but more sudden death of seedlings and young trees. It is most likely to attack trees stressed by other problems. For controls see "Armillaria Root Rot" on page 301.

ALMONDS
Prunus amygdalus

ALMONDS AT A GLANCE

Botanical Name: *Prunus amygdalus*
Height: To 40 feet; dwarf, 8–10 feet
Spread: To 30 feet; dwarf, 6–8 feet
Shade Tolerance: Full sun (partial shade in hot climates)
Hardiness: Zones 6–9
Preferred Soil: Fertile, well-drained

Most Common Almond Pests

Symptom: New shoots wilted or dying
Causes: **Oriental fruit moths; peach twig borers**

These pests may also feed in developing fruit. Mature fruit may look undamaged outside, but you will find the caterpillars inside near the pit. For controls see "Peaches and Nectarines" on page 92.

Symptom: Silken webs inside nuts
Cause: **Navel orangeworms**

These caterpillars enter the nuts when the husks split. For this reason, harvest nuts early to avoid damage. Pick up fallen nuts, and knock all mummified nuts out of trees in winter before the adults emerge. Growing a cover crop under trees has been shown to attract beneficial insects that control orangeworms and to hasten the decomposition of fallen nuts, which kills the larvae inside. Spray *Bacillus thuringiensis* var. *kurstaki* (BTK) several times to control newly hatched larvae, before they bore into fruit or into almonds at the hull-split stage.

Most Common Almond Diseases

Symptom: Blossoms shriveled and covered with a fuzzy, grayish mold

Cause: **Brown rot**

This disease is most serious in humid climates. Avoid brown rot by planting resistant cultivars, such as 'Nonpareil', 'Peerless', and Texas'. For controls see "Brown Rot" on page 306.

Symptoms: Small, dark spots on leaves; some with missing centers

Cause: **Shothole disease (*Coccomyces hiemalis*)**

Infected leaves become perforated as spots age. Protect plants by spacing widely for good air circulation and light exposure. Keep trees well pruned.

Almond (Prunus amygdalus)

APPLES
Malus hybrids

APPLES AT A GLANCE

Botanical Name: *Malus* hybrids
Height: To 40 feet; dwarf, 6–12 feet
Spread: 30 to 40 feet; dwarf, 6–12 feet
Shade Tolerance: Full sun
Hardiness: Zones 3–9
Preferred Soil: Moderately fertile, well-drained, slightly acidic; can tolerate widely varying conditions, depending on rootstock

Most Common Apple Pests

Symptom: Half-circle brown scars on fruit

Cause: **Plum curculios**

Egg-laying scars appear as crescent-shaped flaps of skin on young fruit. Later in the season, adults feed on the surface of maturing fruit, creating corky brown scars. Look for the ⅓-inch-long, fat, white larvae with brown heads feeding near the core of fallen fruit. For controls see "Plum Curculio" on page 280.

Symptom: Leaves distorted and sticky

Cause: **Aphids**

Look for colonies of tiny, pear-shaped insects on undersides of affected leaves. Native beneficial insects usually provide sufficient control. For controls see "Aphids" on page 244.

Symptom: Fruit with indented dimples

Cause: **Apple maggots**

The tiny, white larvae of these flies bore brown, winding tunnels in the flesh of the fruit, which may rot entirely. Collect and destroy or use up dropped fruit daily to eliminate larvae. Hang sticky red ball traps in trees from mid-June onward to catch adults.

Symptom: Holes bored in fruit, plugged
         with brown castings
Causes: **Codling moths; oriental
         fruit moths**

Apples attacked by codling moths usually have a single hole, bored from the blossom end, with wet, dark brown castings present. This may not be noticeable until the fruit is cut open. Fruit moth caterpillars enter from the stem end and produce masses of gummy castings. Once caterpillars are in the fruit, they are out of reach, but any undamaged part of fruit is edible. To protect the next crop, intercept codling moth caterpillars by banding trunks with canvas, sticky trap glue, or corrugated cardboard, or tie small paper bags over fruit after thinning in June to prevent codling moth damage. In early summer, control eggs of both, and early fruit moth caterpillars, with summer oil sprays.

Symptom: Yellow speckles on leaves
Cause: **European red mites**

Use a hand lens to look for these minute, reddish spider mites on undersides of leaves. These do not cover the lower leaf surface with webs. Native predatory spider mites usually provide sufficient control. For light infestations, spray water or insecticidal soap. For heavy infestations where leaves are turning brown and brittle, spray summer oil when leaf buds are developing. Release predatory spider mites (*Metaseiulus occidentalis* or other species adapted to the local climate). Spray dormant oil and lime-sulfur in late winter.

Symptom: Cracked bark with cottony fluff
         around edges
Causes: **Woolly apple aphids**

These aphids feed on twigs and branches, causing galled, open cracks in the bark. In light infestations, prune out attacked branches, remove suckers at the base of the tree, and prune water sprouts on limbs to eliminate breeding sites. Spot-spray summer oil or neem on affected branches early in the season. Spray dormant oil in late winter for good control next season.

Symptom: Leaves turn yellow along whole
         branches, which may die
Cause: **San Jose scale**

Look for clusters of tiny, gray bumps on the bark. On fruit, San Jose scale makes small red or whitish spots. Prune out the most infested branches and, in late winter, spray dormant oil.

Symptoms: Tree is weak; no pests or
          diseases obvious
Causes: **Roundheaded apple tree borers;
         other boring insects**

Carefully examine the base of the trunk for sawdust and holes in the bark. Slide a fine wire into holes to kill borers, or inject a solution of insect parasitic nematodes.

Symptom: Leaves at branch tips pulled
         together by fine webs
Cause: **Fruit tree leafrollers**

These caterpillars feed on young foliage and fruit for a month in spring. You can find the caterpillars (which are up to 1 inch long with dark heads) inside the webbed foliage, protected from predators and sprays. For controls see "Fruit Tree Leafroller" on page 264.

Symptom: Irregular, deep brown scars in fruit

Causes: **Oriental fruit moths; leafroller caterpillars**

Although unsightly, fruit with scars from earlier feeding by various insects is still edible, although it may not store well. Where a high proportion of apples were scarred, spray dormant oil in winter. Inspect trees carefully in spring to determine whether sprays of *Bacillus thuringiensis* var. *kurstaki* (BTK), neem, or pyrethrins are needed to control larvae while they are small. Destroy fruit moth pupae around trees by shallow cultivation before blossoms open in spring.

Apple (Malus hybrid)

Most Common Apple Diseases

Symptom: Brown, velvety, or corky spots on leaves and fruit skin

Cause: **Apple scab**

Infected fruit may also be cracked, deformed, or russetted. Infected leaves drop early. Minimize apple scab problems by planting resistant cultivars, such as 'Freedom', 'Golden Delicious', 'Grimes Golden', 'Liberty', and 'Redfree'. For controls see "Apple Scab" on page 300.

Symptom: Fruit is small, often distorted, and has yellow or orange spots

Cause: **Cedar-apple rust**

The small, yellow spots on the leaves and apples can become numerous and as they age become brown and sunken, disfiguring fruit. Reduce the chances of cedar-apple rust by growing resistant cultivars, such as 'Arkansas Black', 'Empire', 'Freedom', 'Grimes Golden', 'Redfree', and 'Winesap'. For controls see "Cedar-Apple Rust" on page 307.

Symptoms: Spots on leaves; rotting spots on fruit

Cause: **Summer disease (various fungi)**

To prevent problems, try resistant cultivars, such as 'Freedom' and 'Liberty'. For controls see "Summer Diseases" on page 331.

Symptom: White, powdery growth on leaves

Cause: **Powdery mildew**

If powdery mildew is a common problem in your area, look for resistant cultivars, such as 'Empire', 'Freedom', 'Golden Delicious', and 'Liberty'. For controls see "Powdery Mildew" on page 323.

Symptom: Leaves and twigs blacken

Cause: **Fire blight (*Erwinia amylovora*)**

To minimize the chance of this disease devastating your trees, start with resistant cultivars, such as 'Arkansas Black', 'Empire', 'Freedom', 'Liberty', 'Redfree', and 'Winesap'. For controls see "Fire Blight" on page 314.

Most Common Apple Disorders

Symptoms: Young twigs and branches die; interior wood of branches is darkened and rotted

Cause: **Winter injury**

Trees subjected to sudden or excessively cold temperatures can suffer a number of different types of injury. If the bark in the crotch of a tree is cold-injured and has lifted from the tree, tack it back in place and paint over the edges with an asphalt paint meant for trees. Similarly, tack bark back onto trunks that have split from the cold. Cover the bark with asphalt tree paint. Prune injured trees more lightly than normal in late winter. In spring, give the injured trees extra fertilizers and moisture and thin the blossoms out drastically. Preventive measures include fertilizing only in spring and early summer. Paint trunks with a diluted white interior latex paint (equal parts paint and water) or cover them with white plastic guards. Choose cultivars and rootstocks that are known to be hardy in your region or, preferably, one region colder.

Symptoms: Blossoms darken and become limp; no fruit sets

Cause: **Freezing**

Freezing temperatures when blossoms are open may kill them. To protect yourself against losses due to freezing, choose cultivars that are known to grow successfully in your area. Plant trees on northern slopes when possible to prevent their blooming too early in the season. When frost threatens, drape small trees with sheets or blankets to protect the blooms. On large trees, sprinkle frosted blossoms with water from just before dawn to several hours afterward to slow their thawing and possibly minimize damage.

APRICOTS

Prunus armeniaca

APRICOTS AT A GLANCE

Botanical Name: *Prunus armeniaca*
Height: To 30 feet; dwarf, 8–10 feet
Spread: To 30 feet; dwarf, 6–8 feet
Shade Tolerance: Full sun
Hardiness: Zones 5–9
Preferred Soil: Fertile, well-drained

Most Common Apricot Pests

Same pests as peaches. See "Peaches and Nectarines" on page 92.

Most Common Apricot Diseases

Symptoms: Blossoms brown and wither; leaves brown; fruit develops rotting spots

Cause: **Brown rot**

Minimize this problem by growing 'Harcot', 'Harlayne', or another resistant cultivar. For controls see "Brown Rot" on page 306.

Symptoms: Small angular spots on leaves; branches wilt and die; bark cracks and exudes a gummy, sour-smelling material

Causes: **Bacterial canker; valsa canker**

Both of these diseases are also called gummosis. Prune off wilted or dying branches several inches below the obvious site of infection. Sterilize tools between cuts. If the lesion is on a large limb or the trunk, cut out the canker down to healthy wood. Infected wood is darker than healthy wood, so you'll be able to see the difference. Copper sprays help to control canker when it first infects leaves. Prevent valsa canker in new plantings by starting with resistant cultivars, such as 'Harcot' and 'Harlayne'.

Symptom: Small, dark, sunken spots or cracks on fruit skin

Cause: **Bacterial leaf spot**

Plant resistant cultivars, such as 'Harcot' and 'Harlayne'. Common in the Southeast, this disease is very difficult to control. Infected trees may also develop water-soaked twig cankers that reinfect the leaves in the spring. Rake up and remove all fallen leaves at the end of the growing season to reduce problems in the following year. Prune out twig cankers. Spray infected trees with copper in late spring.

Apricot (Prunus armeniaca)

BLACKBERRIES
Rubus hybrids

BLACKBERRIES AT A GLANCE

Botanical Name: *Rubus* hybrids
Height: To 6 feet
Spread: To 40 feet
(usually pruned to 6–8 feet)
Shade Tolerance: Full sun (partial shade in South)
Hardiness: Zones 5–9 (marginal in Zones 4 and 10)
Preferred Soil: Deep, sandy loam, high in organic matter; widely tolerant if soil is well-drained with a pH of 6.0–7.0

Most Common Blackberry Pests
Same pests as raspberries. See "Raspberries" on page 98.

Most Common Blackberry Diseases

Symptoms: Light-colored cracks in bark; lateral shoots wilt and die

Cause: **Cane blight**
(*Leptosphaeria coniothyrium*)

This fungus enters the plant through wounds caused by insects or pruning tools. For controls see "Cane Blight" on page 306.

Symptoms: Whole plant is weak; growth is stunted

Cause: **Pest nematodes (many, but *Pratylenchus* spp. most common)**

Pest nematodes attack the feeder roots of plants, causing the plant to lose the ability to take in water and nutrients. While digging up

Blackberry (Rubus fruticosus)

a plant won't reveal the microscopic worms, you can see the damage. If pest nematodes attack, dig up your plant, taking as much surrounding soil as possible. Fill the area with fully finished compost and cover-crop it with grasses for a few years before replanting with new brambles. Be certain to buy bramble stock that is certified disease-free.

Symptom: Orange or yellow pustules on leaf undersides or bark

Causes: **Orange rust (*Gymnoconia peckiana*); cane and leaf rust (*Kuehneola uredinis*)**

The orange pustules appear in early spring and new shoots are weak and spindly. The pustules grow on both bark and leaf undersides of fruiting canes and appear in early summer. Avoid problems by growing rust-resistant cultivars, such as 'Boysenberry', 'Cheyenne', 'Comanche', and 'Evergreen'. For controls see "Rust" on page 327.

Symptoms: Plant stunted; greenish yellow blisters on leaves

Cause: **Mosaic**

Aphids, leafhoppers, and other insects spread viruses as they feed. For controls see "Mosaic" on page 319.

Symptoms: Little or no fruit set; clusters of small twigs with pale leaves on fruiting canes

Cause: **Rosette or double blossom (*Cercosporella rubi*)**

"Witches-brooms" of densely growing twigs with small, pale leaves are the first symptom of rosette. Elongated flower buds soon appear. These buds are sterile and will not set fruit. At the first sign of this disease, cut out the infected canes. Spray the whole planting with copper two or three times at 10-day intervals. Watch carefully in subsequent seasons so that you can act quickly.

Symptoms: Young canes wilt; leaves yellow; fruiting canes collapse as fruit ripens

Cause: **Verticillium wilt (*Verticillium albo-atrum*)**

Verticillium wilt fungi overwinter in crop debris. For controls see "Verticillium Wilt" on page 332.

Symptoms: Warty swellings on crown and canes; canes split and die

Cause: **Crown gall**

Crown gall bacteria enter canes through wounds caused by insects or pruning tools. Look for large, irregularly shaped galls near the soil line. Crown gall is difficult to control once it occurs, so prevention does pay off.

Closely examine purchased plants for galls. Soak seeds and roots of susceptible plants in a solution containing the beneficial bacteria *Agrobacterium radiobacter* before planting. If infection does occur, dig out diseased plants, taking as much surrounding soil as possible. Where infection is mild and localized, you can try cutting out only the infected areas, sterilizing your pruning tools between cuts.

Symptom: Gray mold on fruit
Cause: **Gray mold**

Botrytis fungi can enter plants only through wounds, bruises, and natural openings (such as dying blossoms). A fuzzy, gray mold grows on the exposed tissues. Prevent problems by choosing a planting site with good air circulation. Remove and destroy infected plants and take care not to injure plants when transplanting or pruning.

Symptom: White, powdery coating on fruit
Cause: **Powdery mildew (*Sphaerotheca humuli*)**

Affected fruit is inedible, and whole canes may be weakened or killed. Compost all plant debris. For controls see "Powdery Mildew" on page 323.

Symptom: Purple spots on canes and leaves
Causes: **Anthracnose (*Elsinoe veneta*); cane and leaf spot disease (*Septoria rubi*)**

Remove and destroy infected canes immediately after harvest. Prune well to encourage good air circulation. Spray with lime-sulfur before buds break in spring. Prevent future problems by planting resistant cultivars, such as 'Black Satin' and 'Dirksen Thornless'.

BLUEBERRIES
Vaccinium hybrids

BLUEBERRIES AT A GLANCE

Botanical Name: *Vaccinium* hybrids
Height: 1½–7 feet
Spread: 2–8 feet
Shade Tolerance: Full sun (partial shade in hot climates)
Hardiness: Zones 3–9
Preferred Soil: Moist, well-drained, loose, loamy or sandy soil with a pH of 4.5–5.2

Most Common Blueberry Pests

Symptom: Soft, shriveled berries that drop early
Cause: **Blueberry maggots**

You may see small, whitish maggots in berries or on the surface of picked berries. Destroy all soft or dropped berries and delay harvesting until berries are ripe. This avoids harvest of infested berries, which drop early. For heavy infestations, cover bushes with screen in spring, after fruit set, to prevent egg-laying by female flies. Hang sticky traps baited with fruit-fly (*Rhagoletes*) attractant in plants to trap adults.

Symptom: Berries webbed together
Causes: **Cherry fruitworms; cranberry fruitworms**

If you see ½-inch-long, white or greenish caterpillars feeding inside the webs, it is likely to be fruitworms. Handpick damaged fruit. Harvest berries daily to minimize damage. For heavy infestations, spray plants with pyrethrins after bloom period is over.

Blueberry (Vaccinium hybrid)

Symptom: Fruit disappears
Causes: **Birds**

Birds can strip bushes very quickly before berries are fully ripe. Before berries start to turn blue, cover bushes with bird netting.

Symptom: Leaves webbed together
Causes: **Blueberry leafrollers; other leafrollers**

Leafrollers are usually sufficiently controlled by native parasites. In light infestations, handpick leaves with webbing. Spray *Bacillus thuringiensis* var. *kurstaki* (BTK) or neem if defoliation is serious. Larvae drop readily when mature, about the time berries are ripe, and can be shaken from plants onto a ground sheet and destroyed just before you start to pick.

Symptom: Half-circle notches in leaf edges
Cause: **Black vine weevils**

A large number of notches is an indicator that damage may be occurring from weevil larvae, which feed on roots and girdle stems. For controls see "Black Vine Weevil" on page 248.

Symptom: Leaves skeletonized
Cause: **Japanese beetles**

These blue-green beetles with bronze wing covers are easy to see. For controls see "Japanese Beetle" on page 268.

Most Common Blueberry Diseases

Symptom: Berries are gray, dry, and hard and may drop prematurely
Cause: **Mummyberry (*Monilinia vaccinii-corymbosi*)**

The fungus that causes mummyberry overwinters on infected berries that dropped to the ground the previous season. Wilting flower clusters that turn brown are usually the first sign. Berries that grow from infected ovaries shrivel and dry about midway through their growth. Each year, rake up all mulch and plant debris under the bushes. Cover exposed soil with compost and top with fresh mulch. Minimize the chances of this disease by growing resistant cultivars, such as 'Burlington', 'Collins', 'Jersey', and 'Rubel'.

Symptom: Stems weaken and die
Cause: **Stem canker (*Botryosphaeria corticis; Fusicoccum putrefaciens*)**

The first of these diseases is most prevalent in the southeast. It causes swellings on the stem that are somewhat reddish the first year and turn black and blisterlike in the second year.

Plant resistant cultivars, such as 'Atlantic' and 'Jersey', to avoid this disease. In colder areas, the second organism is prevalent. It causes reddish, circular spots on the stem that can look like targets. Prune off all diseased stems. Rake under the bushes to remove infected twigs that may have dropped to the ground. Prevent this canker by planting 'Burlington', 'Coville', 'Rubel', or another resistant cultivar.

Symptom: Gray mold on twigs and
              blossoms
Cause: **Botrytis blight (*Botrytis cinerea*)**

On leaves, stems, and fruit, the first signs of infection are tiny, water-soaked spots. Stem and leaf tissues become light brown and crack open, allowing the gray spores to emerge. For controls see "Botrytis Blight" on page 305.

Symptom: Orange-colored mold on fruit
Cause: **Anthracnose**
              (*Glomerella cingulata*)

This disease spreads quickly in wet weather. For controls see "Anthracnose" on page 300.

Most Common Blueberry Disorders

Symptom: Leaves are yellow with
              green veins
Cause: **Iron deficiency**

Blueberries require very low pH soil, roughly 4.5–5.2. If they grow in a soil with a pH higher than 5.2, they are likely to become iron-deficient. To alleviate immediate symptoms, spray iron chelates on the foliage. Longer-term solutions require your reducing the soil pH. Effective methods include adding sulfur to the soil (get your soil tested to find out how much sulfur you need) or mulching with an acidic material such as pine needles.

CHERRIES
Prunus spp. and hybrids

CHERRIES AT A GLANCE

Botanical Name: *Prunus* spp. and hybrids
Height: Pie cherry, to 20 feet; sweet cherry, to 35 feet
Spread: To 30 feet
Shade Tolerance: Pie cherry, full sun or light shade; sweet cherry, full sun
Hardiness: Pie cherry, Zones 5–9; Sweet cherry, Zones 5–8
Preferred Soil: Moist, well-drained

Most Common Cherry Pests

Symptom: Shriveled, soft fruit drops early
Cause: **Cherry fruit flies**

Look for white maggots feeding inside the fruit. Destroy dropped fruit daily. Where infestations are always heavy, starting in May, hang yellow sticky traps in trees to intercept females before they lay eggs. Collect and destroy dropped fruit daily.

Symptom: Half-circle scars on young fruit
Cause: **Plum curculios**

Feeding and egg-laying by adults damage fruit skin, leaving a characteristic half-circle scar. The larvae tunnel in fruit, which causes the fruit to rot or drop prematurely. You may find the ⅓-inch-long, fat grubs with brown heads feeding inside. The larvae feed for 2–3 weeks and, when the fruit drops, they leave to pupate in soil. For controls see "Plum Curculio" on page 280.

Sweet cherry (Prunus avium)

Symptom: Leaves curled and sticky
Cause: **Black cherry aphids**

Look for colonies of tiny, shiny, black insects on undersides of leaves. Both adults and nymphs suck plant sap. Severely infested leaves and flowers may drop. Treatment is usually not necessary, as cherry aphids leave the trees by midsummer. For controls see "Aphids" on page 244.

Symptom: Leaves chewed and webbed
                together
Cause: **Green fruitworms**

Look for pale green, 1¼-inch-long caterpillars feeding on the leaves. They usually do not cause serious damage to leaves, but later they bite into fruit and may completely consume it. Where infestations are heavy, spray *Bacillus thuringiensis* var. *kurstaki* (BTK) or neem as soon as leaf damage is noticed.

Most Common Cherry Diseases

Symptom: Small purplish or reddish spots
                on leaves
Cause: **Cherry leaf spot**
                (*Coccomyces* spp.)

The fungus that causes this disease overwinters on fallen leaves and fruit. Waxy bumps grow on leaf undersides and infected leaves turn yellow and drop. Practice good fall sanitation, raking up and destroying all dropped leaves and prune tree to promote good air circulation. Avoid problems with this disease by growing resistant cultivars, such as 'Lambert', 'Meteor', and 'Northstar'.

Symptom: Wilting when soil is moist
Cause: **Verticillium wilt**

Prevent problems by planting cherries in well-drained soil in full sun. The first symptoms of this fungus wilt may be yellow or brown, wilting leaves at branch tips. Clean up fallen leaves and fruits in the fall.

Symptom: Fruit rots during ripening or
                soon after being picked
Cause: **Brown rot**
                (*Monolinia fructicola; M. laxa*)

Minimize the development of this disease by planting resistant cultivars, such as 'Northstar' and 'Windsor'. Brown rot is most serious in warm, humid climates. Tiny, brown specks cover the flower and its stem. The fungus soon spreads to growing fruit, where it produces small brown spots. Prune trees to promote good air circulation. Avoid overfertilizing, since high nitrogen levels encourage this fungus. Control insects as much as possible to avoid wounds that admit disease. In fall, gather and destroy all mummified fruit and fallen leaves and twigs. Apply sulfur sprays when blossoms show pink to petal fall and again before harvest to control brown rot.

Symptoms: Leaves grow in compact rosettes; few fruit form
Cause: **Peach rosette (virus)**

This virus causes trees to develop abnormally short internodes on new branches. Rosettes of up to a hundred small, discolored leaves form on these branches. Leaves turn yellow, and no fruit forms on infected branches. Buy only certified disease-free trees from your nursery. Control leafhoppers, aphids, and other sucking insects to help prevent the spread of the disease, and eliminate all wild chokecherries where possible. Remove infected trees.

Symptoms: Growth distortions such as dwarfing, discoloration, or leaf rolling
Causes: **Little cherry, X-disease, and small-bitter cherry (viruses)**

Aphids, leafhoppers, and other insects can spread viruses as they feed on your plants. For controls see "Peach Rosette" above.

Symptom: White, powdery coating on leaves
Cause: **Powdery mildew**

Powdery mildew infections are unsightly and weaken host plants. Infected fruit usually develops a soft rot under the coating of white fungal threads and spores. To prevent problems, choose a resistant cultivar, such as 'Northstar'. Plant in well-drained soil and pick off and destroy infected tissues. For further controls see "Powdery Mildew" on page 323.

Symptom: Sunken, oozing cankers on branches, twigs, or trunk
Cause: **Canker (*Valsa leucostoma; V. cincta*)**

Leaves on infected branches may wilt, and dieback is common. To control, cut out all cankers and paint wounds with a mixture of equal parts lime-sulfur and white interior latex paint. 'Sam' and 'Sue' are cultivars with some canker resistance.

Most Common Cherry Disorders

Symptom: Fruit is hard, shriveled, and blotchy
Cause: **Boron deficiency**

Cherries require moderate levels of boron. If you suspect a deficiency, call your Cooperative Extension Service and ask for information about the nearest laboratories that perform tissue analyses. You'll want a recommendation from them before adding borax to your soils because boron can be lethal in high doses.

Symptom: Fruit cracks at or just before maturity
Cause: **Environmental factors**

Heavy rains just before harvest are often blamed for cracking. However, temperature, sugar content, and permeability of the fruit skin all play a part. When buying trees, ask your supplier for information about the cultivar's susceptibility to cracking. Resistant cultivars include 'Stella', 'Sam', and 'Northstar'. As further protection, after heavy rains, shake the branches of your trees to jar water off the fruit. Small trees can be covered with plastic if rain threatens when the fruit has begun to color.

CITRUS
Citrus spp. and hybrids

CITRUS AT A GLANCE

Botanical Name: *Citrus* spp. and hybrids
Height: 20–30 feet; dwarf, 3–12 feet
Spread: About as wide as tall
Shade Tolerance: Full sun
Hardiness: Zones 9–11
Preferred Soil: Moderately fertile, moist,
  well-drained soil with a pH of 6.0–6.5

Most Common Citrus Pests

Symptom: Small, round, reddish bumps on fruit
Cause: **California red scale**

The fruit is unharmed, as scale is only on the rind. Native predators usually control scale sufficiently. If an infestation is heavy enough to cause leaves to yellow and drop, spray summer oil once in late summer or early fall. For severe infestations, release the parasitic wasp *Aphytis melinus.*

Symptom: Flowers and fruit deformed
Cause: **Citrus bud mites**

This is mostly a pest of lemons in western coastal areas. Damage is cosmetic. If damage is severe, spray summer oil once, either in early summer or in fall (not in hot, dry weather).

Symptom: Fruit has scarred skin around stem end
Cause: **Citrus thrips**

Fruit is unharmed and the scars are only cosmetic. No control is necessary.

Symptom: Leaves curled and sticky
Cause: **Aphids**

Aphids feed in clusters on growing tips and the undersides of leaves. For controls see "Aphids" on page 244.

Symptom: Leaves sticky
Causes: **Citrus whiteflies; citrus mealybugs**

If whiteflies are the problem, you'll see tiny, white insects fly up from undersides of leaves. Mealybugs are oval, powdery white, crawling insects, usually found in clusters. Native parasites and predators usually provide sufficient control. Control ants, which remove the native predators of both pests. Wash leaves with water to knock off whiteflies and mealybugs and to remove the sticky coating and black mold that may have developed. For further controls see "Whiteflies" on page 297 and "Mealybugs" on page 272.

Symptom: Holes chewed in leaves and fruit
Cause: **Snails**

If the culprit is not visible but slimy trails are left behind, snails may be the problem. Permanently prevent them from climbing trees by fastening copper bands around trunks. Prune low branches so they do not touch the ground and give snails an alternative route.

Symptom: Pale yellow speckles on leaves
Cause: **Citrus red mites**

Use a hand lens to look for these minute, red mites on young leaves. Native predatory mites usually provide sufficient control. For heavy infestations spray summer oil once in early fall (not in hot, dry weather, which damages leaves).

Most Common Citrus Diseases

Symptoms: Leaves yellow; gum oozes from
              bark near soil line
Cause: **Collar rot**
              (*Phytophthora citrophthora*)

Collar rot, while caused by a fungus, only strikes when humidity levels are excessive near the trunk. The brown, oozing lesions will spread to girdle the trunk if the disease is not halted. To prevent collar rot, plant in well-drained conditions. Prune off low-hanging branches, leave several inches of bare ground between mulch and the trunk, and avoid wetting the trunk when watering. Plant citrus trees so the graft union is well above the soil line. If collar rot appears, cut off all damaged bark and paint the wound with white latex paint.

Symptom: Irregular, raised, grayish scabs
             on fruit
Cause: **Citrus scab**

Citrus scab spores are carried by wind, rain, and insects. For controls see "Citrus Scab" on page 308.

Symptom: Brown, sunken spots on fruit
Cause: **Melanose (*Diaporthe citri*)**

The first symptoms of this disease are dark brown or reddish brown leaf spots. For controls see "Melanose" on page 318.

Symptoms: Leaves drop prematurely;
              grayish brown or yellowish
              brown spots on fruit
Cause: **Brown rot (*Phytophthora* spp.)**

Brown rot is most common in humid conditions. It lives in the soil but is spread to fruit by splashing rain or irrigation water. Prune off low-hanging branches and mulch under the trees. Water trees carefully to avoid splashing soil on leaves.

Symptoms: Abnormal growth patterns;
              mottled coloration on leaves
Cause: **Viral diseases**

A number of different viruses infect citrus trees. Choose certified disease-free trees. Control sucking insects such as mites because they spread viruses. Destroy infected trees.

Most Common Citrus Disorders

Symptom: Bark peels or splits
Cause: **Sunburn**

Citrus bark is thin and very easily sunburned. To protect your trees, paint the bark with equal parts water and white latex paint or wrap them with commercial tree wrap.

'Valencia' orange (<u>*Citrus sinensis*</u> 'Valencia')

CURRANTS AND GOOSEBERRIES

Ribes spp.

CURRANTS AT A GLANCE

Botanical Name: *Ribes* spp.
Height: To 6 feet
Spread: 2–4 feet
Shade Tolerance: Full sun
Hardiness: Zones 4–7
Preferred Soil: Moderately fertile, moderately moist, well-drained, loam or clay soil with a pH of 5.0–7.0

GOOSEBERRIES AT A GLANCE

Botanical Name: *Ribes hirtellum* and *R. uva-crispa*
Height: 6–8 feet
Spread: 2–4 feet
Shade Tolerance: Full sun (partial shade in hot climates)
Hardiness: Zones 3–8
Preferred Soil: Moderately fertile, moderately moist, well-drained, sandy to clay soil with a pH of 5.0–7.0

Most Common Currant and Gooseberry Pests

Symptom: Yellow leaves and stems die back
Cause: **Currant borers**

Infested canes have smaller, yellowing leaves in the spring. If you cut open the base of the cane, you may see the yellowish, ½-inch-long borer grubs. Prune out and destroy infested canes at the first sign of injury. Red currants are somewhat less attacked than black cultivars.

Symptom: Fruit drops early
Cause: **Currant fruit flies**

The ⅖-inch-long maggots of this fly feeding in the currants cause them to color early and drop. Collect and destroy all dropped fruit.

Symptom: Leaves chewed from edges inward
Cause: **Imported currantworms**

These sawfly larvae are ⅕ inch in size and look like pale green caterpillars with black spots. They start feeding in the center of the bush about the time plants leaf out. They may completely defoliate plants. Handpick light infestations or spray pyrethrins thoroughly to ensure the first generation is controlled. (These are not true caterpillars, therefore *Bacillus thuringiensis* var. *kurstaki* (BTK) has no effect.)

Symptom: Red, puckered, or wrinkled patches on leaves
Cause: **Currant aphids**

Look for colonies of tiny, yellowish green insects on undersides of affected leaves. For controls see "Aphids" on page 244.

Most Common Currant and Gooseberry Diseases

Symptom: Leaves, blooms, and shoots coated with white, powdery growth
Cause: **Powdery mildew (*Sphaerotheca mors-uva; Microsphaera grossulariae*)**

Powdery mildew is common on currants but usually not serious enough to threaten the life of your plant. For controls see "Powdery Mildew" on page 323.

Symptoms: Leaves have brown spots which enlarge and dry; leaves die and drop

Cause: **Leaf spot (*Mycosphaerella ribis, Cercospora angulata,* or *Pseudopeziza ribis*)**

Most leaf spot diseases start as tiny specks that you hardly notice. However, it doesn't take long for the organisms to spread, killing whole leaves. In severe cases, the bushes become defoliated by mid- to late summer. Spray copper or sulfur at the first sign of infection in spring. Continue to spray every 10–14 days until new growth does not show spots.

Symptom: Brown, orange, or reddish spots on leaves

Cause: **Rust (*Cronartium ribicola*)**

Minimize rust problems by choosing a planting site with good air circulation. Avoid excessive applications of nitrogen. Water carefully to keep leaves dry. Pick off and destroy infected leaves. Sulfur spray, used when rust spots first appear, kills new spores.

Currant (<u>Ribes fasciculatum</u>)

FIGS
Ficus carica

FIGS AT A GLANCE

Botanical Name: *Ficus carica*
Height: To 10 feet in cold climates; 40 feet where mild; usually pruned smaller
Spread: In mild climates, 25–60 feet if unpruned
Shade Tolerance: Full sun
Hardiness: Zones 7–11
Preferred Soil: Fertile, very well-drained loam; but widely tolerant

---

Most Common Fig Pests

Symptoms: Tree grows poorly; leaves of whole branches wilt

Cause: **Scale**

Look for clusters of tiny, reddish, purple, white, yellowish, or brown bumps on bark of branches. Prune out most severely affected branches. Spray dormant oil in winter.

Most Common Fig Diseases

Symptom: Yellow or yellow-orange spots on leaves

Cause: **Rust**

Early rust symptoms are a general lack of vigor and slow growth. Later, the fungus produces yellow or yellow-orange pustules, often on leaf undersides. Affected leaves may turn completely yellow and die. Spring weather blows spores to new hosts, sometimes hundreds of miles from their original site. To prevent rust, avoid excessive nitrogen applications. Prune to improve air circulation; water

Fig (Ficus carica)

problems by planting resistant cultivars, such as 'Black Mission' and 'Brown Turkey'.

Symptom: Tree grows poorly
Cause: **Root knot nematodes**

Maintain vigorous growth and mulch with organic mulches. Turn in green manure crops to stimulate growth of soil fungi that control nematodes, or dig in chitosan, a natural polymer derived from the chitin components of the shells of crabs and shrimp. Chitosan is available through mail-order and organic gardening specialty sources. Try drenching soil around the roots with neem. Choose resistant cultivars such as 'Celeste' and 'Hunt'.

Symptoms: Roughened bark; light-colored
               spore masses on bark lesions
Cause: **Canker (*Phomopsis cinerescens*)**

Canker usually infects figs at pruning cuts or where a branch or twig has dropped. Prevent canker by pruning only in bright, dry weather. To control this disease, prune off and destroy infected branches. Cut at least 3 inches below the canker site and sterilize all pruning tools between cuts.

Symptom: Fruits and young shoots covered
              with gray mold
Cause: **Gray mold**

Minimize the chances of this disease by growing resistant cultivars, such as 'Black Mission' and 'Brown Turkey'. Botrytis fungi can enter plants only through wounds, bruises, and natural openings (such as dying blossoms). Prevent problems by choosing a planting site with good air circulation. Remove and destroy infected plant parts and take care to avoid injuring plants when transplanting or pruning.

carefully to keep leaves dry. Pick off and destroy infected leaves. Sulfur spray, used when spots first appear, kills new spores.

Symptom: Spots on leaves
Cause: **Leaf blight (many fungi)**

Most of these fungi spread fairly rapidly to fruit, twigs, and branches. Leaf blights are favored by high-humidity, low-light conditions. Keep trees pruned to allow sunlight to strike inner branches. Rake up and destroy all dropped leaves and fruit. Prune off and destroy infected branches. Prevent future

FILBERTS (HAZELNUTS)
Corylus spp. and hybrids

> ### FILBERTS (HAZELNUTS) AT A GLANCE
>
> **Botanical Name:** *Corylus* spp. and hybrids
> **Height:** To 20 feet
> **Spread:** 15–20 feet
> **Shade Tolerance:** Full sun (partial shade in hot climates)
> **Hardiness:** Zones 4–8
> **Preferred Soil:** Fertile, light, well-drained

Most Common Filbert Pests

Symptom: Kernels of nuts stained black
Cause: **Filbertworms**

These ½-inch-long caterpillars feed in nuts and pupate on the ground in winter. Collect and use or destroy all fallen nuts. Rake up and compost fallen leaves.

Symptom: Leaves distorted and sticky
Cause: **Aphids**

Aphids are particularly attracted to new growth. For controls see "Aphids" on page 244.

Symptom: Abnormally swollen flower buds
Cause: **Bud mites**

You will need a magnifying glass to see these minute mites in the bud scales. They feed on buds in spring, and infested buds do not produce nuts. Where infestations have been heavy, spray summer oil in May. Plant resistant cultivars such as 'Barcelona', 'Cosford', 'Italian Red', and 'Purple Aveline'.

Most Common Filbert Diseases

Symptoms: Bark shows lesions; branches and then whole bush die
Cause: **Eastern filbert blight (*Anisogramma anomala*)**

There is no cure for this fungal disease. It doesn't affect American filberts but kills European cultivars. Infected bushes should be removed and destroyed. Plant resistant hybrids or American filberts if you live in the eastern United States.

Symptoms: Small spots appear on leaves; cankers form on branches
Cause: **Western filbert blight (*Xanthomonas corylina*)**

Western filbert blight is caused by a bacteria rather than a fungus. Prevent the disease with good cultural care, guarding particularly against winter sunburn. If new twigs or leaves show spots, spray with copper. Prune and destroy all infected twigs and branches.

Filbert (Corylus maxima)

GRAPES

Vitis spp. and hybrids

GRAPES AT A GLANCE

Botanical Name: *Vitis* spp. and hybrids
Height: 4–5 feet
Spread: To 100 feet, but usually pruned to
   6–12 feet
Shade Tolerance: Full sun
Hardiness: Zones 4–10
Preferred Soil: Deep, moderately fertile,
   well-drained, slightly acidic

Most Common Grape Pests

Symptoms: Grapes with holes; grapes
           webbed together
Cause: **Grape berry moths**

Berry moth caterpillars are ⅓ inch long and
feed in flowers as well as fruit, causing young
berries to turn dark and drop. Pick and
destroy infested berries and rolled sections of
leaves, which contain cocoons. In fall, destroy
fallen leaves to remove overwintering pupae.
Where heavy infestations are a problem, spray
Bacillus thuringiensis var. *kurstaki* (BTK),
starting shortly after fruit has set in spring.

Symptom: Leaves sticky
Causes: **Grape whiteflies; grape
           mealybugs**

If whiteflies are the problem, you will see tiny,
white insects fly up from undersides of leaves.
Mealybugs are oval, powdery white, crawling
insects found on the grape canes. Native
parasites and predators usually provide sufficient control of both. A low infestation of

whiteflies does little damage. Wash leaves with
water to knock off whiteflies and mealybugs and
to remove the sticky coating and black mold
that may have developed. Control ants, which
remove the native predators, by using sticky
bands around grape trunks. For heavy infestations spray neem for whiteflies, or insecticidal
soap for both pests. For mealybugs, scrape off all
loose bark to expose mealybugs to high summer
temperatures, which kills them. Release
Australian lady beetles (*Cryptolaemus
montrouzieri*). Spray dormant oil in late winter.

Symptom: Small, round, rough galls on
           undersides of leaves
Cause: **Grape phylloxera**

If you cut open these green and reddish galls,
you will see numerous minute, yellowish eggs
and insects inside. Prune out and destroy
leaves with galls. Leaf gall phylloxera cause
little direct damage unless they are numerous;
however, they are an indicator that the much
more damaging root-attacking form of
phylloxera may be present on susceptible cultivars. There is no treatment for root phylloxera.
Provide good irrigation and fertile soil to slow
the decline of infested vines. Replant with
grapes grafted onto resistant rootstock.
American or French hybrids are resistant to
root phylloxera. Cultivars tolerant to leaf galls
are 'Aurora', 'Seyval Blanc', 'Duchess',
'Delaware', 'Agawam', and 'Catawba'.

Symptom: Leaves skeletonized
Cause: **Japanese beetles**

These pests are a serious problem in many
areas. Adults are metallic blue-green beetles
with bronze wings that feed on plants during
the day, especially in warm weather. For
controls see "Japanese Beetle" on page 268.

Symptom: Leaves lose color and dry up
Cause: **Leafhoppers**

Leafhopper damage is first noticeable as pale green stipples along the leaf veins. Both adults and nymphs suck juices from stems and undersides of leaves. Plants may have tipburn and yellowed, curled leaves with white spots on undersides. When leafhoppers are numerous, the whole plant may be stunted. Plants also react to the insect's toxic saliva by producing distorted leaves. Serious damage from leafhoppers is rare because native parasites and predators usually provide sufficient control. If infestation is severe enough to cause leaves to turn yellow and drop, spray neem, insecticidal soap, pyrethrins, or summer oil (use this while berries are still small).

Symptoms: Vines stunted; low yields
Cause: **Grape phylloxera**

Check the roots for small, rough, brown galls near the root tips and minute yellowish insects. Damage from the root-attacking form of phylloxera is limited to European cultivars not grafted on resistant rootstock. There is no treatment. Provide good care to slow the decline of affected vines. Replant with grapes grafted onto phylloxera-resistant rootstock. American or French hybrids are resistant to root phylloxera. Cultivars tolerant to leaf galls are 'Aurora', 'Seyval Blanc', 'Duchess', 'Delaware', 'Agawam', and 'Catawba'.

Symptom: Vines slowly decline in vigor
Cause: **Grape scale**

Check for tiny, light gray bumps on bark and scrape off loose bark to expose immature scales on or under bark. Spray dormant oil in late winter and radically prune back old growth to remove scales and renew vines.

Most Common Grape Diseases

Symptoms: Brown circular spots on leaves; grapes brown, then blacken and shrivel
Cause: **Black rot**

This fungus overwinters on infected leaves, vines and mummified grapes. Red spots on the upper leaf surfaces soon become brown and enlarge. Infections on shoots and vines are elongated, sunken and purple to black. Keep vines well-pruned and trellised to facilitate air movement. Spray a copper fungicide or Bordeaux mixture before and after bloom and again 10 days later. If past infections have been severe, spray again in early June.

Symptom: Galls on roots, trunk, or vine
Cause: **Crown gall**

Crown gall bacteria can enter stems through wounds caused by insects or pruning tools. For controls see "Crown Gall" on page 309.

'Concord' grape (*Vitis labrusca* 'Concord')

Symptom: Leaves become yellow along
              margins and then dry
Cause: **Pierce's disease**

This bacteria survives on infected plant tissue. Portions of fruit clusters wilt and dry and often the entire cluster is ruined. Prevent problems by choosing hybrid cultivars and keep vines pruned, trellised, and growing vigorously. Leafhoppers can spread this disease as they feed on your plants. so cover vines with row cover material early in the season. Prune out and destroy all infected plant tissues, cutting well below the obvious signs of infection.

Symptom: White, powdery growth on
              leaves and shoots
Cause: **Powdery mildew**
              (*Uncinula necator*)

Minimize the development of this disease by planting a resistant cultivar, such as 'Candice'. Plant grapes in well-drained soil, and space them widely enough to promote good air circulation. Clean up and compost all plant debris in the fall. Spraying compost tea on leaves every 2–4 weeks can help prevent powdery mildew infection. Pick off and destroy infected leaves and stems. Sprays of baking soda solution or baking soda plus oil (see "Oils Sprays" on page 361) are often an effective control.

Symptoms: Yellowish green spots on leaves;
              white spores on leaf undersides
Cause: **Downy mildew**
              (*Plasmopara viticola*)

Prevent problems by growing resistant cultvars, such as 'Canadice', 'Concord', and 'Mars'. Space plants to encourage good air circulation, and water early in the day to give foliage time to dry. Clean up plant debris in fall to remove overwintering spores. Remove and destroy infected plant parts. Bordeaux mixture, sprayed at weekly intervals in spring and just before rain, controls some of the fungi that cause downy mildew.

Symptom: Ripening berries rot, sometimes   showing a fuzzy mold
Cause: **Botrytis fruit rot**
              (*Botrytis cinerea*)

Botrytis fungi are almost always present in the environment and enter plants through wounds, bruises and natural openings such as dying blossoms. A fuzzy, gray mold characterizes botrytis infections. Plant in well-drained soil and space to facilitate air circulation. Remove and destroy infected plants as soon as possible. Some cultivars are more resistant than others; try 'Concord', 'Mars', and 'Niagara'.

Most Common Grape Disorders

Symptom: Flowers appear but no fruit sets
Cause: **Excess nitrogen**

High nitrogen levels also cause the plant to become overly leafy, making it more susceptible to diseases because of high humidity levels. Do not add compost to the planting hole when you set out your vines. Moderate amounts of compost can be used as a mulch if you suspect nutrient deficiencies, but avoid high-nitrogen fertilizers.

Note

Good air circulation prevents many grape diseases. Whenever possible, plant so that rows parallel prevailing winds. Remove and burn or dispose of all prunings and dropped leaves.

KIWIS

Actinidia s p p .

KIWIS AT A GLANCE

Botanical Name: *Actinidia* spp.
Height: To 30 feet
Spread: To 6 feet
Shade Tolerance: Full sun; tolerate partial shade
Hardiness: Fuzzy kiwis (*A. deliciosa*), Zones 7–10; hardy kiwis (*A. arguta* and *A. kolomikta*), Zones 3–9
Preferred Soil: High in organic matter, neutral pH; tolerate various well-drained soils

Kiwi (Actinidia deliciosa)

Most Common Kiwi Pests

Symptom: Leaves skeletonized
Cause: **Japanese beetles**

These blue-green beetles are ½ inch long with bronze wing covers and are easy to see. They feed on plants during the day, especially in warm weather. For controls see "Japanese Beetle" on page 268.

Most Common Kiwi Diseases

Symptom: Roots and base of stem rot
Cause: **Collar rot (*Phytophthora* spp.)**

This fungus grows well in damp conditions and thrives where weeds have been allowed to grow too near. Yellowing foliage may be an early symptom of collar rot. Improve air circulation near the base of the plant so that humidity is decreased and avoid wetting stems when watering.

Symptoms: Flowers rot and die; stored fruit rot
Cause: **Storage rot**

Prevent this fungal disease by selecting a planting site with good air circulation. Botrytis fungi are almost always present in the environment and enter plants through wounds, bruises, and natural openings such as dying blossoms. A fuzzy, gray mold characterizes botrytis infections. Remove and destroy infected plants as soon as possible.

Most Common Kiwi Disorders

Symptom: Bark at base of vine chewed and torn up
Cause: **Cat damage**

Cats like kiwi vines as much as they like catnip. Prevent cat damage by enclosing the vine in a wire cage that they can't penetrate.

PEACHES AND NECTARINES

Prunus persica

PEACHES AND NECTARINES AT A GLANCE

Botanical Name: *Prunus persica*
Height: To 25 feet; dwarf, 6–10 feet
Spread: To 25 feet
Shade Tolerance: Full sun
Hardiness: Zones 5–9; some cultivars hardy in Zones 4 and 10
Preferred Soil: Fertile, well-drained

Most Common Peach and Nectarine Pests

Symptom: Deformed, "catfaced" fruit with corky scars
Cause: **Tarnished plant bugs**

Though blemished, the fruit is edible. For controls see "Tarnished Plant Bug" on page 291.

Symptom: Curled, puckered, sticky leaves
Cause: **Green peach aphids**

Look for colonies of tiny, greenish insects on undersides of affected leaves. For controls see "Aphids" on page 244.

Symptom: Masses of gummy castings on fruit
Causes: **Oriental fruit moths; peach twig borers**

Mature fruit may look undamaged outside, but you will find the caterpillars near the fruit pit.

Fruit moth caterpillars are up to ½ inch long and pinkish with a brown head, while peach twig borers are light brown with darker bands and a dark head. Destroy immature fruit with entry holes (usually near the stem end) to kill the larvae inside. Cultivate the soil 4 inches deep around trees before bloom to destroy overwintering fruit moth pupae. Where peach twig borers are a serious problem, spray dormant oil during winter to kill larvae overwintering under bark. Spray *Bacillus thuringiensis* var. *kurstaki* (BTK) at bloom time and several times during summer to control the first generation of caterpillars before they bore into shoots.

Symptom: Tips of shoots wilt and die back
Causes: **Oriental fruit moths; peach twig borers**

If you suspect the cause is an insect rather than a disease, look for a caterpillar inside the stem just below the wilted section. Fruit moth caterpillars are pinkish with a brown head, while borer larvae are light brown with darker bands and a dark head. Control as above.

Symptom: Yellow speckles on leaves
Cause: **European red mites**

These tiny pests suck the juices out of plant leaves. For controls see "Spider Mites" on page 286.

Symptom: Tree loses vigor
Cause: **Peachtree borers**

Caked sawdust and gummy castings at the base of the trunk are evidence that borers are at work. Remove the soil several inches deep around base of trunk and look for borer holes containing cream-colored larvae. Dig out larvae with a sharp knife or kill them by working a flexible wire into the holes. Cultivate the soil around the trunk in June and July to kill pupae. Weak or injured trees are most attacked; maintain vigorous growth and avoid injuring bark.

Most Common Peach and Nectarine Diseases

Symptoms: Spots on flowers and fruit; brown growth on fruit

Cause: **Brown rot**

Prevent problems by planting resistant cultivars, such as 'Elberta' and 'Sunbeam'. For controls see "Brown Rot" on page 306.

Symptoms: Leaves and fruit with olive-black spots and blotches; fruits are malformed, scabby; skin is cracked

Cause: **Peach scab (Cladosporium carpophilum)**

Peach scab usually becomes visible on the fruit about 6 weeks after the petals drop. Destroy leaves, unharvested fruit, and old mulch in fall. Sulfur, sprayed every 10–20 days from the time that flower buds show green until they open, helps to prevent the disease. Spray at the same intervals until harvest as long as weather is warm and humid.

Symptom: New leaves redden and arch unnaturally

Cause: **Peach leaf curl (Taphrina deformans)**

To prevent this disease, look for a resistant cultivar, such as 'Frost'. For controls see "Peach Leaf Curl" on page 323.

Symptoms: Leaves grow in compact rosettes; few fruit form

Cause: **Peach rosette (virus)**

This virus causes trees to develop abnormally short internodes on new branches. Rosettes of up to a hundred small, discolored leaves form on these branches. Infected leaves turn yellow and no fruit forms on infected branches. Buy only certified disease-free trees. Control leafhoppers, aphids and other sucking insects and eliminate all wild chokecherries where possible. Remove affected trees.

Most Common Peach and Nectarine Disorders

Symptom: Leaf buds do not open in spring

Cause: **Inadequate chilling hours**

Peaches require between 200 and 1,200 chilling hours, depending on the cultivar. Choose cultivars carefully, matching their requirements to your environment. Check with your local extension office for any recommended cultivars.

Peach (Prunus persica)

PEANUTS

See "Peanuts" on page 39.

PEARS

Pyrus communis cultivars

PEARS AT A GLANCE

Botanical Name: *Pyrus communis* cultivars
Height: To 40 feet; dwarf, to 25 feet
Spread: To 25 feet; dwarf, to 15 feet
Shade Tolerance: Full sun
Hardiness: Zones 5–8; some cultivars hardy in Zones 3, 4, and 9
Preferred Soil: Fertile, moist, well-drained, slightly acidic; more tolerant of heavy, wet soil than most fruit trees

---

Most Common Pear Pests

Symptom: Holes bored into fruit
Cause: **Codling moths**

Pears attacked by codling moths usually have a single hole bored from the blossom end and plugged with dark brown castings. Once caterpillars are in the fruit, they are out of reach. For controls see "Apples" on page 71.

Symptom: Foliage browning by
            midsummer
Cause: **Pear psylla**

Look for small, oval, wingless insects sucking sap from leaf twigs and exuding sticky honeydew onto fruit and leaves. For heavy infestations, spray insecticidal soap or summer oil. Spray dormant oil as soon as leaves drop in fall and again, mixed with lime-sulfur, just before buds swell in spring.

Symptom: Leaves skeletonized, with a
            scorched appearance
Cause: **Pear sawflies**

The larvae of this sawfly are soft, slimy, and dark green to yellowish. They look like small slugs and feed on the upper surfaces of leaves. Wash larvae from trees with a strong stream of water (this is very effective). Spray insecticidal soap, neem, or summer oil.

Symptom: Reddish brown blisters on
            undersides of leaves
Cause: **Pearleaf blister mites**

You will need a magnifying glass to see these 1/100-inch-long gall mites inside the blisters. They rarely harm the tree and are usually sufficiently controlled by dormant oil–lime-sulfur sprays before buds open. Where heavy infestations reoccur, spray summer oil as buds swell.

Symptom: Leaves turn yellow along whole
            branches, which may die
Cause: **San Jose scale**

Look for clusters of tiny gray bumps on the bark to find out whether these sucking insects are the problem. Prune dying branches and, in late winter, spray dormant oil.

Most Common Pear Diseases

Symptoms: Branches show blackened,
            rough lesions; shoot tips wilt
            and blacken
Cause: **Fire blight**

Affected shoots bend downward, and young fruit are darkened and remain on the tree. Plant resistant cultivars, such as 'Mericourt' and 'Seckel'. For controls see "Fire Blight" on page 314.

Symptom: Scabby lesions on fruit
Cause: **Pear scab (*Ventura pirina*)**

To prevent scab in a susceptible cultivar, spray with lime-sulfur before bud break in spring. Rake up and destroy leaves, old mulch, and dropped fruit in fall. Avoid scab problems by growing a resistant cultivar, such as 'Bartlett'.

Symptoms: Small purple or black spots on leaves and fruit; infected leaves drop prematurely; fruit crack
Causes: **Leaf blight; fruit spot (*Fabraea maculata*)**

Infected twigs and branches show dark-colored lesions any time from midseason to fall. Prune off and destroy all infected branches. Rake up and destroy all dropped leaves, twigs, and fruit. Spray copper at bud break, 2 weeks later, and finally, a month after the leaves open.

Note
Asian pears are similar to European pears in both culture and susceptibility to pests and diseases. However, they often bloom earlier in spring because they have chilling requirements that range from 400 to 900 hours (depending on cultivar), rather than the 900 to 1,000 hours required by European pear cultivars.

'Beurre Bosc' pear (<u>Pyrus communis</u>* 'Beurre Bosc')*

PECANS
Carya illinoensis

PECANS AT A GLANCE

Botanical Name: *Carya illinoensis*
Height: To 100 feet
Spread: To 50 feet
Shade Tolerance: Full sun
Hardiness: Zones 6–9
Preferred Soil: Deep, fertile, moist; tolerate less fertile soils, intolerant of salinity

Most Common Pecan Pests

Symptom: Larvae in nuts
Causes: **Pecan weevils; caterpillars**

Several species of caterpillars, as well as the grubs of pecan weevils, may infest nuts. Pecan weevils are ¼–⅓-inch-long, dark gray, snout beetles that lay eggs in immature nuts. The larvae feed inside, then exit through holes bored in the shells. The damaged nuts usually stay on the tree. To reduce weevil damage, knock the adults from trees onto a ground sheet by sharply tapping branches with a padded stick. Do this every 2 weeks from midsummer onward. If you see caterpillars inside nuts that drop early, collect and destroy all dropped nuts.

Most Common Pecan Diseases

Symptoms: Leaves yellow and drop prematurely; nuts mummify
Cause: **Scab (*Cladosporium effusum*)**

High-humidity conditions favor pecan scab. Spores are produced from old lesions and are carried by wind or rain to new growth.

This fungus infects growing tissue only; mature leaves and nuts are immune. Prevent problems with good sanitation. Knock old leaves and nuts off the tree in fall. Prune to improve both air movement and exposure to sunlight. If scab has been a problem in the past, spray with Bordeaux mixture as blossoms open in spring and again 7–10 days later.

Symptoms:	Spots appear on leaves; fuzzy fungal growth is visible on spots
Cause:	**Downy spot** (*Mycosphaerella caryigena*)

Downy spot is one of many leaf spot diseases that attack pecans. Each disease is capable of defoliating the tree, preventing it from providing the nutrition necessary to mature the nut crop. Prevent problems by spacing trees widely so that none are shaded. Prune to improve air circulation. Bordeaux mixture will usually control mild infections.

Note
Most pecan cultivars require a suitable pollinator to set nuts. When buying trees, check that you are choosing an appropriate pair since not every pecan pollinates every other.

Pecan (<u>Carya illinoensis</u>)

PLUMS
Prunus spp. and hybrids

PLUMS AT A GLANCE

Botanical Name: *Prunus* spp. and hybrids
Height: To 30 feet
Spread: To 25 feet
Shade Tolerance: Full sun
Hardiness: Japanese, Zones 6–11; European, Zones 4–9
Preferred Soil: Moderately fertile, moist, well-drained; somewhat drought-tolerant when established

Most Common Plum Pests

Symptom:	Tips of shoots wilt and die back
Cause:	**Oriental fruit moths**

If this pest is the cause, you will find pinkish caterpillars up to ½ inch long inside the stem just below the wilted section. Prune out and destroy all affected branches to reduce later damaging generations that feed inside fruit. Cultivate the soil 4 inches deep around trees next spring before bloom to destroy all overwintering pupae.

Symptom:	Curled, puckered, sticky leaves
Cause:	**Aphids**

Look for colonies of tiny, greenish insects on undersides of affected leaves. Severely infested leaves and flowers may drop. As they feed, aphids excrete a sweet, sticky honeydew onto leaves below. This allows sooty mold to grow, which is unsightly and blocks light from the leaves. For controls see "Aphids" on page 244.

Most Common Plum Diseases

Symptom: Blackened galls appear on branches

Cause: **Black knot**

This fungus lives and reproduces in infected wood, and twigs and branches have large, elongated, rough-textured swellings. If unchecked they increase every year; the tree becomes stunted and productivity declines. Prune infected branches and twigs to 4–6 inches below the swellings, disinfecting tools between cuts, then burn prunings. Spray with lime sulfur or Bordeaux mix before buds break in early spring. Choose a resistant cultivar, such as 'Santa Rosa'.

Symptoms: Narrow, distorted leaves; new growth stunted; fruit drop prematurely or are abnormally large

Cause: **Plum dwarf (viruses)**

Plum dwarf is carried by aphids and leafhoppers. There is no control for this disease. Remove and destroy infected trees.

Symptom: Fruit with fuzzy, brown, rotting areas

Cause: **Brown rot** (*Monilinia fructicola; Sclerotinia laxa*)

Minimize brown rot by choosing resistant cultivars, such as 'Au-Rosa' and 'Crimson'. Prune to ensure good air circulation. Don't overfertilize, since high nitrogen levels encourage this fungus. Control insects as much as possible to avoid wounds. In fall, gather and destroy all mummified fruit and fallen leaves and twigs. Sulfur, sprayed twice from when blossoms show pink to petal fall, and again before harvest, helps to control the disease.

Symptoms: Small purple or red leaf spots; centers of spots often fall out

Cause: **Leaf spot** (*Xanthomonas pruni*)

Prevent problems by planting a resistant cultivar, such as 'Green Gage'. For controls see "Beeches" on page 173.

Most Common Plum Disorders

Symptom: Brown areas in fruit flesh

Cause: **Boron deficiency**

European plums are sensitive to boron deficiencies. However, since an excess of boron is toxic, have leaf tissue analyzed before adding boron to the soil and follow recommendations carefully. Check with your local extension office for information.

Note

Japanese plums often require fruit thinning to achieve their full size. When fruits are jellybean-sized, thin to leave 4–6 inches between fruits.

'Blufire' plum (*Prunus* hybrid)

RASPBERRIES

Rubus spp.

RASPBERRIES AT A GLANCE

Botanical Name: *Rubus* spp.
Height: 6–10 feet
Spread: Usually 2–4 feet
Shade Tolerance: Full sun
Hardiness: Zones 3–9
Preferred Soil: Deep, sandy loam, high in
    organic matter; widely tolerant if soil is
    well-drained

Most Common Raspberry Pests

Symptom: Small, white larvae in berries
Cause: **Raspberry fruitworms**

Check early dropped fruit for these ¼-inch-long larvae. Collect and destroy dropped fruit daily. For heavy infestations, spray pyrethrins in late May to early April when flower buds are developing. Spraying just before blossoms open to kill the adult beetles before they lay eggs (to protect bees, do not spray during bloom).

Symptom: Light yellow speckles on leaves
Cause: **Spider mites**

Look for fine webbing on undersides of leaves. For controls see "Spider Mites" on page 286.

Symptom: Leaves skeletonized
Causes: **Raspberry sawflies; Japanese beetles**

The sawfly larvae are ⅗ inch long and pale green with white spines. They are found on undersides and edges of leaves and rarely cause significant damage to healthy canes. For heavy infestations, spray neem or pyrethrins. Japanese beetles are blue-green, with bronze wing covers. The beetles feed on plants during the day, especially in warm weather. They chew on flowers and skeletonize leaves. For controls see "Japanese Beetle" on page 268.

Symptom: Canes are weak and break easily
Cause: **Raspberry crown borers**

These ⅞-inch-long borer larvae tunnel into the base of canes and into main roots. They prefer stressed plants, and their feeding stunts some canes and kills others. Dig and destroy severely infested plants in late fall. Next spring, if more than 5 percent of canes break easily while you are tying up canes, spray plants with pyrethrins when new growth is about 4 inches long to control early-stage borer larvae.

Symptom: Tips of shoots wilt and die back
Cause: **Cane borers**

Look for slightly swollen galls below the wilted part of the cane and for ¾-inch-long, white grubs inside the canes. Prune out and destroy infested canes. Where borers damage many canes, spray pyrethrins in spring, just before flowers open, to intercept adults as they lay eggs.

Most Common Raspberry Diseases

Symptoms: Reddish brown discoloration
    around buds; leaves fall pre-
    maturely; fruit branches stunted
Cause: **Spur blight**
    (*Didymella applanata*)

Spur blight attacks red raspberries. Plant resistant cultivars, such as 'Algonquin', 'Amity', and 'Haida', to avoid the problem. Good air circulation and soil drainage also help to prevent this disease. Prune out and destroy all infected growth. The following year, spray with copper at bud break in spring.

Symptoms: Plants lack vigor and are stunted; leaves are small and yellow

Cause: **Root rot**

To prevent problems, choose a planting site with good drainage and grow resistant cultivars, such as 'Algonquin', 'Amity' and, 'Haida'. For controls see "Root Rot" on page 326.

Symptom: Galls on canes or roots near the soil surface

Cause: **Crown gall**

Look for large, irregularly shaped galls near the soil line. Crown gall bacteria exude acetic acids that promote abnormal and excessive growth of nearby cells. The bacteria enter stems through wounds caused by insects and tools. For controls see "Crown Gall" on page 309.

Symptom: Small, gray spots with red or purple margins on canes

Cause: **Anthracnose (*Elsinoe veneta*)**

Prevent damage by planting resistant cultivars, such as 'Jewel' and 'Lowden'. For controls see "Anthracnose" on page 300.

Symptom: Leaves have light green or yellow mottling

Cause: **Mosaic virus**

Prevent problems by planting resistant cultivars, such as 'Algonquin' and 'Haida'. For controls see "Mosaic" on page 319.

Symptom: Ripe berries fall apart

Cause: **Crumbly berry virus**

This virus can remain dormant but viable in dead plant material for years. Once the virus enters a plant it spreads through the entire system. Berries of infected plants fall apart into individual drupelets when touched. Buy certified stock and place new plantings at least 200 yards away from older brambles. Aphids can spread this virus as they feed on your plants. For controls see "Aphids" on page 244.

Symptom: Gray mold on fruit

Cause: **Gray mold (*Botrytis* spp.)**

Prevent problems by selecting a planting site with good air circulation. For controls see "Blackberries" on page 75.

Symptom: White, powdery coating on fruit

Cause: **Powdery mildew (*Sphaerotheca humuli*)**

To prevent problems grow resistant cultivars, such as 'Heritage' and 'Ruby'. For controls see "Powdery Mildew" on page 323.

Raspberries (Rubus idaeus)

STRAWBERRIES

Fragaria x *ananassa*

STRAWBERRIES AT A GLANCE

Botanical Name: *Fragaria* x *ananassa*
Height: To 1 foot
Spread: To 1 foot; spread by runners
to 2–3 feet
Shade Tolerance: Full sun
Hardiness: Zones 3–10
Preferred Soil: Fairly fertile, moist, well-
drained; intolerant of salinity

Most Common Strawberry Pests

Symptom: Pinched, distorted berries
Cause: **Tarnished plant bugs**

Frost damage to flowers or poor pollination
during cool weather can both cause deformed,
"catfaced" fruits. When these conditions are
absent, suspect tarnished plant bug feeding as
the cause of fruit damage. Plant bugs suck the
juice from leaves and fruits. For controls see
"Tarnished Plant Bug" on page 291.

Symptom: Young leaves crinkled
                or puckered
Cause: **Cyclamen mites**

Feeding by these mites, which are only
$\frac{1}{50}$ inch long, makes plants produce compact,
stunted growth. In heavy infestations, leaves
become bronzed. Remove and destroy
affected plants as soon as you notice damage.
Replant annually with uninfested plants to
reduce losses to this mite. Where heavy infestations recur, try releases of the predatory
mite *Amblyseius cucumeris.*

Symptoms: Small holes in blossoms;
                blossom stalks cut
Cause: **Strawberry clipper weevils**

This weevil is ⅖ inch in size and causes serious
damage in some areas by clipping the stalks of
flower buds, causing them to dry up. Control
weeds in strawberry beds. After the final
fruiting year, dig under plants as soon as they
are finished yielding. For heavy infestations,
spray pyrethrins in early spring, before the first
blossoms open (sprays will harm pollinators
and beneficial insects).

Symptom: Leaves sticky
Cause: **Strawberry aphids**

Look for clusters of small, pale green or
yellowish insects on undersides of leaves.
Large numbers of aphids can spread strawberry viruses in some areas. Wash aphids from
plants with a strong spray of water or, where
virus is a concern, spray neem or pyrethrins.
Cut and destroy old leaves in fall to remove
overwintering aphid eggs.

Symptom: Leaves rolled or webbed together
Cause: **Leafrollers**

Check for small, greenish caterpillars inside
the webbing. Leafrollers rarely cause significant damage to plants or berries. Handpick
rolled leaves containing caterpillars. For heavy
infestations, spray *Bacillus thuringiensis* var.
kurstaki (BTK) or neem. Remove dead leaves
and debris from beds before winter to remove
overwintering sites.

Symptom: White foam on leaves and stems
Cause: **Spittle bugs**

In April and May, the nymphs of these
leafhoppers feed inside a protective mass of

bubbles, which is easily washed off plants with water. Although their feeding also causes leaf distortions, there are rarely enough spittle bugs to cause significant damage.

Symptom: Light yellow speckles on leaves
Cause: **Spider mites**

Look for fine webbing on undersides of leaves. Both adults and nymphs feed by sucking the juice from plant cells. In severe infestations, leaves become bronzed or turn yellow. The webs may cover both sides of the leaves. Native predatory mites usually sufficiently suppress spider mites. For controls see "Spider Mites" on page 286.

Symptom: Half-circle notches in leaf edges
Cause: **Root weevils**

Adult weevils feed on leaves and cause little direct damage, whereas larvae feed on roots and are much more damaging. Spray pyrethrins to control adults if you see fresh notches on leaves (do not spray during bloom period). Apply neem or insect parasitic nematodes to the soil around the roots in early May and again in August to control larvae. Where heavy infestations recur, spray pyrethrins before the bloom period to control emerging adults moving onto plants in spring.

Symptom: Plants wilt and collapse
Causes: **Strawberry crown borers;**
              strawberry root weevils

Dig a plant and look for fat, white grubs in a hollowed-out crown and roots. Destroy all infested plants. Adult crown borers are weevils that do not fly; plant the next crop in a new location at least 300 feet away. Control root weevils as above.

Most Common Strawberry Diseases

Symptoms: Plants are stunted; leaves have a gray or purplish cast; yields diminish
Cause: **Red stele**

Prevent this troublesome disease by planting resistant cultivars, such as 'Allstar' and 'Guardian'. For controls see "Red Stele" on page 325.

Symptoms: Dark patches on leaves; grayish white patches on leaf undersides and on fruit
Cause: **Strawberry mildew**
               (***Sphaerotheca humuli***)

Planting in well-drained soil can help prevent this disease. In extremely wet springs, spray with sulfur just before the blossoms open and again several weeks afterward.

Strawberry (Fragaria x ananassa)

Symptom: Fruit is soft and becomes covered with gray fuzz

Cause: **Gray mold**

To minimize problems, plant a resistant cultivar, such as 'Jewell'. Botrytis fungi can enter plants only through wounds, bruises, and natural openings. A fuzzy gray mold grows on exposed tissues. Prevent problems by choosing a planting site with good air circulation. Remove and destroy infected plants and take care not to injure plants when transplanting.

Symptom: Plants yellow, drop leaves, and die

Cause: **Verticillium wilt** (*Verticillium albo-atrum*)

Verticillium fungi overwinter in crop debris. Resting spores of this fungus are quite long-lived; they can survive on old organic matter in soil for as long as 15 years. Minimize the chances of this disease developing by growing resistant cultivars, such as 'Allstar' and 'Guardian'. Plant in well-drained soil that warms quickly in spring. Remove crop debris and compost it in piles that reach 150°–160°F for several days. Row covers and other season-extending materials that warm the air around plants may inhibit spore germination, which is optimal at temperatures of 70°–75°F.

Symptoms: Leaves mottled and distorted; low yields

Cause: **Viral diseases**

Strawberries are prey to many viral species, some of which cause general dwarfing and some of which cause leaf distortions. Aphids and mites transmit viruses, so controlling them may prevent problems. If your plants become infected, remove and destroy them. Do not replant strawberries in the same location for at least 3 years.

WALNUTS
Juglans spp.

WALNUTS AT A GLANCE

Botanical Name: *Juglans* spp.
Height: To 60 feet
Spread: To 50 feet
Shade Tolerance: Full sun
Hardiness: English, Zones 6–9; black and Persian, Zones 5–9; eastern black, Zones 4–8
Preferred Soil: Fertile, deep soil

Most Common Walnut Pests

Symptom: Husks with black spots; shells stained black

Cause: **Walnut husk flies**

You may see the small, white maggots inside the husks (they do not bore into the nut itself). Although they stain the shells, the maggots otherwise do no damage. Collect and destroy husks to reduce population of flies.

Symptom: Curled, puckered, sticky leaves

Cause: **Aphids**

For controls see "Aphids" on page 244. Some walnut cultivars are sensitive to oil sprays; test-spray before making a full application.

Symptom: Foliage stripped from branches

Cause: **Walnut caterpillars**

Look for black caterpillars up to 2 inches long, covered with long, white hairs. They move down the trunk in groups to shed their skins and can often be seen in clusters on the trunk.

Watch trees daily and destroy caterpillars as they descend to molt. Prune out infested branches as soon as you notice the caterpillars. Spray *Bacillus thuringiensis* var. *kurstaki* (BTK), neem, or pyrethrins to protect small trees with heavy infestations.

Most Common Walnut Diseases

Symptom: Small, reddish brown spots on young leaves or leaf margins
Cause: **Bacterial blight**
(*Xanthomonas juglandis*)

This disease is most severe during warm, wet springs. For controls see "Pseudomonas Leaf Blight" on page 325.

Persian walnut (<u>Juglans regia</u>)

Symptom: Dark-colored cankers and decayed areas appear on the trunk
Cause: **Crown rot**
(*Phytophthora cactorum*)

Crown rot attacks the bark of the walnut tree. Telltale symptoms include sponginess of the bark and weeping dark fluids. The tree is stunted and dies back. High soil moisture levels favor this disease. If you suspect it, expose the crown and basal parts of the main roots an inch or two to let in air and sunlight during summer, reburying before winter cold arrives.

Symptom: Clusters of honey-colored mushrooms appear around the trunk
Cause: **Mushroom root rot**
(*Armillaria mellea*)

You may also notice that the leaves are smaller than normal, or that they are yellow, brown, or wilted. For controls see "Armillaria Root Rot" on page 301.

Symptom: Galls form at and just below the soil line
Cause: **Crown gall**

Crown gall bacteria enter stems through wounds. Examine purchased plants carefully for galls. Before planting, soak roots in a solution containing the beneficial bacteria *Agrobacterium radiobacter.* Dig out infected plants, taking as much surrounding soil as possible. Cut out mild, localized infections, sterilizing tools between cuts.

Most Common Walnut Disorders

Symptom: Tree loses vigor for no apparent reason
Cause: **Overwatering**

Walnut trees require regular deep watering but suffer if their soil is consistently wet. Do not water your walnut tree on the same schedule as your lawn and garden. Instead, let the soil surface dry well between irrigations. Plant walnuts in well-drained soil only.

ANNUALS

Most Common Annual Pests

Symptom: Leaves and new shoots
              distorted and sticky
Cause: **Aphids**

Look for clusters of 1/16–3/8-inch-long, pear-shaped insects on undersides of leaves, on new shoots, and in flower buds. Their feeding causes curled leaves and deformed buds, and they produce sticky honeydew, which covers leaves and allows sooty molds to grow. Wash honeydew and aphids from leaves with a strong stream of water, repeating several times as necessary. For heavy infestations, spray insecticidal soap, neem, or pyrethrins.

Symptoms: Large, irregular holes in leaves;
               slime trails present
Causes: **Slugs; snails**

Both slugs and snails prefer moist or shady parts of the garden and rasp large holes in soft, tender plants. They are most damaging in spring when wet weather favors their development and plants are small and easily damaged. In high-rainfall regions they can be a problem all season. The best controls for slugs are garter snakes, toads, ground beetles, fireflies, and other natural enemies. Where slugs or snails are severe pests, it may be worth it to band flower beds with copper flashing to keep them off particularly valued plants.

Symptom: Foliage sticky
Cause: **Whiteflies**

Look for tiny, white, flying insects. The tiny, pearly white nymphs look like scales on undersides of leaves. A light infestation of whiteflies does little damage outdoors where natural enemies are present, but it can quickly become a heavy infestation in greenhouse plants. For a heavy infestation, pick off lower leaves, where the nymphs are concentrated, and spray insecticidal soap, neem, or pyrethrins. In greenhouses, releasing parasitic wasps (*Encarsia formosa*) in early spring is an effective control.

Symptom: Brown streaks and scars on
              leaves and flowers
Cause: **Thrips**

You will need a magnifying lens to see if these minute, quick-moving insects are present on leaves and between flower petals. For heavy infestations, spray insecticidal soap, neem, or pyrethrins. As a last resort, dust diatomaceous earth on undersides of leaves and on the soil at the base of the plant. Keep nearby weeds pulled to eliminate thrips' host plants.

Symptoms: Holes chewed in leaves; webs
               may be present
Cause: **Caterpillars**

Many species of caterpillars feed on annuals. Some only chew holes in leaves and usually can be seen feeding on the foliage. Others roll or tie leaves together and hide inside to feed. Handpick light infestations. For heavy infestations, spray *Bacillus thuringiensis* var. *kurstaki* (BTK) or neem, first plucking open webbed-together leaves to allow sprays to penetrate.

Symptom: Light yellow speckles on leaves
Cause: **Spider mites**

With the exception of European red mites, most species of spider mites spin fine webbing on undersides of leaves. The tiny mites (under

⅟₅₀ inch long) may be visible crawling on the webbing. Native predatory mites and beetles usually provide sufficient control. Spider mites are most damaging in hot, dry weather and where natural enemies have been destroyed by sulfur or other pesticides. For light infestations, spray foliage with water or insecticidal soap. For heavy infestations, which cause leaf edges to curl, turn brown and dry up, spray neem or summer oil. Release predatory mites (*Metaseiulus occidentalis* or other species adapted to the local climate). Plan to spray lime-sulfur in late winter.

Symptoms: Holes in leaves; flowers chewed
Causes: **Japanese beetles; leaf-eating beetles**

The large, blue-green Japanese beetles are ½ inch long with bronze wing covers are easy to see, and so is the damage from their feeding, which skeletonizes leaves. Knock beetles onto ground sheets early in the morning and destroy. Handpick these and other leaf- and flower-eating beetles.

Symptom: Young plants or shoots cut off or girdled at soil level
Cause: **Cutworms**

During the day, search for and destroy the fat, gray caterpillars hiding in soil around the base of freshly damaged plants, or go out at night with a flashlight to catch feeding cutworms. Where infestations are always heavy, drench soil with neem or a solution of insect parasitic nematodes before planting, or use a bran bait mixed with *Bacillus thuringiensis* var. *kurstaki* (BTK) sprinkled over the soil. Setting plants out later also avoids the main generation of cutworms. To prevent problems, always use cutworm collars around transplants.

Symptom: Pinched, scarred, or distorted leaves and buds
Causes: **Tarnished plant bugs; four-lined plant bugs; other true bugs**

When true bugs pierce and suck plant sap, their toxic saliva causes plants to react with distorted foliage and flowers. You may not see the bugs feeding because they fly away or drop quickly when disturbed. For light infestations, keeping the weeds down around flower beds may be sufficient. For heavy infestations, spray pyrethrins to control both nymphs and adults.

Most Common Annual Diseases

Symptom: Sooty black material coats leaves
Cause: **Sooty mold**

Sooty mold grows in the honeydew deposited on leaves by insect infestations. Leaves become covered with a dark gray to black mold. When you see the mold, gently wipe plant leaves with a cloth moistened with warm water. Most of the mold will come off, but spores will be released. Next control the aphids and whiteflies. For controls see "Sooty Mold" on page 330.

Symptom: Spots on leaves
Cause: **Leaf spot disease**

Many fungi and bacteria cause leaf spots. Prevent these diseases by spacing plants to improve air circulation and light exposure. Use drip irrigation or water the soil by hand to avoid wetting leaves. When sprinkling, do it early in the day so leaves dry by nightfall. Inspect plants frequently and remove diseased leaves. Dig out and destroy severely infected plants. Wash tools when moving from one part of the garden to another and after any contact with contaminated soil or plants.

AGERATUM/FLOSSFLOWER

Ageratum houstonianum

AGERATUM/FLOSSFLOWER AT A GLANCE

Botanical Name: *Ageratum houstonianum*
Height: Dwarf, 6–8 inches; tall, 12–30 inches
Spread: 6–10 inches
Shade Tolerance: Full sun or light shade
Hardiness: Damaged or killed by frost
Preferred Soil: Fertile, moist, well-drained

Most Common Ageratum Pests

Symptoms: Foliage sticky; tiny, white insects present on undersides of leaves
Cause: **Whiteflies**

Look for tiny (1/20 inch), white, flying insects. Their tiny, pearly white nymphs look like scales on undersides of leaves. Whiteflies suck plant juices, weakening plants. They can spread plant

Ageratum (Ageratum houstonianum)

viruses as they feed. They also exude honeydew, which promotes the growth of sooty mold on plants. Native parasitic wasps, lacewings, lady beetles, and pirate bugs attack whitefly nymphs outdoors. Capture adults on yellow sticky traps. For a few plants, use a handheld vacuum to remove adults from undersides of leaves. To control nymphs, spray neem, insecticidal soap, or kinoprene (Enstar). As a last resort, try spraying pyrethrins.

Symptoms: Holes chewed in leaves; webs may be present
Cause: **Caterpillars**

Many species of caterpillars feed on ageratums. Some only chew holes in leaves and usually can be seen feeding on the foliage. Others roll or tie leaves together and hide inside to feed. Handpick light infestations. For heavy infestations, spray *Bacillus thuringiensis* var. *kurstaki* (BTK) or neem, first plucking open webbed-together leaves to allow sprays to penetrate.

Most Common Ageratum Diseases

Symptoms: Plants wilt; growth slows
Causes: **Fusarium wilt; verticillium wilt (*Verticillium albo-atrum*)**

Plants that wilt when the ground is moist should be suspected of having one of these wilt diseases. It's easier to prevent wilt diseases than it is to control them. Plant in well-drained soil, and water carefully to avoid splashing spores from soil and plant debris onto uninfected plants. Clean up plant residues in fall to remove overwintering fungal spores. Remove and destroy infected plants. For controls see "Verticillium Wilt" on page 332 and "Fusarium Wilt" on page 315.

BLACK-EYED SUSAN

Rudbeckia hirta

COLEUS

Coleus x *hybridus*

BLACK-EYED SUSAN AT A GLANCE

Botanical Name: *Rudbeckia hirta*
Height: 1–3 feet
Spread: To 2½ feet
Shade Tolerance: Full sun
Hardiness: Damaged by light frost
Preferred Soil: Fertile, moist, well-drained, high in organic matter

---

COLEUS AT A GLANCE

Botanical Name: *Coleus* x *hybridus*
Height: 6–24 inches
Spread: 6–24 inches
Shade Tolerance: Full sun, partial shade, or full shade
Hardiness: Damaged or killed by light frost
Preferred Soil: Fertile, moist, well-drained

Most Common Black-Eyed Susan Pests

Same pests as orange coneflower. See "Orange Coneflower" on page 151.

Most Common Black-Eyed Susan Diseases

Same diseases as orange coneflower. See "Orange Coneflower" on page 151.

Most Common Coleus Pests

Symptoms: White, cottony masses on stems; leaves sticky
Cause: **Mealybugs**

These tiny, oval, pinkish insects cluster under waxy fluff, which protects them from sprays. Wash plants with water to dislodge mealybugs. Spray insecticidal soap repeatedly to control all stages.

Black-eyed Susan (<u>Rudbeckia hirta</u>)

Coleus (<u>Coleus</u> x <u>hybridus</u>)

Symptoms: Foliage sticky; tiny, white insects
present on undersides of leaves
Cause: **Whiteflies**

Look for tiny (1/20 inch), white, flying insects.
The tiny, pearly white nymphs look like scales
on undersides of leaves. Whiteflies suck plant
juices, weakening plants. They also exude
honeydew, which promotes the growth of sooty
mold on plants. For controls see "Whiteflies"
on page 297.

Most Common Coleus Diseases

Symptoms: Abnormal leaf coloring and
mottling; leaves pucker
Cause: **Mosaic**

Mottling is the telltale sign that a mosaic virus
is attacking your plant. The following information is generally applicable to any virus that
attacks plants. Viruses cause many plant
problems, including distorted growth, spots
on plant tissues, stunting, yellowing, and
mottled plant tissue. We call the viruses that
cause mottling "mosaics." Mosaic-infected
leaves are usually cupped or puckered. The
plant grows slowly or is stunted. In some cases,
stems are unusually brittle and break easily.
Infected flowers also display a mottled
coloration. Prevent viruses by keeping plants
growing vigorously. Choose resistant cultivars
and certified disease-free planting stock. Do
not touch wet plants. Control sucking insects
as much as possible. Remove and destroy
virus-infected plants immediately.

Note

*Coleus is quite sensitive to the phytotoxic compounds that
can linger in unfinished compost. Commercial compost
producers use it as a "test crop" to determine if the compost
is ready to be used in a potting mix.*

COSMOS
Cosmos spp.

COSMOS AT A GLANCE

Botanical Name: *Cosmos* spp.
Height: 2–6 feet
Spread: 1–4 feet
Shade Tolerance: Full sun
Hardiness: Damaged by light frost
Preferred Soil: Average to infertile,
well-drained

Most Common Cosmos Pests

Symptom: Leaves and new shoots distorted
and sticky
Cause: **Aphids**

Look for clusters of small, pear-shaped insects
on undersides of leaves, on new shoots, and in
flower buds. For controls see "Aphids" on
page 244.

Symptom: Stalks weakened and falling over
or breaking
Cause: **Stalk borers**

If stalk borers are the problem, you should be
able to find small holes in the base of stems
marked by sawdustlike castings around the hole.
For controls see "Delphiniums" on page 141.

Symptoms: Holes in leaves; flowers chewed
Causes: **Japanese beetles; leaf-
eating beetles**

Beetle damage—ragged holes and skeletonized leaves—is easy to see. For controls see
"Japanese Beetle" on page 268.

Most Common Cosmos Diseases

Symptom: Plants wilt suddenly, collapse, and die within a few days

Cause: **Bacterial wilt**
    (*Pseudomonas solanacearum*)

Young cosmos plants are more prone to this disease than older plants. Destroy infected plants. Do not replant cosmos in that area.

Symptoms: Brown spots on stem; stem, leaves, and flowers above the lesion wilt

Cause: **Stem blight**
    (*Diaporthe stewartii*)

Portions of the plant above the stem lesions become brittle and break off the plant. Prevent this disease with good sanitation and 2- to 3-year crop rotations. Remove and destroy all plants with stem blight symptoms.

Symptom: Spots on leaves

Cause: **Leaf spot**
    (*Cercospora* spp.; *Septoria* spp.)

Leaf spots may spread to cover entire leaves, stunting plant growth. For controls see "Most Common Annual Diseases" on page 105.

'Sensation Mixed' cosmos (*Cosmos bipinnatus*)

FLOWERING TOBACCO
Nicotiana alata

FLOWERING TOBACCO AT A GLANCE

Botanical Name: *Nicotiana alata*
Height: 12 inches–3 feet
Spread: 8–15 inches
Shade Tolerance: Light shade; tolerates full sun in humid air
Hardiness: Damaged by light frost
Preferred Soil: Fertile, moderately moist, well-drained

Most Common Flowering Tobacco Pests

Symptom: Leaves and new shoots distorted and sticky

Cause: **Aphids**

Look for clusters of small, pear-shaped insects on undersides of leaves. For controls see "Aphids" on page 244.

Symptom: Foliage sticky

Cause: **Whiteflies**

Look for tiny, white, flying insects on undersides of leaves. For controls see "Whiteflies" on page 297.

Symptom: Young plants cut off or girdled at soil level

Cause: **Cutworms**

Cutworms feed at night, usually cutting the stem at the soil line so that the plant topples over. For controls see "Cutworms" on page 259.

Most Common Flowering Tobacco Diseases

See also "Petunias" on page 116.

Symptom: Plants stunted and growing poorly
Cause: **Southern root knot nematodes**

Heavily infested plants wilt in the midday sun, do not grow well, and their leaves turn yellow. Infestation appears as small, hard knobs and swollen galls on the fine roots. For controls see "Peonies" on page 152.

Flowering tobacco (<u>Nicotiana alata</u>)

GERANIUMS

Pelargonium spp. and hybrids

ANNUAL OR ZONAL GERANIUMS AT A GLANCE

Botanical Name: *Pelargonium* spp. and hybrids
Height: 1–2 feet
Spread: 1–3 feet
Shade Tolerance: Full sun
Hardiness: Zones 8–11
Preferred Soil: Moderately moist, well-drained; prefer sandy loam

---

Most Common Geranium Pests

Symptom: Light yellow speckles on leaves
Cause: **Two-spotted spider mites**

Look for very fine webbing on undersides of leaves. For controls see "Spider Mites" on page 286.

Symptom: Leaves and new shoots distorted and sticky
Cause: **Aphids**

Look for clusters of small, pear-shaped insects on undersides of leaves, on new shoots, and in flower buds. For controls see "Aphids" on page 244.

Symptom: Foliage sticky
Cause: **Greenhouse whiteflies**

Look for tiny, white flying insects on undersides of leaves. For controls see "Whiteflies" on page 297.

Symptoms: Large, irregular holes in leaves; slime trails present

Causes: **Slugs; snails**

Snails and slugs rasp large holes in soft, tender plants. For controls see "Slugs and Snails" on page 283.

Most Common Geranium Diseases

Symptom: Spots on leaves

Causes: **Alternaria leaf spot (*Alternaria tenuis*); bacterial blight (*Xanthomonas pelargonii*); cercospora leaf spot (*Cercospora brunkii*)**

Leaf spots may spread to cover entire leaves. For controls see "Most Common Annual Diseases" on page 105.

Symptoms: Young leaves wrinkled and deformed; coloration abnormal; plant stunted

Causes: **Crinkle virus, leaf breaking virus, leafy cup (beet curly top virus)**

Leafhoppers, aphids, and other insects can spread viruses. For controls see "Mosaic" on page 319.

Symptoms: Small yellow spots on leaves; orange blisters on leaf undersides

Cause: **Rust (*Puccinia pelargonii-zonalis*)**

Moderately infected plants are usually stunted, while seriously infected plants die. Watch for very slow growth and lack of vigor. Prevent problems by buying disease-free plants. For controls see "Rust" on page 327.

Symptom: Numerous short, fleshy stems and leaves growing from main stem

Cause: **Fasciation (*Rhodococcus fascians*)**

The distorted stems and leaves grow into a gall-shaped structure that is generally just at the soil line. There is no cure for this disease so infected plants must be destroyed. Do not take cuttings from plants with symptoms.

Most Common Geranium Disorders

Symptoms: Water-soaked spots on leaves; corky spots or ridges on leaves and stems

Cause: **Edema**

Edema occurs when the soil is moist and warm but the air is moist and cool. The plant takes in more water than it releases through transpiration, so cells become swollen and burst. Prevent this by good environmental management; in greenhouses or coldframes, water sparingly when days are cool and humidity is high.

'Harlequin Mahogany' geranium (<u>*Pelargonium*</u> *'Harlequin Mahogany'*)

IMPATIENS AND GARDEN BALSAM

Impatiens spp.

IMPATIENS AT A GLANCE

Botanical Name: *Impatiens wallerana*
Height: 6–15 inches
Spread: 10–18 inches
Shade Tolerance: Partial to deep shade
Hardiness: Damaged by light frost
Preferred Soil: Fertile, moist, well-drained, sandy, high in organic matter

GARDEN BALSAM AT A GLANCE

Botanical Name: *Impatiens balsamina*
Height: 1–3 feet
Spread: 10 inches–2½ feet
Shade Tolerance: Full sun; partial shade in hot climates
Hardiness: Damaged by light frost
Preferred Soil: Fertile, moist, light, well-drained

Most Common Impatiens Pests

Symptom: Light yellow speckles on leaves
Cause: **Spider mites**

For controls see "Spider Mites" on page 286. Some impatiens cultivars are sensitive to insecticidal soap; if you decide to try soap, test-spray a few leaves before treating plants.

Symptom: Leaves and new shoots distorted and sticky
Cause: **Aphids**

For controls see "Aphids" on page 244.

Symptom: Foliage sticky
Cause: **Whiteflies**

Look for tiny, white, winged insects on undersides of leaves. For controls see "Whiteflies" on page 297. Test-spray a few leaves before treating plants.

Most Common Impatiens Diseases

Symptom: Plants stunted and growing poorly
Cause: **Southern root knot nematodes**

Heavily infested plants wilt in the midday sun, do not grow well, and their leaves turn yellow. For controls see "Peonies" on page 152.

Symptom: Spots on leaves
Causes: **Leaf spot (various fungi, including *Stemphylium botryosum*, *Cercospora fucushiana*, *Phyllosticta* spp.; *Septoria noli-tangeris*)**

Leaf spots may spread to cover entire leaves, stunting plant growth. For controls see "Most Common Annual Diseases" on page 105.

*Impatiens (*Impatiens wallerana*)*

LOBELIA
Lobelia erinus

> ### EDGING LOBELIA AT A GLANCE
>
> **Botanical Name:** *Lobelia erinus*
> **Height:** 4–8 inches
> **Spread:** To 12 inches
> **Shade Tolerance:** Full sun or partial shade
> **Hardiness:** Tolerates light frost
> **Preferred Soil:** Fertile, moist, well-drained, sandy, high in organic matter

Most Common Lobelia Pests

Symptom: Leaves and new shoots distorted and sticky
Cause: **Aphids**

Look for clusters of small, pear-shaped insects on undersides of leaves, on new shoots, and in flower buds. Both adults and nymphs suck plant sap. Severely infested leaves and flowers may drop. As they feed, aphids excrete a sweet, sticky honeydew onto leaves below. Aphids have a large number of native predators which usually control them sufficiently to prevent serious plant damage. For controls see "Aphids" on page 244.

Symptoms: Shoots turn yellow; bases of stems damaged
Cause: **Wireworms**

These yellowish brown, leathery, wormlike beetle larvae are occasionally damaging to lobelias. Plants may be stunted or killed. Wireworms are worst in newly turned sod. For controls see "Wireworms" on page 298.

Most Common Lobelia Diseases

Symptoms: Lower leaves yellow; stems rot
Cause: **Stem rot (Rhizoctonia solani)**

The causal organism is widespread in soils, so the best control is prevention. Leave enough space between plants for good air circulation and choose locations with well-drained soil. Remove and destroy infected plants.

Symptom: Spots on leaves
Causes: **Leaf spot (Cercospora lobeliae; Phyllosticta bridgesii; Septoria lobeliae)**

Leaf spots may spread to cover entire leaves, stunting plant growth. Prevent leaf spot by spacing plants for good air circulation and light exposure. Water early in the day so leaves dry by nightfall; as much as possible, avoid wetting leaves. For controls see "Most Common Annual Diseases" on page 105.

Edging lobelia (<u>Lobelia erinus</u>)

MARIGOLDS
Tagetes spp. and hybrids

MARIGOLDS AT A GLANCE

Botanical Name: *Tagetes* spp. and hybrids
Height: 6 inches–3 feet
Spread: 6 inches–2 feet
Shade Tolerance: Full sun; partial shade in hot summer areas
Hardiness: Damaged by light frosts
Preferred Soil: Average to fertile, moderately moist, well-drained

---

Most Common Marigold Pests

Symptom: Leaves and new shoots distorted and sticky
Cause: **Aphids**

Look for clusters of pear-shaped insects on undersides of leaves, on new shoots, and in flower buds. For controls see "Aphids" on page 244.

'Golden Girls' marigold (<u>Tagetes</u> 'Golden Girls')

Symptoms: Foliage sticky; tiny, white insects present on undersides of leaves
Cause: **Whiteflies**

Look for tiny, white, flying insects. The tiny, pearly white nymphs look like scales on undersides of leaves. For controls see "Whiteflies" on page 297.

Most Common Marigold Diseases

Symptoms: Leaves wilt; stems have blackened, sunken lesions
Cause: **Stem rot (Phytophthora cryptogea)**

Stem rot starts at the soil level and works upward. Remove and destroy infected plants. Avoid replanting marigolds in that area unless you sterilize the soil.

Symptom: Spots on leaves
Cause: **Leaf spot (Septoria tageticola)**

Leaf spots may spread to cover entire leaves, stunting plant growth. For controls see "Most Common Annual Diseases" on page 105.

Symptoms: Yellowed foliage; leaves distorted or mottled; stunted growth
Cause: **Aster yellows**

Leafhoppers carry the mycoplasma-like organism that causes this disease. Leaves yellow without spotting first. Growth is usually dwarfed, and shoots and internodes may be abnormally short. Flowers are misshapen, sometimes only on one side. For controls see "Yellows" on page 333.

NASTURTIUMS

Tropaeolum spp. and hybrids

NASTURTIUMS AT A GLANCE

Botanical Name: *Tropaeolum* spp.
  and hybrids
Height: To 2 feet
Spread: Dwarf, 6–12 inches; trailer, to 6
  feet or more
Shade Tolerance: Full sun or partial shade
Hardiness: Damaged by light frosts
Preferred Soil: Infertile to average, well-
  drained

Most Common Nasturtium Pests

Symptom: Leaves and new shoots distorted
  and sticky

Cause: **Aphids**

Look for clusters of small, pear-shaped insects on undersides of leaves. For controls see "Aphids" on page 244. Do not use insecticidal soap on nasturtiums as it damages the foliage.

Symptom: Winding white tunnels in leaves

Cause: **Serpentine leafminers**

The tiny larvae of this small fly mine between the upper and lower surfaces of the leaves, out of reach of sprays. Handpick all infested leaves as soon as you see them. In fall rake up and destroy all fallen leaves and plant debris to remove overwintering miners. For heavy infestations, spray neem.

Symptom: Holes chewed in leaves

Causes: **Cabbage loopers; imported cabbageworms**

These green caterpillars may completely defoliate plants. Handpick light infestations. For heavy infestations, spray *Bacillus thuringiensis* var. *kurstaki* (BTK).

Most Common Nasturtium Diseases

Symptom: Leaves wilt, yellow, and die

Cause: **Bacterial wilt (Pseudomonas solanacearum)**

There is no cure for this disease; remove and destroy infected plants. Solarize the soil before replanting nasturtiums or other susceptible plants in that area.

Symptom: Tiny, red spots on leaves that quickly enlarge and dry

Cause: **Heterosporium disease (Heterosporium tropaeoli)**

Leaf spots on red-flowered cultivars have brown centers and dark borders, while those on yellow-flowered cultivars are tan. This disease is carried on seeds and on the wind. If you collect nasturtium seed, treat it with a hot-water bath at 125°F for 30 minutes before planting.

Nasturtiums (Tropaeolum majus)

PETUNIAS

Petunia x *hybrida*

PETUNIAS AT A GLANCE

Botanical Name: *Petunia* x *hybrida*
Height: 8–18 inches
Spread: 1–3 feet
Shade Tolerance: Full sun
Hardiness: Damaged by light frost
Preferred Soil: Fertile, moderately moist, well-drained, sandy

---

Most Common Petunia Pests

Symptom: Leaves and new shoots distorted and sticky
Cause: **Aphids**

Look for clusters of small, pear-shaped insects on undersides of leaves, on new shoots, and in flower buds. For controls see "Aphids" on page 244.

*Petunias (*Petunia* x *hybrida*)*

Symptom: Holes chewed in leaves and flowers
Causes: **Beetles; caterpillars; slugs**

Japanese beetles, Colorado potato beetles, flea beetles, and other beetles may attack petunias. Also, several species of caterpillars, as well as slugs, may damage plants especially in early spring. For most infestations, handpicking is sufficient as petunias are vigorous and usually outgrow the damage. For control of heavy infestations see entries in "What Garden Pest or Disease is That?" beginning on page 242.

Most Common Petunia Diseases

Symptom: Spots with concentric rings on leaves
Cause: **Alternaria blight (*Alternaria tenuis*)**

Infected leaves may die but remain attached to the stem of the plant. Pick them off as soon as you see them. This disease can spread from the leaves to the stems, killing the plant. Prevent by allowing good air circulation around plants and avoiding overwatering. Zonal geraniums (*Pelargonium* spp.) also contract this disease.

Symptom: Crown and bottom branches rot and die
Cause: **Crown rot (*Phytophthora* spp.)**

Prevent crown rot by planting petunias in well-drained soil. When transplanting, set each plant at the same level it grew in the pot. Space plants far enough apart for good air circulation and don't overwater. Remove and destroy affected plants.

Symptom: Short, fleshy stems and leaves
form on main stem near the
soil line
Cause: **Fasciation
(*Rhodococcus fascians*)**

Affected plants tend to be stunted and bloom
less than normal. For controls see
"Geraniums" on page 110.

Symptom: Plants wilt when soil is moist
Cause: **Fusarium wilt**

Symptoms often first appear on the lower or
outer parts of the plant. For controls see
"Fusarium Wilt" on page 315.

Symptoms: Mottled leaves; deformed leaves
and blossoms; plant is stunted
Cause: **Various viruses, including
mosaic**

Aphids, leafhoppers, and other insects can
spread viruses as they feed on your plants. For
controls see "Mosaic" on page 319.

Scarlet sage (Salvia splendens)

SCARLET SAGE
Salvia splendens

SCARLET SAGE AT A GLANCE

Botanical Name: *Salvia splendens*
Height: 6 inches–3 feet
Spread: To 1½ feet
Shade Tolerance: Full sun or partial shade
Hardiness: Damaged or killed by light frost
Preferred Soil: Fertile, moist, well-drained,
high in organic matter

Most Common Scarlet Sage Pests
Not troubled by pests.

Most Common Scarlet Sage Diseases

Symptoms: Spots on leaves; sometimes
yellow and dry and sometimes
dark
Cause: **Leaf spot (many fungi)**

Leaf spots may spread to cover entire leaves,
stunting plant growth. For controls see "Most
Common Annual Diseases" on page 105.

Symptom: Reddish or light brown spots
on leaves
Cause: **Rust (several fungal species)**

Keep soil evenly moist to promote vigorous
growth. For controls see "Rust" on page 327.

Symptoms: Growth is stunted or too bushy;
leaves yellow
Cause: **Aster yellows**

Insect pests may spread this disease as they
feed. For controls see "Yellows" on page 333.

SNAPDRAGON

Antirrhinum majus

SNAPDRAGON AT A GLANCE

Botanical Name: *Antirrhinum majus*
Height: Dwarf, 7–12 inches; tall, to 3 feet
Spread: 10–15 inches
Shade Tolerance: Full sun
Hardiness: Tolerates light frost
Preferred Soil: Poor to fertile, moderately moist, well-drained

---

Most Common Snapdragon Pests

Symptom: Leaves and new shoots distorted and sticky
Cause: **Aphids**

Look for clusters of pear-shaped insects on undersides of leaves. Severely infested leaves and flowers may drop For controls see "Aphids" on page 244.

Snapdragon (<u>Antirrhinum majus</u>)

Symptoms: Holes chewed in leaves; webs may be present
Cause: **Caterpillars**

Many species of caterpillars feed on snapdragons. For controls see "Most Common Annual Pests" on page 104.

Symptoms: Light yellow speckles on leaves
Cause: **Spider mites**

Look for fine webbing on undersides of leaves. Spider mites are most damaging in hot, dry weather and where natural enemies have been destroyed by sulfur or other pesticides. For controls see "Spider Mites" on page 286.

Most Common Snapdragon Diseases

Symptom: Large dark spots with concentric ridges, generally near tips or margins of the leaves
Cause: **Blight (*Phyllosticta antirrhini*)**

As spots from this blight disease age, they become light-colored and sunken before browning and dying. Stems develop lesions. Good sanitation helps to prevent the disease. In the greenhouse, hold temperatures at 60°F or below to inhibit spore germination. Plant snaps in well-drained soil and water the soil, not the plants, when watering. Spray plants with Bordeaux mixture to control.

Symptom: Reddish brown powdery pustules on leaves and stems
Cause: **Rust (*Puccinia antirrhini*)**

To minimize the chances of rust developing, plant rust-resistant cultivars and keep the soil evenly moist to promote vigorous growth. For controls see "Rust" on page 327.

SUNFLOWER

Helianthus annuus

> ## SUNFLOWER AT A GLANCE
>
> **Botanical Name:** *Helianthus annuus*
> **Height:** 2–10 feet
> **Spread:** 2–3 feet
> **Shade Tolerance:** Full sun
> **Hardiness:** Injured or killed by light frost
> **Preferred Soil:** Fertile to poor, moist, well-drained

Most Common Sunflower Pests

Symptom: Leaves and new shoots distorted and sticky
Cause: **Aphids**

Look for clusters of small, pear-shaped insects on undersides of leaves. Plant pollen and nectar plants to attract native predators and parasites; these usually control aphids sufficiently to prevent serious damage. Keep plants healthy, but avoid overfertilizing with nitrogen. Knock aphids off plants with a strong stream of water; repeat as needed. If further control is necessary, spray with insecticidal soap, neem, or homemade garlic sprays.

Symptom: Holes chewed in leaves
Cause: **Caterpillars**

Many species of caterpillars feed on sunflowers. Some only chew holes in leaves and usually can be seen feeding on the foliage. Others roll or tie leaves together and hide inside to feed. For controls see "Most Common Annual Pests" on page 104.

Most Common Sunflower Diseases

Symptom: Plants wilt when soil is moist
Cause: **Fungal wilt**

Wilt symptoms generally first appear on the lower or outer parts of the plant. Plant in well-drained soil, and water carefully to avoid splashing spores from soil and plant debris onto uninfected plants. Clean up plant residues in fall to remove overwintering fungal spores. Remove and destroy infected plants. For controls see "Verticillium Wilt" on page 332 and "Fusarium Wilt" on page 315.

Sunflower (Helianthus annuus)

Sweet Alyssum

Lobularia maritima

Sweet Alyssum at a Glance

Botanical Name: *Lobularia maritima*
Height: 3–6 inches
Spread: To 2 feet
Shade Tolerance: Full sun or light shade
Hardiness: Tolerates light frost
Preferred Soil: Average to poor fertility, moderately moist, well-drained

Most Common Sweet Alyssum Pests

Not troubled by pests.

Most Common Sweet Alyssum Diseases

Symptom: Lower leaves and stems rot and shrivel
Cause: **Stem rot**

Stem rot can attack seedlings and established plants. For controls see "Lobelia" on page 113.

Sweet alyssum (<u>Lobularia maritima</u>)

Verbena

Verbena x *hybrida*

Verbena at a Glance

Botanical Name: *Verbena* x *hybrida*
Height: 6–8 inches
Spread: 12–18 inches
Shade Tolerance: Full sun
Hardiness: Killed by light frost
Preferred Soil: Fertile, well-drained, sandy

Most Common Verbena Pests

Symptom: Leaves and new shoots distorted and sticky
Cause: **Aphids**

Look for clusters of pear-shaped insects on undersides of leaves. For controls see "Aphids" on page 244.

Symptom: Light yellow speckles on leaves
Cause: **Spider mites**

Look for fine webbing on undersides of leaves. Both adults and nymphs feed by sucking the juice from plant cells. When numerous, their feeding weakens plants, causing leaves to drop. For controls see "Spider Mites" on page 286.

Symptom: Foliage sticky
Cause: **Whiteflies**

Look for tiny, white, winged insects on undersides of leaves. The tiny, pearly white nymphs look like scales on undersides of leaves. These can quickly become a heavy infestation in greenhouse plants. For controls see "Whiteflies" on page 297.

Symptom: Winding white tunnels in leaves
Cause: **Verbena leafminers**

The ¹⁄₁₀–¹⁄₁₆-inch-long larvae of this small fly mine between the upper and lower surfaces of the leaves, out of reach of sprays. Handpick all infested leaves as soon as you see them. In fall, rake up and destroy all fallen leaves and plant debris to remove overwintering miners. For heavy infestations, spray neem.

Most Common Verbena Diseases

Symptom: White powdery coating
on leaves
Cause: **Powdery mildew**

Powdery mildew can spread quickly to cover whole leaves, stems, and flowers. Plant in well-drained soil, and space widely enough for good air circulation. Compost all plant debris. Spraying compost tea on leaves every 2–4 weeks can help prevent attack. Pick off and destroy infected plant tissues. Baking soda or baking soda plus oil sprays are often an effective control.

Verbena (Verbena x hybrida)

VIOLETS AND PANSIES

Viola spp. and hybrids

VIOLETS AND PANSIES AT A GLANCE

Botanical Name: *Viola* spp. and hybrids
Height: 4–9 inches
Spread: 6–12 inches
Shade Tolerance: Full sun or partial shade
Hardiness: Tolerate light frost
Preferred Soil: Fertile, moist, well-drained, high in organic matter

---

Most Common Violet and Pansy Pests

Symptom: Leaves and new shoots distorted
and sticky
Cause: **Aphids**

Look for clusters of small, pear-shaped insects on undersides of leaves. For controls see "Aphids" on page 244.

Symptom: Light yellow speckles on leaves
Cause: **Spider mites**

Look for fine webbing on undersides of leaves. For controls see "Spider Mites" on page 286.

Symptom: Young plants or shoots cut off or
girdled at soil level
Cause: **Cutworms**

Destroy the fat, gray caterpillars hiding in soil around the base of freshly damaged plants, or go out at night with a flashlight to catch feeding cutworms. For more controls see "Cutworms" on page 258.

Symptoms: Large, irregular holes in leaves; slime trails present
Causes: **Slugs; snails**

Slugs are gray, tan, black, or olive green and have no shells, while snails carry a coiled shell on their backs. Both prefer moist or shady parts of the garden and rasp large holes in soft, tender plants. Slugs have many natural enemies in organically managed yards, including birds, garter snakes, toads, and lizards. Ground beetles and fireflies are important predators of slug eggs. Maintain permanent walkways of clover, sod, or stone mulches to harbor ground beetles and garter snakes. Repel slugs and snails with copper strips fastened around trunks of trees or shrubs. Edge garden beds with copper flashing or screening, first making sure you have removed all slugs from the enclosed area. Wrap commercial snail and slug tapes around tree trunks. For further controls see "Slugs and Snails" on page 283.

Pansies (Viola x wittrockiana)

Symptom: Leaves with distortions and galls
Cause: **Violet gall midges**

The maggots of this ⅙-inch-long fly attack the growing points of the leaves, which are galled and may later rot. For light infestations, pick off all infested leaves. Keep fallen leaves picked up. Discard heavily infested plants.

Most Common Violet and Pansy Diseases

Symptom: Dead spots on leaves, usually with a dark border or concentric zones
Cause: **Anthracnose (Colletotrichum violae-tricoloris)**

Anthracnose fungi cause watery, rotting spots on foliage, stems, flowers, or fruits of many plants. Spots darken and merge as they age. For controls see "Anthracnose" on page 300.

Symptom: Plants wilt suddenly
Cause: **Wilt (Aphanomyces cladogamus; Myrothecium roridum; Fusarium oxysporum)**

Plant in well-drained, compost-amended soil and space widely enough so air can circulate freely. Remove severely infected or dead plants. Grow other plants in that site for at least 2 years before replanting violets or pansies, or solarize the soil.

Symptoms: Dark spots on leaves; spots fall out giving a shothole appearance
Cause: **Leaf spot (Centrospora acerina)**

Leaf spots can merge to cover the entire leaf, stunting plant growth. For controls see "Most Common Annual Diseases" on page 105.

WAX BEGONIAS

Begonia x *semperflorens –
cultorum*

WAX BEGONIAS AT A GLANCE

Botanical Name: *Begonia* x *semperflorens –
cultorum*

Height: 6–12 inches

Spread: 6–12 inches

Shade Tolerance: Light shade; full sun in
cool climates

Hardiness: Killed by light frost

Preferred Soil: Fertile, moist, well-drained

Most Common Begonia Pests

Symptom: Irregular brown blotches
on leaves

Cause: **Leaf nematodes**

As these microscopic worms feed in the leaf
tissue, the brown blotches expand until the
entire leaf dies, usually starting with the lower
leaves. The growth of infested plants is
stunted. Nematodes travel to new leaves in a
film of water and are spread in soil and plant
cuttings; do not wet foliage or take cuttings
from infested plants. Do not replant begonias
in soil where infested plants have grown. For
heavy infestations, discard plants and start
with clean cuttings in new soil.

Symptom: Leaves and new shoots distorted
and sticky

Cause: **Aphids**

Look for clusters of pear-shaped insects on
undersides of leaves. For controls see "Aphids"
on page 244.

Symptom: Powdery white, crawling insects
on stems

Cause: **Mealybugs**

You can see clusters of the small white mealybugs on stems and foliage. They produce
sticky honeydew as they feed and, if
numerous, cause leaves to wilt and turn yellow.
They are difficult to control with sprays,
although light infestations can be kept in
check with insecticidal soap. For heavy infestations, either discard infested plants or try
caging Australian lady beetles (*Cryptolaemus
montrouzieri*) on the plants using sheer curtain
material or window screen.

Symptom: Foliage sticky

Cause: **Whiteflies**

Look for tiny, white-winged insects on undersides of leaves. A light infestation of whiteflies
does little damage outdoors where natural
enemies are present, but it can quickly
become a heavy infestation in greenhouse
plants. The tiny, pearly white nymphs look like
scales on undersides of leaves. For a heavy
infestation, pick off lower leaves where the
nymphs are concentrated and spray insecticidal soap, neem, or pyrethrins. For smooth-
leaved cultivars in greenhouses, release the
parasitic wasp *Encarsia formosa* in spring.

Symptom: Brown streaks and scars in leaves
and flowers

Cause: **Thrips**

You will need a magnifying lens to see if these
minute, quick-moving insects are present on
leaves and between flower petals. Both adults
and nymphs suck the contents of plant cells,
which creates speckling or streaks on leaves. In
severe infestations, plants are stunted and
distorted. For controls see "Thrips" on page 293.

Symptoms: Large, irregular holes in leaves; slime trails present

Causes: **Slugs; snails**

Slugs are gray, tan, black, or olive green and have no shells, while snails carry a coiled shell on their backs. Both prefer moist or shady parts of the garden and rasp large holes in soft, tender plants. Slugs have many natural enemies in organically managed yards, including birds, garter snakes, toads, and lizards. Ground beetles and fireflies are important predators of slug eggs. Maintain permanent walkways of clover, sod, or stone mulches to harbor ground beetles and garter snakes. Repel slugs and snails with copper strips fastened around trunks of trees or shrubs. Edge garden beds with copper flashing or screening, first making sure you have removed all slugs from the enclosed area. Wrap commercial snail and slug tapes around tree trunks. For further controls see "Slugs and Snails" on page 283.

Wax begonias (<u>Begonia</u> x <u>semperflorens</u> – <u>cultorum</u>)

Most Common Begonia Diseases

Symptoms: Crown and lower stems are soft and discolored; stems collapse

Cause: **Pythium rot (*Pythium* spp.)**

Pythium usually attacks plants at the crown, but the infection spreads up the stems of the plant. Leaves on infected stems are water-soaked and limp. To prevent this disease, plant begonias only in well-drained soils, space them widely, and avoid overwatering or wetting the leaves or crown when watering.

Symptom: Small, blisterlike spots on leaves

Cause: **Bacterial leaf spot (*Xanthomonas begoniae*)**

Look for round spots, unless infection is between veins—then spots are angular. For controls see "Most Common Annual Diseases" on page 105.

Symptom: Gray or purplish fuzzy growth on leaves

Cause: **Botrytis blight (*Botrytis cinerea*)**

In spring, spores form and are carried by wind, water, and dirty tools to new plants. This fungus spreads rapidly to infect petioles, stems, and entire branches. On leaves, stems, and fruit, the first signs of infection are tiny, water-soaked spots. The spots enlarge and become soft and watery. Infected stem and leaf tissues become light brown and crack open, allowing the fuzzy gray spores to emerge. Lower leaves of infected lettuce plants rot first. Plant in well-drained soil and keep air circulation high with proper spacing. In greenhouses, increase air circulation and ventilation. Remove faded flowers and destroy infected plant parts to reduce the spread of the disease.

ZINNIA
Zinnia elegans

Most Common Zinnia Pests

Symptom: Light yellow speckles on leaves
Cause: **Spider mites**

Look for fine webbing on undersides of leaves. Mites are most damaging in hot, dry weather. For controls see "Spider Mites" on page 286.

Symptom: Stalks weakened and falling over or breaking
Cause: **Stalk borers**

If stalk borers are the problem, you should be able to find small holes in the base of stems marked by sawdustlike castings around the hole. For controls see "Delphiniums" on page 141.

Symptom: Young plants cut off or girdled at soil level
Cause: **Cutworms**

During the day, search for and destroy the fat, gray caterpillars hiding in soil around the base of freshly damaged plants, or go out at night with a flashlight to catch feeding cutworms. For controls see "Cutworms" on page 258.

Symptoms: Holes in leaves; flowers chewed
Causes: **Japanese beetles; leaf-eating beetles**

Several species of chewing beetles may attack zinnias. For controls see "Japanese Beetle" on page 268.

Most Common Zinnia Diseases

Symptoms: Spots on leaves; affected leaves brown and dry
Cause: **Alternaria blight (Alternaria zinniae)**

This disease may also attack the flowers, causing brown spots on the petals. For controls see "Petunias" on page 116.

Symptom: White, powdery coating on leaves
Cause: **Powdery mildew (Erysiphe cichoracearum)**

Powdery mildew can spread quickly to cover whole leaves, stems, and flowers. For controls see "Powdery Mildew" on page 323.

Zinnia (Zinnia elegans)

PERENNIALS

Most Common Perennial Pests

Symptom: Leaves and new shoots distorted
and sticky
Cause: **Aphids**

Look for clusters of 1/16–3/8-inch-long, pear-shaped insects on the undersides of leaves, on new shoots, and in flower buds. Their feeding causes curled leaves and deformed buds, and they produce sticky honeydew, which covers leaves and allows sooty molds to grow. Wash honeydew and aphids from leaves with a strong stream of water, repeating several times as necessary. For heavy infestations, spray insecticidal soap, neem, or pyrethrins.

Symptoms: Large, irregular holes in leaves;
slime trails present
Causes: **Slugs; snails**

Both slugs and snails prefer moist or shady parts of the garden and rasp large holes in soft, tender plants. They are most damaging in spring when wet weather favors their development and plants are small and easily damaged. Where slugs or snails are severe pests, it may be worth it to band flower beds with copper flashing to keep them out of particularly valued plants. Perennials generally grow quickly and are robust enough to withstand slug attack after the initial sprouting period in spring.

Symptom: Brown streaks and scars in leaves
and flowers
Cause: **Thrips**

You will need a magnifying lens to see if these minute, quick-moving insects are present on leaves and between flower petals. For heavy infestations, spray insectical soap, neem, or pyrethrins. As a last resort, dust diatomaceous earth on undersides of leaves and on the soil at the base of the plant. Keep nearby weeds pulled to eliminate thrips' host plants.

Symptoms: Holes chewed in leaves; webs
may be present
Cause: **Caterpillars**

Many species of caterpillars feed on perennials. Some only chew holes in leaves and are usually visible on the leaf. Others roll or tie together leaves and hide inside to feed. Handpick light infestations. For heavy infestations, spray *Bacillus thuringiensis* var. *kurstaki* (BTK) or neem, first plucking open webbed-together leaves to allow sprays to penetrate.

Symptom: Light yellow speckles on leaves
Cause: **Spider mites**

Most species of spider mites spin fine webbing on undersides of leaves. Spider mites are most damaging in hot, dry weather and where natural enemies have been destroyed by sulfur or other pesticides. For light infestations, spray foliage with water or insecticidal soap. For heavy infestations, which cause leaf edges to curl, turn brown, and dry up, spray neem or summer oil. Release predatory mites (*Metaseiulus occidentalis* or other species adapted to the local climate). Plan to spray lime-sulfur in late winter.

Symptoms: Holes in leaves; flowers chewed
Causes: **Japanese beetles; leaf-
eating beetles**

The large, 1/2-inch-long, blue-green Japanese beetles, with bronze wing covers are easy to see, as is the damage from their feeding, which skeletonizes leaves. Knock beetles onto ground sheets early in the morning and destroy. Handpick light infestations of these and other leaf- and flower-eating beetles, such as rose chafers.

Symptom: Young plants or shoots cut off or girdled at soil level

Cause: **Cutworms**

During the day, search for and destroy the fat, greasy, gray caterpillars hiding in soil around the base of freshly damaged plants, or go out at night with a flashlight to catch feeding cutworms. Where infestations are severe, apply neem or a solution of insect parasitic nematodes to soil or use a bran bait mixed with *Bacillus thuringiensis* var. *kurstaki* (BTK) sprinkled between plants. Protect small plants with cutworm collars.

Symptom: Pinched, scarred, or distorted leaves and buds

Causes: **Tarnished plant bugs; four-lined plant bugs; other true bugs**

When true bugs pierce and suck plant sap, their toxic saliva causes plants to react with distorted foliage and flowers. You may not see the bugs feeding because they fly away or drop quickly when disturbed. For light infestations, keeping the weeds down around flower beds may be sufficient. For heavy infestations, spray pyrethrins to control both nymphs and adults.

Most Common Perennial Diseases

Symptom: Wilting when soil is moist

Cause: **Fusarium wilt (*Fusarium* spp.)**

Symptoms often first appear on the lower or outer parts of the plant. For controls see "Fusarium Wilt" on page 315.

Symptom: White, powdery coating on leaves

Cause: **Powdery mildew**

This fungal disease can spread quickly to cover leaves, stems and buds. For controls see "Powdery Mildew" on page 323.

Symptoms: Watery spots on leaves, buds and flowers; gray mold sometimes visible

Cause: **Botrytis blight (*Botrytis cinerea*)**

Affected plant parts eventually turn brown and dry. For controls see "Botrytis Blight" on page 305.

Symptoms: Pale spots on leaf surfaces; orange pustules on leaf undersides

Cause: **Rust (several fungi)**

The first symptoms of rust diseases are general lack of vigor. Minimize rust problems by choosing a planting site with good air circulation. For controls see "Rust" on page 327.

Symptom: Galls on stem bases

Cause: **Crown gall (*Agrobacterium gypsophilae*)**

Shoot tips of affected plants may turn yellow and die. For controls see "Crown Gall" on page 309.

Symptom: Spots on leaves, sometimes dropping out to give a shothole effect

Cause: **Leaf spot (many fungi)**

Leaf spots may run together to cover whole leaves and stunt plant growth. For controls see "Most Common Annual Diseases" on page 105.

ASTERS

Aster spp. and hybrids

> ### ASTERS AT A GLANCE
>
> **Botanical Name:** *Aster* spp. and hybrids
> **Height:** 6 inches–6 feet
> **Spread:** 6 inches–3 feet
> **Shade Tolerance:** Full sun; partial shade in hot climates
> **Hardiness:** Zones 5–8
> **Preferred Soil:** Fertile, moist, well-drained, sandy or sandy loam

Most Common Aster Pests

Symptom: Leaves and new shoots distorted and sticky
Cause: **Aphids**

Look for clusters of small, pear-shaped insects on undersides of leaves, on new shoots, and in flower buds. For controls see "Aphids" on page 244.

New England aster (Aster novae-angliae)

Symptom: Holes in leaves
Cause: **Japanese beetles**

The large, blue-green Japanese beetles with bronze wing covers are easy to see, and so is the damage from their feeding, which skeletonizes leaves. For controls see "Japanese Beetle" on page 268.

Symptom: Yellowish brown spots and blotches on leaves
Cause: **Chrysanthemum lace bugs**

Look for black specks of excrement on undersides of leaves and for tiny insects with lacy wings. Their feeding also distorts stems, but light infestations are not very noticeable. For heavy infestations, spray insecticidal soap, summer oil, or pyrethrins.

Most Common Aster Diseases

Symptoms: Water-soaked areas on leaves; rotting stems
Cause: **Leaf blight (Rhizoctonia solani)**

This fungus causes blight symptoms on both leaves and stems. For controls see "Lobelia" on page 113.

Symptom: Orange-red pustules on leaf undersides
Cause: **Rust (Coleosporium solidaginis; Puccinia asteris)**

The first symptoms of rust diseases are a general lack of vigor and slow growth. Moderately infected plants are usually stunted; seriously infected plants die. Minimize rust problems by choosing a planting site with good air circulation. For controls see "Rust" on page 327.

ASTILBES

Astilbe spp. and hybrids

ASTILBES AT A GLANCE

Botanical Name: *Astilbe* spp. and hybrids
Height: 1–4 feet
Spread: 1–3 feet
Shade Tolerance: Partial or light shade; full sun with consistent watering
Hardiness: Zones 4–9 (most kinds)
Preferred Soil: Fertile, deep, moist, well-drained, high in organic matter

---

Most Common Astilbe Pests

Symptom: Holes in leaves
Cause: **Japanese beetles**

Astilbes are very attractive to Japanese beetles, which are their only notable pest. The large, blue-green Japanese beetles with bronze wing covers are easy to see, and so is the damage from their feeding, which skeletonizes leaves. The beetles feed during the day, especially in warm weather. They chew on flowers and when peak numbers of beetles are present, they may completely defoliate plants. For controls see "Japanese Beetle" on page 268.

Most Common Astilbe Diseases

Symptom: Wilting when soil is moist
Cause: **Fusarium wilt** (*Fusarium oxysporum* f. *callistephi*)

Symptoms often first appear on the lower or outer parts of the plant. Often, only one side or branch of a plant will wilt. For controls see "Fusarium Wilt" on page 315.

Symptom: White, powdery coating on leaf undersides
Cause: **Powdery mildew** (*Erysiphe polygoni*)

Powdery mildew can spread quickly to cover whole leaves, stems, and flowers. This disease is unsightly and also weakens host plants. Powdery white or gray spots on leaves and flowers enlarge quickly, finally covering the entire leaf, flower, or shoot. Infected tissues become brown and shrivel. Plant in well-drained soils, and space widely for good air circulation. Compost all plant debris and pick off and destroy infected plants tissues. Foliar compost tea sprays at intervals of 2–4 weeks can help prevent attack. Sprays of baking soda solution or baking soda plus oil (see "Oil Sprays" on page 361) are often an effective powdery mildew control.

Astilbe (Astilbe x arendsii)

BABY'S-BREATH

Gypsophila paniculata

BABY'S-BREATH AT A GLANCE

Botanical Name: *Gypsophila paniculata*
Height: 2–3 feet
Spread: To 3 feet
Shade Tolerance: Full sun
Hardiness: Zones 3–9
Preferred Soil: Relatively infertile, well-drained, alkaline

Most Common Baby's-Breath Pests

Symptom: Yellow and brown spots and edges on leaves
Cause: **Aster leafhoppers**

Early leafhopper damage starts as light green stipples, then leaves turn brown and may drop. You may be able to see the quick, wedge-shaped insects on undersides of leaves. For controls see "Leafhoppers" on page 270.

Most Common Baby's-Breath Diseases

Symptom: Plants rot at soil line and topple over
Cause: **Root rot (*Pythium debaryanum; Pellicularia filamentosa*)**

The first signs of root rot are subtle; the plants just don't look vigorous. Plants then wilt easily, leaves yellow or discolor, and the plants grow slowly. Prevent root rot problems by choosing a well-drained planting site. For controls see "Root Rot" on page 326.

Symptom: Galls on stem bases
Cause: **Crown gall (*Agrobacterium gypsophilae*)**

Shoot tips of infected plants may turn yellow and wilt. For controls see "Crown Gall" on page 309.

Symptom: Gray spots on buds, leaves, and stems
Cause: **Botrytis blight (*Botrytis cinerea*)**

Affected plant parts eventually turn brown and dry. For controls see "Botrytis Blight" on page 305.

*Baby's-breath (*Gypsophila paniculata*)*

BEE BALM

Monarda didyma

BEE BALM AT A GLANCE

Botanical Name: *Monarda didyma*
Height: 2–4 feet
Spread: To 3 feet
Shade Tolerance: Full sun or partial shade
Hardiness: Zones 4–9
Preferred Soil: Moderately fertile, moist, well-drained, high in organic matter

Most Common Bee Balm Pests

Not troubled by pests.

Most Common Bee Balm Diseases

Symptom:	White, powdery coating on leaves
Cause:	**Powdery mildew** (***Erysiphe polygoni***)

Powdery mildew can spread quickly to cover whole leaves, stems, and flowers. This disease is unsightly and also weakens host plants. Powdery white or gray spots on leaves and flowers enlarge quickly, finally covering the entire leaf, flower, or shoot. Infected tissues become brown and shrivel. Plant in well-drained soils, and space widely for good air circulation. Compost all plant debris and pick off and destroy infected plants tissues. Foliar compost tea sprays at intervals of 2–4 weeks can help prevent attack. Sprays of baking soda solution or baking soda plus oil (see "Oil Sprays" on page 361) are often an effective powdery mildew control.

Most Common Bee Balm Disorders

Symptom:	Center of plant dies out
Cause:	**Age**

Bee balm spreads rapidly whenever given good soil and adequate moisture levels. But when the center of the plant becomes too crowded, stems die out. Reinvigorate bee balm by lifting and dividing entire clumps every 3 years to keep your plants contained and looking their best. Divide plants in either early spring or fall. For best results, replant divisions as soon as possible after you've taken them, and keep their roots moist until you replant them.

Bee balm (<u>Monarda didyma</u>) (center of photo)

BELLFLOWERS
Campanula spp.

CLUSTERED BELLFLOWER AT A GLANCE

Botanical Name: *Campanula glomerata*
Height: 1–2 ½ feet
Spread: To 2 feet
Shade Tolerance: Full sun; partial shade in hot climates
Hardiness: Zones 3–8
Preferred Soil: Fertile, moist, well-drained

CARPATHIAN HAREBELL AT A GLANCE

Botanical Name: *Campanula carpatica*
Height: To 1 foot
Spread: To 1 foot
Shade Tolerance: Full sun
Hardiness: Zones 3–8
Preferred Soil: Average or poor fertility, moderately moist, well-drained, drought-tolerant

---

Most Common Bellflower Pests

Symptom: Leaves and new shoots distorted and sticky
Cause: **Aphids**

Look for clusters of small, pear-shaped insects on undersides of leaves, on new shoots, and in flower buds. Both adults and nymphs suck plant sap. Their feeding usually causes distorted leaves, buds, branch tips, and flowers. Severely infested leaves and flowers may drop. As they feed, aphids excrete a sweet, sticky honeydew onto leaves below. For controls see "Aphids" on page 244.

Symptom: Brown streaks and scars in leaves and flowers
Cause: **Thrips**

You will need a magnifying lens to see if these minute, quick-moving insects are present on leaves and between flower petals. Both adults and nymphs suck the contents of plant cells, creating silvery speckling or streaks on leaves. In severe infestations, plants are stunted and distorted, and flowers are damaged. Spray neem, insecticidal soap, or pyrethrins. As a last resort, dust undersides of leaves with diatomaceous earth. Use bright blue or yellow sticky traps to catch adults in greenhouses. To control thrips on fruit trees, spray dormant oil. In greenhouses, for onion or western flower thrips, release predatory mites (*Amblyseius cucumeris*) or minute pirate bugs.

Clustered bellflowers (<u>Campanula glomerata</u>)

Symptoms: Large, irregular holes in leaves and exposed bulbs; slime trails present

Causes: **Slugs; snails**

Slugs are gray, tan, black, or olive green and have no shells, while snails carry a coiled shell on their backs. Both prefer moist or shady parts of the garden and rasp large holes in soft, tender plants. For controls see "Slugs and Snails" on page 283.

Most Common Bellflower Diseases

Symptoms: Leaves spotted or yellow and wilting; dark colored lesions on stems; plant collapses

Causes: **Crown rot *(Pellicularia rolfsii)*; stem rot *(Sclerotinia sclerotiorum)***

Poor drainage, particularly in warm weather, favors these diseases. Stem rot produces a visible white mold at the base of plants and usually follows infection with crown rot. Plant in raised beds if your soil is poorly drained. Space widely for good air circulation. Organic mulches can reduce splashing water that spreads disease organisms. Boost disease resistance by spraying foliage with kelp extract early in the season. Remove and destroy infected plants.

Symptom: Orange or reddish brown pustules on leaf undersides

Cause: **Rust *(Coleosporium campanulae; Puccinia campanulae; Aecidium campanulastri)***

The first symptoms of rust diseases are lack of vigor and slow growth. Minimize rust problems by choosing a planting site with good air circulation. For controls see "Rust" on page 327.

BLEEDING HEARTS
Dicentra spp.

Most Common Bleeding Heart Pests
Not troubled by pests.

Most Common Bleeding Heart Diseases

Symptoms: Stems darken at base; leaves wilt; plant collapses

Causes: **Wilt *(Fusarium* spp.; *Verticillium albo-atrum)*; stem rot *(Pseudomonas solanacearum)***

For controls see "Fusarium Wilt" on page 315; "Verticillium Wilt" on page 332; and "Bacterial Wilt" on page 303.

Fringed bleeding heart (<u>Dicentra eximia</u>)

CHRYSANTHEMUMS

Chrysanthemum spp.
and hybrids

GARDEN MUMS AT A GLANCE

Botanical Name: *Chrysanthemum* spp. and hybrids
Height: Cushion, 1–1½ feet; upright, 2–3 feet
Spread: 1–3 feet
Shade Tolerance: Full sun to partial shade
Hardiness: Zones 5–9
Preferred Soil: Fertile, well-drained (especially in winter), high in organic matter

SHASTA DAISY AT A GLANCE

Botanical Name: *Chrysanthemum* x *superbum*, also sold as *Leucanthemum* x *superbum*
Height: 1–3 feet
Spread: To 2 feet or more
Shade Tolerance: Full sun or partial shade
Hardiness: Zones 4–8
Preferred Soil: Fertile, moist, and well-drained; good drainage is especially important in winter

Most Common Chrysanthemum Pests

Symptom: Leaves and new shoots distorted and sticky
Cause: **Aphids**

Look for clusters of small, pear-shaped insects on undersides of leaves, on new shoots, and in flower buds. For controls see "Aphids" on page 244. Avoid spraying oil on plants in bloom as it damages the flowers.

Symptom: Winding, white tunnels in leaves
Cause: **Chrysanthemum leafminers**

The larvae of this ⅒-inch-long fly mine between the upper and lower leaf surfaces, out of reach of sprays. For controls see "Columbines" on page 136.

Symptoms: Light yellow speckles on leaves; webbing present
Cause: **Two-spotted spider mites**

Look for very fine webbing on undersides of leaves. For controls see "Spider Mites" on page 286. Avoid spraying oil on plants in bloom as it damages the flowers.

Symptom: Brown streaks and scars in leaves and flowers
Cause: **Thrips**

You will need a magnifying lens to see if these minute, quick-moving insects are present on leaves and between flower petals. They move quickly and like to hide in tight crevices in plant stems and flowers. Both adults and nymphs suck the contents of plant cells, which creates silvery speckling or streaks on leaves. In severe infestations, plants are stunted and distorted, flowers are damaged. For controls see "Thrips" on page 293. Avoid spraying oil on plants in bloom as it damages the flowers.

Symptom: Yellowish brown spots and blotches on leaves
Cause: **Chrysanthemum lace bugs**

Look for black specks of excrement on undersides of leaves and for ⅒-inch-long insects with lacy wings. Their feeding also distorts stems, but light infestations are not very noticeable. For heavy infestations, spray insecticidal soap, summer oil, or pyrethrins.

Most Common Chrysanthemum Diseases

Symptoms: Flower bases turn tan or brownish and wither; flower stems are blackened

Cause: **Ray blight (Ascochyta chrysanthemi)**

This disease generally attacks blossoms, sometimes only on one side, but can also cause reddish brown stem lesions. Infections usually come in on purchased plants, so check all nursery-grown chrysanthemums carefully for symptoms before buying them. Ray blight is hard to control once it's in the soil, so remove and destroy infected plants as soon as possible.

Symptoms: Wet spots on stem; stem tips wilt; internal stem tissues become jellylike

Cause: **Bacterial blight (Erwinia chrysanthemi)**

Gray, water-soaked spots on stems are followed by brown to reddish-brown rot that moves down the stems. Sterilize tools between cuts to avoid spreading blight between plants. There is no cure for this disease; remove and destroy infected plants. Solarize the soil before replanting chrysanthemums or other susceptible plants in that area.

Symptoms: Yellow patches on lower leaves; deformed flowers; shoots are stunted

Cause: **Foliar nematodes**

Nematode damage usually begins near the base of the plant first. As these microscopic worms feed in the leaf tissue, yellow to brown blotches expand between the leaf veins until the entire leaf dies, starting with lower leaves.

Shasta daisy (Chrysanthemum x superbum)

The nematodes also attack flowers, which do not continue to develop. There is no cure for infected plants, which should be discarded along with all fallen leaves and debris. These nematodes travel up plants and onto new leaves in a film of water. They are also spread in soil and on cuttings; do not wet foliage or take cuttings from infected plants. Do not replant chrysanthemums in infected soil.

Symptom: Spots on leaves

Cause: **Leaf spot (Pseudomonas cichorii; Septoria chrysanthemi; S. leucanthemi; Cylindrosporium chrysanthemi)**

Leaf spots can grow together and cover whole leaves, stunting plant growth. For controls see "Most Common Annual Diseases" on page 105.

Symptoms: Pale spots on leaf surfaces; dark
pustules on leaf undersides

Cause: **Rust (Puccinia chrysanthemi)**

The first symptoms of rust attack are lack of
vigor and slow growth. Minimize rust
problems by choosing a planting site with
good air circulation. For controls see "Rust"
on page 327.

Symptom: Water-soaked or brown spots
on petals

Cause: **Botrytis blight (Botrytis cinerea)**

Frequently, this disease starts as a blight on
aging blossoms. Once established on a plant,
this fungus spreads rapidly to infect petioles,
stems, and entire branches. Affected flower
heads tend to droop. Infected stem and leaf
tissues become light brown and crack open,
allowing gray mold spores to emerge. For
controls see "Botrytis Blight" on page 305.

Symptoms: Flowers decay; plants wilt

Cause: **Wilt (Fusarium tricinctum f.
poae; F. oxysporum;
Verticillium albo-atrum)**

Wilt symptoms tend to start at the base of the
plant and work upwards. For controls see
"Fusarium Wilt" on page 315 and "Verticillium
Wilt" on page 332.

Symptoms: Flowers are green; foliage is
distorted or mottled

Cause: **Aster yellows**

Leafhoppers carry the organism that causes this
disease. Leaves yellow without spotting first.
Growth is usually dwarfed, and shoots and
internodes may be abnormally short. Flowers
are misshapen, sometimes only on one side. For
controls see "Yellows" on page 333.

COLUMBINES

Aquilegia spp.

COLUMBINES AT A GLANCE

Botanical Name: *Aquilegia* spp.
Height: 1–3 feet
Spread: 1–1½ feet
Shade Tolerance: Partial or light shade; full
sun in cool climates
Hardiness: Zones 3–9
Preferred Soil: Fertile, moist, well-drained,
high in organic matter

Most Common Columbine Pests

Symptom: Leaves and new shoots distorted and sticky

Cause: **Aphids**

Look for clusters of small, pear-shaped insects
on undersides of leaves, on new shoots, and in
flower buds. Both adults and nymphs suck
plant sap. Their feeding usually causes
distorted leaves, buds, branch tips, and
flowers. Severely infested leaves and flowers
may drop. As they feed, aphids excrete a
sweet, sticky honeydew onto leaves below. For
controls see "Aphids" on page 244.

Symptom: Winding white tunnels in leaves

Cause: **Columbine leafminers**

The light green larvae of this ¹⁄₁₀-inch-long fly
mine between the upper and lower surfaces
of the leaves, out of reach of sprays. Handpick
all infested leaves as soon as you see them. In
fall rake up and destroy all fallen leaves and
plant debris to remove overwintering miners.
For heavy infestations, spray neem.

Most Common Columbine Diseases

Symptoms: Leaves and shoots wilt;
branches dry

Cause: **Crown rot or wilt
(*Sclerotinia sclerotiorum*)**

Only one or two stems may show the infection at first, but if you see wilting, look closely at the affected leaves. The white web of fungal mycelium is large enough to see without magnification. To prevent this disease, plant columbines in sandy, well-drained soil. Remove and destroy diseased plants immediately to prevent the disease from spreading.

Symptom: Spots on leaves

Cause: **Leaf spot
(various fungi)**

Leaf spots may run together to cover entire leaves; growth of infected plants may be stunted. For controls see "Septoria Leaf Spot" on page 328.

Columbines (Aquilegia vulgaris)

CORAL BELLS

Heuchera spp.

CORAL BELLS AT A GLANCE

Botanical Name: *Heuchera sanguinea*
Height: 1–2 feet
Spread: To 1 foot
Shade Tolerance: Full sun or partial shade
Hardiness: Zones 3–8
Preferred Soil: Fertile, moist, very well-drained, neutral pH, high in organic matter

AMERICAN ALUMROOT AT A GLANCE

Botanical Name: *Heuchera americana*
Height: 1½–3 feet
Spread: 1½ feet
Shade Tolerance: Full or partial shade
Hardiness: Zones 4–9
Preferred Soil: Fertile, moist, well-drained, high in organic

---

Most Common Coral Bells Pests

Symptom: Half-circle notches in leaf edges

Cause: **Strawberry root weevils**

These small, black weevils feed on leaves at night, while the fat, white larvae attack the roots in early spring, killing the crowns. The larvae cause the worst damage by boring into the crowns and roots of plants. In heavy infestations, all plants in a section of the bed may turn black and die. Drench soil with neem or insect parasitic nematodes to control larvae. Spray plants with pyrethrins to kill adults. Remove and destroy badly infested plants.

Most Common Coral Bells Diseases

Symptom: White, powdery coating on
leaves

Cause: **Powdery mildew**

Powdery mildew can spread quickly to cover
whole leaves, stems, and flowers. This disease
is unsightly and also weakens host plants.
Powdery white or gray spots on leaves and
flowers enlarge quickly, finally covering the
entire leaf, flower, or shoot. Infected tissues
become brown and shrivel. Plant in well-
drained soils, and space widely for good air
circulation. Compost all plant debris and pick
off and destroy infected plants tissues. Foliar
compost tea sprays at intervals of 2–4 weeks
can help prevent attack.

Coral bells (<u>Heuchera sanguinea</u>)

COREOPSIS
Coreopsis spp.

LANCELEAF COREOPSIS AT A GLANCE

Botanical Name: *Coreopsis lanceolata*
Height: To 2 feet
Spread: 1–3 feet
Shade Tolerance: Full sun
Hardiness: Zones 3–8
Preferred Soil: Average fertility, well-
drained soil; plants are drought-tolerant
when established

THREADLEAF COREOPSIS AT A GLANCE

Botanical Name: *Coreopsis verticillata*
Height: 1–3 feet
Spread: To 3 feet
Shade Tolerance: Full sun
Hardiness: Zones 3-9
Preferred Soil: Average to relatively
infertile, well-drained soil; plants are
somewhat drought tolerant

Most Common Coreopsis Pests

Symptom: Leaves and new shoots distorted
and sticky

Cause: **Aphids**

Look for clusters of small, pear-shaped insects
on undersides of leaves, on new shoots, and in
flower buds. Their feeding usually causes
distorted leaves, buds, branch tips, and flowers.
Severely infested leaves and flowers may drop.
As they feed, aphids excrete a sweet, sticky
honeydew onto leaves below. For controls see
"Aphids" on page 244.

Symptom: Pinched, scarred, or distorted
              leaves and buds
Cause: **Four-lined plant bugs**

When true bugs pierce and suck plant sap, their toxic saliva causes plants to react with distorted foliage and flowers. Where plant bugs are very numerous, cover small plants with floating row covers. Spray pyrethrins to control nymphs and adults.

Symptoms: Yellow and brown spots; brown
              edges on leaves
Cause: **Aster leafhoppers**

Early leafhopper damage starts as light green stipples, then leaves turn brown and may drop. You may be able to see the quick, wedge-shaped, ⅛-inch-long insects on undersides of leaves. Leafhoppers spread aster yellows, which causes stunted, yellowish plants. Native parasitic flies, damsel bugs, minute pirate bugs, lady beetles, lacewings, parasitic wasps, and spiders are important in keeping leafhopper numbers down. Some leafhopper damage is tolerable and control measures are usually not necessary. Wash nymphs from plants with a stiff spray of water. You can also control nymphs while they are still small with sprays of neem, insecticidal soap, or pyrethrins.

Most Common Coreopsis Diseases

Symptom: Yellowish, stunted plants;
              distorted or mottled leaves;
              greenish flowers
Cause: **Aster yellows**

Leafhoppers carry the mycoplasma-like organism that causes this disease and spread it through their feeding. Control leafhoppers as much as possible (see above). Leaves yellow without spotting first. Growth is usually dwarfed, and shoots and internodes may be abnormally short. Flowers are greenish and misshapen, sometimes only on one side. For controls see "Yellows" on page 333.

Most Common Coreopsis Disorders

Symptoms: Plants leggy; blooms
              decrease after several years
Cause: **Overcrowding**

Coreopsis self-seeds extraordinarily well, quickly crowding itself out of adequate room. Avoid problems by spacing a minimum of 12 inches apart when you first plant or transplant. Each spring, remove extra seedlings. Divide clumps every 3 or 4 years.

*Lanceleaf coreopsis (*Coreopsis lanceolata*)*

DAYLILIES

Hemerocallis spp.
and hybrids

DAYLILIES AT A GLANCE

Botanical Name: *Hemerocallis* spp.
and hybrids
Height: 20 inches–4 feet
Spread: To 2½ feet
Shade Tolerance: Full sun; partial shade
in hot climates
Hardiness: Zones 3–9
Preferred Soil: Moderately fertile, moist,
well-drained, high in organic matter;
somewhat drought-tolerant

Daylily (*Hemerocallis* cultivar)

Most Common Daylily Pests

Symptom: Light yellow or reddish speckles
on leaves
Cause: **Two-spotted spider mite**

Look for very fine webbing on the undersides
of leaves. Both adults and nymphs feed by
sucking the juice from plant cells. For controls
see "Spider Mites" on page 286.

Symptoms: Scarred or dead flower buds;
corky scars on stems
Cause: **Thrips**

You will need a magnifying lens to see if these
minute, quick-moving insects are present on
leaves and between flower petals. Both adults
and nymphs suck the contents of plant cells,
creating silvery speckling or streaks on leaves.
In severe infestations, plants are stunted and
distorted, and flowers are damaged. To control
thrips on fruit trees, spray dormant oil. Spray
neem, insecticidal soap, or pyrethrins. As a last
resort, dust undersides of leaves with diatomaceous earth. Use bright blue or yellow sticky
traps to catch adults in greenhouses. In greenhouses, for onion or western flower thrips,
release predatory mites (*Amblyseius cucumeris*)
or minute pirate bugs.

Most Common Daylily Disorders

Symptom: Yellowing leaves, plant dies
from crown
Cause: **Soggy soil conditions**

Daylilies require good drainage. In consistently wet soils, they may contract one of the
root rot diseases. To prevent problems, plant
in well-drained soil or raised beds. For other
tips see "Waterlogged Soil" on page 339.

DELPHINIUMS

Delphinium spp. and hybrids

> ## DELPHINIUMS AT A GLANCE
>
> **Botanical Name:** *Delphinium* spp. and hybrids
> **Height:** 3–6 feet
> **Spread:** 3 feet
> **Shade Tolerance:** Full sun, partial shade in hot summers
> **Hardiness:** Zones 3–7
> **Preferred Soil:** Fertile, moist, well-drained, high in organic matter, neutral to slightly alkaline

Most Common Delphinium Pests

Symptoms: Large, irregular holes in leaves and shoots; slime trails present
Causes: **Slugs; snails**

Slugs are gray, tan, black, or olive green and have no shells, while snails carry a coiled shell on their backs. Both prefer moist or shady parts of the garden and rasp large holes in soft, tender plants. For controls see "Slugs and Snails" on page 283.

Symptom: Plants cut off at soil line
Cause: **Cutworms**

During the day, search for and destroy the fat, greasy, gray caterpillars hiding in soil around the base of freshly damaged plants, or go out at night with a flashlight to catch feeding cutworms. Protect transplants from damage by using cutworm collars around the stems. Avoid the main population of cutworms by planting later in the season. For further controls see "Cutworms" on page 258.

Symptom: Leaves and new shoots distorted and sticky
Cause: **Aphids**

Look for clusters of pear-shaped insects on undersides of leaves, on new shoots, and in flower buds. For controls see "Aphids" on page 244.

Symptom: Light yellow speckles on leaves
Cause: **Two-spotted spider mites**

Look for very fine webbing on undersides of leaves. Both adults and nymphs feed by sucking the juice from plant cells on undersides of leaves. When numerous, their feeding weakens plants, causes leaves to drop, and results in stunted fruit. Early damage appears as yellow speckled areas on leaves. In severe infestations, leaves become bronzed or turn yellow or white with brown edges. For controls see "Spider Mites" on page 286.

Symptom: Blotchy, brown tunnels in leaves
Cause: **Larkspur leafminers**

The larvae of this $\frac{1}{10}$-inch-long fly mine between the upper and lower leaf surfaces. For controls see "Columbines" on page 136.

Symptom: Stalks weakened and falling over or breaking
Cause: **Stalk borers**

If stalk borers are the problem, you should be able to find small holes in the base of stems marked by fine sawdustlike castings around the holes. Kill them by sticking a fine pin through the stalk in several places above the bored hole or by inserting a fine, flexible wire in the hole. To reduce the overwintering population, cut down and destroy all stalks and nearby weeds in the fall.

Most Common Delphinium Diseases

Symptom: Tarry black spots on leaves
Cause: **Bacterial leaf spot**
(*Pseudomonas delphinii*)

The black leaf spots may run together to form large black patches. Infected tissue often drops out producing a "shothole" look. For controls see "Bacterial Spot" on page 303.

Symptoms: Leaves yellow; stems blackened; plants stunted
Cause: **Bacterial rot (*Erwinia atroseptica, E. chrysanthemi*)**

Look for a black discoloration near the base of the plant. For controls see "Bacterial Soft Rot" on page 302.

Candle larkspur (Delphinium elatum)(center right of photo)

Symptoms: Cankers on crown; cracks in stem; tissue at leaf stem bases is dark
Cause: **Phoma crown rot (*Phoma* spp.)**

Prevent this disease by planting in raised beds and applying compost each spring. Do not allow plants to become overcrowded. Practice 3- or 4-year rotations. In warm climates, solarize soils before planting.

Symptoms: Flowers green; a cluster of succulent leaves or shoots forms on the plant
Cause: **Aster yellows**

Leafhoppers carry this organism and spread it as they feed. For controls see "Yellows" on page 333.

Symptoms: Small, gray, water-soaked spots on leaves; plants wilt
Cause: **Fusarium canker and wilt (*Fusarium oxysporum* f. *delphinii*)**

Symptoms tend to appear on the lower or outer parts of the plant first. For controls see "Fusarium Wilt" on page 315.

Symptom: White, powdery coating on leaves
Cause: **Powdery mildew (*Erysiphe polygoni*)**

Powdery mildew can spread quickly to cover whole leaves, stems, and flowers. Infected tissues become brown and shrivel. Plant in well-drained soils, and space widely for good air circulation. Compost all plant debris and pick off and destroy infected plants tissues. Foliar compost tea sprays at intervals of 2–4 weeks can help prevent attack.

FOXGLOVE

Digitalis purpurea

> ## FOXGLOVE AT A GLANCE
>
> **Botanical Name:** *Digitalis purpurea*
> **Height:** 1–5 feet
> **Spread:** To 1½ feet
> **Shade Tolerance:** Partial shade
> **Hardiness:** Zones 4–9
> **Preferred Soil:** Moderately fertile, moist, well-drained, acidic, high in organic matter

Most Common Foxglove Pests

Symptom: Leaves and new shoots distorted and sticky

Cause: **Foxglove aphids**

Foxglove aphids overwinter only on foxglove; collect and destroy plant tops in the fall. Look for clusters of ¹⁄₁₀–¹⁄₆-inch-long, pear-shaped insects on the undersides of leaves, on new shoots, and in flower buds. For controls see "Aphids" on page 244.

Symptom: Holes in leaves

Causes: **Japanese beetles; leaf-eating beetles**

Foxgloves are a favorite host plant for Japanese beetles. The large, blue-green Japanese beetles with bronze wing covers are easy to see, and so is the damage from their feeding, which skeletonizes leaves. Asiatic garden beetles and rose chafers also feed on leaves. For controls see "Japanese Beetle" on page 268.

Most Common Foxglove Diseases

Symptom: White, powdery coating on leaves

Cause: **Powdery mildew**

Powdery mildew can spread quickly to cover whole leaves, stems, and flowers. Powdery white or gray spots on leaves and flowers enlarge quickly, finally covering the entire leaf, flower, or shoot. Infected tissues become brown and shrivel. Plant in well-drained soils, and space widely for good air circulation. Compost all plant debris and pick off and destroy infected plants tissues. Foliar compost tea sprays at intervals of 2–4 weeks can help prevent mildew attack.

'Foxy' foxglove (*Digitalis purpurea* 'Foxy')

HARDY GERANIUMS

Geranium spp.

HARDY GERANIUMS AT A GLANCE

Botanical Name: *Geranium* spp.
Height: 6–36 inches
Spread: 6–24 inches
Shade Tolerance: Full sun, partial shade in hot climates
Hardiness: Zones 3–8
Preferred Soil: Average to fertile, moist, well-drained

Most Common Geranium Pests

Symptom: Leaves and new shoots distorted and sticky
Cause: **Aphids**

Look for clusters of pear-shaped insects on undersides of leaves, on new shoots, and in flower buds. Native predators and parasites

Hardy geranium (Geranium incanum)

usually control aphids sufficiently to prevent serious damage. Keep plants healthy, but avoid overfertilizing with nitrogen. Knock aphids off plants with a strong stream of water; repeat as needed. If further control is necessary, spray with insecticidal soap, neem, or homemade garlic sprays.

Symptom: Pinched, scarred or distorted leaves and buds
Cause: **Four-lined plant bug**

When these bugs pierce and suck plant sap, their toxic saliva causes plants to react with distorted foliage and flowers. Where plant bugs are very numerous, cover small plants with floating row covers. Spray pyrethrins to control nymphs and adults.

Symptoms: Shoots turn yellow; bases of stems damaged
Cause: **Wireworms**

These larvae of click beetles look like leathery, light brown, jointed worms (up to 1 inch long). The larvae live in the soil and bore into corms and the base of the stem, causing them to rot. Where wireworms are usually damaging, delay planting until soil is warm and wireworms have moved deeper into the soil. Clear wireworms from intended planting areas by burying pieces of potato and carrot below the soil surface. Check these baits every few days and destroy wireworms. For heavy infestations of wireworms, drench soil with insect parasitic nematodes.

Most Common Geranium Diseases

Same diseases as zonal geraniums. See "Annual or Zonal Geraniums at a Glance" on page 110.

HOLLYHOCK

Alcea rosea

HOLLYHOCK AT A GLANCE

Botanical Name: *Alcea rosea*
Height: 2–9 feet
Spread: 1–2 feet
Shade Tolerance: Full sun
Hardiness: Tolerates light frost
Preferred Soil: Fertile, moist, well-drained

Most Common Hollyhock Pests

Symptom: Holes in leaves
Cause: **Japanese beetles**

Hollyhocks are a favorite of these ½-inch-long, metallic blue-green beetles with bronze wing covers. As they feed, Japanese beetles skeletonize leaves; in large numbers, they can easily defoliate plants. In the early morning, handpick beetles or vacuum them from plants, or shake them from the plants onto ground sheets and destroy. Trapping is most effective on a community-wide basis.

Most Common Hollyhock Diseases

Symptoms: Orange spots on leaf undersides;
               leaves deformed
Cause: **Rust (*Puccinia malvacearum*)**

Minimize rust problems by choosing a planting site with good air circulation. For controls see "Rust" on page 327.

Symptom: Water-soaked lesions appear on
              stem near the soil line
Cause: **Stem canker
              (*Sclerotinia sclerotiorum*)**

Plants growing in poorly drained soil are prime targets for stem canker. For controls see "Bellflowers" on page 132.

Symptom: Veins, leaf blades, stems, and
              petioles spotted with black lesions
Cause: **Anthracnose
              (*Colletotrichum malvarum*)**

In serious cases, this disease can spread on a plant to cover whole leaves. For controls see "Anthracnose" on page 300.

Symptoms: Spots on leaves; spots sometimes
               drop out leaving a shothole effect
Cause: **Leaf spot (*Cercospora althaeina;
               Phyllosticta althaeina*)**

Leaf spots can run together and cover entire leaves, stunting plant growth. For controls see "Most Common Annual Diseases" on page 105.

Hollyhocks (*Alcea rosea*)

Hostas

Hosta spp. and hybrids

Hostas at a Glance

Botanical Name: *Hosta* spp. and hybrids
Height: To 3 feet
Spread: To 4 feet
Shade Tolerance: Partial or full shade
Hardiness: Zones 3–9
Preferred Soil: Fertile, moderately moist, well-drained

Most Common Hosta Pests

Symptoms: Large, irregular holes in leaves and shoots; slime trails present
Causes: **Slugs; snails**

Both slugs and snails eat soft, tender plant tissue and rasp large holes in foliage. The moist,

Hosta (<u>Hosta</u> hybrid)

shady conditions in which hostas thrive also favor these slimy pests. Repel slugs and snails by edging garden beds with copper flashing or screening, first removing all slugs and snails from the enclosed area. Where they are an occasional problem, spread wide bands of cinders, woods ashes, or diatomaceous earth around plantings to protect tender seedlings and transplants. For further controls see "Slugs and Snails" on page 283.

Most Common Hosta Diseases

Symptoms: Leaves yellow and wilt; crowns rot
Cause: **Crown rot (various fungi and bacteria)**

Poor drainage, particularly in warm weather, favors these diseases. Stem rot produces a visible white mold at the base of plants and usually follows infection with crown rot. Plant in raised beds if your soil is poorly drained. Space widely for good air circulation. Organic mulches can reduce splashing water that spreads disease organisms. Boost disease resistance by spraying foliage with kelp extract early in the season. Remove and destroy infected plants.

Most Common Hosta Disorders

Symptoms: Scorched or bleached-looking, light brown, papery leaves; leaves small
Causes: **Lack of water; too much sun**

An easy way to ruin hostas is to let them dry out, even for a little while. Even if they continue to grow, plants will be stunted. Sunburned edges or spots reduce hostas' ornamental value significantly and are best prevented by planting hostas in shady sites.

IRISES

Iris hybrids

Most Common Iris Pests

Symptom: Tunnels bored in leaves
        and buds
Cause: **Iris borers**

This is a serious pest of iris in eastern North America. The caterpillars of this moth bore into early leaves and buds, then into crowns and rhizomes. Soft rot usually follows larval destruction. Destroy larvae in the leaves by crushing them. Destroy all iris leaves and debris in fall to remove overwintering sites. In light infestations, save rhizomes by digging the borers out of the roots, dusting the rhizomes with sulfur, and replanting. Plant resistant species such as Siberian iris (*Iris sibirica*).

Symptoms: Large, irregular holes in leaves
        and shoots; slime trails present
Causes: **Slugs; snails**

Both slugs and snails eat soft, tender plant tissue and rasp large holes in foliage. Slugs have many natural enemies in organically managed yards. Maintain permanent walkways of clover, sod, or stone mulches to harbor ground beetles and garter snakes. Repel slugs and snails with copper strips fastened around trunks of trees or shrubs. Edge garden beds with copper flashing or screening, first removing all slugs from the enclosed area. For further controls see "Slugs and Snails" on page 283.

Bearded iris (<u>Iris</u> hybrid)

Symptoms: Brown or silvery streaks; scars
and distortions in leaves
and flowers
Cause: **Thrips**

Several species of thrips feed on irises. You will need a magnifying lens to see these minute, quick-moving insects hiding between flower petals and leaf sheaths. Feeding by thrips causes blackening or russeting of the leaves, and in heavy infestations the plant is stunted and may die. Spray neem, insecticidal soap, or pyrethrins. As a last resort, dust undersides of leaves with diatomaceous earth. Use bright blue or yellow sticky traps to catch adults in greenhouses. In greenhouses, for onion or western flower thrips, release predatory mites (*Amblyseius cucumeris*) or minute pirate bugs.

Most Common Iris Diseases

Symptoms: Rot at base of bulb; scales of
bulb rotted
Cause: **Basal rot; blue mold
(*Penicillium* spp.)**

Choose a planting site with good drainage to help prevent these diseases. For controls see "Most Common Bulb Diseases" on page 157.

Symptom: Black, irregularly shaped spots
with reddish borders on leaves
Cause: **Ink spot
(*Mystrosporium adustum*)**

This disease travels through the soil, infecting adjacent healthy bulbs. Check bulbs for black stains, yellow spots, or sunken, black areas before planting. Don't plant damaged bulbs. If the young foliage is spotted, dig up and destroy the bulb and the surrounding soil. Amend the planting area with compost and don't replant with iris bulbs.

Symptoms: Water-woaked spots on leaves;
rhizomes rotted and soft
Cause: **Bacterial soft rot
(*Erwinia* spp., *Pseudomonas* spp.)**

Soft rot attacks iris rhizomes, entering through wounds made by early leaf removal or cultivation or carried on the bodies of iris borers. Infected rhizomes are dry on the outside but wet, smelly, and slimy inside. Water-soaked streaks appear on leaves, which then turn yellow and wilt from the tips. Control borers to reduce soft rot. Remove and destroy rotting rhizomes. Wash tools when cultivating or dividing irises. Plant healthy rhizomes in well-drained soil with adequate sunlight.

Symptoms: Leaves are mottled; flowers
show spots or featherlike
markings
Cause: **Mosaic (many viruses)**

Aphids, leafhoppers, and other insects can spread viruses as they feed on your plants. For controls see "Mosaic" on page 319.

Symptoms: Tips of outside leaves brown
and die; leaf bases rot; white
mold may appear on the stem
Cause: **Crown rot (*Sclerotium rolfsii*)**

Crown rot symptoms usually start at ground level and work upward. For controls see "Petunias" on page 116.

Symptom: Spots that expand and merge on
leaves after plants have bloomed
Cause: **Leaf spot
(*Didymellina macrospora*)**

Leaf spots may spread to cover entire leaves, stunting plant growth. For controls see "Most Common Annual Diseases" on page 105.

JAPANESE ANEMONE

Anemone x *hybrida*

> ## JAPANESE ANEMONE AT A GLANCE
>
> **Botanical Name:** *Anemone* x *hybrida*
> **Height:** 2½–4 feet
> **Spread:** To 1½ feet, but clumps enlarge
> **Shade Tolerance:** Partial shade
> **Hardiness:** Zones 4–8
> **Preferred Soil:** Fertile, moist, well-drained, high in organic matter

Most Common Anemone Pests

Symptom: Leaves and new shoots distorted and sticky
Cause: **Aphids**

Aphids feeding on anemone flowers cause streaks. Look for clusters of small, pear-shaped insects on undersides of leaves, on new shoots, and in flower buds. Their feeding usually causes distorted leaves, buds, branch tips, and flowers. As they feed, aphids excrete a sweet, sticky honeydew onto leaves below. For controls see "Aphids" on page 244.

Symptoms: Large, irregular holes in leaves; slime trails present
Causes: **Slugs; snails**

Slugs are gray, tan, black, or olive green and have no shells, while snails carry a coiled shell on their backs. Both prefer moist or shady parts of the garden and rasp large holes in soft, tender plants. They may completely demolish seedlings. Birds, garter snakes, toads, and lizards all prey on slugs; ground beetles and fireflies are important predators of slug eggs. Maintain permanent paths of clover, sod, or stones to harbor ground beetles and garter snakes. For further controls see "Slugs and Snails" on page 283.

Symptom: Plants cut off at soil line
Cause: **Cutworms**

During the day, search for and destroy the fat, gray caterpillars hiding in soil around the base of freshly damaged plants, or go out at night with a flashlight to catch feeding cutworms. Protect transplants from damage by using cutworm collars around the stems. Avoid the main population of cutworms by planting later in the season. For further controls see "Cutworms" on page 259.

'Elegance' Japanese anemones (*Anemone* x *hybrida*)

LUPINES

Lupinus Russell Hybrids

RUSSELL HYBRID LUPINES AT A GLANCE

Botanical Name: *Lupinus* Russell hybrids
Height: 15 inches–3 feet
Spread: 1–2 feet
Shade Tolerance: Full sun
Hardiness: Zones 4–7
Preferred Soil: Moist, well-drained, acidic, humus-rich

Most Common Lupine Pests

Symptom: Leaves and new shoots distorted and sticky
Cause: **Aphids**

Look for clusters of small, pear-shaped insects on undersides of leaves, on new shoots, and in

Russell hybrid lupines (Lupinus Russell Hybrids)

flower buds. Aphid nymphs and adults suck plant sap, causing distorted leaves, buds, and flowers. Severely infested leaves and flowers may drop. As aphids feed, they excrete a sweet, sticky honeydew onto leaves below. Black sooty mold often grows on the honeydew, blocking light to the leaves. Plant pollen and nectar plants to attract native predators and parasites; these usually control aphids sufficiently to prevent serious damage. Keep plants healthy, but avoid overfertilizing with nitrogen. Knock aphids off plants with a strong stream of water; repeat as needed. If further control is necessary, spray with insecticidal soap, neem, or homemade garlic sprays.

Most Common Lupine Diseases

Symptom: White, powdery coating on leaves
Cause: **Powdery mildew**

Powdery mildew can spread quickly to cover whole leaves, stems, and flowers. This disease is unsightly and also weakens host plants. Powdery white or gray spots on leaves and flowers enlarge quickly, finally covering the entire leaf, flower, or shoot. Infected tissues become brown and shrivel. Plant in well-drained soils, and space widely for good air circulation. Compost all plant debris and pick off and destroy infected plant tissues. Foliar compost tea sprays at intervals of 2–4 weeks can help prevent attack.

Symptom: Spots on leaves
Cause: **Leaf spot diseases (many fungi)**

Leaf spot diseases rarely cause serious damage to lupines, but they may diminish lupines' ornamental value. For controls see "Most Common Annual Diseases" on page 105.

ORANGE CONEFLOWER
Rudbeckia fulgida

ORANGE CONEFLOWER AT A GLANCE

Botanical Name: *Rudbeckia fulgida*
Height: 1½–2½ feet
Spread: To 2 feet
Shade Tolerance: Full sun or partial shade
Hardiness: Zones 3–9
Preferred Soil: Moderately fertile, moist, well-drained

Orange coneflower (Rudbeckia fulgida)

Most Common Coneflower Pests

Symptom: Leaves and new shoots distorted and sticky
Cause: **Brown ambrosia aphids**

This ⅒-inch-long, bright red aphid with long legs is one of the very few pests of coneflowers. Look for clusters of small, pear-shaped insects on undersides of leaves, on new shoots, and in flower buds. Aphid nymphs and adults suck plant sap, causing distorted leaves, buds, and flowers. Severely infested leaves and flowers may drop. As aphids feed, they excrete a sweet, sticky honeydew onto leaves below. Black sooty mold often grows on the honeydew, blocking light to the leaves. Plant pollen and nectar plants to attract native predators and parasites; these usually control aphids sufficiently to prevent serious damage. Keep plants healthy, but avoid overfertilizing with nitrogen. Knock aphids off plants with a strong stream of water; repeat as needed. If further control is necessary, spray with insecticidal soap, neem, or homemade garlic sprays.

Most Common Coneflower Diseases

Symptom: White, powdery coating on leaves
Cause: **Powdery mildew**

Powdery mildew can spread quickly to cover whole leaves and stems. This disease is unsightly and weakens host plants. Powdery white or gray spots on leaves and flowers enlarge quickly, finally covering the entire leaf, flower, or shoot. Infected tissues become brown and shrivel. Plant in well-drained soil; space widely for good air circulation. Compost all plant debris; pick off and destroy infected plant parts. Sprays of compost tea every 2–4 weeks can help prevent infection.

Symptom: Pale spots on leaves; orange pustules on leaf undersides
Cause: **Rust (several fungi)**

General lack of vigor is an early symptom of rust infection. For controls see "Rust" on page 327.

PEONIES

Paeonia spp. and hybrids

PEONIES AT A GLANCE

Botanical Name: *Paeonia* spp. and hybrids
Height: To 3 feet
Spread: To 3 feet
Shade Tolerance: Full sun or partial shade
Hardiness: Zones 3–8
Preferred Soil: Deep, fertile, well-drained, high in organic matter

---

Most Common Peony Pests

Symptoms: Brown or silvery streaks; scars and distortions in leaves and flowers
Cause: **Thrips**

You will need a magnifying lens to see if these minute, quick-moving insects are present. Adult thrips are yellowish, brown, or black and have narrow, fringed wings. Light yellow or green nymphs are similar to adults but smaller. Both adults and nymphs suck the contents of plant cells. For controls see "Thrips" on page 293.

Symptoms: Holes in leaves; flowers chewed
Causes: **Japanese beetles; leaf-eating beetles**

Late-blooming peony flowers are attacked by Japanese beetles. The large, blue-green Japanese beetles with bronze wing covers are easy to see, and so is the damage from their feeding, which skeletonizes leaves. In late May and June, rose chafers may also attack flowers and leaves. For controls see "Japanese Beetle" on page 268.

Most Common Peony Diseases

Symptoms: Leaves spotted; buds turn brown and fail to open; reddish spots on stems; distorted growth patterns
Cause: **Anthracnose (*Gloeosporium* spp.)**

In serious cases, anthracnose spots may run together to cover the leaves. For controls see "Anthracnose" on page 300.

Symptom: Plants stunted and growing poorly
Cause: **Southern root knot nematodes**

Heavily infected plants wilt in the midday sun, do not grow well, and their leaves turn yellow.

Peony (*Paeonia lactiflora*)

Check the roots for signs of nematode infection, which will appear as small, hard knobs and swollen galls on the fine roots. Drench soil with neem solution. Dig in chitosan, a natural polymer derived from the chitin components of the shells of crabs and shrimp, or green manure crops to encourage beneficial fungi that control nematodes. For heavy infections, discard plants and solarize soil to suppress nematodes in the top layer of soil.

Symptoms: Shiny, purple spots near leaf margins; reddish streaks on stems
Cause: **Measles (Cladosporium paeoniae)**

Spots on leaf undersides are chestnut brown. On stems, spots are most numerous near branch and leaf stem bases. For controls, see "Anthracnose" on page 300.

Symptom: Dark, leathery spots on leaves, stems, and buds
Cause: **Phytophthora blight (Phytophthora cactorum)**

This disease is hard to distinguish from botrytis blight, but control is similar. Plant in well-drained soil where air circulates freely. If one of these diseases strikes, prune and destroy all infected growth. In fall, remove several inches of topsoil around the plant and replace with washed sand to increase drainage.

Symptoms: Young stems wilt and collapse; buds turn black; gray mold appears
Cause: **Botrytis blight (Botrytis cinerea)**

This disease can also attack open flowers and then move down the stem. For controls see "Botrytis Blight" on page 305.

PHLOX
Phlox spp.

GARDEN PHLOX AT A GLANCE

Botanical Name: *Phlox paniculata*
Height: 3–4 feet
Spread: To 2 feet
Shade Tolerance: Full sun
Hardiness: Zones 4–8
Preferred Soil: Deep, fertile, moist, well-drained, high in organic matter

MOSS PINK AT A GLANCE

Botanical Name: *Phlox subulata*
Height: 6–9 inches
Spread: To 12 inches
Shade Tolerance: Full sun
Hardiness: Zones 2–9
Preferred Soil: Moderately fertile, moist, light, sandy

Most Common Phlox Pests

Symptom: Pinched, scarred, or distorted upper leaves and buds
Cause: **Phlox plant bugs**

These plant bugs are greenish yellow, ¼ inch long, with four black stripes down their back. Their toxic saliva causes the plant's foliage and flowers to become distorted. For controls see "Most Common Perennial Pests" on page 126.

Symptom: Light yellow speckles on leaves
Cause: **Spider mites**

Look for fine webbing on undersides of leaves. When numerous, their feeding weakens plants. For controls see "Spider Mites" on page 286.

Most Common Phlox Diseases

Symptoms: Stunted plants with highly distorted leaves; swollen stems
Cause: **Stem and bulb nematodes**

These microscopic nematodes enter the foliage of the new shoots and work upward through the stems. Their feeding causes abnormal development, including shoestring leaves; crinkled, twisted, or curled leaves; and bulges in stems. There is no control. Remove and destroy affected plants and all leaf debris, and do not replant phlox in that site.

Garden phlox (<u>Phlox paniculata</u>)

Symptom: Stem base and crown rot
Cause: **Crown rot (*Puccinia* spp.; *Sclerotium* spp.; *Thielaviopsis* spp.)**

Prevent problems by planting phlox in well-drained soil and spacing plants for good air circulation. Organic mulches can reduce splashing water that spreads disease organisms. Boost resistance by spraying foliage with kelp extract early in the season. Remove and destroy infected plants.

Symptom: White, powdery coating on leaves
Cause: **Powdery mildew**

Powdery mildew can spread quickly to cover leaves and stems. Infected tissues become brown and shriveld. Plant phlox in well-drained soils, and space plants widely for good air circulation. Compost all plant debris and pick off and destroy infected plant parts. Sprays of compost tea every 2–4 weeks can help prevent infection. Sprays of baking soda solution or baking soda plus oil (see "Oil Sprays" on page 361) are often an effective powdery mildew control.

Most Common Phlox Disorders

Symptom: Leaves die, progressing from the base of the plant upward
Cause: **Leaf blight**

Leaf blight appears only on old clumps that need division. It occurs because old stems that new leaves are growing from are unable to keep up with the water needs of the leaves. To correct this situation, divide the plant in early spring, removing some stems as you do so. Give extra water while plants are putting on new spring growth.

POPPIES

Papaver s p p .

Oriental poppy (*Papaver orientale*)

Most Common Poppy Pests

Symptom: Leaves and new shoots distorted and sticky
Cause: **Aphids**

Look for clusters of small, pear-shaped insects on undersides of leaves. Their feeding usually causes distorted leaves, buds, and branch tips, Aphids have a large number of natural enemies, which usually control aphids sufficiently to prevent serious damage. Aphids may be protected from these enemies by ants, which "farm," or care for the aphids, to obtain the sweet honeydew they produce. Maintain healthy plant growth, but do not overfertilize with nitrogen. Knock aphids off plants with a strong stream of water; repeat frequently as needed. Attract native predators and parasites by planting pollen and nectar plants. Release purchased aphid midges, lacewings, lady beetles (these fly away, so they're best for greenhouses), or parasitic wasps. Spray insecticidal soap, neem, summer oil (on tolerant plants), homemade garlic sprays, or, as a last resort, pyrethrins. Repeat as required for effective control.

Most Common Poppy Diseases

Symptoms: Small, black lesions on leaves, stems, and flowers; plant wilts
Cause: **Bacterial blight (Xanthomonas papavericola)**

The lesions caused by this disease often give off a slimy material. Infected plants turn brown and lose leaves; girdled stems die. Dig and destroy infected plants and surrounding soil. Solarize soil before replanting with disease-free seed; water early in the day, so leaves dry quickly.

Symptoms: Stems darken at base; leaves wilt; plant collapses
Cause: **Verticillium wilt (Verticillium albo-atrum)**

Wilt symptoms tend to start at the base of the plant and move upward. Prevent problems by planting in well-drained soil that warms quickly in the spring. For controls see "Verticillium Wilt" on page 332.

SEDUMS

Sedum spp. and hybrids

SEDUMS AT A GLANCE

Botanical Name: *Sedum* spp. and hybrids
Height: 1–2 feet
Spread: 2 feet
Shade Tolerance: Full sun
Hardiness: Zones 3–10
Preferred Soil: Moderately fertile,
    moderately moist, well-drained

Most Common Sedum Pests

Not troubled by pests.

Most Common Sedum Diseases

Symptom: Plants yellow and die
Cause: **Root rot**

Plants wilt easily, leaves yellow or discolor, and
the plant grows quite slowly. For controls see
"Root Rot" on page 326.

'Ruby Glow' sedum (Sedum 'Ruby Glow')

YARROW

Achillea spp.

YARROWS AT A GLANCE

Botanical Name: *Achillea* spp.
Height: 6 inches–3 feet (species vary)
Spread: Forms a mat 1–3 feet or more wide
Shade Tolerance: Full sun
Hardiness: Zones 3–9
Preferred Soil: Poor to moderately fertile,
    moderately moist

Most Common Yarrow Pests

Not troubled by pests.

Most Common Yarrow Diseases

Symptom: White, powdery coating on
    leaves
Cause: **Powdery mildew**

Powdery mildew can spread quickly to cover
whole leaves, stems, and flowers. For controls
see "Powdery Mildew" on page 323.

Common yarrow (Achillea millefolium)

BULBS

Most Common Bulb Pests

Symptom: Stunted, sickly, deformed plants
Cause: **Bulb mites**

These minute mites feed on the bulb scales, weakening and stunting plants, and causing soft, dying areas in the bulb. Pull and discard all infested bulbs. Solarize the soil or avoid planting bulbs in infested soil. Check new bulbs for signs of mite damage before purchase and buy hot-water-treated bulbs. To kill mites before planting, dip cured bulbs in hot water (120°F) for 2 minutes.

Symptom: Leaves and new shoots
distorted and sticky
Cause: **Aphids**

Look for clusters of small, pear-shaped insects on undersides of leaves, on new shoots, and in flower buds. Aphids produce sticky honeydew, which covers leaves and allows sooty molds to grow. Wash honeydew and aphids from leaves with a strong stream of water, repeating several times as necessary. For heavy infestations, spray insecticidal soap, neem, or pyrethrins.

Symptoms: Large, irregular holes in leaves
and bulbs; slime trails present
Causes: **Slugs; snails**

Both slugs and snails prefer moist or shady parts of the garden and rasp large holes in soft, tender plants. The best controls for slugs are garter snakes, toads, ground beetles, fireflies, and other natural enemies. Where slugs or snails are severe pests, it may be worth it to band flower beds with copper flashing to keep them out of particularly valued plants.

Most Common Bulb Diseases

Symptoms: Small, yellowish spots on leaves;
shoots twisted
Causes: **Stem and bulb nematodes**

Dig an infected bulb and cut it open to look for the telltale dark-colored scales with yellowish pockets that contain these microscopic worms. Dig infected bulbs, along with the layer of soil surrounding the bulb, and destroy. Cure mildly infected bulbs for 3 weeks and then dip in hot water (110°F) for 3 hours to kill nematodes. Treat infected soil by solarization or avoid planting bulbs in infected soil.

Symptoms: Bulbs rot; pink or white mold
is visible
Cause: **Basal rot (*Fusarium oxysporum*)**

Basal rot is common on bulbs planted in locations with soggy soils. When digging and replanting bulbs, check each one for disease and discard any with spots or soft areas.

Symptom: Water-soaked lesions on leaves
Cause: **Anthracnose (*Gloeosporium*
spp.; *Colletotrichum* spp.)**

In serious cases, whole leaves can show anthracnose damage. Infected leaves may die prematurely and plants may be defoliated. For controls see "Anthracnose" on page 300.

Symptoms: Leaves or flowers mottled or discolored; growth distorted
Cause: **Various viruses**

Viral infections usually strike plants that are weakened by poor environmental conditions. Control aphids and other sucking insects which can spread viruses. Dig and destroy infected plants.

ALLIUMS
Allium spp.

GIANT ONION AT A GLANCE

Botanical Name: *Allium giganteum*
Height: 3–5½ feet
Spread: Leaves to 1½ feet;
    1 flower stem per plant
Shade Tolerance: Full sun or
    partial shade
Hardiness: Zones 4–8
Preferred Soil: Moderately fertile, moist,
    well-drained, sandy

LILY LEEK AT A GLANCE

Botanical Name: *Allium moly*
Height: 6–8 inches
Spread: 12 inches; multiplies to
    form wide clumps
Shade Tolerance: Full sun or light shade
Hardiness: Zones 4–8
Preferred Soil: Moderately fertile, moist,
    well-drained, sandy

Giant onions (<u>Allium giganteum</u>)

Most Common Allium Pests

Symptom: Large, irregular holes in leaves;
        slime trails present
Cause: **Slugs; snails**

These pests rasp large holes in plant tissues. For controls see "Slugs and Snails" on page 283.

Most Common Allium Diseases

Symptom: Leaves turn yellow and wilt
Cause: **Basal rot**

If you dig up infected bulbs, you may see that they are soft and brown. When digging and replanting bulbs, check each one for disease and discard any with spots or soft areas.

Symptoms: Leaves with white specks;
        tips die
Cause: **Botrytis leaf blast**

Symptoms first appear at the tips of the leaves and work downward. Plant in well-drained soil and keep air circulation high with proper spacing. Destroy infected plant parts to reduce the spread of the disease.

Most Common Allium Disorders

Symptom: Leaves with pale green, yellow,
        or brown spots
Cause: **Downy mildew or ozone injury**

The initial symptoms of ozone injury and downy mildew infection are so similar that you can tell them apart only by pattern of occurance. Ozone injury will affect all of the plants while downy mildew will occur only in spots. If spores form on old spots, you can be certain that the disease is the culprit.

CANNA

Canna x *generalis*

CANNA AT A GLANCE

Botanical Name: *Canna* x *generalis*
Height: 1½–6 feet; cultivars vary
Spread: 1–3 feet
Shade Tolerance: Full sun
Hardiness: Zones 9–11; to Zone 7
   with winter mulch
Preferred Soil: Fertile, moist,
   well-drained, high in organic matter

Most Common Canna Pests

Symptoms: Large, irregular holes in leaves
      and exposed rhizomes; slime
      trails present
Causes: **Slugs; snails**

Both slugs and snails rasp large holes in soft, tender plants. For controls see "Slugs and Snails" on page 283.

Symptom: Holes in leaves and flowers
Cause: **Japanese beetles**

The large, blue-green Japanese beetles are easy to see and so is the damage from their feeding, which skeletonizes leaves. For controls see "Japanese Beetle" on page 268.

Symptoms: Holes chewed in leaves; webs
      may be present
Cause: **Caterpillars**

Several species of caterpillars feed on canna leaves. Yellow woollybear caterpillars chew huge, side-by-side holes in the leaves. Other species roll or tie the leaves together as they feed. For controls see "Most Common Perennial Pests" on page 126.

Most Common Canna Diseases

Symptom: Tiny white spots on leaves
Cause: **Bud rot (*Xanthomonas cannae*)**

If your cannas have a severe case of bud rot, leaves may be blackened and rotting when they unfold. Bud rot can spoil the flower stems, too, making them collapse before bloom. To protect against this disease, do not wet foliage when watering. Keep air circulation high in the greenhouse and, when transplanting outside, do not crowd the planting.

Symptom: Yellow lines or spindle-shaped
      areas on leaves
Cause: **Mosaic**

Aphids, leafhoppers, and other insects can spread viruses as they feed on your plants. For controls see "Mosaic" on page 319.

'Indian Shot' canna (<u>Canna</u> x <u>generalis</u>)

CROCUS

Crocus vernus

DUTCH CROCUS AT A GLANCE

Botanical Name: *Crocus vernus*
Height: 4–6 inches
Spread: To 4 inches
Shade Tolerance: Sun or light shade
Hardiness: Zones 3–9
Preferred Soil: Average fertility, moist, well-drained, sandy, acid to neutral

Most Common Crocus Pests

See "Most Common Bulb Pests" on page 157.

Most Common Crocus Disorders

Symptom: Plants stop blooming prolifically
Causes: **Overcrowding; age; severe winters**

Crocus corms reproduce well in suitable environments, so it isn't long before they become crowded. Divide clumps every 3–4 years for the best performance. The tiny cormels require 2–3 years to reach blooming size but can be replanted, 6 inches apart, for future enjoyment.

Dutch crocus (<u>Crocus</u> <u>vernus</u>)

DAFFODILS

Narcissus spp. and hybrids

DAFFODILS AT A GLANCE

Botanical Name: *Narcissus* spp. and hybrids
Height: 14–20 inches; miniatures, as short as 8 inches
Spread: To 12 inches
Shade Tolerance: Full sun or light shade
Hardiness: Zones 3–8
Preferred Soil: Average fertility, moderately moist, well-drained, high in organic matter

Most Common Daffodil Pests

See "Most Common Bulb Pests" on page 157.

Symptoms: Bulbs rot; shoots do not grow
Cause: **Bulb flies**

Two species of these robust flies lay their eggs on the leaves and necks of bulbs. The ½–¾-inch-long, yellowish larvae bore into the bulbs, which often allows rot organisms to enter. Discard infested bulbs. For heavy infestations, cover bulbs with floating row covers from mid-May to June to prevent flies from laying eggs. Spray or dust bases of stems with pyrethrins or neem weekly during this period.

Symptoms: Brown or silvery streaks; scars and distortions in leaves and flowers
Cause: **Thrips**

You will need a magnifying lens to see these minute insects. They move quickly and like to hide in tight crevices in plant stems and flowers.

The nymphs are light green or yellow, similar to adults, but smaller. There are many generations of thrips per year, and they breed year-round in greenhouses, creating silvery speckling or streaks on leaves. Native predators attack thrips, including minute pirate bugs and lacewings. Spray neem, insecticidal soap, or pyrethrins. As a last resort, dust undersides of leaves with diatomaceous earth. Use bright blue or yellow sticky traps to catch adults in greenhouses.

Most Common Daffodil Diseases

Symptom: Watery spots on leaves and flowers

Cause: **Fire (*Sclerotinia polyblastis*)**

Fire disease shows first on the flowers. In high-humidity conditions, the disease spreads rapidly. Gray, watery spots develop on the stems below the flowers, and elongated yellow spots with reddish brown centers show on the leaves. Bulbs are not attacked, but the disease restricts their growth. To control, pick flowers before they open. Rake and destroy all old foliage. Use copper sprays as a last resort.

Symptoms: Shoots are deformed when they emerge from the soil; brown leaf tips

Cause: **Smolder (*Sclerotinia narcissicola*)**

This soilborne disease attacks plants growing in poorly drained soil or in unusually wet spring weather. Avoid it by planting in well-drained areas or raised beds. Spray with Bordeaux mixture to control the disease. If infection is severe, remove and destroy the bulbs to reduce a population buildup. Do not replant daffodils for several years in that area.

'Palmy Days' daffodils (<u>Narcissus</u> 'Palmy Days')

Symptom: Leaves have white, yellow, or silver streaks

Cause: **Decline (virus complex)**

Decline reduces bulb size and plant vigor, but usually does not strike healthy plants. Decline is probably spread by aphids. Control them as directed in "Aphids" on page 244. Dig and destroy infected bulbs.

Symptoms: Plant fails to grow and/or flower; swollen spots on leaves

Cause: **Stem and bulb nematodes**

Nematode feeding causes deformed leaves with yellow-green spots and small, swollen areas. Bulbs develop dark internal circles or blotches and may fail to grow or bloom in spring. Dig and destroy severely infected bulbs and foliage. Cure mildly infected bulbs, soak them in hot (110°F) water for 3 hours, and then plunge them immediately into cold water. Let them dry and store in a cool, dark place until replanting in fall. Solarize infected soil or dig in a chitin source.

GLADIOLUS

Gladiolus x *hortulanus*

GLADIOLUS AT A GLANCE

Botanical Name: *Gladiolus* x *hortulanus*
Height: 3–6 feet
Spread: To 1 foot
Shade Tolerance: Full sun
Hardiness: Zones 8–11
Preferred Soil: Average fertility, moist, well-drained, high in organic matter

Most Common Gladiolus Pests

Symptoms: Brown or silvery streaks; scars and distortions in leaves and flowers
Cause: **Thrips**

Four species of thrips commonly attack gladiolus. In severe infestations, flowers are spotted and may shrivel up completely. You will need a magnifying lens to see these minute, quick-moving insects. Gladiolus thrips attack and overwinter on corms. When digging corms for storage, dust thoroughly with diatomaceous earth or a mixture of pyrethrins and diatomaceous earth. For additional controls see "Thrips" on page 293.

Symptom: Leaves and new shoots distorted and sticky
Cause: **Aphids**

Aphids are common pests on gladiolus. Look for clusters of small, pear-shaped insects on undersides of leaves, on new shoots, and in flower buds. For controls see "Aphids" on page 244.

Symptom: Stunted, sickly, deformed plants
Cause: **Bulb mites**

It is hard to see these minute mites, even with a hand lens, as they are only $\frac{1}{50}$–$\frac{1}{25}$ inch long. For controls see "Most Common Bulb Pests" on page 157.

Symptom: Pinched, scarred, or distorted leaves and buds
Cause: **Tarnished plant bugs**

These small bugs pierce and suck plant sap. For controls see "Tarnished Plant Bug" on page 291.

Most Common Gladiolus Diseases

Symptoms: Leaves turn brown; flowers are spotted
Cause: **Botrytis dry rot (*Botrytis gladiolorum*)**

Botrytis can attack corms, leaves, and flowers. For controls see "Botrytis Blight" on page 305.

Symptoms: Corms have spots and rot in the ground; corms shrivel and dry in storage
Cause: **Corm rot (*Fusarium oxysporum* f. *gladioli*; *Penicillium gladioli*)**

Plants growing from infected corms may be stunted and discolored. For controls see "Most Common Bulb Diseases" on page 157.

Symptom: Oval tan spots on leaves and flowers
Cause: **Leaf spot (*Curvularia trifolii* f. *gladioli*)**

Black spores are visible in the center of the spots as the disease progresses. In severe cases flowers fail to open. Good garden care, including planting in well-drained soil, careful watering, and using 2- to 3-year rotations, can prevent this disease. If it builds up in your soil, solarize the area by removing all the plants, tilling, and then covering the bare soil surface with clear plastic for a month to six weeks. Afterwards, dig or till in a 1-inch layer of fully finished compost. Spray affected plants with copper or sulfur as a last resort.

Symptom: Leaves and flowers streaked and mottled

Causes: **Cucumber mosaic virus; tobacco mosaic virus**

Aphids, leafhoppers, and other insects can spread viruses as they feed on your plants. For controls see "Mosaic" on page 319.

Gladiolus (Gladiolus x hortulanus)

HYACINTH
Hyacinthus orientalis

HYACINTH AT A GLANCE

Botanical Name: *Hyacinthus orientalis*
Height: Flower stem, to 18 inches; leaves, to 12 inches
Spread: To 10 inches
Shade Tolerance: Full sun or light shade
Hardiness: Zones 3–8
Preferred Soil: Average fertility, moist, well-drained, acid to neutral, high in organic matter

Most Common Hyacinth Pests
See "Most Common Bulb Pests" on page 157.

Most Common Hyacinth Diseases

Symptoms: Yellow, water-soaked stripes on leaves; flowers brown and shrivel

Cause: **Yellow rot (*Xanthomonas hyacinthi*)**

If symptoms appear, immediately dig and destroy the bulb and the surrounding soil.

Symptoms: Flowers fail to develop; buds open irregularly; flowers rot

Cause: **Soft rot (*Erwinia carotovora*)**

Plant parts that are infected with this bacterial disease tend to have a foul odor. Soft rot initially creates a small, water-soaked spot. As the bacteria feed, the spot enlarges. For controls see "Bacterial Soft Rot" on page 302.

Symptoms: Leaves are mottled; flowers show spots or featherlike markings
Cause: **Mosaic**

Aphids, leafhoppers, and other insects can spread viruses as they feed on your plants. For controls see "Mosaic" on page 319.

Symptoms: Tips of outside leaves brown and die; leaf bases rot; white mold may appear on the stem
Cause: **Crown rot (*Sclerotium rolfsii*)**

Crown rot symptoms usually start at ground level and work upwards. For controls see "Petunias" on page 116.

Symptom: Spots that expand and merge on leaves after plants have bloomed
Cause: **Leaf spot (*Didymellina macrospora*)**

Leaf spots may spread to cover entire leaves, stunting plant growth. For controls see "Most Common Annual Diseases" on page 105.

Hyacinth (<u>Hyacinthus orientalis</u>)

LILIES
Lilium s p p. a n d h y b r i d s

> ### LILIES AT A GLANCE
>
> **Botanical Name:** *Lilium* spp. and hybrids
> **Height:** 2–7 feet
> **Spread:** To 1 foot
> **Shade Tolerance:** Full sun or partial shade
> **Hardiness:** Zones 3–8
> **Preferred Soil:** Deep, fertile, moist, well-drained, high in organic matter

Most Common Lily Pests
See "Most Common Bulb Pests" on page 157.

Most Common Lily Diseases

Symptoms: Basal roots rot; leaves yellow and wilt; plant is stunted
Cause: **Root rot**

Minimize the chances of root rot by choosing a planting site with good drainage. Since root rot fungi are in all soils, prevention is the best course. Do not overwater plants and keep air circulation high.

Symptoms: Oval or round, orange or reddish brown spots on leaves; gray mold develops on leaves, stems, or flowers
Cause: **Botrytis blight (*Botrytis elliptica*)**

On lilies, botrytis blight symptoms tend to start at the base of the plant and work up the stem. For controls see "Botrytis Blight" on page 305.

Symptom: Small orange or reddish brown pustules on lower sides of leaves

Cause: **Rust (*Uromyces holwayi*)**

Spring weather stimulates reproduction of rust spores, which wind and rain carry to new host plants. Rainfall may bring spores down hundreds of miles from their original site. Minimize rust problems by choosing a planting site with good air circulation. The first symptoms of rust diseases are general lack of vigor and slow growth. Moderately infected plants are usually stunted; seriously infected plants die. Avoid amendments high in nitrogen, and prune, space, and water carefully to increase air circulation and keep leaves dry. Pick off and destroy infected leaves. Sulfur spray, used when spots first appear, kills new spores.

Symptom: Leaves mottled; plants stunted

Cause: **Various viruses, including lily mosaic virus and cucumber mosaic virus**

Aphids, leafhoppers, and other insects can spread viruses as they feed on your plants. Most viruses are transmitted to plants by insects, although some are seedborne. They can also enter through bruises and wounds. Viruses are composed of DNA or RNA and a protein coating. Rather than dividing to reproduce, they cause the host cell to replicate them, so they build populations only in living tissues. However, they can remain in an inactive but viable state in dead tissues for as long as 50 years. They easily survive composting and freezing temperatures. Prevent viruses by keeping plants growing vigorously. Choose certified disease-free bulbs. Do not touch wet plants. Try to control sucking insects such as aphids and leafhoppers. Remove and destroy virus-infected plants immediately.

*Lilies (*Lilium* hybrid)*

Most Common Lily Disorders

Symptom: Leaf margins yellow, brown, and die

Cause: **Leaf scorch**

Leaf scorch can be caused by a number of factors. The most common are imbalanced nutrition and fluoride toxicity, particularly in acid soils. Protect plants by adding a handful of bone meal to the holes when you plant. Avoid high-nitrogen soil amendments. Have your soil tested and amend it appropriately to supply missing nutrients and to maintain a pH of 6.5–7.0. If your water contains fluoride, don't use it to water the lilies. Instead, collect rainwater for this area of the garden.

LILY-OF-THE-VALLEY

Convallaria majalis

**LILY-OF-THE-VALLEY
AT A GLANCE**

Botanical Name: *Convallaria majalis*
Height: 6–8 inches
Spread: Each plant 6 inches, in
  spreading clumps
Shade Tolerance: Partial shade
Hardiness: Zones 2–8
Preferred Soil: Moderately fertile, moist,
  well-drained, acid

Lily-of-the-valley (Convallaria majalis)

Most Common Lily-of-the-Valley Pests

Symptoms: Large, irregular holes in leaves;
  slime trails present
Causes: **Slugs; snails**

Both slugs and snails rasp large holes in soft, tender plants. Slugs and snails thrive in the moist, shady conditions within a dense planting of lily-of-the-valley. Encourage natural predators, such as birds, garter snakes, toads, and lizards. Trap slugs and snails under boards laid in the garden; destroy trapped pests daily. For further controls see "Slugs and Snails" on page 283.

Most Common Lily-of-the-Valley Diseases

Symptoms: Oval or round, orange or red
  dish brown spots on leaves; gray
  mold develops on affected
  plant parts
Cause: **Botrytis blight**

Botrytis blight symptoms can also spread to the flowers. Plant in well-drained soil and keep air circulation high with proper spacing. Remove faded flowers and destroy infected plant parts to reduce the spread of the disease.

Most Common Lily-of-the-Valley Disorders

Symptom: Few blooms
Cause: **Lack of light**

Filtered shade provides a good environment for these plants, but in dense shade plants may not receive enough light to flower well. Choose locations that provide several hours of sunlight a day.

TULIPS

Tulipa spp.

> ### TULIPS AT A GLANCE
>
> **Botanical Name:** *Tulipa* spp. and hybrids
> **Height:** 10 inches–2½ feet
> **Spread:** To 1 foot
> **Shade Tolerance:** Full sun or light shade
> **Hardiness:** Zones 4–7
> **Preferred Soil:** Fertile, moist, well-drained, high in organic matter

*Tulips (*Tulipa* hybrids)*

Most Common Tulip Pests

See "Most Common Bulb Pests" on page 157.

Most Common Tulip Diseases

Symptom:	Watery spots on leaves and flowers
Cause:	**Fire (*Botrytis tulipae*)**

Fire disease in tulips first appears on leaves. Spots on flowers are tiny and white or light brown. Tulip bulbs are also attacked and you can sometimes see tiny, dark-colored spots on the outer scales. To prevent damage, remove old foliage and stems below the soil surface, as soon as they yellow. Dig and destroy infected plants. Rotate tulips, and don't plant tulips in infected beds for 2–3 years.

Symptoms:	Flower stalk shrivels; blossoms wither or decay
Cause:	**Blossom blight (*Phytophthora cactorum*)**

This disease infects only tulips planted in unsuitable locations. Always plant tulips in areas where they receive 6 or more hours of sunlight a day. Well-drained soil is essential since bulbs rot easily in wet conditions. Dig and destroy infected plants.

Symptom:	Blossoms have unexpected color variegation
Cause:	**Breaking (various viruses)**

"Broken" tulips can be quite beautiful. (The old Rembrandt tulips are a case in point.) However, virus infection results in smaller flowers and reduced plant vigor, so it's best to eliminate it from your beds. It is probably spread by aphids and leafhoppers. Control them as directed in "Aphids" on page 244. Dig and destroy all plants on which viral symptoms appear. Sterilize your tools after working around infected plants.

TREES, SHRUBS, AND VINES

Most Common Tree, Shrub, and Vine Pests

Symptom: Leaves distorted and sticky
Cause: **Aphids**

Look for colonies of 1/16–3/8-inch-long, pear-shaped insects on undersides of affected leaves. Aphids do not harm most deciduous trees, but their copious production of honeydew, which is sprayed onto leaves and objects (such as parked cars) below the tree, is a nuisance. Unsightly sooty molds also grow on the honeydew. Wash honeydew and aphids from leaves with a strong stream of water or spray insecticidal soap. For very tall trees or heavy infestations, spray neem or pyrethrins. Try releasing aphid midges (*Aphidoletes aphidimyza*) in early spring.

Symptom: Leaves or needles turn yellow along whole branch
Cause: **Scale**

Many species of scale attack trees and shrubs. Look for clusters of 1/10–1/5 inch, reddish, purple, white, gray, yellowish or brown bumps on bark of branches. Their feeding weakens and kills branches and makes the plants more susceptible to borer attack. Scale is usually controlled well by dormant oil or lime-sulfur sprays in late winter and by sprays of summer oil or insecticidal soap as buds start to open. To control scale crawlers in midsummer or later, spray summer oil or insecticidal soap, but only for heavy infestations because these sprays will harm the many species of native beneficial insects that usually control scale. Always test-spray oils on a branch first to check for damage. Do not use oil sprays on blue spruce or junipers since it removes the blue "bloom" on the needles.

Symptoms: Holes chewed in leaves; webs present in foliage
Causes: **Tent caterpillars; fall webworms; other caterpillars**

Several caterpillars spin silken tents in trees. First, find out whether caterpillars are still present in or around the webs, which remain in trees long after the larvae are gone. Prune out infested branches, or remove webs and caterpillars by hand (wear gloves). For heavy infestations, spray *Bacillus thuringiensis* var. *kurstaki* (BTK) or neem early in the season while caterpillars are still small. Use sticky tree bands to catch caterpillars leaving the tree to pupate. Spray dormant oil in the winter to kill overwintering eggs.

Symptom: Gray, lacy blotches on leaves
Cause: **Lace bugs**

Lace bugs are tiny, oval bugs with lacy wings. Look on undersides of leaves for the specks of dark excrement that show lace bugs have been feeding. Light infestations are not damaging. For heavy infestations of lace bugs, which cause leaves to dry up and drop, spray insecticidal soap, pyrethrins, or summer oil (on plants that tolerate oil).

Symptoms: Branches die or break; trees are weak
Cause: **Borers**

If borers are causing the decline of a tree or shrub, you should be able to see small holes bored through the bark of limbs or the trunk. Work a fine wire into the holes to kill larvae, or inject a solution of insect parasitic nematodes. Prune out damaged branches and provide the best of care—the best defense against borers is a vigorous tree.

Symptom: Holes in leaves
Cause: **Japanese beetles**

These ½-inch-long, blue–green beetles with bronze wing covers are easy to see, as is their feeding damage, which skeletonizes leaves. Knock beetles from the parts of the tree you can reach onto groundsheets early in the morning and destroy them. Apply milky disease or parasitic nematodes to the lawn for long–term control.

Symptom: Leaves or needles stripped from branches
Cause: **Bagworms**

Bagworms hang from twigs and branches in 2½-inch-long, tough, silken bags studded with pieces of leaf and plant debris. Handpick the bags by cutting the silk attachment from the branch, making sure to remove any silk that encircles the branch. For heavy infestations, spray *Bacillus thuringiensis* var. *kurstaki* (BTK) at 7- to 10-day intervals from early spring to early summer.

Symptom: Light yellow speckles on leaves or needles
Cause: **Spider mites**

With the exception of European red mites, most species of spider mites spin fine webbing on undersides of leaves. The tiny mites (under ¹⁄₅₀ inch long) may be visible crawling on the webbing. Native predatory mites and beetles usually provide sufficient control of these pests. Spider mites are most damaging in hot, dry weather and where natural enemies have been destroyed by sulfur or other pesticides. For light infestations, spray foliage with water or insecticidal soap. For heavy infestations, which cause leaf edges to curl, turn brown and dry up, spray neem or summer oil. Release predatory mites (*Metaseiulus occidentalis* or other species adapted to the local climate). Plan to spray lime-sulfur in late winter.

Most Common Tree, Shrub, and Vine Diseases

Symptoms: Spots on leaves; tree loses vigor
Cause: **Leaf spot diseases (many fungi, bacteria, and viruses)**

To control these problems, rake up and destroy all fallen leaves at the end of the season. If the disease persists and you can't identify it, take a leaf to your Extension Service plant pathologist, who should also be able to tell you if copper or sulfur sprays are effective as a last–resort remedy.

Symptom: White, powdery coating on upper leaf surfaces
Cause: **Powdery mildew (several fungal species)**

Powdery mildew is unsightly but doesn't usually cause serious damage. For controls see "Powdery Mildew" on page 323.

Symptom: Orange or reddish spots on leaves
Cause: **Rust (several fungal species)**

The first symptoms of rust diseases are general lack of vigor and slow growth. Choose a planting site with good air circulation. For controls see "Rust" on page 327.

ARBORVITAES

Thuja spp.

> ### AMERICAN ARBORVITAE/EASTERN WHITE CEDAR AT A GLANCE
>
> **Botanical Name:** *Thuja occidentalis*
> **Height:** 40–60 feet (many cultivars shorter)
> **Spread:** 10–15 feet (short cultivars vary in shape)
> **Shade Tolerance:** Full sun
> **Hardiness:** Zones 3–7
> **Preferred Soil:** Deep, moist, well-drained
>
> ### ORIENTAL ARBORVITAE AT A GLANCE
>
> **Botanical Name:** *Thuja orientalis* (*Platycladus orientalis*)
> **Height:** 30–40 feet (usually 18–25 feet)
> **Spread:** 15–20 feet (usually 10–15 feet)
> **Shade Tolerance:** Full sun or light shade
> **Hardiness:** Zones 6–9
> **Preferred Soil:** Tolerates various soils if they are well-drained

Oriental arborvitae (Thuja orientalis)

Most Common Arborvitae Pests

Symptom: Branches stripped of needles
Cause: **Bagworms**

Bagworms hang from twigs and branches in 2½-inch-long tough, silken bags. For controls see "Bagworm" on page 247.

Most Common Arborvitae Diseases

Symptom: Twig tips turn brown and die back in late spring and early summer
Cause: **Tip blight (many fungi, particularly *Coryneum berckmanii*)**

Prune off and destroy all infected growth. Spray two or three times, at weekly intervals, with copper. Copper discolors the shrub, but new healthy growth will soon mask this damage.

Symptom: Needles turn pale yellow and drop
Cause: **Leaf spot (many fungi)**

Leaf spots can spread to cover whole leaves. For controls see "Beeches" on page 173.

Most Common Arborvitae Disorders

Symptom: Needles dry and turn brown
Cause: **Environmental stress**

Arborvitaes suffer from drought and exposure to drying winds and hot sun. When you plant, soak the soil thoroughly and mulch with a thick layer of straw to retard moisture loss. In fall, spray plants with an antitranspirant to protect them from drying winter winds. In Zones 3–5, wrap young shrubs in exposed locations with burlap for winter.

ASHES
Fraxinus spp.

GREEN ASH AT A GLANCE

Botanical Name: *Fraxinus pennsylvanica*
Height: 50–80 feet
Spread: 25–80 feet
Shade Tolerance: Full sun
Hardiness: Zones 4–9
Preferred Soil: Moist, well-drained; tolerates high pH, salt, and poor soil once established

WHITE ASH AT A GLANCE

Botanical Name: *Fraxinus americana*
Height: 50–80 feet
Spread: 50–80 feet
Shade Tolerance: Full sun
Hardiness: Zones 4–9
Preferred Soil: Deep, moist, well-drained soil; tolerates dry, rocky soil

Most Common Ash Pests

Symptom: Leaves turn yellow along whole branch
Causes: **Oystershell scale; other scale species**

Look for masses of tiny, elongated bumps on the bark. For controls see "Most Common Tree, Shrub, and Vine Pests" on page 168.

Symptoms: Branches die or break; plants are weak
Cause: **Borers**

If borers are causing the decline of the tree, you will see small holes bored through the bark of limbs or the trunk, or around the base of the trunk. For controls see "Most Common Tree, Shrub, and Vine Pests" on page 168.

Symptom: Distorted flowers with clusters of irregular galls
Cause: **Ash flower gall mites**

These microscopic gall mites are only $\frac{1}{50}$ inch long and feed in the male flowers of white ash. This causes very rough, irregular galls in the flowers. These dry out and stay on the tree during winter. Spray dormant oil in late winter, especially targeting galls.

Most Common Ash Diseases

Symptom: Yellow–orange spots on upper surfaces of leaflets in spring
Cause: **Rust (*Puccinia peridermiospora*)**

Minimize rust problems by choosing a planting site with good air circulation. For controls see "Rust" on page 327.

Green ash (*Fraxinus pennsylvanica*)

BARBERRIES

Berberis spp.

JAPANESE BARBERRY AT A GLANCE

Botanical Name: *Berberis thunbergii*
Height: 4–6 feet; dwarf cultivars to 2 feet
Spread: 4–7 feet; dwarf cultivars to 5 feet
Shade Tolerance: Full sun
Hardiness: Zones 4–8
Preferred Soil: Very adaptable; withstands dry conditions or low fertility, but not extremely moist conditions

KOREAN BARBERRY AT A GLANCE

Botanical Name: *Berberis koreana*
Height: 4–6 feet
Spread: Slightly more narrow than tall
Shade Tolerance: Full sun or light shade
Hardiness: Zones 4–7
Preferred Soil: Tolerates most soils that aren't permanently wet

---

Japanese barberry (Berberis thunbergii)

Most Common Barberry Pests

Symptoms: Holes chewed in leaves; webs present in foliage
Causes: **Barberry webworms; tent caterpillars; other webworms**

Several caterpillars that spin silken tents attack barberries. For controls see "Most Common Tree, Shrub, and Vine Pests" on page 168.

Symptom: Leaves distorted and yellowish
Cause: **Aphids**

Several species of aphids attack barberries. For controls see "Aphids" on page 244.

Symptom: Leaves turn yellow along branches
Cause: **Scale**

Barberry scale looks like tiny, reddish brown bumps on the bark of twigs. Prune out heavily infested branches and spray summer oil or insecticidal soap. Spray dormant oil before buds break to control overwintering scale.

Most Common Barberry Diseases

Symptom: Orange powdery spots on leaves
Cause: **Rust (*Puccinia graminis*)**

The first symptoms of rust diseases are general lack of vigor and slow growth. Minimize rust by choosing a planting site with good air circulation. For controls see "Rust" on page 327.

Symptoms: Wilting when soil is moist;
Cause: **Wilt (*Verticillium albo–atrum*)**

Wilt symptoms usually appear on lower or outer portions first. For controls see "Verticillium Wilt" on page 332.

BEECHES

Fagus spp.

AMERICAN BEECH AT A GLANCE

Botanical Name: *Fagus grandifolia*
Height: 50–70 feet
Spread: To 70 feet
Shade Tolerance: Full sun or light shade
Hardiness: Zones 4–8
Preferred Soil: Moist, well-drained, preferably acidic (pH 5.5–6.5), not constantly wet or compacted

EUROPEAN BEECH AT A GLANCE

Botanical Name: *Fagus sylvatica*
Height: 50–60 feet
Spread: 35–45 feet (narrower and weeping cultivars available)
Shade Tolerance: Full sun or partial shade
Hardiness: Zones 5–9
Preferred Soil: Moist, well-drained, slightly acidic

Most Common Beech Pests

Symptom: Leaves distorted and yellowish
Cause: **Aphids**

Look for bluish, pear-shaped insects covered with white, waxy fluff. Knock aphids off plants with a strong stream of water; repeat frequently as needed. Attract native predators and parasites by planting pollen and nectar plants. Control the ants that guard aphid colonies in trees by placing sticky bands around trunks. For further controls see "Aphids" on page 244.

Symptoms: Branches die or break; plants are weak
Cause: **Borers**

If borers are causing the decline of the tree, you will see small holes bored through the bark of limbs or the trunk. For controls see "Most Common Tree, Shrub, and Vine Pests" on page 168.

Symptoms: Holes in leaves; webbing may be present
Cause: **Caterpillars**

Many species of caterpillars attack beeches, including tent caterpillars, which spin webs. Natural enemies usually keep caterpillars in check. For heavy infestations, spray *Bacillus thuringiensis* var. *kurstaki* (BTK) or neem.

European beech (Fagus sylvatica)

Symptom: White fluff on bark
Cause: **Woolly beech scale**

These minute yellowish, immature scale insects, ¹⁄₁₀ inch long, spread over the tree during late summer, then become stationary and secrete the white fluffy covering you see in late fall. You must control them because they spread beech bark disease. Spray dormant lime-sulfur sprays on trunk and branches (don't use oil sprays on beech).

Most Common Beech Diseases

Symptom: Lesions on branches ooze light
             brown or reddish brown liquid
Cause: **Canker (*Phytophthora cactorum*)**

Canker enters the tree through wounds caused by insects or gardening tools. For controls see "Cytospora Canker" on page 310.

Symptom: Spots appear on leaves in mid-
             to late summer
Cause: **Leaf spot (*Gloeosporium fagi*;
             Phyllosticta faginea)**

Leaf spot is fairly common but rarely life threatening to the tree. Rake up and destroy all fallen leaves at the end of the season to reduce the problem next year. To control leaf spot, spray with copper in late spring.

Symptom: White, powdery coating
             on leaves
Cause: **Powdery mildew (*Microsphaera
             alni*; *Phyllactinia corylea*)**

Powdery mildew is unsightly but seldom causes serious damage, especially if it appears late in the season. The powdery spots on leaves enlarge quickly. For controls see "Powdery Mildew" on page 323.

BIRCHES
Betula spp.

EUROPEAN WHITE BIRCH AT A GLANCE

Botanical Name: *Betula pendula*
Height: 40–50 feet
Spread: 20–35 feet
Shade Tolerance: Full sun
Hardiness: Zones 3–5
Preferred Soil: Moist, well-drained, sandy or loamy soil; tolerates wet or dry soil

PAPER BIRCH AT A GLANCE

Botanical Name: *Betula papyrifera*
Height: 50–70 feet
Spread: 35–50 feet
Shade Tolerance: Full sun or partial shade
Hardiness: Zones 2–7
Preferred Soil: Moist, well-drained, acidic, sandy or silty loam; adapts to a variety of soils

RIVER BIRCH AT A GLANCE

Botanical Name: *Betula nigra*
Height: 40–70 feet
Spread: 40–60 feet
Shade Tolerance: Full sun or partial shade
Hardiness: Zones 4–8
Preferred Soil: Fertile, moist soil with a pH of 6.5 or lower; tolerates widely different moisture levels

Most Common Birch Pests

Symptom: Brown, wrinkled blotches
on leaves

Cause: **Birch leafminers**

Look for the white larvae, ⅒ inch in length, of these leafminer sawflies inside the leaf blisters. Trees usually withstand light to moderate attack year after year. Trees should be given good care to maintain vigor and avoid borer attacks. Handpick infested leaves as soon as you see them to reduce the next generation. Spray neem to control larvae. Where infestations are usually heavy, spray three times at 10–day intervals in April with pyrethrins or neem.

Symptoms: Leaves turn yellow; upper
branches dying

Cause: **Bronze birch borers**

The whitish, ¼–½-inch-long, larvae of this serious birch pest burrow in the inner bark, leaving zigzag tunnels. They start at the top of the tree and often go unnoticed until it is too late. If damage seems confined to the top of the tree, try pruning out all affected wood. Where this borer is common, do not plant European white birch (*B. pendula*) or paper birch (*B. papyrifera*), which are very susceptible. 'Heritage' river birch and 'Whitespire' birch are resistant to borers.

Symptom: Leaves curled and sticky

Cause: **Birch aphids**

Look for these ⅒-inch-long, greenish insects on undersides of leaves. Knock aphids off plants with a strong stream of water; repeat frequently as needed. Control the ants that guard aphid colonies in trees by placing sticky bands around trunks. For further controls see "Aphids" on page 244.

Symptom: Holes chewed in leaves

Causes: **Caterpillars; Japanese beetles**

Several cankerworms and other caterpillars attack birch. Gray birch (*B. populifolia*) may be severely attacked by Japanese beetles. For control of both see "Most Common Tree, Shrub, and Vine Pests" on page 168.

Most Common Birch Diseases

Symptom: Swelling, cracking, or callusing
of branch bases

Cause: **Canker (*Nectria galligena*)**

Canker fungi enter the tree through bark cracks and other wounds. For controls see "Cytospora Canker" on page 310.

*European white birch (*Betula pendula*)*

Symptom: Galls form on branches, trunks, or roots

Cause: **Crown gall**

Wounds produced by insects or lawn-care equipment provide access for this bacteria. For controls see "Crown Gall" on page 309.

Symptom: Branches at the top of the tree weaken and die

Cause: **Dieback (*Melanconium betulinum*)**

This disease strikes when the tree is stressed by nutrient deficiencies, drought, or insect attacks. Prune off and destroy infected branches. Restore the tree's vigor by watering and mulching with compost.

Symptom: Reddish yellow, raised pustules on leaves

Cause: **Rust (*Melampsora betulinum*)**

The first symptoms of rust diseases are general lack of vigor and slow growth. Plants that are moderately infected are usually stunted; while seriously infected plants die. The fungus then produces pustules, often on leaf undersides. Minimize rust problems by choosing a planting site with good air circulation. For controls see "Rust" on page 327.

Symptom: Shelflike fungal growths on trunk

Cause: **Wood rot (*Polyporus betulinus*; *Torula* spp.; *Fomes* spp.; *Poria* spp.)**

While *P. betulinus* infects only dead or dying trees, the other organisms infect stressed but living trees. The "shelf" is the fruiting body of the fungus. There is no control, but you can slow it down by pruning off infected wood. Prevent attacks with good cultural care.

BOXWOODS

Buxus spp.

COMMON BOXWOOD AT A GLANCE

Botanical Name: *Buxus sempervirens*
Height: 15–20 feet (usually pruned shorter)
Spread: 8–20 feet
Shade Tolerance: Full sun or light shade
Hardiness: Zones 5–8
Preferred Soil: Fertile, moist, well-drained, amended with organic matter; tolerates moderate fertility and moisture

Most Common Boxwood Pests

Symptom: Brown, wrinkled blotches on leaves

Cause: **Boxwood leafminers**

These leafminers are the tiny, orange larvae of flies and grow up to ⅛ inch. As soon as you notice the first damage, pick off leaves and destroy to reduce the next generation. Spray neem to control larvae. For heavy infestations, spray summer oil or neem in early May when adults are starting to lay eggs on leaves.

Symptom: Leaves curled down over stem
Cause: **Boxwood psyllids**

Look for tiny, green, aphidlike insects, ⅛ inch long, on undersides of leaves at the growing tips. Spray insecticidal soap, neem, pyrethrins, or summer oil for heavy infestations.

Symptom: Light yellow speckles on leaves
Cause: **Spider mites**

Both adults and nymphs feed by sucking the juice from plant cells on undersides of leaves. Extremely fine webbing may be visible on the undersides of leaves (some species do not spin webs). In severe infestations, leaves become bronzed or turn yellow or white with brown edges. The webs may cover both sides of the leaves and eventually cover the tips of branches. Long skeins of webbing carrying hundreds of mites may hang down from the infested tips, allowing the mites to be blown to the next plant. Spider mite outbreaks can be sudden and severe in hot, dry conditions. Native predatory mites usually suppress spider mites sufficiently in organically managed orchards. Spray neem, insecticidal soap, or pyrethrins as needed. Spray summer oil on woody shrubs and trees that can tolerate it.

Symptom: Leaves turn yellow along whole branch
Cause: **Scale**

Look for small, grayish bumps on bark. Prune out heavily infested branches and spray summer oil or insecticidal soap. Spray dormant oil before buds break to control overwintering scale.

Most Common Boxwood Diseases

Symptom: Leaves and twigs die at branch tips
Cause: **Blight (*Phoma conidiogena*; *Hyponectria buxi*)**

Prune off infected growth. Spray with copper four times during the year: in later winter, when plants are dormant; in mid-spring; in early summer; and in late fall.

Symptoms: Lesions on leaves and twigs; leaves are pale-colored
Cause: **Canker (*Pseudonectria rousselliana*)**

Canker fungi can enter the plant through wounds caused by insects, pruning tools, and lawn-care equipment. Prevent this disease with good cultural care. Prune only in dry weather and avoid unnecessary wounds. Remove severely infected branches. On trunks and large branches, remove cankers, cutting about 2 inches beyond the infected area. Sterilize all pruning tools between cuts and leave them open to the air. Protect the trunks of young trees from sunscald in winter by covering with tree paint.

Common boxwood (<u>Buxus sempervirens</u>)

BUCKEYES AND HORSE CHESTNUTS

Aesculus spp.

BOTTLEBRUSH BUCKEYE AT A GLANCE

Botanical Name: *Aesculus parviflora*
Height: 8–12 feet
Spread: 8–15 feet
Shade Tolerance: Full sun or partial shade
Hardiness: Zones 5–8
Preferred Soil: Moist, well-drained, high in organic matter; acidic best, but tolerates varying pH

OHIO BUCKEYE AT A GLANCE

Botanical Name: *Aesculus glabra*
Height: 20–40 feet
Spread: 20–40 feet
Shade Tolerance: Full sun or partial shade
Hardiness: Zones 3–8
Preferred Soil: Moist, well-drained, high in organic matter; acidic best, but tolerates varying pH

RED HORSE CHESTNUT AT A GLANCE

Botanical Name: *Aesculus* x *carnea*
Height: To 45 feet
Spread: 35–40 feet
Shade Tolerance: Full sun or light shade
Hardiness: Zones 5–8
Preferred Soil: Moist, well-drained; tolerates varying pH

Most Common Buckeye and Horse Chestnut Pests

Symptom: Holes in leaves
Causes: **Japanese beetles; caterpillars**

The caterpillars of several moths may feed on horse chestnut. They are usually controlled by natural enemies and rarely cause enough damage to warrant treatment. Horse chestnut, however, is a favorite host plant for Japanese beetles. These ½-inch-long, blue–green beetles with bronze wing covers are easy to see, as is their feeding damage, which skeletonizes leaves. For controls see "Most Common Tree, Shrub, and Vine Pests" on page 168.

Symptom: Leaves stripped from branches
Cause: **Bagworms**

Bagworms hang from twigs and branches in 2½-inch, tough, silken bags. For controls see "Bagworm" on page 247.

Most Common Buckeye and Horse Chestnut Diseases

Symptoms: Moist-looking dark spots on leaves; shoots blackened
Cause: **Anthracnose**

This fungal disease is particularly a problem during cool, wet springs. Leaf spots darken and merge as they age, covering entire leaves in some cases. Infected leaves may drop prematurely, and the entire tree may be defoliated. Stem spots often enlarge to girdle and kill trees. On trees, branch tips may die. Rake up and destroy fallen leaves and twigs. Prune out and destroy any infected growth within reach. Use copper fungicides to protect young or valuable plants. Apply sprays before symptoms appear.

Symptoms: Weeping lesions on trunk or branches; branch tips die back

Cause: **Canker**

Canker fungi can enter a tree through wounds caused by insects, pruning tools, and lawn-care equipment. Long, sunken cankers form on branches or the trunk, generally starting at a wound or branch stub. Bark beneath the canker is often cracked and darkened and may be surrounded by a raised callus. Smaller branches may be girdled and killed. For controls see "Cytospora Canker" on page 310.

Most Common Buckeye and Horse Chestnut Disorders

Symptom: Leaf margins are yellow or brown and dry

Cause: **Leaf scorch**

This symptom indicates weak or damaged roots or poor soil conditions. Newly planted trees are particularly susceptible. Prevent damage and help affected plants recover by keeping the soil evenly moist and by mulching with organic matter to keep the roots cool.

Bottlebrush buckeye (Aesculus parviflora)

CAMELLIAS
Camellia spp.

COMMON CAMELLIA AT A GLANCE

Botanical Name: *Camellia japonica*
Height: 8–15 feet
Spread: 6–10 feet
Shade Tolerance: Light shade or partial shade
Hardiness: Zones 7–10
Preferred Soil: Fertile, moist, well-drained, acidic (pH 5.0–6.0), high in organic matter

SASANQUA CAMELLIA AT A GLANCE

Botanical Name: *Camellia sasanqua*
Height: 6–10 feet
Spread: 4–8 feet
Shade Tolerance: Light shade or partial shade
Hardiness: Zones 7–10
Preferred Soil: Fertile, moist, acidic (pH 5.0–6.0)

Most Common Camellia Pests

Symptom: Leaves and new shoots distorted and sticky

Cause: **Aphids**

Look for clusters of small, pear-shaped insects on undersides of leaves, on new shoots, and in flower buds. Maintain healthy plant growth, but do not overfertilize with nitrogen. Knock aphids off plants with a strong stream of water; repeat as needed. For further controls see "Aphids" on page 244.

Symptom: Leaves turn yellow along
whole branch
Cause: **Scale**

A large number of scale species attack camellia. Look for clusters of tiny, whitish, grayish, reddish, or brown bumps on stems and bark. For controls see "Most Common Tree, Shrub, and Vine Pests" on page 168.

Symptom: Half–circle notches in leaf edges
Causes: **Black vine weevils; strawberry
root weevils**

Adult weevils feed on leaves, while their larvae feed on roots. For controls for both see "Rhododendrons and Azaleas" on page 220.

Sasanqua camellia (Camellia sasanqua)

Symptom: Powdery white crawling
insects on stems
Cause: **Mealybugs**

If you find small, oval insects, ¹⁄₁₀ inch long, covered with white, waxy fluff on the bark, mealybugs are the problem. They feed on all parts of the plant, especially new growth, and some species also feed on roots. For controls see "Mealybugs" on page 272.

Symptoms: Holes chewed in leaves;
webs may be present
Cause: **Caterpillars**

Several species of caterpillar feed on camellia leaves. Some roll or tie the leaves together as they feed. For controls see "Most Common Tree, Shrub, and Vine Pests" on page 168.

Most Common Camellia Diseases

Symptoms: Leaves wilt; young growth dies;
cankers form on branches
and twigs
Cause: **Canker (*Glomerella cingulata*)**

Prune off and destroy all infected parts. Spray copper or Bordeaux mixture on scars left by fallen leaves.

Symptoms: Brownish specks appear on
flowers; flowers brown and drop
Cause: **Flower blight
(*Sclerotinia camelliae*)**

Dropped flowers develop shiny black streaks of spore masses. Destroy all infected flowers before they drop. The organism can survive for 2 years in soil; throw out potted medium and sterilize containers of greenhouse crops. Outside, do not replant camellias where infected plants grew.

CLEMATIS

Clematis s p p .

LARGE-FLOWERED CLEMATIS AT A GLANCE

Botanical Name: *Clematis* hybrids
Height: 10–15 feet
Spread: To 4 feet
Shade Tolerance: Full sun
Hardiness: Zones 4–9
Preferred Soil: Fertile, moist

SWEET AUTUMN CLEMATIS AT A GLANCE

Botanical Name: *Clematis maximowicziana*
   (*C. paniculata*)
Height: To 30 feet if support is provided
Spread: To 30 feet if support is provided
Shade Tolerance: Full sun or light shade
Hardiness: Zones 4–9
Preferred Soil: Fertile, moist

Most Common Clematis Pests

Symptoms: Poor growth, tops die back
Cause: **Clematis borers**

Dig down and look for plump, white grubs up to ⅔ inch long with brown heads feeding in the crown and roots. Destroy badly infested plants. Dig borers out of lightly infested plants and cut back stems.

Symptom: Leaves turn yellow along
        whole branch
Cause: **Scale**

For controls see "Most Common Tree, Shrub, and Vine Pests" on page 168.

Most Common Clematis Diseases

Symptoms: Small, water–soaked spots on
        leaves; reddish lesions on stems
Causes: **Leaf spot; stem rot**
        (*Ascochyta clematidina*)

Stem lesions gradually enlarge, finally girdling and killing the stem. Before buying, check all nursery–grown plants for symptoms because they sometimes carry the disease. Provide good air circulation around plants by training them on large trellises and thinning out excess growth. Prune off and destroy all infected growth and spray with sulfur.

Symptom: Plants wilt when soil is moist
Cause: **Wilt**

Setting clematis vines slightly deeper at planting time than they grew in the nursery may help plants recover from wilt attack. For controls see "Bacterial Wilt" on page 303, "Verticillium Wilt" on page 332, and "Fusarium Wilt" on page 315.

*'Ernest Markham' clematis (*Clematis* hybrid)*

COTONEASTERS

Cotoneaster spp.

ROCKSPRAY COTONEASTER AT A GLANCE

Botanical Name: *Cotoneaster horizontalis*
Height: 2–3 feet
Spread: 5–8 feet
Shade Tolerance: Full sun
Hardiness: Zones 5–8
Preferred Soil: Tolerates most soils if well-drained

SPREADING COTONEASTER AT A GLANCE

Botanical Name: *Cotoneaster divaricatus*
Height: 5–6 feet
Spread: 6–8 feet
Shade Tolerance: Full sun or light shade
Hardiness: Zones 5–8
Preferred Soil: Fertile, loose, well-drained soils; tolerates poor, dry soils

Rockspray cotoneaster (Cotoneaster horizontalis)

Most Common Cotoneaster Pests

Symptoms: Skeletonized leaves; webbing present
Cause: **Cotoneaster webworms**

Look for yellowish green caterpillars, ¼–½ inch in length, in silken webs around the foliage. They cause the most damage in early spring, when plants are leafing out. A heavy infestation can kill young plants and weaken older plants. Pull the webs off the foliage to expose the caterpillars and spray *Bacillus thuringiensis* var. *kurstaki* (BTK) or neem. Where infestations have been serious, spray dormant oil and lime-sulfur when plants are dormant.

Symptom: Leaves distorted and yellowish
Cause: **Aphids**

You will see the small, pear-shaped insects on undersides of leaves and in growing tips. Knock aphids off plants with a strong stream of water; repeat frequently as needed. For further controls see "Aphids" on page 244.

Symptom: Light yellow speckles on leaves
Cause: **Spider mites**

Look for fine webbing on undersides of leaves. For controls see "Spider Mites" on page 286.

Symptom: Gray, lacy blotches on leaves
Cause: **Lace bugs**

Lace bugs are tiny, oval bugs with lacy wings. Look on undersides of leaves for the specks of dark excrement that show lace bugs have been feeding. For controls see "Lace Bugs" on page 270. Plant resistant species such as Parney cotoneaster (*C. lacteus*), *C. buxifolius*, and wintergreen cotoneaster (*C. conspicuus*).

Symptom: Reddish warts or blisters
             on leaves
Cause: **Pear leaf blister mites**

Feeding by these 1/100-inch-long gall mites produces galls that are greenish yellow in spring, turning red, purple, and then brown by August. These rarely harm the plant. Handpick damaged leaves. After an unusually heavy infestation of pear leaf blister mites, spray dormant oil or lime-sulfur just before buds swell in early spring.

Symptoms: Branches die or break; plants
             are weak
Cause: **Borers**

If borers are causing the decline of the shrub, you will see small holes bored through the bark of limbs or the trunk. For controls see "Most Common Tree, Shrub, and Vine Pests" on page 168.

Most Common Cotoneaster Diseases

Symptom: New growth wilts, blackens,
             and dies
Cause: **Fire blight (*Erwinia amylovora*)**

This devastating disease can spread quickly. Infected blossoms look water-soaked, then brown and shriveled. Leaves turn brown or black and curl upward, remaining on the twigs as if scorched by fire. Cankers have distinct margins; the wood beneath them is water-soaked, then darkened. Warm spring rains stimulate overwintering bacteria into growth. Cankers produce bacterial ooze that attracts many insects, which carry the bacteria to susceptible plants. Rain, splashing water, and contaminated tools also transmit fire blight. For controls see "Fire Blight" on page 314.

CRABAPPLES
Malus spp. and hybrids

CRABAPPLES AT A GLANCE

Botanical Name: *Malus* spp. and hybrids
Height: Usually 10–25 feet
Spread: To 25 feet
Shade Tolerance: Full sun or light shade
Hardiness: Zones 3–9 (varies by cultivar)
Preferred Soil: Evenly moist, well-drained,
    acidic (pH 5.0–6.5)

Most Common Crabapple Pests
See "Apples" on page 71.

Crabapple (<u>Malus floribunda</u>)

Most Common Crabapple Diseases

Symptom: Sunken lesions on branches and trunk
Cause: **Canker** (*Physalospora obtusa*; *Phoma mali*)

Canker fungi enter the tree through wounds caused by insects, pruning tools, or lawn-care equipment. For controls see "Cytospora Canker" on page 310.

Symptoms: Dark brown cankers on bark; leaves wilt suddenly and dry on the twig
Cause: **Fire blight** (*Erwinia amylovora*)

This devastating disease can spread quickly through susceptible trees. For controls see "Fire Blight" on page 314.

Symptom: Brown or orange spots on leaves
Cause: **Cedar-apple rust** (*Gymnosporangium juniperi-virginianae*)

This fungal disease can cause stunted growth and early leaf drop. For controls see "Cedar-Apple Rust" on page 307.

Symptoms: Dark-colored, rough-looking spots on leaves and fruit; premature leaf drop
Cause: **Apple scab** (*Venturia inaequalis*)

Apple scab spores overwinter on fallen apple and crabapple leaves. Apple scab manifests itself as light gray spots on sepals and undersides of early leaves. As spots age, they change from green to brown. Infected fruit may be cracked, deformed, or russetted. Infected leaves drop early. For controls see "Apple Scab" on page 300 .

DOGWOODS
Cornus spp.

FLOWERING DOGWOOD AT A GLANCE

Botanical Name: *Cornus florida*
Height: To 25 feet
Spread: To 25 feet or more
Shade Tolerance: Light shade or partial shade
Hardiness: Zones 5–9
Preferred Soil: Average to fertile, moist, well-drained, acidic

KOUSA DOGWOOD AT A GLANCE

Botanical Name: *Cornus kousa*
Height: 25–30 feet
Spread: 25–30 feet
Shade Tolerance: Full sun
Hardiness: Zones 5–7
Preferred Soil: Average to fertile, moist, well-drained, acidic, high in organic matter

RED-OSIER DOGWOOD AT A GLANCE

Botanical Name: *Cornus sericea*
Height: 7–9 feet
Spread: 10 feet or more
Shade Tolerance: Full sun or light shade
Hardiness: Zones 3–8
Preferred Soil: Adaptable to various soil conditions; best if moist

Most Common Dogwood Pests

Symptoms: Loose bark peels away; branches
die or break
Cause: **Borers**

At least seven species of borer may attack
dogwood, especially when the plants are in full
sun. If they are causing the plant to decline,
you should see holes bored through the bark
of limbs or the trunk. For controls see "Most
Common Tree, Shrub, and Vine Pests" on
page 168.

Symptom: Swollen galls on twigs
Cause: **Gall midges**

The orange larvae of these tiny midges
burrow in twigs in late May, causing ½-inch-
long, club-shaped swellings. The leaves on the
shoot may also wilt. Prune out and destroy
galls in summer.

Symptom: Leaves turn yellow along
whole branch
Cause: **Scale**

Look for small, grayish bumps on bark. Scale
is usually controlled well by dormant oil or
lime-sulfur sprays in late winter and by sprays
of summer oil or insecticidal soap as buds start
to open. To control scale crawlers in
midsummer or later, spray summer oil or
insecticidal soap, but only for heavy infestations. For controls see "Most Common Tree,
Shrub, and Vine Pests" on page 168.

Symptom: Tunnels between upper and
lower leaf surfaces
Cause: **Leafminers**

Several different insects may mine within
leaves. For controls see "Birches" on page 174.

Most Common Dogwood Diseases

Symptom: Sunken black spots on leaves
Cause: **Anthracnose**

Dogwood anthracnose causes purple-rimmed
leaf spots and twig dieback. Symptoms often
appear on the lower branches first. For
controls see "Anthracnose" on page 300.

Symptoms: Flowers or leaves discolor and
wilt; cankers on twigs
Cause: **Blight (*Botrytis cinerea*;
Myxosporium spp.;
Cryptostitis spp.;
Sphaeropsis spp.)**

To control blight, prune off all infected wood
several inches below cankers. Spray once with
copper during the flowering period in spring.
Continue to watch the plant during summer,
pruning off any diseased growth you see.

*Flowering dogwood (*Cornus florida*)*

Symptoms: Branches with leaves that are small and pale; swollen growth on lower trunk or roots

Cause: **Crown canker (*Phytophthora cactorum*)**

This disease is most common in transplanted trees, so watch all new dogwoods carefully. Prune off and destroy all infected branches. If a small canker has formed on the trunk, dig out all of the discolored bark and wood and remove a 1-inch strip of healthy bark all around the cankerous spot. Paint the area where you removed the bark with shellac and cover the gouged–out area with white interior latex paint.

Symptom: White, powdery–looking coating on leaves

Cause: **Powdery mildew (*Microsphaera alni; Phyllactinia corylea*)**

Powdery mildew is unsightly but usually doesn't threaten the life of the tree. The powdery white or gray spots enlarge quickly and infected tissues become pale, then turn brown and shrivel. Spraying compost tea on leaves every 2–4 weeks can help prevent attack. For further controls see "Powdery Mildew" on page 323.

Note

Dogwoods in northeastern areas have been suffering from many diseases and dying in unprecedented numbers since about 1977. Researchers believe that current weather patterns are responsible. Protect your trees by providing the very best cultural care. Don't overfertilize them or fertilize or mulch with compost after midsummer. Make certain that their soil receives at least 1 inch of water per week (2 gallons per square foot of area under the dripline), and prune only when humidity is low and leaves are dry. In wet springs, spray with copper when the buds begin to open and continue spraying every 7–10 days while the trees are leafing out. Spray only three times in dry springs.

EUONYMUS

Euonymus spp.

BURNING BUSH/WINGED EUONYMUS AT A GLANCE

Botanical Name: *Euonymus alata*
Height: 15–20 feet
Spread: 15–20 feet
Shade Tolerance: Full sun or light shade
Hardiness: Zones 4–8
Preferred Soil: Average to fertile, moist, well-drained, pH adaptable; does not tolerate waterlogged soil or drought

WINTERCREEPER AT A GLANCE

Botanical Name: *Euonymus fortunei*
Height: Groundcover types, to 2 feet; shrubs, to 5 feet; vines, to 30 feet
Spread: Groundcovers, to 8 feet; shrubs, to 5 feet
Shade Tolerance: Full sun to full shade
Hardiness: Zones 4–9
Preferred Soil: Fertile, moist, well-drained, pH adaptable; does not tolerate water logged soil

Most Common Euonymus Pests

Symptom: Leaves turn yellow along whole branch

Cause: **Scale**

Many species of scale attack euonymus. Look for small, white, grayish, reddish, or brown bumps on bark. Their feeding weakens and kills branches. For controls see "Most Common Tree, Shrub, and Vine Pests" on page 168. Choose resistant species such as spreading euonymus (*E. kiautschovicus*).

Symptom: Leaves distorted and yellowish
Cause: **Aphids**

Look for small, pear-shaped insects on undersides of leaves. Their feeding usually causes distorted leaves and branch tips. For controls see "Aphids" on page 244.

Most Common Euonymus Diseases

Symptom: Leaves have yellow, brown,
              black, or dead spots
Cause: **Leaf spot**

Leaf spots can merge to cover whole leaves. For controls see "Beeches" on page 173.

Symptoms: Sunken spots on leaves; pinkish
              spores on branch lesions
Cause: **Anthracnose (*Colletotrichum*
              spp.; *Gloeosporium* spp.)**

Anthracnose is a problem during cool, wet springs. Preventive tactics include cleaning up garden debris, spacing plants to increase air movement, keeping leaves dry while watering, and not working in the garden when plants are wet. Rake up and destroy leaves and twigs from infected trees. On smaller plants, prune off and destroy all infected growth at the first sign of infection. If you've had previous anthracnose problems, use copper fungicides to protect young or particularly valuable plants. Apply sprays before disease symptoms appear.

Symptom: Galls on roots, trunk,
              or branches
Cause: **Crown gall**

Crown gall bacteria can enter the plant through wounds caused by insects, pruning tools, and lawn-care equipment. Carefully inspect plants for crown gall before you buy.

Soak roots in a solution containing the beneficial bacteria *Agrobacterium radiobacter* before planting. Prune out mild, localized infections, sterilizing tools between cuts. Dig out and destroy severely infected plants, taking as much surrounding soil as possible.

Symptom: White, powdery coating on
              leaves
Cause: **Powdery mildew**

Powdery white or gray spots on leaves enlarge quickly. Infected tissues become brown and shrivel. Plant in well-drained soil, and space plants widely for good air circulation. Compost all plant debris and pick off and destroy infected plant parts. Sprays of compost tea every 2–4 weeks can help prevent infection. Sprays of baking soda solution or baking soda plus oil (see "Oil Sprays" on page 361) are often an effective powdery mildew control.

*Burning bush or winged euonymus
(Euonymus alata)*

FIRETHORNS

Pyracantha spp.

> ### SCARLET FIRETHORN
> ### AT A GLANCE
>
> **Botanical Name:** *Pyracantha coccinea*
> **Height:** 6–18 feet
> **Spread:** 6–18 feet
> **Shade Tolerance:** Full sun or partial shade
> **Hardiness:** Zones 5–9
> **Preferred Soil:** Requires good drainage;
> tolerates poor soils, drought, and broad
> pH range (5.5–7.5)

Most Common Firethorn Pests

Symptom: Leaves turn yellow along
whole branch
Cause: **Scale**

Several species of scale attack firethorns. Look for clusters of tiny, grayish or brown bumps on bark. For controls see "Most Common Tree, Shrub, and Vine Pests" on page 168.

Scarlet firethorn (Pyracantha coccinea)

Symptom: Leaves distorted and sticky
Cause: **Apple aphids**

Aphids do not harm most deciduous shrubs, but their production of honeydew is a nuisance. Knock aphids from plants with a strong spray of water, repeating as frequently as needed. For further controls see "Aphids" on page 244.

Symptom: Gray, lacy blotches on leaves
Cause: **Hawthorn lace bugs**

Lace bugs are 1/10-inch-long, oval bugs with lacy wings. Look on undersides of leaves for the specks of dark excrement that show lace bugs have been feeding. Maintain vigorous plants. For heavy infestations, in mid-May and again 10 days later, spray insecticidal soap or pyrethrins to control both adults and nymphs. Summer oils are also effective on trees and plants that can tolerate oil sprays.

Symptom: Leaves and branch tips webbed
Cause: **Pyracantha webworms**

These striped green caterpillars are 1/4–1/2 inch long, feed on leaves, and spin silk webs to enclose foliage and stems. For a light infestation, handpick webs and caterpillars. For heavy infestations, spray *Bacillus thuringiensis* var. *kurstaki* (BTK), neem, or summer oil, first breaking open webs to ensure spray coverage.

Most Common Firethorn Diseases

Symptoms: Leaves yellow and drop; scabby
lesions form on leaves
and berries
Cause: **Scab (*Fusicladium pyracanthae*)**

Scab infects firethorns that are weakened by poor growing conditions or insect damage.

Prune and destroy all infected wood. In spring, when the buds first break, spray with copper, repeating once or twice 10–14 days apart.

Symptom: Leaves die
Cause: **Blight**

Minimize blight damage by selecting a planting site with good air circulation and well-drained soil. Blight fungi overwinter on plant debris. In spring, spores form and are carried by wind, water, and tools to new plants. Blight fungi enter plants through wounds, bruises, and dying tissue, reproducing rapidly in humid conditions and forming spores that infect other plants. Don't work around plants when they are wet to avoid spreading blight spores; avoid creating wounds that might admit disease. Prune crowded plantings to improve air circulation. Remove faded flowers and destroy infected plant parts to reduce the spread of the disease.

Symptoms: Dark, roughened areas on branches; flowers and shoots wilt in spring
Cause: **Fire blight**
     (*Erwinia amylovora*)

This devastating disease can quickly spread through a plant. Protect plants by avoiding overfertilization with nitrogen. Look for infections on wild plants and destroy them. Control insects as much as possible. In late winter, prune out and destroy infected shoots and branches, cutting at least 6–12 inches below the visible infection. Spray with streptomycin during blossoming, at 7- to 10-day intervals. In late winter, spray with copper or Bordeaux mixture.

FIRS
Abies spp.

BALSAM FIR AT A GLANCE

Botanical Name: *Abies balsamea*
Height: To 75 feet
Spread: 20–25 feet
Shade Tolerance: Full sun or light shade
Hardiness: Zones 2–5
Preferred Soil: Moist, well-drained, acidic

WHITE FIR AT A GLANCE

Botanical Name: *Abies concolor*
Height: To 50 feet
Spread: 15–30 feet
Shade Tolerance: Full sun or light shade
Hardiness: Zones 4–7
Preferred Soil: Moist, well-drained, acidic

White fir (Abies concolor)

Most Common Fir Pests

Symptom: Distorted needles
Cause: **Balsam twig adelgids**

These small, greenish, sucking insects hide between the needles under white, waxy fluff. They suck sap from the needles, causing misshapen growth and exuding sticky honeydew. Blast them out of branch tips with a strong spray of water or, for heavy infestations, spray insecticidal soap, neem, or pyrethrins.

Symptom: Bronzed or grayish needles that
             dry and drop off
Cause: **Spruce spider mites**

These tiny mites spin webbing between needles, especially on undersides of branches. For controls see "Spider Mites" on page 286.

Symptom: Branches stripped of needles
Causes: **Hemlock loopers; bagworms**

Loopers are 1½-inch-long, greenish caterpillars with black spots. They feed on needles at the tips of branches and move along the branch toward the center of the tree. Handpick them or spray *Bacillus thuringiensis* var. *kurstaki* (BTK) or neem. Bagworms hang from twigs and branches in tough, silken bags studded with needles and plant debris. For controls see "Bagworm" on page 247.

Symptom: Needles dead at tips of branches
Cause: **Spruce budworms**

These tiny caterpillars mine into needles, as well as into buds, cones, and twigs. Spray *Bacillus thuringiensis* var. *kurstaki* (BTK) or neem as soon as you find the tiny larvae in late summer. Spray again in early spring when the larvae resume feeding.

HAWTHORNS
Crataegus spp.

COCKSPUR HAWTHORN AT A GLANCE

Botanical Name: *Crataegus crus–galli*
Height: 20–30 feet
Spread: 20–35 feet
Shade Tolerance: Full sun
Hardiness: Zones 4–7
Preferred Soil: Tolerates many soils if
   well-drained

WASHINGTON HAWTHORN AT A GLANCE

Botanical Name: *Crataegus phaenopyrum*
Height: 25–30 feet
Spread: 20–25 feet
Shade Tolerance: Full sun
Hardiness: Zones 4–8
Preferred Soil: Tolerates many soils if
   well-drained

Washington hawthorn (<u>Crataegus phaenopyrum</u>)

Most Common Hawthorn Pests

Hawthorns are susceptible to the same pests as apple. See "Apples" on page 71.

Most Common Hawthorn Diseases

Symptoms: Leaves with pale yellow spots that enlarge and turn orange; stems and fruit may be distorted

Cause: **Hawthorn rust**
(*Gymnosporangium globosum*)

Affected leaves may turn completely yellow and drop early. Hawthorn rust spends part of its life cycle on eastern red cedars (*Juniperus virginiana*) and other junipers, producing spores that are windblown onto susceptible hawthorns, apples, pears, and mountain ashes. On cedars, the fungus forms rounded, red-brown galls, up to ½ inch in diameter. In warm, rainy conditions, the galls produce spore-bearing tendrils. Since spores are windborne, it is necessary to separate hawthorns from cedars by at least 4 miles to prevent rust from spreading. Choose rust-resistant hawthorn species, such as English hawthorn (*C. laevigata*) or cultivars such as 'Crusader' hawthorn (*C. crus-galli* var. *inermis* 'Crusader'). Remove and burn rust galls found on cedars.

Symptoms: Light gray to velvety olive green spots on undersides of leaves; early leaf drop

Cause: **Apple scab**
(*Venturia inaequalis*)

Circular leaf spots age from light gray to olive green, then chocolate brown and metallic black. Infected leaves drop prematurely; severe infection may defoliate a tree. For controls see "Apple Scab" on page 300.

HEMLOCKS
Tsuga spp.

CANADA HEMLOCK AT A GLANCE

Botanical Name: *Tsuga canadensis*
Height: 40–75 feet (many cultivars smaller)
Spread: 25–35 feet (cultivars vary in shape)
Shade Tolerance: Full sun or light shade
Hardiness: Zones 3–8
Preferred Soil: Fertile, moist, well-drained, acidic

CAROLINA HEMLOCK AT A GLANCE

Botanical Name: *Tsuga caroliniana*
Height: 45–60 feet (shorter cultivars available)
Spread: 20–25 feet (shorter cultivars vary in shape)
Shade Tolerance: Partial or light shade
Hardiness: Zones 5–8
Preferred Soil: Moderately fertile, moist, well-drained

Most Common Hemlock Pests

Symptom: Branches stripped of needles
Causes: **Bagworms; hemlock loopers**

Bagworms hang from branches in tough, silken bags. For controls see "Most Common Tree, Shrub, and Vine Pests" on page 168. Loopers are greenish caterpillars with black spots. They start feeding on needles at the tips of branches and move along the branch toward the tree center. For light infestations, handpick the caterpillars. For heavy infestations, spray *Bacillus thuringiensis* var. *kurstaki* (BTK) or neem.

Symptoms: Needles drop; white tufts
between needles and on bark
Cause: **Hemlock woolly adelgid**

If this sucking insect is the problem, you can
see the cottony, white egg masses in late winter
and early spring in the crevices of bark and at
the base of needles. A heavy infestation can kill
a young tree. Spray dormant oil, especially on
the bark of the trunk and branches in early
spring, before buds swell. Spraying in summer
kills the natural predators of this adelgid;
spray only if absolutely necessary, using insecticidal soap or summer oil.

Carolina hemlock (Tsuga caroliniana)

Symptom: Bronzed or grayish needles that
dry and drop off
Cause: **Spruce spider mites**

You will need a magnifying lens to see the tiny
mites among the webbing they spin between
needles, especially on undersides of branches.
For controls see "Firs" on page 189.

Symptom: Needles turn yellow along
whole branch
Cause: **Scale**

Many species of scale attack hemlocks. Look
for clusters of tiny, whitish, grayish, purplish,
or brown bumps on bark. Their feeding
weakens and kills branches and makes the
plants more susceptible to borer attack. For
controls see "Most Common Tree, Shrub, and
Vine Pests" on page 168.

Symptom: Needles dead at tips of branches
Cause: **Spruce budworms**

These tiny caterpillars are hard to see. They
mine into needles, as well as into buds, cones,
and twigs. For controls see "Firs" on page 189.

Most Common Hemlock Diseases

Symptom: Powdery golden pustules
on cones and needles
Cause: **Rust (*Melampsora medusae*; *M.
abietis-canadensis*; *Pucciniastrum
vacinii*)**

Yellow to reddish blisters on needle undersides
are an early sign of rust. Avoid amendments
high in nitrogen, and prune, space, and water
carefully to increase air circulation and keep
needles dry. Pick off and destroy infected
twigs. Sulfur spray, used when spots first
appear, kills new spores.

HIBISCUS

Hibiscus spp.

CHINESE HIBISCUS AT A GLANCE

Botanical Name: *Hibiscus rosa–sinensis*
Height: 8–15 feet
Spread: 6–18 feet
Shade Tolerance: Full sun or partial shade
Hardiness: Zones 9–11
Preferred Soil: Adapts to various soils if well-drained

ROSE-OF-SHARON AT A GLANCE

Botanical Name: *Hibiscus syriacus*
Height: 6–12 feet
Spread: 6–10 feet
Shade Tolerance: Full sun or partial shade
Hardiness: Zones 5–9
Preferred Soil: Moist, well-drained, organic soil; tolerates all but very wet or dry soil

Most Common Hibiscus Pests

Symptom: Leaves distorted and yellowish
Cause: **Aphids**

You will see the small, pear-shaped insects on undersides of leaves and in growing tips. For controls see "Aphids" on page 244.

Symptom: Skeletonized leaves
Cause: **Japanese beetles**

These ½-inch-long, blue-green beetles with bronze wing covers skeletonizes leaves. For controls see "Japanese Beetle" on page 268.

Most Common Hibiscus Disorders

Symptom: Plants die over winter
Cause: **Low temperatures**

Hibiscus breeders are working to extend the range in which cultivars can overwinter. They have succeeded to a remarkable degree, but in extraordinarily cold years, hibiscus plants in Zone 6 may not survive. Protect plants by placing them in sheltered locations and covering with a thick mulch as soon as the ground freezes in the fall.

Chinese hibiscus (<u>Hibiscus rosa–sinensis</u>*)*

HOLLIES
Ilex spp.

AMERICAN HOLLY AT A GLANCE

Botanical Name: *Ilex opaca*
Height: 15–50 feet
Spread: 10–40 feet at base; pyramidal
Shade Tolerance: Full sun or light shade
Hardiness: Zones 6–9
Preferred Soil: Fertile, moist, loose, acidic (pH 5.0–6.0)

JAPANESE HOLLY AT A GLANCE

Botanical Name: *Ilex crenata*
Height: 5–10 feet
Spread: 5–10 feet
Shade Tolerance: Partial shade
Hardiness: Zones 6–9
Preferred Soil: Moderately fertile, moist, well-drained, light, slightly acidic

---

Most Common Holly Pests

Symptom: Brown or translucent blotches on leaves
Cause: **Holly leafminers**

These tiny, white larvae of small flies tunnel between the upper and lower surfaces of the leaves. They are a widespread holly pest. The larvae, which are ⅛ inch long, are found inside the leaf and are protected from most sprays, but most fall prey to parasitic wasps or birds. Handpick infested leaves and rake up and destroy all fallen leaves. For heavy infestations, spray neem.

Symptom: Leaves at branch tips webbed together
Cause: **Bud moth caterpillars**

The caterpillars of this moth are a common problem in the Pacific northwest in May. They feed on the new leaves and buds, enclosing the tips of the branches inside webs. Pull webs and caterpillars out of the foliage. For heavy infestations, spray *Bacillus thuringiensis* var. *kurstaki* (BTK) or neem in April and May while caterpillars are still small. Rake up any fallen leaves to eliminate overwintering sites.

Symptom: Leaves turn yellow along whole branch
Cause: **Scale**

Look for masses of tiny, brownish, elongated or grayish bumps on the bark. For controls see "Most Common Tree, Shrub, and Vine Pests" on page 168.

Symptom: Light yellow speckles on leaves
Cause: **Spider mites**

Look for fine webbing on undersides of leaves. In severe infestations, leaves become bronzed or turn yellow or white with brown edges. The webs may cover both sides of the leaves and eventually cover the tips of branches. For controls see "Spider Mites" on page 286.

Most Common Holly Diseases

Symptom: New leaves and shoots wilt and look scorched
Cause: **Bacterial blight (*Clavibacter ilicis*)**

Cleaning up dropped leaves can help stop the spread of this disease. For controls see "Pseudomonas Leaf Blight" on page 325.

Symptoms: Spots on leaves; black lesions form on stems
Cause: **Dieback (*Phytophthora ilicis*)**

Cool, rainy weather favors this disease, which is most noticeable in fall. If the infection is severe, spray your bushes several times with Bordeaux mixture at intervals of 10–14 days. Holly leaves may be discolored as a result of the copper in the mixture.

Symptoms: New twigs die back
Cause: **Fusarium blight (*Fusarium* spp.)**

You may also notice yellow or browned leaves. For controls see "Fusarium Wilt" on page 315.

Symptom: Yellow, tan, brown, or black spots on leaves
Cause: **Leaf spot (various fungi)**

Leaf spots can merge to cover entire leaves. For controls see "Beeches" on page 173.

Symptom: White, powdery coating on leaves
Cause: **Powdery mildew (*Phyllactinia corylea*; *Microsphaera alni*)**

Powdery mildew may also appear on buds and shoot tips. These fungal infections are unsightly and also weaken host plants. Powdery white or gray spots are usually the first symptoms you will notice. For controls see "Powdery Mildew" on page 323.

Symptom: Moist, tan-colored areas on flowers
Cause: **Botrytis blight (*Botrytis cinerea*)**

Minimize problems with by choosing a planting site with good air circulation. For controls see "Botrytis Blight" on page 305.

Symptom: Sunken spots on leaves
Cause: **Anthracnose**

This fungal disease is a serious problem during cool, wet springs. For controls see "Anthracnose" on page 300.

Symptom: Sunken or swollen lesions on branches and trunk
Cause: **Canker**

Canker fungi can enter plants through wounds caused by insects and tools. For controls see "Cytospora Canker" on page 310.

Most Common Holly Disorders

Symptom: Plants fail to produce berries
Causes: **Lack of pollination; weather conditions**

Pollination problems in hollies can be caused by several factors, including rainy weather at flowering time that severely limits the number of pollinating insects. Hollies need both male and female plants to set fruit; make sure you buy both. It may take a few years for plants to mature enough to produce flowers and fruit.

American holly (Ilex opaca)

HONEYLOCUST
Gleditsia triacanthos

THORNLESS HONEYLOCUST AT A GLANCE

Botanical Name: *Gleditsia triacanthos* var. *inermis*

Height: 30–70 feet

Spread: 30–70 feet

Shade Tolerance: Full sun

Hardiness: Zones 4–9

Preferred Soil: Fertile, moist, well-drained soil; tolerates drought, high pH, limestone, and salt

Most Common Honeylocust Pests

Symptoms: Holes chewed in leaves, webs present in foliage

Causes: **Tent caterpillars; fall webworms**

For controls see "Most Common Tree, Shrub, and Vine Pests" on page 168. Plant cultivars such 'Moraine', which is somewhat resistant to fall webworms.

Thornless honeylocust (Gleditsia triacanthos var. inermis)

Symptom: Leaves stripped from branches

Cause: **Bagworms**

Bagworms hang from twigs and branches in tough, silken bags studded with pieces of leaf and plant debris. Adult males are black moths with clear wings. Females are wingless. The larvae are shiny, dark brown caterpillars. For controls see "Bagworm" on page 247.

Symptom: Branches die or break and plants are weak

Cause: **Borers**

If borers are causing the decline of the tree, you will see small holes bored through the bark of limbs or the trunk. For controls see "Most Common Tree, Shrub, and Vine Pests" on page 168.

Symptom: Light yellow speckles on leaves

Causes: **Spider mites**

Look for fine webbing on undersides of leaves. Spider mites feed by sucking the juice from plant cells on undersides of leaves. When numerous, their feeding weakens plants and causes leaves to drop. In severe infestations, leaves become bronzed or turn yellow or white with brown edges. For controls see "Spider Mites" on page 286.

Most Common Honeylocust Diseases

Symptom: Dark–colored oozing lesions on branches

Cause: **Canker**

The lesions generally start at a wound or the trunk. The canker fungi can enter trees through wounds caused by insects, pruning tools, and lawn-care equipment. For controls see "Cytospora Canker" on page 310.

HONEYSUCKLES

Lonicera spp.

TRUMPET HONEYSUCKLE AT A GLANCE

Botanical Name: *Lonicera sempervirens*
Height: To 20 feet
Spread: 10 feet or more
Shade Tolerance: Full sun or partial shade
Hardiness: Zones 4–9
Preferred Soil: Moist, well-drained, acidic or near neutral

FRAGRANT OR WINTER HONEYSUCKLE AT A GLANCE

Botanical Name: *Lonicera fragrantissima*
Height: 6–10 feet
Spread: 6–10 feet
Shade Tolerance: Full sun or partial shade
Hardiness: Zones 5–9
Preferred Soil: Loamy, moist, well-drained

Most Common Honeysuckle Pests

Symptom: Curling leaves
Cause: **Woolly honeysuckle aphids**

These tiny, yellowish insects are $\frac{1}{10}$ inch long with a black head and midsection. For controls see "Aphids" on page 244.

Symptom: Leaves turn yellow along whole branch
Cause: **Scale**

Look for masses of tiny, brownish, elongated bumps or grayish bumps on the bark. For controls see "Most Common Tree, Shrub, and Vine Pests" on page 168.

Symptom: Irregular brown spots on leaves
Cause: **Four–lined plant bugs**

These yellowish green plant bugs have four black lines down their back and are $\frac{1}{4}$–$\frac{1}{3}$ inch long. The nymphs are orange. They usually start feeding on the upper leaves first in early summer. Handpick light infestations. For heavy infestations, spray insecticidal soap to control nymphs, and pyrethrins to control adults.

Most Common Honeysuckle Diseases

Symptom: Raised, sometimes oozing lesions on stems
Cause: **Canker**

Canker-causing organisms can enter stems through wounds caused by insects, pruning tools, or lawn-care equipment. For controls see "Cytospora Canker" on page 310.

Symptom: White powdery coating on leaves
Cause: **Powdery mildew**

Minimize mildew problems by planting in a site with good air circulation. For controls see "Powdery Mildew" on page 323.

*Fragrant or winter honeysuckle (*Lonicera fragrantissima*)*

HYDRANGEAS

Hydrangea spp.

BIGLEAF HYDRANGEA AT A GLANCE

Botanical Name: *Hydrangea macrophylla*
Height: 3–6 feet; dwarf, to 3 feet
Spread: Equal to or greater than height
Shade Tolerance: Full sun or partial shade
Hardiness: Zones 6–8
Preferred Soil: Evenly moist, well-drained, humus rich

PANICLE HYDRANGEA AT A GLANCE

Botanical Name: *Hydrangea paniculata*
Height: 15–25 feet
Spread: Usually 10–20 feet
Shade Tolerance: Full sun or partial shade
Hardiness: Zones 4–9
Preferred Soil: Evenly moist, well-drained, humus-rich

Bigleaf hydrangea (Hydrangea macrophylla)

Most Common Hydrangea Pests

Symptom: Leaves distorted and yellowish
Cause: **Aphids**

You will see the small, pear-shaped insects on undersides of leaves and in growing tips. Their feeding usually causes distorted leaves, buds, branch tips, and flowers. For controls see "Aphids" on page 244.

Symptom: Leaves and buds webbed together
Cause: **Hydrangea leaftier**

These green caterpillars have brown heads and are ¼–½ inch in length. They feed on leaves, spin silk webs to enclose flower buds, and tie together leaves at the tips of shoots. For a light infestation, handpick webs and caterpillars. For heavy infestations, spray *Bacillus thuringiensis* var. *kurstaki* (BTK) or neem, first breaking open the webs to ensure good spray coverage.

Symptom: Chewing damage on leaves and flowers
Cause: **Rose chafers**

Look for small, reddish brown beetles with yellow hairs on their wing covers feeding on leaves and flowers. Usually numbers are not high enough to require control, and handpicking is sufficient for most infestations. For heavy infestations, spray pyrethrins.

Symptom: Light yellow speckles on leaves
Cause: **Spider mites**

To distinguish mite damage from sunscald (they look similar when the leaf edges turn brown), look for fine webbing on undersides of leaves. For controls see "Spider Mites" on page 286.

Most Common Hydrangea Diseases

Symptoms: Round spots on leaves; leaves
distorted and curled; plant
is stunted

Cause: **Ring spot**

Aphids, leafhoppers, and other insects can
spread viruses as they feed on your plants. For
controls see "Mosaic" on page 319.

Symptom: Grayish mold grows on flowers
and leaves

Cause: **Botrytis blight (*Botrytis cinerea*)**

Once established on a plant, this fungus
rapidly spreads to infect petioles, stems, and
entire branches. Infected stem and leaf tissues
become light brown and crack open, allowing
the fuzzy gray spores to emerge. Choose a
planting site with good air circulation. For
controls see "Botrytis Blight" on page 305.

Symptom: White, powdery coating
on leaves

Cause: **Powdery mildew
(*Erysiphe polygoni*)**

Powdery mildew may also appear on buds and
shoot tips. For controls see "Powdery Mildew"
on page 323.

Most Common Hydrangea Disorders

Symptoms: Leaves become yellow; plants
are stunted

Cause: **Soil is too alkaline**

Hydrangeas grow best in soil with a pH of 6.0
or slightly lower. Test your soil and amend it
with sulfur as indicated by the test results to
lower the pH. Mulching with pine needles
helps prevent problems.

IVIES

Hedera spp.

> ### ENGLISH IVY AT A GLANCE
>
> **Botanical Name:** *Hedera helix*
> **Height:** Groundcover, 6–8 inches; vine, to
> 40 feet
> **Spread:** To 90 feet
> **Shade Tolerance:** Full sun to full shade
> **Hardiness:** Zones 5–9
> **Preferred Soil:** Fertile, moist, well-drained,
> organic soil; tolerates acidic or alkaline

Most Common Ivy Pests

Symptom: Leaves distorted and yellowish

Cause: **Aphids**

You will see the small, pear-shaped insects on
undersides of leaves and in growing tips. For
controls see "Aphids" on page 244.

Symptom: Leaves turn yellow along
whole branch

Cause: **Scale**

Look for masses of tiny, brownish, elongated
bumps or grayish bumps on the bark. For
controls see "Most Common Tree, Shrub, and
Vine Pests" on page 168.

Symptom: Light yellow speckles on leaves

Cause: **Spider mites**

Look for fine webbing on undersides of
leaves. Both adults and nymphs feed by
sucking the juice from plant cells on undersides of leaves. For controls see "Spider Mites"
on page 286.

Most Common Ivy Diseases

Symptom: Water–soaked or raised spots
              on leaves
Cause: **Bacterial leaf spot**
             (*Xanthomonas hederae*)

Leaf spots turn brownish black and may spread to form large patches of dead tissue. For controls see "Bacterial Spot" on page 303.

Symptom: Swollen or oozing lesions
              on stems
Cause: **Canker**

Canker-causing organisms can enter stems through wounds. For controls see "Cytospora Canker" on page 310.

Symptom: Pale or brown spots on leaves
Cause: **Fungal leaf spot**

Minimize problems by choosing a planting site with good air circulation. For controls see "Beeches" on page 173.

English ivy (Hedera helix)

JUNIPERS
Juniperus spp.

CHINESE JUNIPER AT A GLANCE

Botanical Name: *Juniperus chinensis*
Height: To 50 feet (many cultivars shorter)
Spread: 15–20 feet (shorter cultivars vary in shape)
Shade Tolerance: Full sun
Hardiness: Zones 4–8
Preferred Soil: Evenly moist, well-drained soil; tolerates soils high in calcium

CREEPING JUNIPER AT A GLANCE

Botanical Name: *Juniperus horizontalis*
Height: To 2 feet
Spread: 4–10 feet
Shade Tolerance: Full sun
Hardiness: Zones 2–8
Preferred Soil: well-drained; tolerates slightly alkaline soil, sand, clay, rocky soil

EASTERN RED CEDAR AT A GLANCE

Botanical Name: *Juniperus virginiana*
Height: 40–50 feet (many cultivars shorter)
Spread: 8–20 feet (shorter cultivars vary in width)
Shade Tolerance: Full sun
Hardiness: Zones 3–9
Preferred Soil: Deep, moist loam, well-drained soil; tolerates poor soil, drought, wide pH range

Most Common Juniper Pests

Symptom: Branches stripped of needles
Cause: **Bagworms**

Bagworms hang from twigs and branches in tough, silken bags studded with plant debris. For controls see "Bagworm" on page 247.

Symptom: Needles turn yellow along whole branch
Causes: **Scale; mealybugs**

Scale are masses of tiny, brownish, elongated bumps or grayish bumps on the bark. For controls see "Most Common Tree, Shrub, and Vine Pests" on page 168. Mealybugs are small, oval insects covered with white, waxy fluff. For controls see "Mealybugs" on page 272.

Symptom: Sticky coating on foliage
Cause: **Juniper aphids**

These ⅛-inch-long, reddish brown, small, pear-shaped insects suck the plant sap. For controls see "Aphids" on page 244.

Symptom: Webbing at tips of branches
Cause: **Juniper webworms**

Look for a small, brown caterpillar feeding inside the webbing in late June. Handpick light infestations. Spray *Bacillus thuringiensis* var. *kurstaki* (BTK) or neem, first breaking open the webs to ensure spray coverage.

Symptom: Weak growth and brown tips on branches
Cause: **Red cedar bark beetles**

These beetles are ¹⁄₁₆ inch long and attack weakened trees, especially those that are newly transplanted or drought-stressed. The adult beetles chew holes in twigs and the larvae tunnel under the bark. Prune out damaged tips to remove borers and maintain healthy, well-watered plants.

Symptoms: Dead needle tips; blisters at the base of needles
Cause: **Juniper leaf midges**

These ¹⁄₁₂-inch-long maggots of tiny flies feed on the needles, causing them to die back. Prune out all infested tips. Cultivate under the plants and remove debris to control the overwintering stages.

Most Common Juniper Diseases

Symptom: Twig and branch tips turn brown in spring, dead foliage turns gray with black spots
Cause: **Twig blight**

Space new plants widely and do not plant susceptible species in heavy shade. Do all pruning in dry weather and avoid touching plants when they are wet. Resistant cultivars are available. Some examples are the Chinese junipers 'Femina' and 'Iowa' and common junipers 'Ashfordii' and 'Prostrata Aurea'.

Creeping juniper (Juniper horizontalis)

LARCHES

Larix spp.

LARCHES AT A GLANCE

Botanical Name: *Larix* spp.
Height: 40–90 feet (depends on species)
Spread: 25–40 feet (depends on species)
Shade Tolerance: Full sun
Hardiness: Zones 2–6 (varies slightly by species)
Preferred Soil: Moist, well-drained, high in organic matter

Most Common Larch Pests

Symptom: Browning, shriveled needles
Cause: **Larch casebearers**

Look very closely for tiny, cigar-shaped cases among the twigs. The reddish brown caterpillars are ¼ inch long with black heads. They live inside the cases and spend the winter on the twigs. They are usually kept in check by native parasites. For heavy infestations, spray lime-sulfur or dormant oil in the winter, when the needles are off the tree.

Symptoms: Branches defoliated; new shoots distorted
Cause: **Larch sawflies**

In June these ¾–1-inch-long, olive-gray larvae with brown spines chew the needles of larches. For heavy infestations, spray horticultural oils to control larvae (they are not true caterpillars, therefore *Bacillus thuringiensis* var. *kurstaki* [BTK] is ineffective). Clean up needles and debris under trees to remove overwintering cocoons on the ground.

Symptom: Fluffy, white patches among needles
Cause: **Woolly larch adelgids**

These ¹⁄₂₀-inch-long, sucking insects are underneath the white fluff. Spray dormant oil before the buds swell or spray summer oil.

Most Common Larch Diseases

Symptom: Oozing lesions on branches or trunk
Cause: **Larch branch canker**

Japanese larch (*L. kaempferi*) is less susceptible to larch branch canker than European larch (*L. decidua*). For controls see "Cytospora Canker" on page 310.

Symptom: Powdery orange pustules on needle undersides
Cause: **Rust (*Melampsora medusae*; *M. abietis-canadensis*)**

Rust can spread quickly during mild, wet weather. For controls see "Rust" on page 327.

European larch (<u>Larix decidua</u>*)*

LILACS

Syringa spp.

COMMON LILAC AT A GLANCE

Botanical Name: *Syringa vulgaris*
Height: 8–20 feet
Spread: 6–15 feet
Shade Tolerance: Full sun
Hardiness: Zones 3–7
Preferred Soil: Loose, well-drained, slightly acidic

MEYER LILAC AT A GLANCE

Botanical Name: *Syringa meyeri*
Height: 4–8 feet
Spread: 6–12 feet
Shade Tolerance: Full sun
Hardiness: Zones 4–7
Preferred Soil: Loose, well-drained, slightly acidic

Most Common Lilac Pests

Symptom: Leaves turn yellow along whole branch
Cause: **Scale**

Many species of scale attack lilacs. Look for clusters of tiny, whitish, grayish, purplish, or brown bumps on bark. Their feeding weakens and kills branches and makes the plants more susceptible to borer attack. For control see "Most Common Tree, Shrub, and Vine Pests" on page 168. Chinese lilacs (*Syringa* x *chinensis*) are more susceptible to scale than other lilacs. Do not spray lilacs annually with dormant oils unless necessary, as they may be damaged.

Symptoms: Holes chewed in leaves; webs may be present
Cause: **Caterpillars**

Several caterpillars spin silken tents in trees. These pests are usually kept in check by native beneficial insects. First, find out whether caterpillars are still present in or around the webs, which remain in trees long after the larvae are gone. Prune out infested branches, or remove webs and caterpillars by hand (wear gloves). For heavy infestations, spray *Bacillus thuringiensis* var. *kurstaki* (BTK) or neem early in the season while caterpillars are still small. Use sticky tree bands to catch caterpillars leaving the tree to pupate. Spray dormant oil on trees in the winter to kill overwintering eggs.

Symptom: Branches die or break
Cause: **Borers**

If borers are causing the decline of a lilac, you should see small holes bored through the bark of limbs or the trunk. Work a fine wire into the holes to kill larvae, or inject a solution of parasitic nematodes. Prune out damaged branches and provide the best of care—the best defense against borers is a vigorous tree.

Symptoms: Leaves skeletonized; webs spun around foliage
Cause: **Lilac leafminers**

The ⅜-inch-long caterpillars mine between the upper and lower surfaces of leaves early in June, then leave the tunnels to web together the foliage and chew on leaves. For heavy infestations of leafminers, spray *Bacillus thuringiensis* var. *kurstaki* (BTK) or neem when caterpillars are feeding outside the leaves before they spin webs. If spraying later, brush open the webs to ensure good coverage.

Most Common Lilac Diseases

Symptoms: Leaves spotted and withered; flowers brown and fail to open; shoots blackened

Causes: **Bacterial blight** (*Pseudomonas syringae*); **fungal blight** (*Phytophthora cactorum*)

Blights can also cause shoots to die back. You can treat both fungal and bacterial blights the same way. For controls see "Pseudomonas Leaf Blight" on page 325.

Symptom: Brown spots and holes in leaves

Cause: **Leaf blight** (*Cladosporium herbarum; Heterosporium syringae*)

Rainy weather in late spring or early summer promotes this disease. Spray with copper just after the flowers drop and again a week later. If the disease continues to spread, spray again.

Common lilac (<u>Syringa vulgaris</u>*)*

Symptom: Clusters of slender, weak shoots at branch tips

Cause: **Witches'-broom (virus)**

Leaves on the shoots that form the "broom" are about one–quarter of the normal size and are pale. There is no cure for this disease. Prune out and destroy all infected growth, cutting well below the "broom" and sterilizing tools between each cut.

Symptom: Galls on stems, crown, and roots of plant

Cause: **Crown gall**

Crown gall bacteria can enter plants through wounds caused by insects, pruning tools, and lawn-care equipment. If plants do contract the disease, dig them out, taking as much surrounding soil as possible. In cases where infection is mild and localized, you can try cutting out only the infected areas, sterilizing tools between cuts.

Symptom: White, powdery coating on leaves late in season

Cause: **Powdery mildew** (*Microsphaera alni*)

Powdery mildew is unsightly but usually not serious enough to threaten the life of your lilac. The spots enlarge quickly, covering the entire leaf, flower, or shoot. Infected tissues become pale, then turn brown and shrivel. For controls see "Powdery Mildew" on page 323.

Symptom: Leaves yellow or brown and wilt

Cause: **Verticillium wilt** (*Verticillium albo-atrum*)

Whole branches on affected plants may wilt and die. For controls see "Verticillium Wilt" on page 332.

LINDENS
Tilia s p p .

AMERICAN LINDEN/ BASSWOOD AT A GLANCE

Botanical Name: *Tilia americana*
Height: 60–80 feet
Spread: 30–60 feet
Shade Tolerance: Full sun or partial shade
Hardiness: Zones 2–7
Preferred Soil: Deep, fertile, moist, well-drained; tolerates drier, heavier soil

LITTLELEAF LINDEN AT A GLANCE

Botanical Name: *Tilia cordata*
Height: 60–80 feet
Spread: 30–60 feet
Shade Tolerance: Full sun
Hardiness: Zones 3–7
Preferred Soil: Fertile, moist, well-drained; adaptable to varying pH

Most Common Linden Pests

Symptom: Branches stripped of leaves
Cause: **Bagworms**

Bagworms hang from twigs and branches in 2½-inch-long, tough, silken bags. For controls see "Bagworm" on page 247.

Symptom: Leaves distorted and sticky
Cause: **Aphids**

Aphids do not harm most deciduous trees, but their production of honeydew is a nuisance. For controls see "Aphids" on page 244.

Symptoms: Branches die or break; trees are weak
Cause: **Borers**

If borers are causing the decline of a tree or shrub, you should see small holes bored through the bark of limbs or the trunk. For controls see "Most Common Tree, Shrub, and Vine Pests" on page 168.

Symptom: Leaves turn yellow along whole branch
Cause: **Scale**

Many species of scale attack lindens. Look for clusters of tiny, whitish, grayish, reddish, or brown bumps on bark. For controls see "Most Common Tree, Shrub, and Vine Pests" on page 168.

Symptoms: Holes chewed in leaves; webs may be present
Cause: **Caterpillars**

Several species of caterpillars, including web-forming species, attack lindens. For controls see "Most Common Tree, Shrub, and Vine Pests" on page 168.

Symptom: Large holes in leaves and flowers
Causes: **Japanese beetles; elm sawflies**

The ½-inch-long, blue-green Japanese beetles with bronze wing covers are easy to see, as is their feeding damage, which skeletonizes leaves. For controls see "Most Common Tree, Shrub, and Vine Pests" on page 168. The smooth, pale green elm sawfly larvae are 1 inch long with a black stripe down their back. Handpick light infestations on a small tree or, for out-of-reach larvae, spray insecticidal soap, neem, or pyrethrins.

Most Common Linden Diseases

Symptoms: Leaves with moist or brown
sunken spots; leaves and shoots
blackened

Cause: **Anthracnose**

This fungal disease is particularly a problem
during cool, wet springs. For controls see
"Anthracnose" on page 300.

Symptom: Leaves with powdery white
coating

Cause: **Powdery mildew**

This disease is unsightly but usually doesn't
threaten the life of your tree. For controls see
"Powdery Mildew" on page 323.

Littleleaf linden (Tilia cordata)

MAGNOLIAS
Magnolia spp.

SAUCER MAGNOLIA AT A GLANCE

Botanical Name: *Magnolia* x *soulangiana*
Height: To 25 feet
Spread: To 25 feet
Shade Tolerance: Full sun
Hardiness: Zones 5–9
Preferred Soil: Moderately fertile, deep,
moist, high in organic matter, acidic
(pH 5.0–6.5)

SOUTHERN MAGNOLIA AT A GLANCE

Botanical Name: *Magnolia grandiflora*
Height: 60–80 feet
Spread: 30–50 feet
Shade Tolerance: Full sun or partial
shade
Hardiness: Zones 6–9
Preferred Soil: Fertile, well-drained, loamy

STAR MAGNOLIA AT A GLANCE

Botanical Name: *Magnolia stellata*
Height: 15–20 feet
Spread: 10–15 feet
Shade Tolerance: Full sun
Hardiness: Zones 5–9
Preferred Soil: Fertile, moist, high in
organic matter

Most Common Magnolia Pests

Symptom: Leaves turn yellow or wilt along whole branch

Causes: **Scale; mealybugs**

Magnolias are susceptible to many different species of scale, which appear as clusters of small, grayish, whitish, purple, brown, or cottony-white bumps on the bark. For controls see "Most Common Tree, Shrub, and Vine Pests" on page 168. Mealybugs also attack magnolias. They are tiny, white, oval insects covered with powdery white fluff, usually on the trunks. Spray insecticidal soap or summer oil, especially on the affected bark (magnolia flowers do not tolerate oil sprays).

Most Common Magnolia Diseases

Symptom: Sunken lesions on trunk and branches

Cause: **Canker (*Nectria magnoliae*)**

The lesions generally start at a wound or a branch stub. The bark under the canker is often cracked and darkened and may be surrounded by a raised callus. Smaller branches are girdled quickly and then die. Canker fungi can enter a tree through wounds caused by insects, pruning tools, or lawn-care equipment. For controls see "Cytospora Canker" on page 310.

Symptoms: Fungal mycelium shows on leaf undersides; leaves are matted together

Cause: **Leaf blight (*Pellicularia koleroga*)**

Prune off and destroy branches with infected leaves and then spray once or twice with copper. Spray again the following spring, just after leaves have fully expanded.

Symptom: Leaves are spotted, turn brown, and drop prematurely

Cause: **Leaf spot**

Leaf spots may run together to cover the whole leaf. For controls see "Beeches" on page 173.

Symptom: Leaves yellow or brown and wilted

Cause: **Wilt (*Verticillium albo-atrum*)**

Wilt symptoms usually appear on the lower or outer parts of the tree first. For controls see "Verticillium Wilt" on page 332.

Symptoms: Foliage is sparse; branch tips die

Cause: **Wood rot (*Fomes geotropus; F. fasciatus*)**

Wood rot fungi can attack both living and dead trees. For controls see "Birches" on page 174.

Note

Magnolias grow best in sheltered spots, particularly in areas with late spring frosts or cold prevailing winds. If you can't provide a sheltered site, plant a windbreak to protect your tree.

Star magnolia (Magnolia stellata)

MAPLES
Acer spp.

SUGAR MAPLE AT A GLANCE

Botanical Name: *Acer saccharum*
Height: 65–85 feet
Spread: Almost as wide as tall
Shade Tolerance: Full sun or partial shade
Hardiness: Zones 3–7
Preferred Soil: Fertile, moist, well-drained, loose, slightly acidic

RED MAPLE AT A GLANCE

Botanical Name: *Acer rubrum*
Height: To 65 feet
Spread: To 45 feet
Shade Tolerance: Full sun
Hardiness: Zones 3–9
Preferred Soil: Widely tolerant; tolerates dry or rather wet soil if slightly acidic

JAPANESE MAPLE AT A GLANCE

Botanical Name: *Acer palmatum*
Height: Most 15–25 feet; some cultivars only 6–8 feet
Spread: Most 15–25 feet; 6–8-foot cultivars wider than tall
Shade Tolerance: Partial shade
Hardiness: Zones 5–8
Preferred Soil: Moist, well-drained, high in organic matter

Most Common Maple Pests

Symptom: Sticky coating on leaves
Cause: **Aphids**

Aphids do not harm maple trees, but their copious production of honeydew, which is sprayed onto leaves and objects (such as parked cars) below the tree, is a nuisance. For controls see "Aphids" on page 244.

Symptom: Fluffy white patches on twigs and branches
Cause: **Maple scale**

Several similar species of scale attack maples. Their feeding weakens and kills branches and makes the trees more susceptible to borer attack. For controls see "Most Common Tree, Shrub, and Vine Pests" on page 168. Test-spray summer oils on a few leaves before spraying, especially on Japanese, sugar, and silver maples, which may be sensitive to oil sprays.

Symptom: Bright red, greenish, or brown warts or puckers on leaves
Cause: **Gall mites**

Several species of gall mites feed on maples, producing red, greenish, or brown galls. These rarely harm the tree. Just handpick damaged leaves. For an unusually heavy infestation, spray dormant oil or lime-sulfur just before buds swell in early spring.

Symptoms: Holes chewed in leaves; webs present in foliage
Causes: **Tent caterpillars; fall webworms**

Several caterpillars spin silken tents in trees. For controls see "Most Common Tree, Shrub, and Vine Pests" on page 168.

Symptom: Holes chewed in leaves
Cause: **Caterpillars**

Several other caterpillars feed on maple leaves, but do not make webs. These are easier to control, as they are not protected by webbing. For heavy infestations, spray *Bacillus thuringiensis* var. *kurstaki* (BTK) or neem.

Most Common Maple Diseases

Symptoms: Leaves or shoots blackened; leaves with brown or moist-looking sunken spots
Cause: **Anthracnose (*Gleosporium* spp.)**

This fungal disease is particularly a problem during cool, wet springs. Anthracnose fungi cause watery, rotting spots on foliage, stems, flowers, or fruits of many plants. Infected leaves may drop prematurely. For controls see "Anthracnose" on page 300.

Symptoms: Leaves wilt; branches die back; weeping lesions show on branches and trunk
Cause: **Canker (*Phytophthora cactorum*)**

Canker fungi can enter a tree through wounds caused by insects, pruning tools, and lawn-care equipment. The lesions generally start at a wound or a branch stub. The bark under the canker is often cracked and darkened and may be surrounded by a raised callus. For controls see "Cytospora Canker" on page 310.

Symptom: Leaves develop small blisters and curl
Cause: **Leaf blister (*Taphrina* spp.)**

Leaf blister usually isn't serious enough to threaten the life of your tree. For controls see "Leaf Blister" on page 316.

Symptoms: Spots on leaves; leaves yellow and wilt
Cause: **Verticillium wilt (*Verticillium albo-atrum*)**

Wilt symptoms often appear on the lower or outer parts of the tree first. For controls see "Verticillium Wilt" on page 332.

Most Common Maple Disorders

Symptom: Leaf margins are yellow or brown and dry
Cause: **Leaf scorch**

Leaf scorch is caused by lack of water or by heat reflected from surrounding pavement. Newly planted trees are particularly susceptible. Prevent damage and help affected plants recover by keeping the soil evenly moist and by mulching with organic matter to keep the roots cool.

Japanese maple (Acer palmatum)

MOUNTAIN ASHES

Sorbus spp.

EUROPEAN MOUNTAIN ASH AT A GLANCE

Botanical Name: *Sorbus aucuparia*
Height: 20–40 feet
Spread: 13–26 feet
Shade Tolerance: Full sun or partial shade
Hardiness: Zones 4–7
Preferred Soil: Loamy, well-drained, acidic; intolerant of chalky or compacted soils

KOREAN MOUNTAIN ASH AT A GLANCE

Botanical Name: *Sorbus alnifolia*
Height: 40–50 feet
Spread: 20–30 feet
Shade Tolerance: Full sun
Hardiness: Zones 4–7
Preferred Soil: Any well-drained soil; very tolerent of varying pH

Most Common Mountain Ash Pests

See also "Apples" on page 71.

Symptom: Leaves distorted and sticky
Cause: **Aphids**

Aphids feed in clusters on new growth. Both adults and nymphs suck plant sap. Their feeding usually causes distorted leaves, buds, branch tips, and flowers. Aphids excrete a sweet, sticky honeydew. This allows sooty mold to grow, which is unsightly and blocks light from the leaves. For controls see "Aphids" on page 244.

Symptoms: Rough, cracked bark; cottony, white fluff around edges
Cause: **Woolly apple aphids**

These aphids feed on twigs and branches, causing galled, open cracks in the bark. For controls see "Apples" on page 71.

Symptom: Reddish blisters on undersides of leaves
Cause: **Pearleaf blister mites**

You will need a magnifying lens to see these tiny gall mites inside the blisters. For controls see "Pears" on page 94.

Symptoms: Tree is weak; no pests or disease are obvious
Causes: **Roundheaded apple tree borers; other borers**

Carefully examine the base of the trunk for sawdust and holes in the bark. For controls see "Apples" on page 71.

Symptom: Leaves turn yellow along whole branch
Cause: **Scale**

Look for tiny, grayish or brown bumps on bark. For controls see "Most Common Tree, Shrub, and Vine Pests" on page 168.

Symptom: Large holes in leaves
Causes: **Japanese beetles; mountain ash sawflies**

The ½-inch-long, blue-green Japanese beetles with bronze wing covers are easy to see, as is their feeding damage, which skeletonizes leaves. For controls see "Most Common Tree, Shrub, and Vine Pests" on page 168. Sluglike green sawfly larvae also skeletonize leaves in early summer. Wash the ¼-inch-long larvae from leaves with a strong spray of water, or spray insecticidal soap or pyrethrins.

Most Common Mountain Ash Diseases

Symptom: Dark-colored, rough-textured lesions on branches

Cause: **Fire blight (*Erwinia amylovora*)**

This devastating disease can spread quickly. For controls see "Fire Blight" on page 314.

Symptom: Oozing lesions on branches and trunk

Cause: **Canker**

Canker fungi can enter a tree through wounds caused by insects, pruning tools, and lawn-care equipment. For controls see "Cytospora Canker" on page 310.

European mountain ash (Sorbus aucuparia)

OAKS
Quercus spp.

LIVE OAK
AT A GLANCE

Botanical Name: *Quercus virginiana*
Height: 40–80 feet
Spread: 60–100 feet
Shade Tolerance: Full sun
Hardiness: Zones 7–10
Preferred Soil: Adapts well to various soils

PIN OAK
AT A GLANCE

Botanical Name: *Quercus palustris*
Height: 60–70 feet
Spread: 25–40 feet
Shade Tolerance: Full sun
Hardiness: Zones 5–8
Preferred Soil: Deep, moist, well-drained soil with a pH of 5.5–6.5; tolerates many soils, including wet, if pH is not alkaline

WHITE OAK
AT A GLANCE

Botanical Name: *Quercus alba*
Height: 60–80 feet
Spread: Equal to or greater than height
Shade Tolerance: Full sun
Hardiness: Zones 3–8
Preferred Soil: Deep, moist soil with a pH of 5.5–6.5; tolerates many soils if well-drained

Most Common Oak Pests

Symptom: Leaves turn yellow along
whole branch

Cause: **Scale**

Look for clusters of tiny grayish or brown bumps on bark. Their feeding weakens and kills branches. For controls see "Most Common Tree, Shrub, and Vine Pests" on page 168. Red oak may be sensitive to summer oil sprays; test-spray first.

Symptom: Swellings or distortion on
leaves, twigs, or branches

Cause: **Gall wasps**

Many different galls of all sizes, colors, and textures are found on oaks; many are quite beautiful. These generally do no harm to the tree. If there are too many to tolerate, prune out new galls before the occupants have emerged.

Symptoms: Holes chewed in leaves; webs
may be present

Cause: **Caterpillars**

Many species of caterpillars attack oaks. Several caterpillars spin silken tents in trees. These pests are usually kept in check by native beneficial insects. For controls see "Most Common Tree, Shrub, and Vine Pests" on page 168.

Symptom: Whitish gray blotches on leaves

Cause: **Oak lace bugs**

Lace bugs are ⅒-inch-long, oval bugs with lacy wings. Look on undersides of leaves for the specks of dark excrement that show lace bugs have been feeding. Maintain vigorous, healthy plant growth. For controls see "Lace Bugs" on page 270.

Symptom: Light yellow speckles on leaves

Cause: **Oak mites**

Look for fine webbing on undersides of leaves. For controls see "Spider Mites" on page 286.

Symptom: Branches or whole tree
defoliated

Cause: **Gypsy moths**

These distinctive caterpillars grow up to 2½ inches long and are covered with tufts of long hair. If you live in an eastern region where gypsy moths are established, trees may be defoliated in a year of peak populations. Trees will leaf out again. To reduce damage, spray *Bacillus thuringiensis* var. *kurstaki* (BTK) or neem two or three times at 1- to 2-week intervals during the caterpillars' spring development period. Wrap tree bands around trunks and check daily to destroy hiding caterpillars.

Symptoms: Branches die or break; trees
are weak

Cause: **Borers**

Several species of borers attack oaks. If borers are causing the decline of an oak, you will see small holes bored through the bark of limbs or the trunk. For controls see "Most Common Tree, Shrub, and Vine Pests" on page 168.

Most Common Oak Diseases

Symptoms: Lesions on twigs and branches;
leaves wilt and die

Cause: **Blight (*Diplodia longispora*)**

Oak blight is spread by insects feeding on the leaves. This disease can kill the tree. Prune off all infected branches, cutting at least 6–12 inches below the infection site. Healthy trees resist infections.

Symptom: Circular, raised, pale-colored blisters on upper leaf surfaces
Cause: **Leaf blister (*Taphrina coerulescens*)**

Leaf blisters are unsightly but usually not serious enough to threaten the health of your tree. For controls see "Leaf Blister" on page 316.

Symptom: Brown, yellow, or dead spots on leaves, usually showing late in the season
Cause: **Leaf spot**

Leaf spots can run together to cover the whole leaf. For controls see "Beeches" on page 173.

Symptom: Honey-colored mushrooms sprout at base of tree trunk
Cause: **Root rot (*Armillaria mellea*)**

Keeping trees healthy with good general care will go a long way toward preventing this disease. For controls see "Armillaria Root Rot" on page 301.

Symptom: Leaves yellow, brown, and droop before dropping
Cause: **Wilt (*Ceratocystis fagacearum*)**

Wilt attacks treetops first, spreading rapidly and killing the tree. Insects and nearby infected roots spread the disease. There is no control. Cut out and destroy all affected branches, cutting well below obvious symptoms. Destroy heavily infected trees, taking roots and surrounding soil. Do not replant with an oak.

Symptom: Shelflike growths on tree
Cause: **Wood rot**

Wood rots can attack both living and dead trees. For controls see "Birches" on page 174.

Symptom: Moist, sunken spots on leaves
Cause: **Anthracnose**

This fungal disease is particularly a problem during cold, wet springs. For controls see "Anthracnose" on page 300.

Symptom: Sunken, moist-looking lesions on branches and trunk
Cause: **Canker**

Canker fungi can enter trees through wounds caused by insects or tools. For controls see "Cytospora Canker" on page 310.

Symptom: White, powdery coating on leaves
Cause: **Powdery mildew (*Microsphaera* spp.; *Sphaerotheca* spp.)**

Powdery mildew is unsightly but usually isn't serious enough to threaten the life of your tree. For controls see "Powdery Mildew" on page 323.

Oak (*Quercus* sp.)

PINES

Pinus spp.

EASTERN WHITE PINE AT A GLANCE

Botanical Name: *Pinus strobus*
Height: 50–80 feet
Spread: 20–40 feet
Shade Tolerance: Full sun or light shade
Hardiness: Zones 3–9
Preferred Soil: Fertile, moist, well-drained, neutral to slightly acidic; tolerates a wide range of soils

SCOTCH PINE AT A GLANCE

Botanical Name: *Pinus sylvestris*
Height: 30–60 feet (shorter cultivars available)
Spread: 30–40 feet (shorter cultivars vary in shape)
Shade Tolerance: Full sun
Hardiness: Zones 3–8
Preferred Soil: Tolerates most well-drained soils; best in acidic soil

SWISS MOUNTAIN PINE/ MUGO PINE AT A GLANCE

Botanical Name: *Pinus mugo, P. mugo* var. *mugo*
Height: 15–20 feet (most popular cultivar, to 3 feet)
Spread: 20–25 feet (most popular cultivar, to 3 feet)
Shade Tolerance: Full sun or partial shade
Hardiness: Zones 3–7
Preferred Soil: Deep, fertile, moist, well-drained

Most Common Pine Pests

Symptom: Branches stripped of needles
Cause: **Bagworms**

Bagworms hang from twigs and branches in tough, silken bags studded with needles and plant debris. For controls see "Bagworm" on page 247.

Symptoms: Terminal shoots crooked; dead tips
Cause: **White pine weevils**

This is a particular pest of young, ornamental pines. The grayish weevils lay their eggs in the stem of the leader and the fat, white grubs developing inside eventually girdle and kill the leader. In summer, prune damaged leaders back just above the first whorl of undamaged branches (burn the infested leaders). Prune the tips off all but one of the strongest branches in the top whorl, which will become the new top. Protect pines until they are 30 feet tall by spraying the terminals regularly throughout April and May with pyrethrins.

Symptom: Bronzed or grayish needles that dry and drop
Cause: **Spruce spider mites**

These tiny mites spin webbing between needles, especially on undersides of branches. For controls see "Spider Mites" on page 286.

Symptom: Needles dead at tips of branches
Causes: **Pine tip moths; pine shoot moths; spruce budworms**

These tiny caterpillars grow up to ¾ inch long and are hard to see. They mine into needles, as well as into buds, cones, and twigs. Handpick the damaged tips and spray *Bacillus thuringiensis* var. *kurstaki* (BTK) or neem. For spruce budworm controls see "Firs" on page 189.

Symptom: Needles covered with tiny, white specks

Cause: **Pine needle scale**

In heavy infestations, the needles turn yellow, are stunted, and may drop early. During June, when the young, $\frac{1}{10}$-inch-long crawlers are present, blast them repeatedly from needles with a strong spray of water or spray insecticidal soap. Native lady beetles and parasites usually control scale, but where infestations are usually heavy, spray summer oil in April before new buds begin to open.

Symptom: Wounds in bark, needles turn yellow

Cause: **Beetles**

Several species of weevils and other beetles attack pines. Maintain vigorous trees with adequate irrigation and fertile soil. Replace heavily infested trees.

Symptom: Branches defoliated

Cause: **Conifer sawflies**

Look for caterpillar-like, grayish green larvae, which are ¼–½ inch long and are usually feeding in groups. Handpick larvae from small trees. For heavy infestations, spray summer oil or neem to control larvae. Spread a ground sheet under tall trees to catch larvae as they drop to the ground to pupate, and destroy them daily.

Most Common Pine Diseases

Symptom: Needles redden and twist or pucker, then drop

Cause: **Blight**

Blight may kill entire shoots and is most common in trees located in shady areas where foliage doesn't dry quickly enough. Provide wide spacing when planting. Prune to allow air circulation and light exposure on your trees. Water only the soil, not the needles.

Symptom: Galls form on branches and trunk

Cause: **Blister rust (*Cronartium quercuum*; *C. comandrae*)**

Blister rust galls can enlarge to girdle the tree, eventually killing it. Cut out all galls the moment you see them. Cut down and destroy seriously infected trees.

Scotch pine (Pinus sylvestris)

Symptom: Reddish orange pustules on
               needles
Cause: **Rust (*Coleosporium asterum*)**

Whitish blisters on the needles are an early sign
of rust. For controls see "Rust" on page 327.

Symptoms: Cankers develop on branches;
                branch tips die; needles brown;
                growth stunted
Cause: **Tip blight (*Diplodia pinea*)**

On young trees, tip blight can begin just below
the soil surface on the trunk. Look for
reddening of the bark and dark streaks on
underlying wood. Destroy infected seedlings.
Older trees are more likely to have infections
on only a branch or two. Prune infected wood
in dry weather. Spray with copper. In spring,
begin spraying when the buds open and
continue, at weekly intervals, until needles have
completely emerged from their sheaths.

Symptom: Shelflike growths on trunk
Cause: **Wood rot**

Wood rot fungi can attack both living and dead
trees. For controls see "Birches" on page 174

Symptom: Needles are distorted,
               turn yellow, and drop
Cause: **Needle cast**

These diseases are most serious on young trees.
For controls see "Needle Cast" on page 320.

Symptom: Sunken or swollen lesions on
               branches and trunk
Cause: **Canker**

Canker fungi can enter trees through wounds
caused by insects and tools. For controls see
"Cytospora Canker" on page 310.

POPLARS
Populus spp.

EASTERN COTTONWOOD AT A GLANCE

Botanical Name: *Populus deltoides*
Height: 75–100 feet
Spread: 50–75 feet
Shade Tolerance: Full sun
Hardiness: Zones 3–9
Preferred Soil: Thrives in moist or even
    wet soil; tolerates drier soils, salts, and
    pollutants

QUAKING ASPEN AT A GLANCE

Botanical Name: *Populus tremuloides*
Height: 40–50 feet
Spread: 20–30 feet
Shade Tolerance: Full sun
Hardiness: Zones 2–6
Preferred Soil: Thrives in moist soils
    ranging from loam to rock or clay

WHITE POPLAR AT A GLANCE

Botanical Name: *Populus alba*
Height: 40–70 feet
Spread: 40–70 feet
Shade Tolerance: Full sun
Hardiness: Zones 3–8
Preferred Soil: Deep, moist, loam; very
    adaptable and tolerant of pollutants
    and salts

Most Common Poplar Pests

Symptom: Swellings on the leaf stems
or twigs
Cause: **Gall aphids**

Several species of gall-forming aphids attack poplars, causing round, irregular, or twisted galls on the leaf stems or twigs. These usually cause little damage, but where infestations are heavy, spray valuable trees with lime-sulfur in the winter to control overwintering stages.

Symptom: Leaves turn yellow along branch
Cause: **Scale**

Many species of scale attack poplars. Look for clusters of whitish, grayish, reddish, or brown bumps on bark. For controls see "Most Common Tree, Shrub, and Vine Pests" on page 168.

Symptoms: Holes chewed in leaves; webs
may be present
Causes: **Caterpillars; leaf beetles**

Several species of caterpillars, including web-forming species, attack poplars. For controls see "Most Common Tree, Shrub, and Vine Pests" on page 168. Leaf beetles skeletonize leaves. Control adults and larvae by spraying pyrethrins or insecticidal soap.

Symptoms: Leaves turn yellow; upper
branches die
Cause: **Bronze birch borers**

The whitish larvae of this serious birch pest burrow in the inner bark, leaving zigzag tunnels. They start at the top of the tree and often go unnoticed until it is too late. If damage seems confined to the top of the tree, try pruning out all affected wood.

Most Common Poplar Diseases

Symptoms: Brown spots on leaves; leaves
drop prematurely
Cause: **Leaf spot (various fungi, particularly *Marssonina populi*)**

Leaf spot fungi can spread to cover whole leaves but is rarely life threatening to the tree. Rake up and destroy all fallen leaves at the end of the season to reduce the problem next year. To control, spray with copper in late spring.

Symptom: Orange, powdery pustules on
leaf undersides
Cause: **Rust (*Melampsora medusae*;
M. abietis-candensis)**

The first symptoms of rust diseases are lack of vigor and slow growth. Whitish blisters on leaf undersides are also an early sign of rust. For controls see "Rust" on page 327.

Eastern cottonwood (Populus deltoides)

Symptom: Sunken or swollen lesions on branches and trunk
Cause: **Canker**

Canker fungi can enter trees through wounds caused by insects, pruning tools, and lawn-care equipment. The bark under the canker is often cracked and darkened and may be surrounded by a raised callus. For controls see "Cytospora Canker" on page 310.

Symptom: Yellow, brown, and pale-colored blisters on leaves
Cause: **Leaf blister (*Taphrina aurea*)**

Mild, moist weather promotes the development of this disease. To reduce disease incidence, rake up all dropped leaves and burn or destroy them. Do not put them in a slowly decomposing leaf compost since temperatures will be too low to kill the organism. In late spring, just before bud break, spray severely infected trees with lime-sulfur or Bordeaux mix.

Symptom: White, powdery coating on leaves
Cause: **Powdery mildew**

Powdery mildew is unsightly but usually isn't serious enough to threaten the health of your tree. Powdery white or gray spots are usually the first symptoms you will notice. The spots enlarge quickly, covering the entire leaf, flower, or shoot. Infected tissues become pale, then turn brown and shrivel. Plant in well-drained soil, and space widely enough for good air circulation. Compost all plant debris. Spraying compost tea on leaves every 2–4 weeks can help prevent attack. Pick off and destroy infected plant tissues. Baking soda or baking soda plus oil sprays (see "Oil Sprays" on page 361) are often an effective control.

PRIVETS
Ligustrum spp.

BORDER PRIVET AT A GLANCE

Botanical Name: *Ligustrum obtusifolium*
Height: 10–12 feet
Spread: 12–15 feet
Shade Tolerance: Full sun to full shade
Hardiness: Zones 4–7
Preferred Soil: Tolerates various soils if well-drained

JAPANESE PRIVET AT A GLANCE

Botanical Name: *Ligustrum japonicum*
Height: 6–12 feet
Spread: 6–8 feet
Shade Tolerance: Full sun to full shade
Hardiness: Zones 7–9
Preferred Soil: Tolerates various soils if well-drained; salt-tolerant

Most Common Privet Pests

Symptom: Dusty, grayish–looking foliage
Cause: **Privet thrips**

You can control these $\frac{1}{20}$-inch-long yellowish, elongated insects with sprays of summer oil.

Symptom: Leaves yellowish and curled lengthwise
Cause: **Privet aphids**

You will see these $\frac{1}{10}$-inch-long, pear-shaped insects on undersides of leaves and in growing tips. For controls see "Aphids" on page 244.

Symptom: Leaves turn yellow along whole branch

Cause: **Scale**

Look for masses of tiny, brownish, elongated bumps or grayish bumps on the bark. For controls see "Most Common Tree, Shrub, and Vine Pests" on page 168.

Symptom: Notched edges on new leaves and shoots

Cause: **Japanese weevils**

Look for ¼-inch-long, brownish snout beetles on the leaves. These indicate the presence of larvae, which feed on the roots. Privet is a favored host plant for these weevils and they may be very damaging. For heavy infestations, spray foliage with pyrethrins. Drench roots with a solution of insect parasitic nematodes to control larvae.

Most Common Privet Diseases

Symptom: Leaves are spotted, turn brown, and drop prematurely

Cause: **Leaf spot**

Leaf spots can merge to cover whole leaves. Leaf spot is fairly common but rarely life threatening to the tree. Rake up and destroy all fallen leaves at the end of the season to reduce the problem next year. To control leaf spot, spray with copper in late spring.

Symptom: Small, sunken spots on leaves

Cause: **Anthracnose (*Glomerella cingulata*)**

This fungal disease is particularly a problem during cool, wet springs. Infected leaves may drop prematurely, and the entire plant may be defoliated. For controls see "Anthracnose" on page 300.

Symptom: White, powdery coating on leaves

Cause: **Powdery mildew (*Microsphaera alni*)**

Powdery mildew is unsightly but usually isn't serious enough to threaten the health of your plant. Spots enlarge quickly, covering entire leaves. Infected tissues become pale, then turn brown and shrivel. To prevent or reduce powdery mildew incidence, choose resistant cultivars. Plant in well-drained soil, and space widely enough for good air circulation. Compost all plant debris. Spraying compost tea on leaves every 2–4 weeks can help prevent attack. Pick off and destroy infected plant tissues. Baking soda or baking soda plus oil sprays (see "Oil Sprays" on page 361) are often an effective control.

Variegated privet (<u>Ligustrum ovalifolium</u> 'Aureum')

RHODODENDRONS AND AZALEAS

Rhododendron spp.

DECIDUOUS AZALEAS AT A GLANCE

Botanical Name: *Rhododendron* spp. and hybrids

Height: 2–8 feet

Spread: 2–10 feet

Shade Tolerance: Partial or light shade

Hardiness: Zones 5–8; some cultivars hardy in Zones 4 and 9

Preferred Soil: Fertile, moist, well-drained, high in organic matter, somewhat acidic (pH 5.0–6.0)

EVERGREEN AZALEAS AT A GLANCE

Botanical Name: *Rhododendron* spp. and hybrids

Height: 6 inches–8 feet

Spread: 1–8 feet

Shade Tolerance: Partial or light shade

Hardiness: Zones 7–9; some cultivars hardy to Zone 5

Preferred Soil: See "Deciduous Azaleas at a Glance"

RHODODENDRONS AT A GLANCE

Botanical Name: *Rhododendron* spp. and hybrids

Height: 2–10 feet

Spread: 2–10 feet

Shade Tolerance: Partial or light shade

Hardiness: Zones 5–8; some cultivars hardy to Zone 4

Preferred Soil: See "Deciduous Azaleas at a Glance"

Most Common Rhododendron Pests

Symptom: Half-circle notches in leaf edges
Cause: **Black vine weevils**

These oval, brownish black weevils are $\frac{1}{3}$ inch long and feed on the leaf edges, while their larvae feed on the roots. Handpick weevils at night or knock them onto a ground sheet and destroy. Lay boards under bushes in April and May when adults are emerging and check under them daily for weevils. For heavy infestations, apply parasitic nematodes to roots to control larvae. Band trunks with plastic wrap painted with sticky trap glue to intercept adults as they emerge. Plant resistant cultivars such as 'P. J. M.', 'Jock', 'Sapphire', 'Rose Elf', 'Cilpinense', and 'Lucky Strike'.

Symptom: Whitish spots on leaves; black flecks on undersides
Cause: **Lace bugs**

Lace bugs are tiny, oval bugs with lacy wings. Look on undersides of leaves for specks of dark excrement. Maintain vigorous plants. For heavy infestations, in mid-May and again 10 days later, spray insecticidal soap or pyrethrins to control both adults and nymphs. Summer oils are also effective on trees and plants that can tolerate oil sprays.

Symptom: Leaves turn yellow along whole branch
Cause: **Scale**

Look for clusters of tiny, grayish or brown bumps on bark. Their feeding weakens and kills branches. For controls see "Most Common Tree, Shrub, and Vine Pests" on page 168. Summer oils may cause leaf spotting on rhododendrons and azaleas; test-spray on a few leaves first.

Symptom: Dead or weakened branches
Cause: **Rhododendron borers**

The ½-inch-long larvae of this wasplike moth bore inside the main stems, scarring or killing the branches. Prune out all affected branches and seal the cut surfaces with grafting wax to prevent more borers from entering. Give plants the best of care—the best defense against borers is a vigorous plant.

Symptom: Yellow, mottled leaves with rolled edges
Cause: **Rhododendron whiteflies**

If you look closely, you can probably see the ¹⁄₂₀-inch-long, white adults resting on undersides of leaves on the top of the plant. The pale green scalelike nymphs live on undersides of leaves. They secrete honeydew that makes leaves sticky and promotes growth of sooty molds. Natural enemies usually control these. For heavy infestations, spray insecticidal soap, neem, or summer oil on a cloudy day. Test insecticidal soap and oil sprays on a few leaves before applying to entire plants.

Most Common Rhododendron Diseases

Symptom: Generalized spotting on plant
Cause: **Blight (many fungi)**

Rhododendrons species are quite susceptible to blights. Some, such as flower petal blight (*Ovulinia azaleae*), attack the flowers, while others infect leaves and wood. Good sanitation is crucial. Destroy infected branches. Do not water with overhead sprinklers, particularly when in flower. Plant in lean soil and don't overfertilize. Copper sprays are effective against some of these diseases. Spray when spotting begins and again 2 weeks later if the outbreak is serious.

Hybrid rhododendron (Rhododendron vireyas)

Symptom: Leaves yellow and wilt
Cause: **Wilt (*Phytophthora cinnamomi*)**

Choosing a planting site with good drainage will help to prevent this problem. For controls see "Root Rot" on page 326.

Symptom: New growth dries out and dies
Cause: **Dieback (*Phytophthora cactorum*)**

Dieback can also cause leaves to brown and wilt. For controls see "Birches" on page 174.

Symptom: Galls form on stems
Cause: **Crown gall**

This bacteria can enter plants through wounds. For controls see "Crown Gall" on page 309.

Symptom: White, powdery growth on leaves
Cause: **Powdery mildew (*Microsphaera alni*)**

Good air circulation can help to prevent powdery mildew. For controls see "Powdery Mildew" on page 323.

Symptom: Yellow or brown pustules on leaf
undersides
Cause: **Rust (*Pucciniastrum vacinii*)**

This rust fungus also attacks hemlocks, so they
should not be planted within 100 yards or so
of each other. The first symptoms of rust
diseases you will notice are general lack of
vigor and slow growth. For controls see "Rust"
on page 327.

Symptom: Honey-colored mushrooms
sprout at base of bush
Cause: **Shoestring root rot
(*Armillaria mellea*)**

Keeping plants healthy can minimize the
development of this disease. For controls see
"Armillaria Root Rot" on page 301.

Most Common Rhododendron Disorders

Symptoms: Leaves yellow; plant loses vigor
Cause: **Iron deficiency**

Iron deficiencies are usually caused by too
alkaline a soil. Members of this family prefer a
low pH, from about 5.0–6.0. To adjust,
sprinkle ¼ cup of elemental sulfur onto the
surface of the soil before you mulch the
plants. Highly acidic mulches such as pine
needles also help to correct the problem. In
serious cases, spray leaves with an iron chelate.

Symptom: Outer leaves or shoot tips of
plant are brown and dry
in spring
Cause: **Winter injury**

Drying winter winds can damage azaleas and
rhododendrons. For controls see "Winter
Injury" on page 340.

ROSES

Rosa spp. and hybrids

CLIMBING ROSES AT A GLANCE

Botanical Name: *Rosa* hybrids (climbers)
Height: 6–8 feet; some to 20 feet
Spread: 6–15 feet
Shade Tolerance: Full sun; partial shade in
hottest summers
Hardiness: Zones 5–8
Preferred Soil: Fertile, moist, well-drained,
slightly acidic; tolerant of any
reasonably good soil

HYBRID TEA AND OTHER GARDEN ROSES AT A GLANCE

Botanical Name: *Rosa* hybrids
Height: 3–6 feet
Spread: 2–4 feet
Shade Tolerance: Full sun; partial shade in
hottest summers
Hardiness: Zones 5–9
Preferred Soil: Fertile, moist, well-drained,
high in organic matter, slightly acidic;
tolerant of any reasonably good soil

RUGOSA ROSES AND OTHER SHRUB ROSES AT A GLANCE

Botanical Name: *Rosa rugosa*, other *Rosa*
spp. and hybrids
Height: 4–8 feet
Spread: 4–8 feet
Shade Tolerance: Full sun; partial shade in
hottest summers
Hardiness: Zones 2–10 (varies by species)
Preferred Soil: Fertile, moist, well-drained,
high in organic matter, slightly acidic;
tolerant of any reasonably good soil;
R. rugosa is drought-tolerant

Most Common Rose Pests

Symptom: Leaves distorted and sticky
Cause: **Aphids**

Several species of aphids attack roses and are usually present in crowded clusters along stems and new shoots. For controls see "Aphids" on page 244.

Symptom: Light yellow speckles on leaves
Cause: **Spider mites**

Look for fine webbing on undersides of leaves. Spider mites are most damaging in hot, dry weather. For controls see "Spider Mites" on page 286.

Symptom: Leaves turn yellow along
               whole branch
Cause: **Scale**

Check for clusters of tiny, grayish or brown bumps on bark. Their feeding weakens and kills branches. For controls see "Most Common Tree, Shrub, and Vine Pests" on page 168.

Symptom: Large holes in leaves and flowers
Causes: **Japanese beetles; rose sawflies**

Roses are a favorite host plant for Japanese beetles. These ½-inch-long, blue-green beetles with bronze wing covers are easy to see, as is their feeding damage, which skeletonizes leaves. Knock beetles onto groundsheets early in the morning and destroy them. Apply milky disease or parasitic nematodes to the lawn for long-term control. The sluglike larvae of several species of rose sawflies skeletonize leaves in early summer. Washing larvae from leaves with a strong spray of water is very effective, or spray insecticidal soap, neem, or pyrethrins.

Symptom: Chewing damage on leaves and
               flowers
Cause: **Rose chafers**

Look for small, reddish brown beetles with yellow hairs on their wing covers feeding on leaves and flowers. Usually chafer numbers are not high enough to require spraying; handpicking is sufficient for most infestations. For heavy infestations, spray pyrethrins.

Symptoms: Holes in flowers; flowers
               don't open
Causes: **Rose curculios; rose leaf beetles**

Rose curculios are ¼-inch-long, bright red, snout beetles. Rose leaf beetles are even smaller, just ⅕-inch-long, blue-green beetles. Both chew petals and tunnel into flower buds. Handpick beetles and prune off damaged buds. For heavy infestations, spray pyrethrins.

'Iceberg' rose (<u>Rosa</u> 'Iceberg')

Symptoms: Dried brown edges on flowers;
              flowers may not open
Cause: **Thrips**

You will need a magnifying lens to see these quick, minute, yellowish brown insects hiding in crevices between the petals. Their sucking damages flowers, causing scars, streaks, and distortions, as well as browning edges. For heavy infestations, spray neem, insecticidal soap, or pyrethrins.

Symptom: Tips of shoots distorted and
             blackened
Cause: **Rose midges**

The 1/12-inch-long, pale orange larvae of these midges feed in leaf and flower buds, causing them to die back. There are many generations each season; diligent pruning and hand picking to remove damaged buds is the best form of control.

Most Common Rose Diseases

Symptoms: Small, black spots on leaves;
              spots develop tan centers as
              they age
Cause: **Anthracnose**
              (*Sphaceloma rosarum*)

Anthracnose spots may run together and cover the entire leaf. Spots darken and merge as they age, covering the entire leaf in some cases. For controls see "Anthracnose" on page 300.

Symptom: Round, black spots with fringed
             margins on leaves
Cause: **Black spot (*Diplocarpon rosae*)**

Hybrid tea, floribunda, and grandiflora roses are particularly susceptible to black spot. For controls see "Black Spot" on page 304.

Symptoms: Flower buds droop and don't
              open; stems have lesions; gray
              mold appears
Cause: **Botrytis blight (*Botrytis cinerea*)**

This blight also attacks already-open flowers. For controls see "Botrytis Blight" on page 305.

Symptom: Gall-like growths on stems,
             near soil line
Cause: **Crown gall**

Galls can form on upper stems and on roots. For controls see "Crown Gall" on page 309.

Symptom: White, powdery coating
             on leaves
Cause: **Powdery mildew (*Sphaerotheca*
             pannosa var. *rosae*)**

This disease spreads quickly to cover whole leaves, stems, and buds. For controls see "Powdery Mildew" on page 323.

Symptom: Small orange or yellow
             pustules on plant
Cause: **Rust (*Phragmidium* spp.)**

Minimize rust problems by choosing a site with good air circulation. For controls see "Rust" on page 327.

Symptoms: Delayed shoot growth in spring;
              downward rolling of leaves;
              abnormal growth
Cause: **Spring dwarf virus**

Spring dwarf is one of several viruses that infect roses. These diseases are usually transmitted during the propagation process. Always inspect plants well before buying. Other viral diseases are mosaic, yellow mosaic, and streak. Destroy all infected plants.

SPIREA

Spiraea spp.

BRIDALWREATH SPIREA AT A GLANCE

Botanical Name: *Spiraea prunifolia*
Height: 4–9 feet
Spread: 6–8 feet
Shade Tolerance: Full sun
Hardiness: Zones 5–9
Preferred Soil: Tolerates many soils if they are moist and well-drained

BUMALD SPIREA AT A GLANCE

Botanical Name: *Spiraea* x *bumalda*
Height: 2–3 feet
Spread: 3–5 feet
Shade Tolerance: Full sun
Hardiness: Zones 4–8
Preferred Soil: Tolerates many soils if they are well-drained

VANHOUTTE SPIREA AT A GLANCE

Botanical Name: *Spiraea* x *vanhouttei*
Height: 6–8 feet; dwarf, to 5 feet
Spread: 10–12 feet
Shade Tolerance: Full sun
Hardiness: Zones 3–8
Preferred Soil: Loamy, moist, well-drained

Most Common Spirea Pests

Symptom: Leaves turn yellow along whole branch
Cause: **Scale**

Look for clusters of grayish or brown bumps on the bark. To control scale crawlers in midsummer, spray summer oil or insecticidal soap, but only for heavy infestations because these sprays will harm the many species of native beneficial insects that usually control scale. Always text-spray oils on a branch first to check for damage. Do not use oil sprays on blue spruce or junipers since it removes the blue "bloom" on the needles.

Symptoms: Leaves distorted and sticky
Causes: **Aphids**

Aphids tend to feed in clusters on new growth. Their feeding usually causes distorted leaves, buds, branch tips, and flowers. Severely infested leaves and flowers may drop. As they feed, aphids excrete a sweet, sticky honeydew onto leaves below. This allows sooty mold to grow, which is unsightly and blocks light from the leaves. For controls see "Aphids" on page 244.

Symptoms: Holes chewed in leaves; webs may be present
Cause: **Caterpillars**

Several caterpillars spin silken tents in trees. For controls see "Most Common Tree, Shrub, and Vine Pests" on page 168.

Symptom: Leaves at branch tips rolled together with fine webs
Cause: **Obliquebanded leafrollers**

You will see these ⅜–1-inch-long, green caterpillars with brown heads feeding inside the rolled-up leaves, safe from predators and sprays. Handpick caterpillars in a light infestation. Where infestations are heavy, spray *Bacillus thuringiensis* var. *kurstaki* (BTK) or neem early in spring before the caterpillars roll the leaves.

Symptom: Branches die or break; shrubs are weak
Cause: **Borers**

If borers are causing the decline of a shrub, you should see small holes bored through the bark of limbs or the trunk. Work a fine wire into the holes to kill larvae, or inject a solution of insect parasitic nematodes. Prune out damaged branches and provide the best of care.

Most Common Spirea Diseases

Symptom: Plant stunted and grows poorly
Cause: **Root knot nematodes**

If you can find no sign of disease or pest infestation or any explanation in soil or watering conditions, the problem may be a nematode infestation in the roots. If so, you will see the small, hard galls on the roots. There is no cure; you must pull and discard the plant. Replant with another tolerant species. For more information see "Nematodes, Root Knot" on page 322.

Bridalwreath spirea (Spiraea prunifolia)

Symptom: Yellow, brown, or dead spots on leaves
Cause: **Leaf spot (many fungi)**

Leaf spots can merge to cover whole leaves. Rake up and destroy all fallen leaves at the end of the season to reduce the problem next year. To control leaf spot spray with copper in late spring.

Symptom: White, powdery coating on leaves
Cause: **Powdery mildew**

Powdery mildew is unsightly but usually not serious enough to threaten the life of your plant. Powdery white or gray spots are usually the first symptoms you will notice. The spots enlarge quickly, covering the entire leaf, flower, or shoot. Infected tissues become pale, then turn brown and shrivel. For controls see "Powdery Mildew" on page 323.

Symptoms: Branches have dark, rough cankers; leaves and twigs die
Cause: **Fire blight (*Erwinia amylovora*)**

This devastating disease can quickly spread through the plant. For controls see "Fire Blight" on page 314.

Most Common Spirea Disorders

Symptoms: Plants lose vigor; leaves yellow
Cause: **Alkaline soil**

Spireas are most healthy in soils with a pH of 5.5–6.0 (slightly more acid than good garden soil). When you plant, mix a tablespoon or so of sulfur with the soil. Mulch with pine needles or chopped oak leaves. If these are unavailable, sprinkle a tablespoon or so of sulfur around the bushes each spring.

SPRUCES

Picea spp.

COLORADO SPRUCE AT A GLANCE

Botanical Name: *Picea pungens*

Height: 30–50 feet (shorter cultivars available)

Spread: 10–20 feet (shorter cultivars vary in shape)

Shade Tolerance: Full sun

Hardiness: Zones 3–7

Preferred Soil: Fertile, moist; more drought-tolerant than other species

NORWAY SPRUCE AT A GLANCE

Botanical Name: *Picea abies*

Height: 40–60 feet (shorter cultivars available)

Spread: 25–30 feet (shorter cultivars vary in shape)

Shade Tolerance: Full sun (light shade in South)

Hardiness: Zones 2–6

Preferred Soil: well-drained, acidic; adaptable to average soil if kept evenly moist

SERBIAN SPRUCE AT A GLANCE

Botanical Name: *Picea omorika*

Height: 50–60 feet (shorter cultivars available)

Spread: 20–25 feet (shorter cultivars similiar in shape to species)

Shade Tolerance: Partial shade

Hardiness: Zones 4–8

Preferred Soil: Deep, fertile, moist, well-drained; alkaline or acidic

Most Common Spruce Pests

Symptom: Branches stripped of needles
Cause: **Bagworms**

Bagworms hang from twigs and branches in tough, silken bags studded with needles and plant debris. For controls see "Bagworm" on page 247.

Symptom: Needles dead at tips of branches
Cause: **Spruce budworms**

These tiny caterpillars are hard to see. They mine into needles, as well as into buds, cones, and twigs. For controls see "Firs" on page 189.

Symptom: Bronzed or grayish needles, which dry and drop
Cause: **Spruce spider mites**

These tiny mites spin between needles, especially on undersides of branches. For controls see "Firs" on page 189. Do not use horticultural oils on Koster blue or Colorado blue spruce because they remove the blue "bloom" from the needles.

Symptom: Cone-shaped galls in branch tips
Cause: **Cooley spruce gall adelgids**

These 1/25-inch-long insects have a complex life cycle, part of which is spent feeding on the new growth of spruces. The galls are greenish at first. They turn purplish red and dry out later in the season, when they look much like a dry cone. Handpick the galls early in summer. Damaging infestations are rare, but if a large number of galls developed the previous year, spray insecticidal soap three times at 10-day intervals, starting just as buds begin to open.

Symptom: Needles dead and webbed
               together
Cause: **Spruce needle miners**

Look for small, green caterpillars, ³⁄₁₀ inch in length, boring into the base of the needles. Spray with a strong stream of water in late fall to remove webs and again in spring before the buds open. Collect and destroy the debris removed by the water spray.

Symptoms: Terminal shoots deformed;
               dead tips
Cause: **White pine weevils**

This is particularly a pest of young, ornamental spruces. The ⅕-inch-long, grayish weevils lay their eggs in the stem of the leader. The fat, white grubs develop inside, eventually girdling and killing the leader. For controls see "Pines" on page 214.

Colorado spruce (Picea pungens)

Most Common Spruce Diseases

Symptom: Needles and twigs distorted
               and shriveled
Cause: **Blight (*Rehmiellopsis balsameae*;
               Botrytis cinerea; other fungi)**

Blight is most common in trees located in shady areas where foliage doesn't dry quickly enough. Avoid problems by allowing wide spacing when planting. Prune to provide good air circulation and light exposure for your trees. Water only the soil, not the needles.

Symptoms: Branches die back; needles
               brown and drop; cankers
               form on bark
Cause: **Canker (*Cytospora* spp.)**

Canker fungi can enter trees through wounds caused by insects, pruning tools, and lawn-care equipment. For controls see "Cytospora Canker" on page 310.

Symptom: White or pale yellow blisters on
               needle undersides
Cause: **Rust (*Chrysomyxa* spp.)**

Severely affected needles may drop. For controls see "Rust" on page 327.

Symptom: Shelflike fungal growths
               on trunk
Cause: **Wood rot**

Wood rot fungi can attack both living and dead trees. While *P. betulinus* infects only dead or dying trees, the other organisms infect stressed but living trees. The "shelf" is the fruiting body of the fungus. There is no control, but you can slow it down by pruning off infected wood. Prevent attacks with good cultural care.

SYCAMORES

Platanus spp.

SYCAMORE/ AMERICAN PLANETREE/ BUTTONWOOD/ AT A GLANCE

Botanical Name: *Platanus occidentalis*
Height: 75–100 feet
Spread: 75–100 feet or more
Shade Tolerance: Full sun
Hardiness: Zones 5–8
Preferred Soil: Deep, fertile, moist, well-drained; less adaptable than London planetree

LONDON PLANETREE AT A GLANCE

Botanical Name: *Platanus* x *acerifolia*
Height: 70–100 feet
Spread: 60–80 feet
Shade Tolerance: Full sun
Hardiness: Zones 6–9
Preferred Soil: Deep, fertile, moist, well-drained; widely adaptable

---

Most Common Sycamore Pests

Symptom: Leaves turn yellow along whole branch

Cause: **Scale**

Many species of scale attack sycamores. Look for tiny, whitish, grayish, reddish, or brown bumps on bark. Scale is usually controlled well by dormant oil or lime-sulfur sprays in late winter and by sprays of summer oil or insecticidal soap. For further controls see "Most Common Tree, Shrub, and Vine Pests" on page 168.

Symptom: Small yellow and red spots on leaves

Cause: **Sycamore lace bugs**

Feeding by these small bugs on undersides of leaves causes the leaf tissue to turn yellow and red around the feeding punctures. For heavy infestations, spray insecticidal soap, pyrethrins, or summer oil.

Symptom: Sticky coating on leaves
Cause: **Aphids**

Look for colonies of small pear-shaped insects on undersides of leaves. For controls see "Aphids" on page 244.

Sycamore (Platanus occidentalis)

Most Common Sycamore Diseases

Symptoms: Elongated, sunken areas on trunk and branches; leaves yellow and drop

Cause: **Canker stain**

The bark on infected trees may crack open. Lesions widen and spread, eventually girdling and killing branches. Prune off and destroy all infected branches. If cankers appear on trunk, cut out the lesions, extending the cut several inches into sound wood. Prune in dry weather, when the tree is dormant.

Symptoms: Oozing lesions on branches or trunk; branch tips die back

Cause: **Canker**

Canker fungi can enter sycamores through wounds caused by insects, pruning tools, and lawn-care equipment. For controls see "Cytospora Canker" on page 310.

Symptom: Powdery coating on leaves

Cause: **Powdery mildew**

Powdery mildew is unsightly but usually isn't serious enough to threaten the life of your tree. For controls see "Powdery Mildew" on page 323.

Symptoms: Moist or sunken spots on leaves; dark-colored leaves and shoots

Cause: **Anthracnose**

Anthracnose fungi cause watery, rotting spots on foliage and stems that darken and merge as they age. This fungal disease is particularly a problem on sycamores during cool, wet springs. Stressed trees are most susceptible to infection. For controls see "Anthracnose" on page 300.

VIBURNUMS
Viburnum spp.

DOUBLEFILE VIBURNUM AT A GLANCE

Botanical Name: *Viburnum plicatum* var. *tomentosum*

Height: 8–10 feet (shorter cultivars available)

Spread: 9–12 feet or wider (shorter cultivars vary in shape)

Shade Tolerance: Partial shade

Hardiness: Zones 6–8

Preferred Soil: Moist, well-drained; intolerant of poorly drained, clay soil

EUROPEAN CRANBERRYBUSH VIBURNUM AT A GLANCE

Botanical Name: *Viburnum opulus*

Height: 8–12 feet

Spread: 10–15 feet

Shade Tolerance: Full sun or partial shade

Hardiness: Zones 4–8

Preferred Soil: Adapted to a wide range of soils and pH levels

KOREANSPICE VIBURNUM AT A GLANCE

Botanical Name: *Viburnum carlesii*

Height: 4–5 feet (shorter cultivars available)

Spread: 4–8 feet

Shade Tolerance: Full sun or partial shade

Hardiness: Zones 5–8

Preferred Soil: Moist, well-drained, slightly acidic

Most Common Viburnum Pests

Symptom: Leaves distorted and sticky
Cause: **Aphids**

Look for colonies of ¹⁄₁₆–³⁄₈-inch-long, pear-shaped insects on undersides of affected leaves. For controls see "Aphids" on page 244.

Symptom: Leaves turn yellow along
          whole branch
Cause: **Scale**

Seven species of scale attack viburnums. Look for clusters of tiny, whitish, grayish, purplish, or brown bumps on bark. Their feeding weakens and kills branches and makes the plants more susceptible to borer attack. Scale is usually controlled well by dormant oil or lime-sulfur sprays in late winter and by sprays of summer oil or insecticidal soap as buds start to open. For controls see "Most Common Tree, Shrub, and Vine Pests" on page 168.

Symptom: Holes in leaves
Cause: **Japanese beetles**

These ¹⁄₂-inch-long, blue-green beetles with bronze wing covers are easy to see, as is their feeding damage, which skeletonizes leaves. For controls see "Japanese Beetle" on page 268.

Symptom: Dried brown edges on flowers,
          which may not open
Cause: **Thrips**

You will need a magnifying lens to see these quick, minute, yellowish brown insects hiding in crevices in the blossoms. Native predators attack thrips, including minute pirate bugs, lacewings, and lady beetles. For controls see "Thrips" on page 293.

Most Common Viburnum Diseases

Symptoms: Rotting spots on flowers, leaves,
          and shoot tips; fuzzy gray mold
          develops
Cause: **Botrytis blight (*Botrytis cinerea*)**

Prevent damage by choosing a planting site with good air circulation. Plant in well-drained soil and keep air circulation high with proper spacing. Remove faded flowers and destroy infected plant parts to reduce the spread of the disease.

Symptoms: Galls on stems; branches
          die back
Cause: **Crown gall**

Crown gall bacteria can enter plants through wounds caused by insects, pruning tools, and lawn-care equipment. Leaves yellow and wilt and branches begin to die back. Look for arge, irregularly shaped galls near the soil line. Inspect plants carefully before you buy.

Doublefile viburnum (Viburnum plicatum)

Soak roots of susceptible plants in a solution containing the beneficial bacteria *Agrobacterium radiobacter* before planting. Dig out infected plants, taking as much of the surrounding soil as possible. Cut out mild, localized infections, sterilizing tools between cuts.

Symptom: White, powdery coating on leaves

Cause: **Powdery mildew (*Microsphaera alni*)**

Powdery mildew is unsightly but usually isn't serious enough to threaten the life of your plant. For controls see "Powdery Mildew" on page 323.

Symptom: Yellow, brown, or dead areas on leaves

Cause: **Leaf spot**

Leaf spots may merge to cover whole leaves. Leaf spot is fairly common but rarely life threatening to the tree. Rake up and destroy all fallen leaves at the end of the season to reduce the problem next year. To control leaf spot, spray with copper in late spring.

Symptom: Orange, yellow, or reddish spots on leaves

Cause: **Rust**

Severely infected leaves may drop. For controls see "Rust" on page 327.

Symptom: Sunken spots on leaves

Cause: **Anthracnose (*Colletotrichum* spp.; *Gloeosporium* spp.)**

This fungal disease is particularly a problem during cool, wet springs. For controls see "Anthracnose" on page 300.

WILLOWS
Salix spp.

WEEPING WILLOW AT A GLANCE

Botanical Name: *Salix babylonica*, *S. alba* 'Tristis', other cultivars
Height: *S. babylonica*, 30–40 feet; *S. alba* 'Tristis', to 70 feet
Spread: *S. babylonica*, 30–40 feet; *S. alba* 'Tristis', to 70 feet
Shade Tolerance: Full sun
Hardiness: *S. babylonica*, Zones 7–9; *S. alba* 'Tristis', Zones 3–9
Preferred Soil: Deep, moist; tolerates various soils

PUSSY WILLOW AT A GLANCE

Botanical Name: *Salix caprea*
Height: To 25 feet
Spread: To 15 feet
Shade Tolerance: Full sun
Hardiness: Zones 4–8
Preferred Soil: Tolerates various soils if moist

Most Common Willow Pests

Symptom: Leaves turn yellow along whole branch

Cause: **Scale**

Look for clusters of tiny, grayish or brown bumps on bark. Their feeding weakens and kills branches and makes the plants more susceptible to borer attack. For controls see "Most Common Tree, Shrub, and Vine Pests" on page 168.

Symptoms: Branches die or break;
trees are weak
Cause: **Borers**

If borers are your problem you will see small holes bored through the bark of limbs or the trunk. For controls see "Most Common Tree, Shrub, and Vine Pests" on page 168.

Symptom: Leaves yellow and distorted
Cause: **Aphids**

Aphids feed in clusters on tender growth. For controls see "Aphids" on page 244.

Symptoms: Holes chewed in leaves; webs
may be present
Cause: **Caterpillars**

Several caterpillars spin silken tents in trees. For controls see "Most Common Tree, Shrub, and Vine Pests" on page 168.

Symptom: Cone-shaped or distorted
galls on twigs
Cause: **Gall midges**

The tiny larvae of these midges feed in twigs, causing them to react by producing galls. They do little damage, but for heavy infestations of gall midges, prune out and destroy new galls in summer.

Symptom: Yellow, mottled blotches on
leaves
Cause: **Willow lace bugs**

Lace bugs are $\frac{1}{10}$–$\frac{1}{15}$-inch, oval bugs with lacy wings. Look on undersides of leaves for the specks of dark excrement that show lace bugs have been feeding. Both adult lace bugs and their nymphs suck juices from leaves and stems of plants. Their feeding causes yellowish patches or a speckled, white or gray blotchy appearance on the leaf surface. Light feeding causes little damage, but large lace bug populations can kill leaves and stems. To prevent injury from lace bug feeding, maintain healthy plants. For heavy infestations, spray insecticidal soap or pyrethrins in mid-May and again 10 days later to control both adults and nymphs.

Symptom: Leaves skeletonized
Cause: **Imported willow leaf beetles**

The $\frac{1}{8}$-inch-long, dark, sluglike larvae of these small, blue-green beetles feed on undersides of foliage, leaving just the veins behind. For heavy infestations, especially on small plants, spray pyrethrins.

Weeping willow (Salix babylonica)

Most Common Willow Diseases

Symptoms: Leaves wilted and brown; branches die back
Cause: **Bacterial blight (*Pseudomonas saliciperda*)**

This bacterial disease is most severe during warm, wet springs. It seriously weakens infected trees and eventually kills them if it is not controlled. Spots on leaves and shoots in early spring may be the first sign of blight. Leaf spots enlarge rapidly, turning dark brown or black. Bacteria spread quickly to branches, causing cankers on willows. To prevent bacterial blight infections, avoid overfertilizing willows with nitrogen. Prune only in dry weather. Prune off and destroy infected branches, cutting at least 6 inches below infection sites and sterilizing tolls between cuts. Spray with an antibiotic after pruning infected growth and again just before buds swell in spring. Copper or lime-sulfur, sprayed when buds swell, is sometimes an effective control.

Symptoms: Dark brown "target" spots on leaves; cankers on twigs
Cause: **Canker (*Physalospora miyabeana*)**

Canker fungi can enter a tree through wounds caused by insects, pruning tools, or lawn-care equipment. For controls see "Cytospora Canker" on page 310.

Symptoms: Leaves wilt and turn dark brown or black before dropping; cankers on twigs
Cause: **Leaf blight (*Venturia saliciperda*)**

Rake up and destroy all fallen leaves to reduce future problems. Beginning in early spring when leaves begin to emerge and repeating at intervals of 10–14 days, spray three or four times with Bordeaux mixture or copper. Choose species such as weeping willow (*Salix babylonica*), purple osier (*S. purpurea*), and bay-leaved willow (*S. pentandra*), which are resistant to leaf blight.

Symptom: Galls with rough surfaces on trunk or branches
Cause: **Crown gall**

Crown gall bacteria enter the tree through wounds caused by insects and garden tools. For controls see "Crown Gall" on page 309.

Symptom: Yellow, brown, or black spots on leaves
Cause: **Leaf spot**

Leaf spots can spread to cover whole leaves. Leaf spot is fairly common but rarely life threatening to the tree. Rake up and destroy all fallen leaves at the end of the season to reduce the problem next year. To control leaf spot, spray with copper in late spring.

Symptom: Powdery coating on leaves
Cause: **Powdery mildew (*Uncinula salicis*)**

These fungal infections are unsightly and also weaken host plants. For controls see "Powdery Mildew" on page 323.

Symptom: Yellowish pustules on leaf undersides
Cause: **Rust (*Melampsora* spp.)**

The first symptoms of rust diseases you will notice are general lack of vigor and slow growth. The fungus then produces pustule. For controls see "Rust" on page 327.

WISTERIAS
Wisteria spp.

JAPANESE WISTERIA AT A GLANCE

Botanical Name: *Wisteria floribunda*
Height: Climbs to 40 feet
Spread: To 6 feet or more
Shade Tolerance: Full sun or partial shade
Hardiness: Zones 5–9
Preferred Soil: Deep, moderately fertile, moist, well-drained, loam; tolerates some drought

---

Most Common Wisteria Pests

Symptoms: Holes chewed in leaves; webs present in foliage
Cause: **Fall webworms**

The larvae are beige caterpillars, covered by dense yellowish brown hairs, with tufts of long white hairs along their sides. The caterpillars chew on leaves and spin large, conspicuous, dirty white webs over the ends of branches. Sometimes several branch tips are held together by one large web. Native parasitic wasps and predators suppress the populations in most years, but localized outbreaks occur. Prune out and destroy branches with webs while caterpillars are still feeding inside. Spray *Bacillus thuringiensis* var. *kurstaki* (BTK) or neem on leaves around the fall webworm webs while the larvae are small or when older larvae start wandering outside of webs to feed. Catch webworm caterpillars in sticky tree bands as they leave to pupate. Spray summer oil to control larvae on trees that can tolerate oil sprays.

Symptom: Half-circle notches in leaf edges
Cause: **Black vine weevils**

At night, knock weevils off plants onto a ground sheet and destroy them. Apply a solution of parasitic nematodes to the soil to control larvae in late spring or early fall. For heavy infestations, try trapping adults starting in April by setting out stakes with 12-inch-high wraps of corrugated plastic or cardboard. Remove paper from one side of the cardboard and face the corrugations inward. Check every few days and destroy trapped weevils. Intercept adult weevils climbing up shrubs by tying a 6-inch-high band of plastic wrap painted with sticky trap glue around the trunk.

Most Common Wisteria Disorders

Symptom: Plant does not bloom
Causes: **Plant is too young; excessive soil nitrogen**

Wisterias must be 3–5 years old before they begin to bloom. Older plants stop blooming if nitrogen levels are too high. Avoid high nitrogen fertilizers.

'Alba' Japanese wisteria (Wisteria floribunda 'Alba')

YEWS

Taxus spp.

ANGLOJAPANESE YEW AT A GLANCE

Botanical Name: *Taxus* x *media*
Height: To 40 feet (most cultivars smaller)
Spread: Varies by cultivar
Shade Tolerance: Full sun to full shade
Hardiness: Zones 5–7
Preferred Soil: Moist, sandy, loam, well-drained, acidic to neutral

JAPANESE YEW AT A GLANCE

Botanical Name: *Taxus cuspidata*
Height: To 40 feet (most cultivars smaller)
Spread: Equal to or greater than height (cultivars vary)
Shade Tolerance: Full sun to full shade
Hardiness: Zones 3–9
Preferred Soil: Moist, sandy, loam; adaptable as long as soil is well-drained

Japanese yew (Taxus cuspidata)

Most Common Yew Pests

Symptom: Needles turn yellow along whole branch
Causes: **Scale; mealybugs; black vine weevils**

Five species of scale attack yews. Look for clusters of tiny, whitish, grayish, purplish, or brown bumps on bark. For controls see "Most Common Tree, Shrub, and Vine Pests" on page 168. If clusters of oval, $\frac{1}{10}$-inch-long, powdery-white, crawling insects are visible on the bark, then mealybugs are the problem. For controls see "Mealybugs" on page 272.

Symptom: Tips of shoots swollen and distorted
Cause: **Bud mites**

These microscopic mites infest the tissue in the buds at the tips of shoots and their feeding distorts the new growth. For severe infestations, spray summer oil in early May.

Most Common Yew Disorders

Symptoms: Leaves yellow; plant loses vigor
Cause: **Acidic soil**

Yews prefer a soil pH of about 6.5–6.8 and will not tolerate greater acidity. Amend your soil as necessary with ground limestone or bonemeal. See "Building Healthy Soil" on page 342. Mulch with nonacidic materials such as straw or fully finished compost.

Symptoms: Leaves yellow; plant loses vigor
Cause: **Overwatering**

Choosing a planting site with good drainage can help to prevent this problem. For controls see "Waterlogged Soil" on page 339.

LAWNS

Most Common Lawn Pests

Symptom: Bare patches in turf
Cause: **Armyworms**

These striped, yellow or brownish green caterpillars grow up to 1½ inches long and skeletonize leaf blades, eventually eating a bare patch in the sod. Outbreaks can appear and disappear suddenly, but are usually worse after drought years. Armyworms are usually kept in check by native predators, including insects, birds, and diseases. When outbreaks occur, try spraying *Bacillus thuringiensis* var. *kurstaki* (BTK) or neem to control the caterpillars. Spray summer oils (on plants that tolerate oil sprays) in July to kill eggs. For heavy infestations, spray BTK or neem where caterpillars are feeding, and reseed the turf. Where outbreaks of armyworms are frequent it may be worth overseeding the lawn with turfgrass cultivars containing endophytic fungi.

Lawn armyworm damage

Symptom: Leaf blades with yellow speckles
Cause: **Banks grass mite**

These ⅟₇₅-inch-long mites occur in turf in most areas except the northeastern United States. As damage increases from this tiny mite, the leaves turn yellow and wither. At the base of leaf blades, you may see webbing produced by the mites. Healthy, vigorous turf is only slightly affected; maintain good irrigation and fertility practices to prevent damage. For heavy infestations of mites, drench areas with insecticidal soap spray.

Symptom: Round, grayish yellow patches
Cause: **Chinch bugs**

Search around the base of plants for these ⅙-inch-long, dark bugs with white wings and red legs. Nymphs are red or black with white spots. Both adults and nymphs suck sap from roots and stems, killing turf in patches. Both adults and nymphs suck juice from roots and stems of grasses, leaving wilted and dying plants. Turf dies in patches in heavily infested lawns. Occasionally, large numbers of chinch bugs migrating from a field can ruin a lawn. In warm spring weather, adults fly from their overwintering sites to fields and turf. Unlike sod damaged by white grubs, the turf is not easily rolled back. There are many native enemies of chinch bugs in organically managed turf. Big-eyed bugs are particularly important enemies of chinch bugs, but look similar. For light infestations, keep turf extremely moist for a month (if diseases are not a problem) to drive out bugs. For heavy infestations, drench turf with neem. Rake up all nearby debris in gardens and under hedgerows to remove overwintering sites. Where heavy infestations are usual, reseed with turfgrass cultivars that contain endophytic fungi, which are toxic to the bugs.

Symptom: Brown streaks of dead turf
Cause: **Mole crickets**

Several introduced species of mole crickets are serious turf pests in southern states and are worst in Florida (native species are not a problem). Researchers have introduced a parasitic fly and a new strain of insect parasitic nematode specifically for mole crickets in Florida and other states, with promising results. For heavy infestations, try drenching the soil with parasitic nematodes.

Note

Researchers at the University of Florida in Gainsville, Florida, have found that the tachinid fly (Ormia depleta), which was introduced in the 1980s from South America to parasitize the pest species of mole crickets, has successfully established itself over a wide area. This parasitic fly has been spreading at an average rate of 36 miles per year from one release site and seems to be established in peninsular Florida. It is providing substantial control of pest mole crickets and has been released in areas of North Carolina and Georgia since 1991. In 1985, University of Florida researchers also found a species of parasitic nematode (Steinernema scapterisci) that kills pest mole crickets. A commercial company (Biosys, Palo Alto, CA) has developed rearing methods, and experimental releases have begun in Florida and other states.

Symptom: Dead patches with webbing in the thatch layer
Cause: **Sod webworms**

The ¾-inch-long caterpillars of these small moths live in tunnels in the thatch, feeding on grass blades, which they cut off and pull down into their tunnels to eat. They are most damaging in late summer when grass growth slows. Sod webworms have many natural enemies in healthy turf. For heavy webworm infestations, apply neem, *Bacillus thuringiensis* var. *kurstaki* (BTK), or parasitic nematodes to kill larvae. Where webworms are a common problem, overseed or reseed with turfgrass cultivars infected with endophytic fungi.

Symptom: Turf sparse with brown patches
Cause: **European crane fly**

Damage is most noticeable in May and June. The 1⅜-inch-long, grayish brown, wormlike larvae (leatherjackets) of this 1-inch, long-legged fly feed on the roots of turf close to the surface of the soil. There must be a large number of larvae present (over 15–25 per square foot) to cause damage, and most healthy, organically managed turf has sufficient natural enemies to keep them in check. Where turf has been damaged in the past, apply parasitic nematodes in spring as soon as soil is over 55°F, or drench turf with neem. Walking over the lawn repeatedly using spiked aerator sandals may reduce populations to below damaging numbers.

Symptom: Irregular dead or wilted patches
Causes: **Japanese beetles; white grubs**

Dead patches show up in August and September. The wilted turf can be easily lifted and pulled back to reveal the white grubs feeding in the roots. To control Japanese beetles and other white grubs (larvae of May and June beetles), in late spring or late summer treat turf with parasitic nematodes, watering well before and after application. Drench soil with neem or walk over the lawn repeatedly using spiked aerator sandals. For long-term control, apply milky disease once between July and first frost (it may take up to 2 years to see results). Do not spread manures or organic fertilizers during summer since they attract May and June beetles, which will lay eggs that hatch into white grubs. Lawns composed of a mixture of turfgrasses, clovers, and some broadleaved weeds are less affected by white grubs than pure turfgrass stands. Creeping bentgrass is less damaged by Japanese beetle grubs than other turfgrasses.

Note

Researchers at Colorado State University found that walking over plots of turfgrass in lawn aerator sandals killed more than half of the white grubs infesting the roots. They walked over the test plot three to five times using the sandals, which attach to regular shoes and have 3-inch-long spikes on the soles.

Most Common Lawn Diseases

Symptom: Brown circular patches 6–24 inches in diameter
Cause: **Brown patch (*Pellicularia filamentosa*)**

This disease occurs as a consequence of close cutting, poor drainage, overwatering, excessive nitrogen, and low pH, especially in hot, humid weather. Prevent brown patch with compost top-dressings and by watering early in the day. Rake out dead grass and replant with resistant grasses.

Symptom: Small tan or straw-colored spots
Cause: **Dollar spot (*Sclerotinia homeocarpa*)**

Dollar spot is most serious when nitrogen is low and drainage is poor. Closely mowed grasses are more susceptible to injury. Aerate the soil and apply compost or a high-nitrogen blend organic fertilizer. Water deeply, but less frequently, and avoid cutting shorter than the recommended height.

*Dollar spot (*Sclerotinia homeocarpa*)*

Symptoms: Bright green, circular areas with brown margins; fast growth inside the ring
Cause: **Fairy ring (several species of fungi)**

Mushrooms often grow on the margins of fairy rings. Eventually, the grass in the ring browns and dies. Removing mushrooms as they appear is usually all the control that's needed. To eradicate the fungi, dig out the soil, 2 feet deep and 1 foot beyond the ring, and remove it. Refill with humusy topsoil, then compost and reseed.

Fairy ring

Symptoms: Reddish brown, tan, or yellow patches; pink mold develops

Cause: **Fusarium blight (*Fusarium* spp.)**

Dethatch and aerate the lawn. Raise mowing height and water with 1–2 inches of water (2–4 gallons per square foot) each week. Fusarium is common on Kentucky bluegrass, so replant dead areas with another species.

Symptom: Dark spots on grass blades

Causes: **Leaf spots and leaf blights (various fungi)**

Hot, humid conditions favor these diseases. Build soil fertility with organic fertilizers and compost. Set mowing height as high as possible. Keep soil evenly moist. Reseed with resistant grasses.

Symptom: Yellow, orange, or red powdery pustules on blades

Cause: **Rust (various fungi)**

Dry lawns with nitrogen deficiency are most susceptible, particularly in late summer. Water in the morning. Fertilize with an organic blend that's high in nitrogen. Mow regularly. Reseed with resistant grasses.

Symptom: Blades with water-soaked, blackened areas that enlarge

Cause: **Cottony blight (*Pythium aphanidermatum*)**

A white mold develops in humid conditions. This fast-spreading disease is most common on poorly drained, overfertilized lawns. Calcium deficiencies and high pH levels favor it. Aerate and adjust nutrient supplies by adding finished compost.

Symptom: Circular patches of scorched-looking or pink, gelatinous masses on lawn

Cause: **Red thread (*Corticium fuciforme*)**

This fungus produces red or rusty-looking threads that cover leaf blades. Red thread fungi grow best in cool, moist weather conditions. Grasses that are growing slowly because of low temperatures, drought, or low soil fertility are most susceptible. To prevent its spread, mow frequently and collect the clippings. Apply compost or an organic fertilizer formulated for lawns. Water thoroughly early in the day to avoid leaving the grass wet for extended periods.

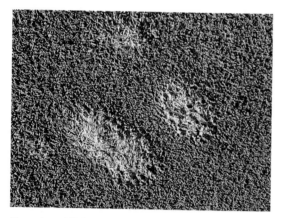

Fusarium blight (Fusarium spp.)

Red thread (Corticium fuciforme)

What Garden Pest or Disease is That?

A field guide to more than 100 pests, diseases, and disorders, with descriptions, plants attacked, and prevention and controls for each.

ALL ABOUT PESTS

This section is all about common yard and garden pests in the United States, with descriptions, plants they attack, prevention strategies, and control tactics. It's where you'll turn to find your plant's pest and what to do about it. But before you start, make sure your problem really is a pest.

When you're trying to find out what's wrong with a plant, you may be surprised to learn that the culprit usually isn't a pest or disease. The fact is that most plant problems are cultural or environmental disorders. This means that you need to consider soil conditions, light levels, watering practices, temperatures, pruning methods, nutrient deficiencies, and other conditions when diagnosing a problem. Another thing to keep in mind is that, while there are many insects and other animals in our gardens, most of them are not harmful. Use this guide to identify a suspected pest before you decide to take action. For more information, refer to "Controlling Pests and Diseases" on page 353, "All About Diseases" on page 299, and "Disorders: When is A Disease Not A Disease?" on page 334.

Even when pests are at work, most insect and mite feeding doesn't particularly endanger a garden crop or flower, or threaten an ornamental tree or shrub. Your plants can tolerate some damage, especially if they're not going to be eaten. For example, holes in the leaves of a potato plant or an apple tree only affect the crop if quite a bit of damage is done. For this type of pest, controls may never be necessary, or they may be needed only in years with particularly heavy outbreaks. Many insect populations rise and fall over a period of years, so outbreaks over a few years may be followed by several years without damage.

Although many different pests are described in this book, experienced organic gardeners know that only a few of these are a problem for any given crop or region. (See "Where's That Pest?" on page 368.) Once you find out which pests are regular problems, you can plan to prevent the problem next year. Preventing pest damage is easier and more effective than treating your plants or trying to control the pests after the damage occurs.

How Do Pests Live?

There are many different types of plant pests, including insects, mites, nematodes, sowbugs and pillbugs, millipedes and centipedes and mollusks (slugs and snails). All but the nematodes (which are a type of worm), and mollusks are arthropods. This means they have a hard-shelled body, which serves as a skeleton, and jointed legs. Generally, insects have six legs, mites have eight legs, and sowbugs, pillbugs, millipedes, and centipedes have many legs.

Insects are an incredibly diverse group, but they have two basic kinds of life cycles. In one kind of life cycle, the insect passes through a stage of complete change, called metamorphosis, between the immature (larval) stage and the adult stage. Insects with a complete metamorphosis pass through four stages as they develop. Development starts with an egg, which hatches into a larva, such as a caterpillar, maggot, or grub. When the larva has grown to full size, it becomes a pupa. This is an immobile stage, and inside its pupal case, such as a cocoon, the insect changes into an adult that looks nothing like the larva. The adult insect splits or chews open the pupal case and crawls out.

The other main life cycle pattern is called gradual metamorphosis. These insects start with an egg that hatches into an immature insect, often called a nymph. Nymphs usually look somewhat like the adults. As a nymph grows, it molts its skin, and with each molt it looks more and more like an adult. With the final molt nymphs become adults, complete with wings and reproductive organs. Instead of a clear difference between the larva and adult with a pupal stage in between, these insects gradually develop into adults.

Insect life cycles can be short—just a few weeks—or they can be long, even taking years. For those species with more than one generation in a year, the number of generations per year varies with the length of the growing season. This means that there are usually fewer generations in northern regions than in the South. An insect's growth rate depends on the temperature of its environment, so a generation takes longer to mature in spring and fall than in summer. In unusually warm weather or long growing seasons, you may find some pests will squeeze in an extra generation in your garden.

Pest Damage and Control

Insects and related pests damage plants by feeding on foliage and fruit, by boring into stems and trunks, and by feeding on or in the roots. Generally, a particular species causes only one type of damage. For example, leaf-eating caterpillars, such as imported cabbageworms or tent caterpillars, never feed on roots, while root maggots do not climb plants to feed among the leaves. Some insects, however, cause somewhat different types of damage depending on the time of year. For example, an early generation of oriental fruit moth caterpillars bores into twigs, whereas larvae in the midsummer generation bore into fruit.

Damage caused by insects that chew leaves is often more unsightly than harmful to the plant, especially on ornamentals. Before deciding to treat a pest problem, it is important to monitor the situation by close inspections for several days or weeks to decide whether there is really any need to take action. The need for treatment will depend on whether the plant part being damaged is the part that will be eaten. For example, potato plants can tolerate a lot of damage to the leaves before it affects the yield of potatoes. On the other hand, it only takes one codling moth caterpillar to ruin an apple.

Organic gardeners have a wide range of controls to choose from. The most important step you can take is to prevent pest problems to begin with by choosing resistant, well-adapted plants for your location, providing the best possible care, and using good garden-cleaning practices. Biological control, which is the use of living organisms to control pests, is particularly effective in organic gardens, where the natural enemies of pests are not killed by insecticides and fungicides. Barriers, screens, and sticky tree bands to prevent pests from reaching plants are effective, non-chemical controls. Simple water sprays can provide good control of some pests, like aphids. Botanical pest control may be toxic to beneficials as well as pest species. Even a mild product, such as insecticidal soap, will damage the leaves of some plants if used too often. Use controls only if absolutely necessary, and only on affected plants. Always follow label directions and wear appropriate protective clothing and gloves when handling any control.

APHIDS
Order Homoptera: Family Aphididae

Aphids on grain

Aphids are soft, pear-shaped insects, 1/16–3/8 inch long. Most species develop crowded colonies on plants. All aphids have two short tubes, called cornicles, projecting backward from the tip of their abdomen. They have long antennae and may be green, pink, yellowish, black, or powdery gray. Most attack leaves, but some feed on plant roots. Aphids may be wingless or winged. The winged form appears in response to crowding or to changes in plant quality. Their abdomens are dark. Their wings are transparent, longer than their body, and held rooflike over their back. Nymphs resemble adults, but are smaller and wingless.

Both adults and nymphs suck plant sap. Their feeding usually causes distorted leaves, buds, branch tips, and flowers. Severely infested leaves and flowers may drop. As they feed, aphids excrete a sweet, sticky honeydew onto leaves below. This allows sooty mold to grow, which is unsightly and blocks light from the leaves. Some aphids spread plant viruses as they feed. In the fall, late feeding by aphids may benefit young fruit trees by helping to harden off new growth.

In colder regions, aphid eggs overwinter on stems or in crevices in bark. They hatch in spring into "stem" females that reproduce without mating, giving birth continuously to live nymphs. Nymphs mature in 1–2 weeks and start producing offspring. Aphid colonies develop very quickly because of their phenomenal reproductive rate. This makes them very difficult to control with sprays—a single surviving aphid can generate a new colony. When days become shorter in the fall, both males and females are born. These mate and produce eggs that overwinter. In very mild climates and in greenhouses, aphids may reproduce year-round.

Small sucking insects related to aphids include adelgids, such as balsam twig adelgid and woolly larch adelgid, and psyllids, such as boxwood psyllids. Control as for aphids.

Plants Attacked
Aphids feed on most fruit and vegetable plants, flowers, ornamentals, nuts, herbs, fruit and shade trees, and conifers. Some species feed on only one kind of plant, others alternate between two species of host plants, while still others, such as the green peach aphid (*Myzus persicae*), attack a wide range of plants. Some, like corn root aphids, live on the roots of host plants.

Organic Controls
Hard, driving rainstorms will kill aphids. Aphids also have a large number of natural enemies, both predators and parasites, which usually control them sufficiently to prevent serious plant damage. Aphids also may be protected from these enemies by ants, which "farm" or care for the aphids to obtain the sweet honeydew they produce.

Maintain healthy plant growth, but do not overfertilize with nitrogen. Spray dormant oil to control overwintering eggs on fruit trees. Knock aphids off plants with a strong stream of water; repeat frequently as needed. Attract native predators and parasites by planting pollen and nectar plants. Control the ants that guard aphid colonies in trees by placing sticky bands around trunks. Release purchased aphid midges, lacewings, lady beetles (these fly away, so they're best for greenhouses), or parasitic wasps. Spray insecticidal soap, neem, summer oil (on tolerant plants), homemade garlic sprays, or, as a last resort, pyrethrins. Repeat as needed for control.

Research Notes

J. F. Walgenbach of North Carolina State University has found that black plastic mulches (as compared to no mulch or a living mulch of white clover) reduced the number of potato aphids on tomatoes and the number of green peach aphids on peppers. The percentage of aphids parasitized by native parasitic wasps was also higher in the black plastic-mulched plots.

Several researchers have investigated the effect of living mulches on aphid numbers in cabbage-family crops. M. Costello at the Kearny Agricultural Center, University of California, found that clover or birdsfoot trefoil grown between broccoli plants resulted in lower numbers of cabbage aphids and green peach aphids on the crop.

APPLE MAGGOT
Rhagoletis pomonella

Adult apple maggots are dark-colored flies up to ¼ inch long. They have yellow legs and transparent wings with characteristic dark, crosswise bands. The fly larvae are known as "railroad worms," and are small, white maggots that develop inside fruit. The apple maggots tunnel through fruit, leaving brown, winding tunnels in the flesh. This usually causes the fruit to drop early. Thin-skinned and early-maturing cultivars are most severely affected by apple maggots.

Apple maggot pupae overwinter in the soil and adults emerge from mid-June to July. The females lay eggs in punctures in the skin of fruit. The eggs hatch in 5–7 days and the maggots tunnel inside the fruit until it drops. The maggots complete their development in the fallen fruit, then crawl several inches deep into the soil to pupate. There is one generation per year in most areas, but in southern regions there may be a partial second generation, with adults emerging in early fall. Some pupae remain dormant in the soil for some years.

Related fruit flies include cherry fruit fly, blueberry fruit fly, currant fruit fly, and walnut husk fly. Although traps are not available for all of them, destroying dropped fruit is an effective way to reduce populations.

Apple maggot larvae (Rhagoletis pomonella)

Plants Attacked

These are serious pests of apples, crabapples, and blueberries. Cherries and plums are occasionally attacked.

Organic Controls

Avoid the main damage by planting late-ripening cultivars. Pick up and destroy all dropped fruit daily until September, then twice a month in the fall. Trap females using sticky red apple-maggot traps. Hang traps in trees from mid-June until harvest (one trap per dwarf tree, up to six traps per full-size tree). Plant groundcovers in the orchard to conserve ground beetles that prey on pupae.

ARMYWORMS
Order Lepidoptera: Family Noctuidae

Adult armyworms are pale, grayish brown moths with 1½–2-inch wingspans. They have a white dot in the center of each forewing. Because they fly at night, they are seldom seen. The young caterpillars, or armyworms, are smooth, pale green, and up to 1½ inches long. Older armyworms are greenish brown with white side stripes and dark or light stripes along their backs. The moths lay their greenish white egg masses on lower leaves.

Armyworms feed together in groups at night and hide during the day in the centers of plants or under leaf litter. In corn, the caterpillars feed in leaf whorls and ears. They can devour whole plants overnight, then move as a group to another field. The first-generation larvae are most damaging and most numerous in years with cold, wet spring weather. Armyworms are found east of the Rockies and in southeastern Canada. They also occur in New Mexico, Arizona, and California. Beet armyworm is a common pest in the southern United States. Armyworms do not overwinter in northern areas, but the moths are blown into these regions by storms.

Armyworms produce two or three generations per year. Depending on the species, armyworms overwinter as caterpillars or pupae in soil or litter around roots. They resume feeding in spring, then pupate. Moths emerge in two weeks.

Armyworm larva

Plants Attacked

Corn is their favorite host, but armyworms will also feed on lawn grasses and other crops, particularly asparagus, beans, beets, cabbage, cucumbers, lettuce, spinach, and tomatoes.

Organic Controls

Armyworms are usually kept in check by native predators, including insects, birds, and diseases. When outbreaks occur, try spraying *Bacillus thuringiensis* var. *kurstaki* (BTK) or neem to control the caterpillars. Spray summer oils (on plants that tolerate oil sprays) in July to kill eggs. After harvest, cultivate the soil to expose pupae to predators.

ASPARAGUS BEETLE
Crioceris asparagi
(also C. duodecimpunctata)

Adult beetles are elongated, shiny, bluish black, and ¼ inch long. They have a reddish brown thorax and wing covers bordered in red and marked with four cream-colored blotches. The larvae are plump, wrinkled, grayish grubs with dark heads and legs. The female beetles lay their shiny black eggs on end, glued to stems and young spears. Spotted asparagus beetles (C. duodecimpunctata) are red-orange with 12 black spots on their wing covers; their larvae are orange grubs.

Both adults and larvae chew holes in green spears, causing brownish blemishes. Later, they attack the stems and strip leaves from asparagus fronds, leaving bare branches.

There are up to five generations in warmer areas. In early spring, hibernating adults emerge when the first asparagus spears are ready to cut. They feed and lay eggs on the spears. Eggs hatch in 3–8 days. The larvae crawl up the plants to feed for 2 weeks, then down to burrow just beneath the soil surface to pupate. The adult beetles emerge in about 10 days.

Plants Attacked
These beetles only attack asparagus.

Organic Controls
Starting in early spring, cover asparagus spears with floating row covers until the end of harvest. Harvest spears often, before beetle eggs hatch. Handpick beetles and larvae, especially in early spring when this has the greatest impact on reducing the second generation. Where beetles are numerous, spray pyrethrins. In fall, remove and destroy old fronds, weeds, and garden trash where beetles overwinter.

Asparagus beetle (Crioceris asparagi) on asparagus stem

BAGWORM
Thyridopteryx ephemeraeformis

Adult males are black moths with clear wings and 1-inch wingspans. Females are wingless. The larvae are shiny, dark brown caterpillars. They are called bagworms because of the silken bags that they spin and hide inside. The bags are up to 2½ inches long; you'll find them attached to trees.

The silken bags that bagworm caterpillars (Thyridopteryx ephemeraeformis) spin and hide inside

Black vine weevil (<u>Otiorhynchus sulcatus</u>)

The female moths lay their light tan eggs inside the bags, where the eggs overwinter. The eggs hatch in late spring, after trees have fully leafed out. The larvae immediately spin their protective silken sacks. They enlarge the bags as they grow and attach bits of tree foliage to the bag. In September, the full-grown larvae attach the bag to a twig with silk, then pupate. After several days, the males emerge and fly to the females, which remain in their bags for mating.

Bagworm caterpillars eat tree foliage, leaving a ragged appearance. They often cause little lasting harm, but the bags attached to foliage and branches are unsightly. In heavy infestations, a tree may be defoliated, which kills conifers.

Plants Attacked

Bagworms attack deciduous and evergreen trees. They are most damaging to arborvitaes and junipers.

Organic Controls

Handpick the bags during winter, when they are easy to see. Cut them away with a knife to avoid leaving a band of silk girdling the twig.

Where the infestation is heavy or the bagworms are out of reach in a tall tree, spray with *Bacillus thuringiensis* var. *kurstaki* (BTK) every 7–10 days from early spring to early summer to kill larvae.

BLACK VINE WEEVIL
Otiorhynchus sulcatus

Adult weevils are flightless, oval, brownish gray or black "snout beetles," and are 1/3 inch long. They have a pattern of small yellow patches on their backs. There are only females (no males), so every weevil lays eggs. The larvae are fat, white grubs up to 1/2 inch long, with yellowish brown heads that live on plant roots in the soil.

The weevils chew along leaf edges, leaving characteristic small, scalloped bite marks on the edges. The adults rarely cause serious damage, but the larvae can be very damaging because they feed on roots. Their feeding stunts plants and may indirectly kill them by allowing disease organisms to enter injured roots.

There is one generation of weevils per year. The adults emerge in June and feed for several weeks to build up their body reserves before laying eggs in the soil around the host plants. The eggs hatch in about 10 days and the larvae immediately burrow into the roots to feed for the rest of the year. They stay in the soil over the winter, then resume feeding on roots the following spring. They pupate in early spring.

Plants Attacked

Black vine weevils most commonly attack blackberry, blueberry, cranberry, and strawberry plants, as well as some ornamentals, particularly azaleas, rhododendrons, camellias, wisteria, and yews. Potted nursery stock is often attacked.

Organic Controls

At night, knock weevils off plants onto a ground sheet and destroy them. Lay boards under plants and check for weevils hiding under them during the day. If leaf damage is severe, cover beds of small plants with floating row covers to stop weevils from reaching the plants to lay eggs. Apply a solution of insect parasitic nematodes (well watered-in) to the soil to control larvae in late spring or early fall. Plant resistant rhododendron and azalea cultivars, which have rolled leaf edges that prevent weevils from grasping the edge to feed. Where weevil infestations are usually heavy, try trapping adults starting in April by setting out stakes with 12-inch-high wraps of corrugated plastic or cardboard. Remove paper from one side of the cardboard and face the corrugations inward. Check these every few days and destroy all accumulated weevils. Intercept adult weevils climbing up shrubs by tying a 6-inch-high band of plastic wrap painted with sticky trap glue around the trunk.

CABBAGE LOOPER

Trichoplusia ni

Adult cabbage loopers are mottled gray-brown moths with a silvery, V-shaped spot in the middle of each forewing and wingspans of 1½ inches. They are rarely seen because they fly late in the evening. Larvae are green caterpillars with a pair of wavy, white or light yellow lines down their backs and one line along each side. They are called loopers because of their habit of humping their bodies up into a loop, especially when disturbed. The females lay their light green, dome-shaped eggs singly or in groups of 2–3 on undersides of leaves.

The caterpillars damage plants by chewing large holes in leaves. If they are numerous, they can ruin whole plants. Larvae are most damaging during the last few days of their development. Many native parasites and predators attack cabbage loopers.

There are three to four generations per year in most areas, although there may be only one generation in northern regions. The adult moths emerge in May from their overwintering cocoons to lay eggs. The eggs hatch in 3–4 days and the larvae feed for 2–3 weeks. They pupate for up to 2 weeks in thin silk cocoons attached to the stems or undersides of leaves. The ½ inch long, green caterpillars of the diamondback moth are also found on cabbage. They look similar, though they do not loop their bodies to move. There are also a number of different "loopers" that are similar to cabbage loopers. Control is the same as for cabbage loopers.

Plants Attacked

Cabbage loopers mainly attack cabbage and cabbage-family plants, but will also feed on beets, celery, lettuce, peas, spinach, tomatoes, and flowers, including carnations, nasturtiums, and mignonette.

Cabbage looper (Trichoplusia ni) on tomato foliage

Organic Controls

For small gardens, handpick caterpillars several times weekly. *Bacillus thuringiensis* var. *kurstaki* (BTK) sprays are very effective, or you can spray neem or pyrethrins. Attract predatory and parasitic insects to the garden with pollen and nectar plants. In northern gardens, start cabbage indoors and plant out very early to avoid peak populations. Bury cabbage crop residues to destroy cocoons before adults emerge in spring.

CABBAGE MAGGOT

Delia radicum (formerly *Hylemya brassicae*)

Adult cabbage maggots are nondescript gray flies, ¼ inch long, with long legs. The white, tapering larvae burrow into the roots of plants, where they cause serious damage.

The first sign of injury is usually plants that wilt in the midday heat. Young plants often die, either from maggot feeding or from rot organisms that enter through root injuries. Older plants may survive to produce a small crop.

Cabbage maggot (Delia radicum)

Cabbage-family root crops, such as turnips and radishes, may be ruined. The maggots do the most damage early in the season when the weather is cool and moist. In hot, dry summers, few eggs from later generations may survive.

There are two to four generations per year in most regions. In warmer regions, the adult flies begin emerging in late March. The females lay eggs in the soil beside the plant roots. After they hatch, the larvae feed on the fine roots, then tunnel into the taproots, feeding for 3–4 weeks. They pupate, and adults emerge in 2–3 weeks. The fall generation of pupae overwinters several inches deep in the soil.

Plants Attacked

These are pests of all cabbage-family plants.

Organic Controls

Avoid the most damaging early generation of flies by planting radishes very early and fall cabbages after July 1. Cover seedlings and small plants, such as radishes and Chinese cabbage, with floating row covers, burying the edges well. Recent research has found that the adults fly low and that simple window screen fences 3 feet high with tops flopped over to the outside are sufficient to keep most adults out of the cabbage patch. Set out transplants through slits in 6 inch squares of tar paper to prevent flies from laying eggs near stems, or wrap stems with paper 1–2 inches above and below the soil line before planting. Burn or destroy roots of cabbage-family plants as soon as they are harvested. Apply insect parasitic nematodes to the soil around roots. Where cabbage maggot numbers are usually low, you can sufficiently repel females from laying eggs by mounding wood ashes, diatomaceous earth, hot pepper, or ginger powder around the plant stems.

CANKERWORMS
Order Lepidoptera: Family Geometridae

Adult males are light gray moths, with a wingspan of over 1 inch. They blend into the background as they rest on plants. The females are wingless, with plump, furry bodies, ½ inch long. The larvae are slender, light green, brown, or black caterpillars with white stripes. They loop their bodies as they crawl, hence the nickname "inchworms." The females lay round, grayish brown eggs in compact masses on twigs and branches.

The caterpillars chew on young tree leaves and buds. As they grow, they move on to feed on larger leaves, leaving behind only the midribs and large veins. Heavily damaged trees look scorched.

There is one generation per year. The adult moths are active in early winter. The wingless females crawl up the trunk to lay eggs on dormant trees in November and December. The eggs hatch in spring, about the time the first leaves open on trees. The caterpillars feed 3–4 weeks, then crawl into the soil to pupate until early winter.

Plants Attacked

Cankerworms feed on apple, elm, oak, linden, beech, and other deciduous trees, as well as ornamental shrubs.

Organic Controls

In most years, native ground beetles and parasitic wasps keep cankerworm populations down.

Spray *Bacillus thuringiensis* var. *kurstaki* (BTK) or neem in spring when larvae are present. In October, band trees with sticky bands to trap the females as they climb up trees to lay eggs. Remove bands in February. Scrape off egg masses laid on branches or spray dormant oil in winter.

Cankerworm or "inchworm"

CARROT RUST FLY
Psila rosae

Adults are shiny, metallic, greenish black flies, about ¼ inch long. They have yellow legs and small, reddish heads. The larvae are creamy white, tapering maggots found tunneling in plant roots.

The root maggots start feeding on the fine root hairs, then bore into the main root, filling the tunnels with characteristic rusty brown castings. Feeding in the roots stunts or kills small plants and allows disease organisms to enter. Larger roots may be forked or distorted and cannot be stored because the last generation of maggots continues to feed in stored roots.

Carrot rust fly (Psila rosae) larvae and damage

There are generally two to three generations per year. The first adults emerge from mid-April to May and lay eggs in the soil close to plants. The eggs hatch in 7–10 days, and the tiny maggots burrow in roots for 3–4 weeks, then pupate in the soil beside the root.

Plants Attacked

These are the most serious pests of carrots in some regions. While they also attack celery, parsley, parsnips, and related plants, they usually do not require control on these crops.

Organic Controls

The best control is covering carrot beds with floating row covers before seedlings emerge. Bury the edges under soil and leave the crop covered until harvest. Recent research has shown that adults fly low and that simple window screen fences 3 feet high with tops flopping over to the outside will keep them from laying eggs in the carrot patch (as long as they were not in the soil from a previous crop). Avoid leaving mature carrots in the ground over winter to act as hosts. Sow the mid-season carrots after the first egg-laying period passes, and harvest early. In mild climates, seed fall carrots in September for March harvest, before the first flies emerge. Drenching the soil with a solution of insect parasitic nematodes may give some control of larvae.

CHINCH BUG
Blissus leucopterus

Adult chinch bugs are ⅛ inch long, with reddish legs. They have white forewings with a black triangular spot near the margin. The youngest nymphs are bright red with a white stripe across the back, while older nymphs are black with white spots. All stages move quickly.

Both adults and nymphs suck juice from roots and stems of grasses, leaving wilted and dying plants. Turf dies in patches in heavily infested lawns. Occasionally, large numbers of chinch bugs migrating from a field can devastate a corn or grain crop or ruin a lawn. There are up to three generations per year.

In warm spring weather, adults fly from their overwintering sites to fields and turf. The females lay eggs on the roots of grass or on the lower leaves of grain plants. The chinch bug eggs hatch in 1–3 weeks and the nymphs chew on roots for 4–5 weeks. They reach the adult stage in late June. In fall, the second-generation adults overwinter in clumps of grasses, especially along the south sides of fence rows and hedges.

Plants Attacked

Chinch bugs attack sod and lawn grasses, as well as corn and cereal-grain crops.

Organic Controls

Managing turfgrass organically encourages the many natural enemies of chinch bugs, including predatory bugs, mites, and birds.

Chinch bug (Blissus leucopterus)

For light infestations, drive out chinch bugs by keeping the turf extremely moist for a month. For heavy infestations, drench turf with neem solution. Where chinch bugs continue to be a serious problem, plant lawns with turfgrass cultivars containing endophytic fungi to give long-term control. (Do not use these cultivars for sod where animals will be grazing.) Chinch bugs avoid shade; therefore, shading the roots of cereal-crop plants by interplanting them with legumes reduces damage. Chinch bugs overwinter in nearby garden debris and hedgerows; rake up all debris in fall.

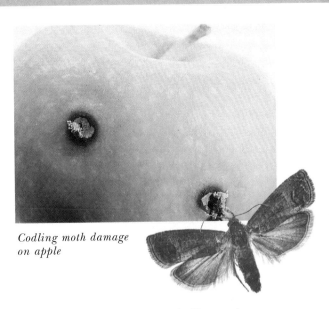

Codling moth damage on apple

Codling moth (Cydia pomonella)

CODLING MOTH

Cydia pomonella

Adults are gray-brown moths with ¾-inch wingspans. The wings have fine, coppery brown, wavy patterns, and the forewings have chocolate brown tips. The larvae are pinkish white, brown-headed caterpillars up to ¾ inch long, found tunneling in fruit. The eggs are white disks, usually laid on the upper surface of leaves.

An apple infested by a codling moth has a hole, usually near the base, which is filled with dark masses of castings. This may not be noticeable until the fruit is cut open and the caterpillar is found feeding at the core. Although infested fruit cannot be stored, the undamaged flesh is edible.

In most regions there are two or three generations of codling moths per year, 5–8 weeks apart. The caterpillars spend the winter in thick cocoons spun under tree bark or in nearby leaf litter. They pupate in the spring and the adult moths emerge when apple trees are in bloom. The females lay eggs on leaves and on fruit when it has formed. The eggs hatch in 1–3 weeks, depending on temperature, and the larvae chew their way into the fruit core, usually starting from the blossom end. They feed for 3–5 weeks, then crawl down the tree to pupate under loose bark or under nearby debris. The pupae are attacked by native predators, such as ground beetles.

Plants Attacked

Codling moths are major pests of apples and pears in fruit-growing regions. In western regions, they are the most damaging pests in orchards. Crabapples and occasionally other fruit may also be attacked.

Organic Controls

In late winter, scrape tree bark to remove cocoons, and spray dormant oil. Use sticky tree bands or bands of corrugated cardboard or canvas tied around tree trunks to trap caterpillars as they leave the tree to pupate. Check the bands daily and destroy larvae and pupae, or replace cardboard bands every 2 weeks and destroy all old bands with larvae inside.

Diligent trapping of the first generation in the spring will reduce the number of moths in the second generation.

Where infestations threaten to damage most fruit, protect your crop by tying a paper lunch bag over each developing fruit in June, after thinning. (Cut a small slit in the bottom of the bag and slip it over the apple, then staple shut the open end.) This prevents moths from laying eggs on the fruit, and also protects it from birds, hail, and other potential hazards.

Attract ground beetles by planting cover crops and using mulches around orchard trees. Apply codling moth granulosis virus sprays where the product is available.

In larger orchards, use pheromone traps to determine the main flight periods for moths (when more than two males are caught for two weeks in a row), and time sprays to coincide with the egg-hatching period, or release trichogramma parasitic wasps to attack eggs. Also, in larger orchards, place twist-tie dispensers of sex pheromones throughout trees to confuse males and prevent mating.

COLORADO POTATO BEETLE
Leptinotarsa decemlineata

Adults are yellowish orange beetles, with ten lengthwise black stripes on their wing covers and black spots on their middle section. They are ⅓ inch long. The larvae are dark orange, humpbacked grubs, ranging from ¹⁄₁₆–½ inch long. They have a row of black spots along each side. The bright yellow eggs are laid on end in upright clusters on undersides of leaves.

Both adults and larvae chew on leaves and stems of potatoes and related plants. Young plants may die, while older plants can be severely defoliated, resulting in loss of the crop. A moderate amount of feeding, however, does not harm plants or reduce potato yields.

There are up to three generations per year. Adult beetles and sometimes pupae overwinter several inches deep in the soil (deeper in colder areas). The beetles emerge in spring to feed on early potato plants as soon as the first shoots are up. Overwintered beetles cannot fly until they have built up their body reserves, so they walk to the host plants. After mating, the females lay up to 1,000 eggs each during their several-month lifespans. The eggs hatch in 4–9 days, and the larvae feed for 2–3 weeks. They burrow into the soil to pupate for another 2–3 weeks, and adults emerge in 5–10 days.

Colorado potato beetle (Leptinotarsa decemlineata)

Plants Attacked

These beetles are major pests of potatoes and, in some areas, also damage tomatoes and eggplants. Related plants, including petunias, are also attacked.

Organic Controls

Plant cultivars with some resistance to potato beetles, such as 'Katahdin' and 'Sequoia'. Mulch plants with deep straw, which seems to impede the movement of beetles in early spring before they have fed enough to be able to fly. You can also trap overwintered beetles in trenches around the potato patch that you have lined with plastic. Cover plants with floating row covers until mid-season.

Good control through the season depends on eliminating the first generation of beetles. Starting in early spring, inspect shoots and undersides of leaves for adults, egg masses, and larvae, and crush them. On older plants, early in the morning, shake adults from plants onto a ground sheet and destroy them. (This is very effective if started as soon as overwintering adults emerge.) To control larvae, spray neem or *Bacillus thuringiensis* var. *san diego* (BTSD) as soon as eggs are present. Control both adults and larvae by spraying weekly with pyrethrins. In the fall, till the soil to kill overwintering beetles.

Biological controls are available, although these are most suited to larger potato patches and should be considered experimental. Try spined soldier bugs (release at a rate of 2–5 bugs per square yard of plants), or the tiny parasitic wasp *Edovum puttleri*, which should be released in time to attack the second-generation larvae.

Research Notes

Researchers at the Agriculture Canada Research Station, Fredericton in New Brunswick, have found that steep-sided, plastic-lined ditches around potato patches provide good control of Colorado potato beetles. When the trench sides are steeper than 45 degrees, the beetles fall into the slippery trenches and very few are able to climb out again.

CORN EARWORM/TOMATO FRUITWORM

Helicoverpa zea (formerly *Heliothis zea*)

Adults are large, yellowish tan moths with a wingspan of 1½–2 inches. The larvae are light yellow, green, pink, or brown caterpillars, 1–2 inches long. They have a paler underside and

Corn earworm (*Helicoverpa zea*) on corn

yellow heads, black legs, and white and dark stripes along their sides. The eggs are round, light green, with a ribbed pattern, and are laid singly on undersides of leaves or on corn silks. The caterpillars feed on fresh corn silks, entering the ear from the tip. They move down the ears, eating kernels and leaving trails of excrement. In tomatoes, the caterpillars eat the flower buds, chew large holes in leaves, and burrow into ripe fruit. The caterpillars also chew leaves of other plants.

There are up to four generations per year. Corn earworm pupae overwinter in the soil and the adults emerge in early spring to lay eggs, which hatch in 2–10 days. The caterpillars feed for 2–4 weeks, then pupate in the soil. The moths emerge 10–25 days later. Earworm pupae are not hardy enough to survive the winter in the northern United States and Canada. The moths, however, fly long distances and migrate north in the spring, where they usually become pests later in the season than in southern regions.

Plants Attacked

These are major pests of corn in the corn belt. Early corn in the north is least affected. Corn, tomatoes, and peppers are the main plants attacked, but earworms/fruitworms have also been reported on beans, cabbage, okra, peanuts, squash, and sunflowers.

Organic Controls

Attract native parasitic wasps, lacewings, and minute pirate bugs by interplanting with pollen and nectar plants. Avoid attracting moths to your garden by keeping nearby lights off at night.

Plant corn cultivars with tight husks that extend beyond the ear, as these prevent earworms from entering. After the corn silks start to dry, apply one of the following to the tip of each ear: *Bacillus thuringiensis* var. *kurstaki* (BTK) sprays, granular BTK, insect parasitic nematodes, or 20 drops of mineral oil. Where earworm populations are low, you can adequately control them by opening the corn husks and digging out larvae in the tip before they damage the main ear. Paint a mixture of pyrethrins and molasses (3 parts water to 1 part molasses) around the base of cornstalks to attract and kill emerging adults. In northern areas, start early corn cultivars indoors and set out early to avoid peak populations. For large corn patches, use sex pheromone traps to monitor the arrival of moths in the area, and time sprays of BTK or neem to coincide with the period when the most eggs should be hatching.

Inspect tomatoes and other plants frequently, and handpick caterpillars or spray BTK or neem.

CUCUMBER BEETLE, SPOTTED

Diabrotica undecimpunctata howardi

Adults are greenish yellow, elongated beetles, about ¼ inch long, with 12 black spots on the wing covers. The larvae, southern corn rootworms, are very slender, white, with reddish brown heads and light brown patches on first and last segments. They are legless and grow up to ¾ inch long.

The larvae tunnel into the base of stems and feed on roots, which often kills young plants. The adult beetles eat holes in leaves and chew on fruit skin. Larvae and adults feeding on older plants generally don't cause much damage, although they may weaken plants so that the stems blow down easily. The cucumber beetles, however, are thought to transmit cucumber mosaic virus and bacterial wilt diseases of corn and cucumber, which can be far more damaging than the direct-feeding injury. As there is no way to tell whether beetles are spreading these diseases, the best policy is to keep beetle populations low.

There are up to three generations of spotted cucumber beetles per year. The beetles spend the winter under crop debris and clumps of grass, emerging in spring to lay eggs in the soil close to plants. When the eggs hatch, the larvae feed in roots and crowns of plants for 2–4 weeks, then pupate. Northern populations of cucumber beetles migrate north and south with the changing seasons, traveling up to 500 miles in a few days.

Plants Attacked
Spotted cucumber beetles can be a major pest of corn and field cucumbers, and they also attack peanuts, potatoes, and ornamentals.

Organic Controls
Plant wilt- and mosaic-resistant cucumber, squash, and melon cultivars to avoid the main damage from these beetles. Where beetles are numerous, cover small and low-growing plants with floating row covers; grow gynoecious cultivars or hand-pollinate cucumbers, melons, and squash. Spray or dust plants with pyrethrins to control adults. For corn, apply insect parasitic nematodes to the soil around roots to control larvae. After harvest, remove and destroy crop residues to eliminate overwintering sites.

Research Notes
M. Hoffman at Cornell University in Ithaca, New York, is working on a trap for cucumber beetles that may be both a control method and a monitoring tool. Large, plastic cups, turned upside down and suspended at various heights above the soil, attracted the adult beetles. The traps were more effective when baited with a mixture of attractant pheromones.

Spotted cucumber beetle (<u>Diabrotica undecimpunctata howardi</u>) on tomato leaf

Striped cucumber beetle (<u>Acalymma vittatum</u>)

CUCUMBER BEETLE, STRIPED
Acalymma vittatum

Adults are yellow, elongated beetles, ¼ inch long. They have black heads and three wide black stripes on their wing covers. The larvae are indistinguishable from spotted cucumber beetle larvae and are also slender and white, with reddish brown heads. They are legless and up to ¾ inch long. When beetles occur in large numbers, they swarm on seedlings, feeding on leaves and young shoots. They also attack the stems and flowers of older plants and eat holes in the fruit.

The beetles are thought to transmit bacterial wilt and mosaic viruses, which often causes more damage than their direct feeding. The larvae feed on the roots of squash-family plants, which stunts and sometimes kills plants.

There are up to four generations per year. The beetles overwinter in dense grass and other vegetation, emerging from April to early June. They feed on weed pollen for 2 weeks, then move into crops to lay their eggs in the soil at the base of the plants.

The eggs hatch in 10 days and larvae burrow down to feed on roots. They feed for 2–6 weeks and pupate in early August. The beetles emerge in 2 weeks and feed on blossoms and maturing fruit.

Plants Attacked
The larvae feed only on cucumbers, melons, pumpkins, and squash. Adults mainly attack these plants, but will also feed on beans, corn, peas, and the blossoms of many plants.

Organic Controls
Plant bacterial wilt- and mosaic-resistant cucumber, squash, and melon cultivars. Where adults are numerous, cover plants with floating row covers (grow gynoecious cultivars or hand-pollinate cucumbers, squash, and melons). Mulch plants with deep straw to impede the movement of adults. Spray or dust with pyrethrins when you see beetles feeding on pollen in flowers.

Apply insect parasitic nematodes to the soil around squash-family plants to help control the larvae.

Research Notes
M. Hoffman at Cornell University in Ithaca, New York, is working on a trap for cucumber beetles that may be promising as both a control method and a monitoring tool. Large, yellow plastic cups, turned upside down and suspended at various heights above the soil, attracted the adult beetles. The traps were more effective when baited with a mixture of attractant pheromones.

A. Radin at the University of Maine in Orono, Maine, has found that squash can be successfully used as a trap crop for striped cucumber beetles to keep them away from cucumbers. The best ratio was planting half squash and half cucumbers. With this ratio, 90 percent of the beetles remained on the trap crop.

CUTWORMS
Order Lepidoptera: Family Noctuidae
Adults are large, brownish or gray moths with 1½-inch wingspans. The larvae are fat, greasy gray or dull brown caterpillars with shiny heads. There are several species of cutworms. Most are found in the soil, although some also climb plants.

Moths do not damage plants, but the cutworm caterpillars can be very destructive in some years. They feed at night on young plants, usually cutting the stem at or just below the soil line so that the plant topples over. They may completely consume seedlings. During the day, cutworms rest just below the soil surface, curled beside the stems of damaged plants.

There is usually one generation per year, but a late second generation may damage plants in years with very warm fall weather. The adult moths emerge from the overwintering pupae and lay their eggs on grass stems or in the soil from early May to early June. The eggs hatch in 5–7 days. The cutworms feed on grass and other plants for 3–5 weeks, then pupate in the soil. Moths emerge from late August to early September. Some cutworm species overwinter as eggs, which hatch during the first warm days, ready to feed on the earliest seedlings.

Plants Attacked

Cutworms attack most early vegetable and flower seedlings, shoots, and transplants.

Organic Controls

Protect transplants from damage by using cutworm collars around the stems. Collars can be cardboard, plastic, or small tin cans with both ends removed. Press them an inch into the soil. Avoid the main population of cutworms by planting later in the season. To clear the soil of cutworms before planting, scatter moist bran mixed with *Bacillus thuringiensis* var. *kurstaki* (BTK) and molasses a week before setting out plants, or drench soil with neem or a solution of insect parasitic nematodes, both before and after transplanting. Dig around the base of damaged transplants in the morning and destroy hiding larvae. To control climbing cutworms, spray plants with neem.

Cultivation can also help to eliminate cutworm larvae from your garden. In fall, remove plant debris from the garden, then thoroughly cultivate the soil to a depth of 6–8 inches. About 2–3 weeks later, turn the top couple of inches of the soil to expose cutworm larvae to hungry birds.

In spring, cultivate lightly as soon as the soil can be worked to reduce damage by the first generation of cutworms, which tends to be the most troublesome. Wait 10–14 days after tilling to plant.

Cutworm collars keep cutworms away from your plants

Cutworm larva

*Smaller European elm bark beetle
(Scolytus multistriatus)*

ELM BARK BEETLES
Scolytus multistriatus and
Hylurgopinus rufipes

Elm bark beetles are compact, cylindrical insects about 1/10 inch long. They are shiny, dark brown with lengthwise rows of fine punctures on their wing covers. Their heads are curved down, under a broad thorax. The larvae are fat, whitish, and C-shaped, without legs. They live under bark.

European corn borer (Ostrinia nubilalis) on corn

The beetles make small entrance and exit holes in the bark of trees. Both the larvae and adults live in galleries they carve in a radiating pattern in the inner bark. They do not cause serious damage directly, but the beetles carry the devastating Dutch elm disease fungi on their bodies and infect healthy trees when they bore into the bark.

There are one to three generations per year. The beetles emerge from holes in the bark in the spring and begin feeding in crotches of elm twigs before moving to recently cut, dead, or dying elms. They engrave galleries between the wood and inner bark and lay eggs. Each larva feeds in a separate branch of the gallery and pupates in a cell at the end. The next generation of adult beetles emerges in 10–14 days. *S. multistriatus* overwinter under the bark as larvae, while *H. rufipes* overwinter either as larvae or adults.

Plants Attacked
These beetles are a major pest of elm trees.

Organic Controls
Replace infected trees with elm cultivars resistant to Dutch elm disease (try 'Prospector' or 'Frontier'), and maintain healthy trees. Bury or burn all diseased or dying elms to eliminate sources of disease. Where infestations are severe, try trapping adult beetles with pheromone traps over a wide area. Braconid wasps (*Dendrosoter protuberans*) parasitize elm bark beetles.

EUROPEAN CORN BORER
Ostrinia nubilalis

Adult females are pale, yellowish brown moths, with 1-inch wingspans. They have dark, zigzag patterns across the wings, whereas male moths are darker and smaller. Larvae are gray or beige, up to 1 inch long, with brown heads. They have small, brown dots on each segment. The eggs are white to tan and laid on undersides of leaves in characteristic masses of 15–20 overlapping eggs.

Young caterpillars feed on the first whorls of leaves, on corn tassels, and beneath the husks of ears. Older larvae burrow into corn stalks and also feed in tassels and ears. Boring weakens stalks, causing them to break easily. There are several different strains of European corn borers. These differ in the number of generations per year (one to three) and the type of feeding damage they do to corn.

The larvae overwinter in corn stalks and plant stems left in fields. They complete pupation in the early spring and the moths generally emerge in June. They lay eggs from late June to mid-July, although some strains can be present much earlier and later than this. The eggs hatch in a week and the larvae feed for 3–4 weeks before spinning a delicate cocoon inside a stalk.

Plants Attacked

Corn is the most important host, and in some regions is the only crop attacked. In other areas, beans, peppers, potatoes, tomatoes, small grains, and other plants, including flowers, may be attacked.

Organic Controls

Start by planting corn cultivars with strong stalks and tight husk covers. Plant to attract native parasitic flies and wasps, which kill large numbers of corn borers. Where populations are high, remove tassels from two-thirds of corn plants before the pollen sheds. This eliminates many larvae in the tassels, while leaving enough tassels for pollination. To control larvae in ears, apply liquid or granular *Bacillus thuringiensis* var. *kurstaki* (BTK) or mineral oil

on the tips of ears. In the fall, shred and compost corn stalks or bury them immediately after harvest. To control larvae on leaves, spray BTK, neem, or pyrethrins.

FLATHEADED APPLETREE BORER

Chrysobothris femorata

Adults are somewhat flattened, dark bronze beetles, about ½ inch long. The larvae are white, legless grubs, up to 1¼ inches long with one very wide segment behind the head. The head is brown and pulled back into the next segment.

The beetles feed on leaves, causing little damage. The larvae, however, tunnel into the sapwood of young trees and under the bark of older trees. They carve out galleries, which are packed with sawdust castings. A gummy sap runs from the bark of an attacked tree and the bark darkens and dies. The tree will die if the bark is killed entirely around the trunk. Young and weakened trees are most susceptible to borers. Most borer attacks are on the sunny sides of trees.

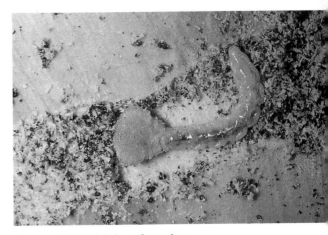

Larva of flatheaded appletree borer (Chrysobothris femorata)

There are one or two generations per year. Borer larvae overwinter in chambers carved 1 inch deep in the wood. They pupate in the spring and the adult beetles emerge from May to July. They lay eggs in cracks in the bark, and when the grubs hatch, they tunnel under the bark for the rest of summer. They usually cannot complete their development on healthy, vigorous trees.

Plants Attacked

This and related species may attack most fruit, shade, and forest trees.

Organic Controls

Maintain vigorous trees, which are least susceptible to borer damage. Avoid mechanical injury to bark and remove any injured limbs promptly. Protect the trunks of young trees from sunscald with white trunk paint. To save an attacked tree, cut out larvae from under dark patches of dying bark in late summer or early fall. (Note that wrapping bark to prevent borers is no longer considered good practice as it can increase borer attack in some plants.)

Flea beetle and damage

FLEA BEETLES
Order Coleoptera: Family Chrysomelidae

Adults are tiny, active black, brown, or bronze beetles, $\frac{1}{10}$ inch long. They have enlarged hind legs and jump like fleas when they are disturbed. The larvae live in the soil and are thin, white, legless grubs with brown heads.

Flea beetle damage is easily recognizable by the small, round holes the adults chew through leaves, which look like they have been peppered with fine shot. Flea beetles are most damaging in the early spring, when seedlings may be killed by a heavy infestation of adults. Larger plants usually survive and outgrow the damage, unless the plants were infected with a plant virus spread by the beetles. The larvae feed on plant roots and, in some species, such as the tuber flea beetle, the larvae cause the greatest losses.

There are up to four generations per year. The adults overwinter in the soil and emerge in spring to feed and lay eggs on the roots of plants. They die out by early July. The eggs hatch in about a week and the larvae feed for 2–3 weeks. They pupate in the soil and the next-generation adults emerge in 2–3 weeks.

Plants Attacked

Flea beetles attack most vegetables, particularly cabbage-family plants, potatoes, and spinach. They also feed on flowers and weeds.

Organic Controls

Plant susceptible plants as late as possible to avoid the most damaging generation. Cover seedlings and potato shoots with floating row covers or fine mesh until adult beetles die off. Flea beetles prefer full sun, so interplant crops to shade susceptible plants. Spray pyrethrins to control adult flea beetles. Drench roots with insect parasitic nematodes to control larvae.

Research Notes

D. Andow and other researchers at Michigan State University have found that interplanting cabbage with living mulches of white clover, creeping bentgrass, red fescue, or Kentucky bluegrass reduced the need to control cabbage flea beetles early in the season. In another study, these researchers found that cabbage flea beetles were slower to find broccoli when it was interplanted with white clover and they were quicker to leave the crop.

FRUIT BORERS

Synanthedon tipuliformis **and related species**

Adults are swift, agile moths that look somewhat like wasps. They have clear wings marked with dark patterns and smooth, black or black-and-yellow striped bodies, up to 1 inch long. The larvae are pale yellow or white caterpillars with dark heads.

The larvae bore into the pith of stems, which kills or weakens canes, causing them to break easily. They also bore into the crowns of plants, girdle canes, and destroy new shoots. There is usually one generation per year. The larvae overwinter inside canes and pupate in early May. The adult moths emerge in 2 weeks. They lay eggs on the canes and these hatch in 10 days. The larvae tunnel in fruit canes all summer, remaining there for the winter. They pupate in the cane, after making an exit hole that will be used by the moth when it emerges later. Rhododendron crownborer larvae spend the winter in crowns and work their way up into plant stems by July. They pupate under the bark, several inches above the soil line, and adults emerge in a month. Other rhododendron borer larvae attack the trunk and branches, causing leaves to wilt and yellow. Look for small holes and sawdust, especially where branches form crotches.

Currant borer moth (Synanthedon tipuliformis)

Plants Attacked

Fruit borers attack blackberries, currants, gooseberries, raspberries, and rhododendrons.

Organic Controls

Before purchasing nursery plants, examine them carefully for signs of borer damage. Maintain vigorous plants, which are less susceptible to borers. Prune out and burn canes infested with borers, dig and destroy infested crowns and roots, or smash remaining stubs with a mallet to kill pupae and larvae. If carefully timed, summer oil sprays provide reasonable control of eggs.

Fruit fly larvae in peach

FRUIT FLIES

Rhagoletes spp., *Ceratitis capitata*

Flies in this group are about ¼ inch long and generally have yellow or white markings on their bodies. They have transparent wings with a characteristic pattern of dark, crosswise bands. Fruit fly larvae are small, white maggots that live in fruit.

These true fruit flies should not be confused with the smaller vinegar flies (often called fruit flies), which hover around rotting fruit. Fruit fly larvae tunnel through fruit, causing it to shrivel and drop early. The earliest cultivars of fruit usually suffer the most damage from these pests. In walnuts, the main injury from walnut husk flies is stained shells.

Most species have one generation per year, but in the South they may reproduce year-round. Adult flies emerge from pupae in mid-June or later. They search for developing fruit and lay eggs in punctures in fruit skin or around stems. The eggs hatch within a week, and the larvae tunnel in the fruit until it drops. The maggots then leave the fruit to pupate and overwinter in the soil. In the soil, both maggots and pupae are preyed upon by ground beetles and rove beetles.

Plants Attacked

Related fruit fly species attack blueberries, currants, plums, cherries, peaches, and walnuts. *Ceratitis capitata* also infests citrus and coffee trees.

Organic Controls

During the summer, collect and destroy fallen fruit every day, before the larvae leave and burrow into the soil. Pick up fallen fruit weekly in the fall. To trap adults, hang yellow sticky traps in fruit trees (1–2 traps per tree) and bait traps with small vials of equal parts ammonia and water, or use commercial fruit fly attractants. Use mulches or groundcovers in the orchard to provide refuges for native predatory beetles.

FRUIT TREE LEAFROLLER

Archips argyrospila

Adult moths have mottled, golden brown forewings, light brown hindwings, and a 1-inch wingspan. The larvae are green caterpillars with brown heads covered with short fine spines. They grow up to 1 inch long and

Fruit tree leafroller (<u>Archips argyrospila</u>)

are found inside rolled-up sections of leaves. The eggs are a light yellowish brown. They are laid in masses of 30–100 on tree branches and trunks and are covered with a brown protective cement.

These caterpillars spin fine webs at the tips of branches, pulling the leaves together into a protective cover. The caterpillars feed on the enclosed buds, leaves, and immature fruit, safe from predators and sprays inside the web. Caterpillars feeding on developing apples leave rough scars or large holes in the fruit. Leafrollers are most damaging to apples in the northern U.S. and Canada.

Fruit tree leafrollers have one generation per year. The eggs overwinter on tree bark and hatch in early spring. The larvae feed for 1 month, then spin webs and pupate within the rolled-up leaves or in a cocoon on the bark. The moths emerge in late June or July and lay eggs, which remain dormant through winter.

Plants Attacked

The fruittree leafroller mainly attacks apple trees, although it is known to feed on most kinds of fruit and ornamental trees, including walnuts in some regions.

Organic Controls

Inspect trees in the winter for egg masses and scrape them from the branches. Spray dormant oil to kill eggs just before buds break. In early spring, inspect young and small trees weekly and handpick the caterpillars from branch tips. Spray *Bacillus thuringiensis* var. *kurstaki* (BTK) while caterpillars are small, before they start to roll leaves, or spray neem or pyrethrins as a last resort. Where infestations are always damaging, start spraying BTK at the blossom stage.

GYPSY MOTH
Lymantria dispar

Adult females are nearly white moths, 1 inch long, with thin brown markings on their wings. Their bodies are plump and furry and, although they have wings, they are unable to fly. The males are smaller, darker, and are strong fliers. Gypsy moth caterpillars have five pairs of blue dots and six pairs of red dots on their backs and are covered with tufts of long hair. They grow up to 2½ inches long. The eggs are laid in masses under a furry, yellowish covering.

Adult female gypsy moth (Lymantria dispar)

Gypsy moth caterpillar on leaf

The caterpillars feed on tree foliage, chewing large holes in the leaves. In years of heavy infestations, which occur periodically, trees may be completely defoliated. Deciduous trees leaf out again, but repeated defoliations may eventually kill them. A single defoliation, however, kills conifers. Some people are allergic to the hairs on larvae and may have allergic reactions when large numbers of caterpillars are present.

The eggs are laid on tree trunks, where they overwinter to hatch in May. The larvae crawl up the tree and feed until mid-July, then pupate for several weeks. The adult moths emerge from late July to early August. The males locate the females by detecting the sex pheromones the females give off. After mating, the female crawls up a nearby tree or other object to deposit her egg mass.

This is an introduced species into North America. Every year its range expands through the movement of the moths. They are also spread widely by people who unknowingly move the egg masses and pupae on camping trailers, outdoor equipment, trucks, and ships. Although the established populations of gypsy

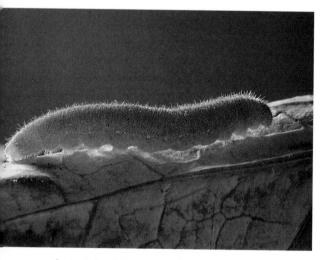

Imported cabbageworm (Artogeia rapae)

moths are mainly in the central and eastern states and Canada, isolated infestations have been recorded in all west-coast states and British Columbia. Gypsy moths have a variety of natural enemies in North America, including flies, ground beetles, parasitic wasps, and diseases; however, these do not prevent periodic outbreaks of high gypsy moth populations.

Plants Attacked

Gypsy moth caterpillars prefer deciduous trees and shrubs, but will feed on conifers.

Organic Controls

Prevent further spread of this pest by checking trailers, boats, camping gear, lawnmowers, and other outdoor equipment for eggs, larvae, and pupae before traveling or moving from an infested region. Use pheromone traps, which catch males, to detect whether populations are present. During outbreaks, spray *Bacillus thuringiensis* var. *kurstaki* (BTK) or neem 2 or 3 times at 1–2 week intervals in early to mid-May to kill caterpillars. Wrap burlap tree bands on orchard and yard trees. Check daily and destroy larvae hiding under bands, or use sticky bands to trap the larvae. In the fall, search for and destroy egg masses on tree trunks, sides of buildings, fence posts, and out-door equipment. Where this species is well established, plant trees less favored by gypsy moth, such as honey locust, basswood, 'Marshall's Seedless' green ash, and 'Deborah' Norway maple.

IMPORTED CABBAGEWORM
Artogeia rapae (formerly *Pieris rapae*)

Adult cabbageworms are the common white butterflies seen in every garden. The wings are white with black tips and with 1 or 2 small black spots on the forewing. They have a wingspan of 1½ inches. The larvae are velvety green caterpillars with a fine, light yellow stripe down the back. The eggs are tiny yellow cones, laid on undersides of leaves.

There are three to five overlapping generations per year in most areas. The adult butterflies emerge in the spring to lay eggs on cabbage-family plants. When the eggs hatch, the caterpillars begin feeding on undersides of leaves. As they grow larger, they bite large, ragged holes in cabbage leaves and chew on florets of cauliflower and broccoli. As they feed, they produce pellets of dark green droppings. The caterpillars feed for 2–3 weeks, then pupate in garden trash on the soil surface. The butterflies emerge from the pupae in 1–2 weeks. Last-generation pupae overwinter in garden debris.

Plants Attacked
Imported cabbageworms feed on nasturtiums and all cabbage-family plants, including broccoli, cabbage, cauliflower, and related plants.

Organic Controls
Plant purple cabbage cultivars, which are less often attacked by cabbageworms. Protect and attract parasitic wasps and other natural enemies, including yellowjacket wasps, which consume large numbers of imported cabbageworm caterpillars. Handpicking caterpillars and eggs provides sufficient control in light infestations. Cover small plants with floating row covers to prevent butterflies from laying eggs on plants. Place yellow sticky traps among host plants to catch female butterflies. Where caterpillars are damaging, spray *Bacillus thuringiensis* var. *kurstaki* (BTK) or neem at 1–2 week intervals. As a last resort, spray pyrethrins.

Iris borer larva (<u>Macronoctua onusta</u>*)*

IRIS BORER
Macronoctua onusta

Adults are large moths with a 2-inch wingspan. They have dark brown forewings and yellowish hindwings. The young larvae are greenish caterpillars that become pinkish with a brown head. They have a light-colored stripe down the back and rows of small black spots along the sides. Larvae grow 1½–2 inches long.

Iris borers have a one-year life cycle. The eggs overwinter on old leaves and hatch in late April to early May. The younger larvae tunnel into the iris leaves, leaf sheaths, and buds. As they get older, the caterpillars bore into the iris crowns and hollow out the rhizomes. Feeding directly injures roots and also leaves them open to soft rot infections. The larvae develop for several weeks, then pupate in the soil near the rhizomes. The moths emerge from the pupae in late August to early September and lay eggs for winter.

Plants Attacked
Where it occurs (mainly eastern North America), this is the most serious pest of iris.

Organic Controls

Inspect plants starting in early spring and pinch leaves at the base to crush larvae feeding inside. Dig and destroy infested rhizomes as soon as you notice damage. To save valuable plants, dig out the larvae and pupae, then dip the roots in an antibiotic or dust with sulfur before replanting to prevent soft rot. Collect and destroy all dead iris leaves and stems in the late fall to eliminate overwintering eggs. Where infestations are usually heavy, spray neem or pyrethrins at the base of plants starting in late April to kill emerging borer larvae.

JAPANESE BEETLE
Popillia japonica

Adults are distinctive, blocky, metallic blue-green beetles, ½ inch long. They have tufts of white hairs along the sides of the abdomen and bronze-colored wing covers. Their legs are relatively long with large claws. The beetle larvae are fat, dirty white, C-shaped grubs with

Japanese beetle (<u>Popillia japonica</u>)

brown heads, up to ¾ inch long and found in the soil.

The beetles feed on plants during the day, especially in warm weather. They chew on flowers and skeletonize leaves, which wilt and drop, and they seem to prefer plants in full sun. When peak numbers of beetles are present in July, they may completely defoliate plants. The beetle larvae feed on roots of lawn turf and other grasses. When populations are high, they cause irregular patches of dead or wilted turf, which is easily lifted as the roots are destroyed. Turf damage is most evident in the spring and fall.

The life cycle takes 1–2 years. As fall approaches, the larvae burrow deeper into the soil to avoid freezing during winter. They move toward the surface again in spring to resume feeding on roots. They pupate in the soil in May and June, and adult beetles emerge from late June to July. The beetles feed on plants until late summer, then burrow under grasses to lay eggs. The eggs hatch into larvae that feed until cold weather arrives.

Plants Attacked

Japanese beetles feed on a wide range of vegetables (especially asparagus, beans, corn, okra, onions, rhubarb, and tomatoes), trees, shrubs, vines, and fruits, as well as many flowers and ornamentals. The larvae damage turfgrass and other grasses.

Organic Controls

Infested turf may be torn up by crows, raccoons, and other animals digging for the plump grubs. In a healthy ecosystem, native species of flies, parasitic wasps, and diseases attack the larvae. In areas where Japanese beetles are common pests, choose ornamental plants that are not attractive to the beetles. When beetle numbers are high in midsummer, cover smaller or more valuable garden plants with floating row covers or screens. In the early morning, handpick beetles or vacuum them from plants with a hand-held vacuum cleaner, or shake them from the plants onto ground sheets and destroy. To reduce beetle numbers in the area, organize a community-wide trapping program (placing traps in a single yard is not effective and may attract additional beetles to the yard).

Destroy beetle eggs in turf by allowing your lawn to dry out well between waterings in mid-summer, or stop watering and allow the turf to go dormant for the summer months. To control larvae, apply insect parasitic nematodes or neem to the sod in late spring or late summer. For long-term control, apply milky disease (*Bacillus popilliae*) to the turf. Aerate the turf with spiked aerator sandals to kill larvae while they are close to the soil surface in late spring and early fall.

White grub and June beetle

JUNE/MAY BEETLES
Phyllophaga spp.

Adults are stout, blocky beetles, mostly shiny brown or black and ¾–1⅜ inches long. Some species have lengthwise stripes on the back or fine hairs over the body. The tip of the abdomen extends past the wing covers. The larvae are fat, C-shaped, white grubs over 1 inch long, with six legs and dark heads.

Adult beetles chew on leaves and, if their numbers are high enough, they may defoliate trees. The larvae feed on roots and may cause serious damage in years when there are large broods, which generally occurs in three-year cycles. Native predators and parasites usually suppress populations sufficiently to prevent serious damage.

Life cycles of May beetles take 1–4 years. The females lay batches of 50–100 eggs in balls of earth formed in the soil. The eggs hatch in 2–3 weeks. The grubs feed on decaying vegetation for their first summer, then hibernate just below the surface of the soil for the winter. They feed on plant roots the second summer. After hibernating again, they feed until June of the third summer, then pupate for 2–3 weeks. Adults remain in the soil until spring of the fourth year, when they emerge to feed and lay eggs.

Plants Attacked
The larvae feed on roots of woody shrubs and trees, garden plants, and grasses. Adult beetles feed on leaves of oak, elm, beech, maple, poplar, willow, and other trees and shrubs, but are rarely damaging.

Organic Controls
Where infestations are severe, apply neem or insect parasitic nematodes to the soil around shrubs and trees to control larvae in late spring or late fall; irrigate before and after applying nematodes. For long-term control, try applying milky disease (*Bacillus popilliae*). Cultivate garden soil to expose the larvae in garden beds to birds and other predators. Avoid spreading manure or other organic amendments on lawns during the summer, as it encourages the female beetles to lay eggs.

Sycamore lace bugs

LACE BUGS
Order Heteroptera: Family Tingidae

Adult lace bugs are tiny, oval or rectangular-shaped bugs, 1/10–1/4 inch long. The body and wings are covered with a characteristic lacy pattern, and the thorax has wide, flattened extensions. The nymphs are smaller, darker, and covered with spines. The eggs are inserted in a slit in the underside of a leaf along a midrib. They are covered by a cone-like cap projecting from the leaf and are marked by spikes of solidified plant juices that ooze from the injury.

Both adults and nymphs suck juices from foliage and stems of trees and other plants. The feeding causes yellowish patches or a speckled, white or gray blotchy appearance on the leaf surface. As they feed, the bugs leave spots of black, pepperlike excrement on undersides of leaves. Light feeding causes little damage, but when large numbers of lace bugs are present, they may cause the death of foliage and stems. Some species feed on flowering plants and suck juice from blossoms.

There are three or more generations per year. Most species of lace bugs overwinter in the egg stage, although some overwinter as adults under tree bark. The eggs hatch into nymphs that feed on plant juices on undersides of leaves for several weeks, before molting to adults.

Plants Attacked

Lace bugs commonly attack oaks, hazel nuts, birches, alders, and plants in the daisy family. Other garden shrubs, flowers, and trees may also be attacked.

Organic Controls

Maintain vigorous plants. For heavy infestations, in mid-May and again 10 days later, spray insecticidal soap or pyrethrins to control both adults and nymphs. Summer oils are also effective on trees and plants that can tolerate oil sprays.

LEAFHOPPERS
Order Homoptera: Family Cicadellidae

Adult leafhoppers are mostly wedge-shaped, slender, and range from 1/10–1/2 inch long. Many leafhopper species have a broadly triangular head or a pronounced forward

Adult leafhopper (Circulliter tenellus)

point to the head. Most are either brown or green and some have bright bands of color on the wings. All have well-developed hind legs and can jump rapidly into flight when disturbed. The nymphs are similar to the adults, but paler in color and wingless. Although they cannot fly, they hop rapidly when disturbed.

Both adults and nymphs suck juices from stems and undersides of leaves, giving leaves a light, mottled appearance. Plants may have tipburn (called "hopper burn" on potatoes) and yellowed, curled leaves with white spots on the undersides. When leafhoppers are numerous, the whole plant may be stunted. Plants also react to the insect's toxic saliva by producing distorted leaves with warty, crinkled, or rolled edges. As they feed, leafhoppers also excrete honeydew on leaves below. Fruit below may be spotted with drops of excrement and honeydew (this can be washed off). Many species of leafhoppers spread viruses and other plant disease organisms.

Most species have two to five generations per year. Adults usually spend the winter on wild host plants; some species overwinter as eggs. Some do not survive winter in northern regions and may migrate over long distances from the South every summer.

The females start laying eggs when the leaves begin to appear on trees. The eggs are laid in rows or clusters, usually within the tissue of leaves, veins, and stems. The eggs hatch in 10–14 days and the nymphs develop for 1–4 weeks. The first fall frosts usually kill any remaining nymphs.

Plants Attacked
Leafhoppers attack flowers, fruit trees, and vegetables, especially apple trees, beans, eggplant, grapes, peanuts, potatoes, and squash-family plants. They also feed on some ornamentals and many kinds of weeds.

Organic Controls
Native parasitic flies, damsel bugs, minute pirate bugs, lady beetles, lacewings, parasitic wasps, and spiders are important in keeping leafhopper numbers down. Some leafhopper damage is tolerable, and control measures are usually not necessary. Apply dormant oil sprays to kill adults overwintering on fruit trees. Wash nymphs from plants with a stiff spray of water. You can also control nymphs while they are still small with sprays of neem, insecticidal soap, or pyrethrins.

Research Notes
B. C. Murphy at the University of California, Davis, California, has found that the native parasitic wasp *Anagrus epos* attacks grape leafhoppers and overwinters in nearby plum trees. This is in addition to the previously known overwintering sites in blackberries.

LEAFMINERS
Order Diptera: Family Agromyzidae
Adult leafminers are mostly black or black and yellow flies, 1/10 inch long (they are rarely seen). The larvae are pale green, stubby, translucent maggots, found in tunnels

Leafminer damage on azalea leaf

between the upper and lower surface of leaves. The eggs are white, cylindrical, and laid side by side in clusters on undersides of leaves.

The larvae tunnel through tissue within the leaf, making hollowed-out, curved, or winding mines, each type characteristic of a particular species. The larval damage may destroy seedlings; however, on older plants, leafminers are often a nuisance rather than a serious problem. Leafminer damage is also unsightly on ornamentals.

Most species have two or three generations per year (more in greenhouse crops). The adult flies emerge from overwintering cocoons in the early spring and lay eggs on leaves. The larvae mine in the leaf tissue for 1–3 weeks, then pupate for 2–4 weeks. Depending on the species, they may pupate in the leaf or drop to the soil to pupate.

Plants Attacked

Common leafminers attack beets, chard, spinach, peas, peppers, tomatoes, and other vegetables, including cabbages and lettuce. Leafminers are also a problem on trees, ivy, and flowers, especially chrysanthemums and nasturtiums.

*Citrus mealybug (*Planococcus citri*)*

Organic Controls

Cover seedlings with floating row covers to prevent adults from laying eggs. Maintain covers all season on small plants, like beets and chard, where leafminers are numerous. Remove nearby dock or lamb's-quarters, which are wild hosts for beet leafminer. Attract native parasitic wasps, which usually suppress leafminers. Handpick and destroy mined leaves and remove egg clusters. If done thoroughly in spring, this is effective in reducing later generations. Most sprays do not reach larvae, as they are protected by the leaf; however, neem sprays are very effective. Some plants (tomatoes, chrysanthemums, beans) take up neem through the roots and can be protected by drenching the soil with neem.

MEALYBUGS
Order Homoptera: Family Pseudococcidae

Adult female mealybugs have soft, oval, pinkish bodies covered with white, powdery, or waxy fluff. Individuals are $\frac{1}{10}$ inch long, and are usually found in groups with all ages of nymphs. The nymphs are similar to females but much smaller. Males are tiny, two-winged insects that are hardly ever noticed.

Both adult females and nymphs suck plant juices. They feed on all parts of the plant, especially new growth, and some species also feed on roots. Attacked leaves wither and turn yellow, and fruit may drop prematurely if the infestation is severe. Mealybugs also excrete honeydew on leaves as they feed, which supports growth of sooty molds.

Mealybugs overwinter outdoors in the warmer, southern areas of North America. In the north, they survive in greenhouses. There are several generations per year outdoors, more in greenhouses. The females lay eggs in a cottony white mass. The eggs hatch in

10 days and the minute "crawlers" wander away to find feeding sites on the plant, where they develop for 1–2 months.

Plants Attacked
Mealybugs feed on citrus and other tree fruits, as well as avocados, grapes, and potatoes. They are major pests of flowers, flowering trees, ornamentals and tropical foliage plants, including arums, oleanders, and poinsettias.

Organic Controls
Attract native parasitic wasps, which often keep populations in check outdoors. Rinse plants with a stiff stream of water to dislodge mealybugs or spray with insecticidal soap. Spray summer oil on plants that tolerate oil sprays. Release mealybug destroyers (*Cryptolaemus montrouzieri*) to control mealybugs on citrus and grapes outdoors and on greenhouse plants. The parasitic wasp *Leptomastix dactylopii* can also be used to control citrus mealybugs.

MEXICAN BEAN BEETLE
Epilachna varivestis

Adults are oval, yellowish brown to copper-colored beetles, ¼ inch long. They have 16 black spots arranged in three rows across the wing covers and look much like beneficial species of lady beetles. The beetle larvae are fat, legless, yellowish orange grubs up to ⅓ inch in length. They have six rows of long, branching spines on their body segments. Eggs are bright yellow ovals laid on end in clusters of 40–60 on the undersides of leaves.

Larvae and adults feed from the underside of leaves on the tissue between the veins. They skeletonize leaves, leaving behind a characteristic lacy appearance. Attacked plants may produce fewer pods and plants may be completely

Mexican bean beetle larva

Adult Mexican bean beetle (Epilachna varivestis)

defoliated and killed in July and August when beetles are most numerous. Bean beetles are most abundant in weedless fields.

There are up to four generations per year. The adults overwinter in garden debris or leaf litter in nearby fields. Some emerge about the time the first bean leaves are up, while others straggle out of hibernation over the next few months. The beetles feed for a couple of weeks before the females lay eggs on bean plants. The eggs hatch in 5–14 days and larvae feed for 2–5 weeks. They pupate in a case attached to the underside of a leaf and the beetles emerge in about a week. When they first emerge, new adults are a solid yellow color. They soon darken and the spots become visible. In late summer, large numbers of beetles can disperse from nearby bean fields.

Plants Attacked

All kinds of beans may be attacked, including cowpeas, lima beans, snap beans, and soybeans.

Millipede

Navel orangeworm larva (<u>Amyelois transitella</u>) in English walnut

Organic Controls

Plant resistant cultivars (such as 'Wade' and 'Logan' snap beans or 'Black Valentine' lima beans). In southern areas, plant early bush beans to avoid the most damaging generation of beetles. This is not practical for northern gardeners, as early plantings grow slowly and may suffer more damage from early generations. Cover beans with floating row covers until plants are well-grown. Leave a few flowering weeds between rows or interplant with flowers and herbs to attract native predators and parasites. Remove or dig in crop debris at harvest to remove overwintering sites. Plant soybeans as a trap crop and destroy plants when they become infested with beetle larvae. In small bean patches, daily handpicking of larvae and adults can considerably reduce damage from the second generation. Check plants as soon as they sprout. Spray weekly with neem or pyrethrins, making sure to cover undersides of leaves. Experiment with releasing spined soldier bugs (*Podisus maculiventris*) to control the early generation, or parasitic wasps (*Pediobius foveolatus*), when the weather warms, to control the second generation.

MILLIPEDES

Class Diplopoda

Millipedes are ½–1½ inches long and slender, with many segments. They are often confused with centipedes, which are beneficial predators. Neither are insects, although they are both related to insects by having hard-shelled bodies and jointed legs. Centipedes have fewer, longer legs that extend outward from their body and they move quickly, whereas millipedes move slowly and have up to 200 pairs of short legs placed under their bodies. Some millipedes curl up into a ball when they are disturbed.

Millipedes feed on decaying plant tissue and on plant roots, germinating seeds, and seedlings. They have a beneficial role in compost, where they break down organic matter. They lay eggs in the soil, which hatch into nymphs similar to adults but shorter, with fewer segments.

Plants Attacked

Millipedes may attack any small or tender plants. They usually feed on leaves and parts in contact with the soil or close to the ground.

Organic Controls

Control is usually not necessary unless populations are unusually high. You can sufficiently deter them by sprinkling wood ashes, natural-grade diatomaceous earth, or cinders along rows of germinating seeds.

NAVEL ORANGEWORM

Amyelois transitella

Adults are light gray moths with ¾-inch wingspans. The wings have darker mottling with a dark border on the hindwings. The larvae are reddish orange caterpillars, with brown heads and two crescent-shaped marks on the segment behind the head.

The caterpillars are a key pest in almonds because they bore into the nuts when the hulls split and spin webs inside to pupate. They also bore into damaged fruit and attack walnuts.

There is one generation per year. The larvae overwinter in mummified nuts remaining on trees or in dropped nuts. They pupate in the spring and the adults emerge over a period of several months. The adults lay eggs in mummified nuts, in the blossom end of injured fruit, and in walnuts with sunburn damage. The larvae feed and overwinter in their web and pupate inside the nuts.

Plants Attacked

Navel orangeworms prefer almonds, but they also attack walnuts, citrus fruits, figs, and other fruits and nuts.

Organic Controls

Harvest nuts early to avoid damage. Pick up fallen nuts and knock all mummified nuts out of trees in winter before the adults emerge. Growing a cover crop under trees has been shown to attract beneficial insects that control orangeworms and to hasten the decomposition of fallen nuts, which kills the larvae inside. Spray *Bacillus thuringiensis* var. *kurstaki* (BTK) several times to control newly hatched larvae, before they bore into fruit or into almonds at the hull-split stage.

NEMATODES
Phylum Nematoda

Nematodes are slender, translucent, unsegmented, microscopic worms. There are many different nematodes, including some beneficial species. Most of the plant-damaging species are under $\frac{1}{50}$ inch long.

Feeding by root-knot nematodes causes knots, lesions, and galls on roots, injures root tips, and stimulates excessive root branching.

Root knot nematode damage on potato

Aboveground parts of plants wilt, growth is stunted, and plants may die. Leaf nematodes cause leaf galls or lesions and twisted, distorted leaves.

Most root knot nematode species have a mobile larval stage that moves through the soil on a film of water to infect plants. The adult stage is reached after several molts. The life cycle takes approximately 3–4 weeks for many plant-feeding species.

Pest or Disease?

Plant-parasitic nematodes are microscopic *animals* that cause disease-like injuries to the plants they feed on. Because nematode damage resembles the damage caused by some diseases, particularly viruses, and because controls for nematodes are similar to those of diseases, these tiny roundworms are considered to be disease organisms rather than pests. For specific information on plant-parasitic nematodes, see "Nematodes, Foliar" on page 321 and "Nematodes, Root Knot" on page 322.

Larvae of northern corn rootworm (Diabrotica longicornis)

Organic Controls

To suppress root knot nematodes, grow cover crops of *Tagetes minutum* marigolds before planting susceptible plants, or dig in chitin. In some soils, turning under green manure crops while they are soft and green stimulates growth of natural soil fungi that parasitize nematodes. Rotate crops annually with non-susceptible crops. Grow trap crops of crotalaria between crop plants to capture root knot nematodes. In regions with hot summers, soil solarization can heat the soil sufficiently to kill nematodes in the top 6–8 inches of soil. Drenching soil with neem may give sufficient control during a growing season.

Research Notes

German researchers have been able to achieve good control of a cyst nematode that attacks sugar beets by turning in green manure crops of oil radish, mustard, or rapeseed (canola). Researchers at Aligarh Muslim University in Aligarh, India, found that they can reduce the root knot nematodes on potatoes by inter-cropping with mustard plants. Researchers from the Departments of Plant Pathology and Crop and Soil Sciences at Washington State University have found that turning under a fall-planted rapeseed crop in spring resulted in a big reduction in the amount of root knot nematode attacks on potatoes planted after the rapeseed.

NORTHERN CORN ROOTWORM
Diabrotica longicornis

Northern corn rootworm adults are active, yellowish green, elongated beetles, ¼ inch long. They have brown antennae and feet; sometimes the head and thorax are also brown. The larvae are slender, wrinkled, and white with a light brown head and grow up to ½ inch long. The larvae cause the most damage by feeding on corn roots and by spreading bacterial wilt disease. The adults feed on pollen from many plants and corn silk, which damages the ears and interferes with pollination. They also feed on corn leaves, producing long, silvery streaks on undersides. Ground beetles and rove beetles prey on the larvae.

There is one generation per year in most regions. The eggs are laid around corn roots in late summer and fall. They hatch the following spring and larvae migrate through the soil to corn roots. They feed until early summer, then pupate in the soil. Adults emerge in July and August and die off in the fall.

Plants Attacked

This species attacks only corn.

Organic Controls

Rotating crops is very effective because rootworm larvae feed only on corn and cannot travel far in search of food. Sow seed early so plants have a good root system before rootworms emerge. Cultivate the soil well after harvest and again before seeding to kill eggs and larvae. Apply insect parasitic nematodes to the soil to control larvae.

ONION MAGGOT

Delia antiqua

Adult onion maggots are pale gray flies, ¼ inch long. The larvae are white maggots, ⅓ inch long, found burrowing inside onion bulbs.

Onion maggots burrow into developing onions, which kills young plants. A single onion maggot can destroy two dozen seedlings during its development. Maggots hollow out or stunt older plants, often causing bulbs to rot. Later in the season, they may infest bulbs

Onion maggot fly (Delia antiqua) with eggs

placed in storage. Infestations are worst in cool, wet weather. There are up to two or three generations per year.

The pupae overwinter several inches deep in soil and the flies emerge from mid-May to late June. They lay eggs at the base of onion plants. The eggs hatch in a week and the maggots burrow into roots for 2–3 weeks, pupating in soil nearby. The flies emerge in 1–2 weeks.

The larvae of bulb flies may also be present, feeding inside the onion bulbs. They are grayish, wrinkled larvae, ½ inch long, and can be effectively controlled in the same way as onion maggots.

Plants Attacked

Onions are the preferred hosts, although onion maggots have been known to attack garlic, shallots, chives, and leeks.

Organic Controls

Native ground beetles and rove beetles prey on the maggots and pupae in the soil. Rotating your crops and planting onion sets late to avoid the first generation are also effective. Plant red onions or Japanese bunching onions, which seem to be somewhat resistant.

Gum mass on twig caused by oriental fruit moth caterpillar

Cover seedlings with floating row covers to prevent flies from laying eggs. Where onion maggot numbers are usually low, you can control them sufficiently by sprinkling rows liberally with ground cayenne pepper, ginger, dill, or chili powder to repel females. Drench soil with insect parasitic nematodes to control maggots. Plant a few of last year's onion bulbs among seedling rows as a trap crop, then destroy the trap onions 2 weeks after they sprout.

Research Notes

R. Vernon of the Agriculture Canada Research Station in Vancouver, British Columbia, has discovered that adult flies of onion maggots, carrot rust flies, and cabbage maggots fly at heights of less than 4 feet above the soil surface. Most could be excluded from reaching plants by a simple nylon window screen fence, 3 feet high, with the top edge bent outward. This baffles the flies, which fly upward once they encounter the fence. The fences must be used with crop rotation to ensure that flies from the previous crop are not trapped inside the fence.

ORIENTAL FRUIT MOTH
Grapholitha molesta

Adult oriental fruit moths are dark gray moths with dark brown, mottled forewings and wingspans of ½ inch. The larvae are white to pinkish gray caterpillars with brown heads, up to ½ inch long. The flat, white eggs are laid on twigs and undersides of leaves.

The caterpillars bore into twigs of fruit trees early in the season, causing them to wilt and die. In midsummer, caterpillars bore into developing fruit, leaving masses of gummy castings on the fruit. Late-summer caterpillars enter the stem end of maturing fruit and bore into the pit.

The oriental fruit moth has a short life cycle, so there are three to seven generations per year. The larvae overwinter in cocoons on the bark or in weeds or soil around the trees. They pupate in early spring and moths emerge from early May to mid-June to lay eggs. The eggs hatch in 10–14 days; the caterpillars feed for 2–3 weeks, then pupate. In northern regions, a second generation appears in mid-July and a third by late August.

Plants Attacked

The oriental fruit moth most commonly attacks fruit trees.

Organic Controls

Plant early peach and apricot cultivars that can be harvested before midsummer larvae bore into the fruit. Cultivate soil 4 inches deep around the trees before bloom to kill overwintering larvae. Spray summer oil to kill eggs and larvae.

PEACHTREE BORERS

Synanthedon exitiosa, Synanthedon pictipes

These unusual moths have narrow, clear wings with 1¼-inch wingspans. They have a blue-black body and males have narrow yellow bands around the body. Female *S. exitiosa* have one broad orange band around the body, which is lacking in *S. pictipes*. The larvae are white grubs, up to 1 inch long, with dark brown heads.

The peachtree borer larvae bore beneath the bark at the base of trees and into the main roots near the surface, often girdling them. These entrance holes are filled with a gum mixed with sawdust. Young or weakened trees may be seriously damaged or killed, whereas older and more vigorous trees are less affected.

One generation of peachtree borer generally takes a year, although some have two-year life cycles. The females lay eggs on trees or soil close to the trunk. The eggs hatch in 12 days and larvae bore under the bark at ground level. They overwinter in bark or nearby soil, and resume feeding in the spring. They pupate in silken cocoons in the soil by late June or July, usually within a few inches of the trunk. The moths emerge in 2–3 weeks.

Plants Attacked

These borers mainly attack peach and occasionally plum, prune, cherry, apricot, and nectarine trees.

Peachtree borer (Synanthedon exitiosa) female moth (left) and male (right)

Organic Controls

Maintain vigorous trees and prevent mechanical injuries to the bark (injuries allow borers to enter). Remove borers by digging them out with a knife, or kill them by inserting a flexible wire into entrance holes. Remove soil several inches deep around the trunk to find borers in the base of a tree. Cultivate the soil shallowly around the trunk to destroy pupae.

PEAR PSYLLA

Cacopsylla pyricola (formerly *Psylla pyricola*)

Adult psylla are dark reddish brown, with green or red markings. They are ¹⁄₁₀ inch long and have transparent wings folded rooflike over their backs. The nymphs are small, oval, and yellowish with red eyes and no wings. The eggs are pear-shaped and yellow.

A major pest of pears, psylla spread diseases, such as "pear decline" virus and fireblight. They suck plant juices, which causes the leaves to turn yellow in reaction to their toxic saliva. On heavily infested trees, leaves turn brown and drop, and fruit is stunted or drops prematurely. Psylla also secrete honeydew, which supports growth of sooty mold. Psylla have three to five generations per year. The adults over-

Pear psylla nymph (<u>Cacopsylla pyricola</u>)

winter under bark and leaf litter and emerge in spring to lay eggs on fruit spurs and buds. The eggs hatch in 2–4 weeks, so by full bloom, there are numerous minute nymphs on stems and undersides of leaves. These take a month to reach the adult stage. The early-stage nymphs move very little and are covered with a droplet of honeydew, while older nymphs are more active.

Plants Attacked

Pear psylla attack pears and quince.

Adult plum curculio (<u>Conotrachelus nenuphar</u>)

Organic Controls

Native insects, such as earwigs, damsel bugs, minute pirate bugs, and other predators, usually keep psylla in check on organically managed trees. Spray dormant oils as soon as leaves drop in fall and again just before buds swell in spring. If there are few native predators present during the growing season, spray insecticidal soap or summer oil to help control nymphs.

PLUM CURCULIO
Conotrachelus nenuphar

Adult curculios are brownish gray "snout" beetles, ⅕ inch long. They have hard, warty wing covers and white hairs on the body. The larvae are plump, white grubs ⅓ inch long, with brown heads. The eggs are round, white, and laid singly under crescent-shaped cuts in fruit skin.

Curculios are the worst pest of apples in eastern regions. Feeding and egg-laying by adults damages fruit skin, leaving a characteristic half-circle scar. The larvae tunnel in fruit, usually feeding near the pit, which causes the fruit to rot or drop prematurely. (Larvae do not live in mature fruit remaining on the tree.)

There are one or two generations per year. In spring, the overwintered adults move to trees as the leaves and flowers appear. They feed and lay eggs, which hatch in 5–10 days. The larvae feed for 2–3 weeks and, when the fruit drops, they leave to pupate in soil. The adults emerge from late July to late October. They feed on ripe or fallen fruit until fall, then migrate to nearby wooded areas or leaf litter to hibernate.

Plants Attacked

A severe pest of apples, plum curculios also attack most tree fruits and blueberries.

Organic Controls

To eliminate larvae, collect and destroy fallen fruit daily, especially the early drops. Curculios drop from trees when disturbed, so knock them from trees onto a ground sheet by sharply tapping branches with a padded stick, then drown them in soapy water. If the infestation is severe, apply pyrethrins when the first scars are seen on developing fruit (not before petals drop, as this kills pollinators), and again 7–10 days later.

ROSE CHAFER

Macrodactylus subspinosus

Adult chafers are reddish brown beetles, ⅓ inch long. They have yellowish hairs on the wing covers and the underside of the body is black. The larvae are small white grubs, found in the soil.

Adult chafers chew on flowers, leaves, and fruits, but are usually damaging only if their numbers are high. When this happens, they can cause serious damage to developing grapes, ripening cherries, and buds of roses. The larvae feed on roots of grass and weeds, which causes little damage. Birds avoid chafers because they are poisonous.

There is just one generation per year. The larvae overwinter in the soil and pupate in spring. The adults emerge from late May to early June. Until early July, they lay groups of eggs among weeds and grasses, in pockets several inches below the soil surface. The eggs hatch in about 2 weeks and grubs feed on roots until fall, then burrow deeper in the soil.

Plants Attacked

Rose chafers attack blackberries, grapes, raspberries, strawberries, and tree fruits. They also feed on garden vegetables, dahlias, hollyhocks, iris, peonies, poppies, and roses.

Rose chafer (Macrodactylus subspinosus) on rose

Organic Controls

Control is usually not necessary. Where infestations are severe, protect small plants with floating row covers until July to prevent adults from laying eggs. Cultivate soil until early June to eliminate pupae. If large numbers of chafers are present, spray pyrethrins as a last resort.

RUST MITES

Order Acarina: Family Eriophyidae

These nearly invisible mites are elongated, pale yellow or tan, and less than ¹⁄₁₀₀ inch long. They have only two pairs of legs, near the front end. Nymphs are similar to adults but smaller.

Rust mites on grape leaf

Rust mites burrow into tissue on the undersides of leaves, causing a russeted appearance. Feeding on fruit also causes a roughened, russeted surface.

There are many overlapping generations all season. The mites overwinter at the base of buds or in cracks in bark, moving onto developing flowers in spring. Rust mite populations usually decline in hot weather. By late August, most species move to overwintering sites.

Plants Attacked

Various species attack apples, pears, and tomatoes, as well as ornamental trees and shrubs.

Organic Controls

Rust mites are an important alternate diet for native predatory mites that control spider mites. Spray dormant oil with lime-sulfur on dormant trees. If it is absolutely necessary to spray leaves during the growing season, any fungicidal spray or dust containing sulfur is effective.

Hard scales on orange fruit

SCALES, ARMORED
Family Coccidae

Adult scales are circular or oval hard bumps, under $\frac{1}{10}$ inch long, with no visible head or legs. Depending on the species, colors are ashy gray, yellow, white, reddish, or purplish brown. Some have a distinct dimple in the center and all secrete an armor of wax in an oyster shell or circular shape. The early-stage nymphs are mobile crawlers, while later stages are legless and hardly move.

Scales suck plant juices. If they are numerous, feeding weakens plants and causes distortion and injury from their toxic saliva. Severe infestations may kill trees.

There are one or two generations per year in the North and up to six generations in the South. Females lay eggs or bear live nymphs. The nymphs wander for several hours or days before settling and becoming immobile. They develop for a month or more to reach the adult stage. Most overwinter as nymphs or eggs on the bark of trees.

Plants Attacked

Armored scales are serious pests of citrus. In the South, armored scales attack citrus, palms, roses, and tropical ornamentals. In the North, scales infest fruit and shade trees, currants, grapes, raspberries, and ornamental shrubs.

Organic Controls

Most pesticides are useless because scales are protected by a waxy covering. Dormant oil sprays during winter provide good control. Summer oil also is effective for plants that tolerate it. Where the cost is warranted, release predatory beetles that feed on scales (*Chilocorus nigritus* or *Lindorus lophanthae*). Release parasitic wasp *Aphytis melinus* to attack California red scale or oleander scale.

SCALES, SOFT
Family Coccidae

Female soft scales are oval or round, legless, wingless bumps, 1/10–1/5 inch long. Males are minute, yellow-winged insects. The youngest larvae are tiny crawlers resembling minute mealybugs, while older larvae settle and become sedentary.

All stages of scales suck plant sap, weakening plants and causing leaves to turn yellow and drop. In severe infestations, plants may die. Soft scales also secrete large quantities of sticky honeydew onto leaves and fruit, which encourages sooty molds. Outdoors there are one or two generations per year, while indoors there may be up to six generations. Females of some species lay as many 2,000 eggs, while others give birth to several nymphs per day. Nymphs move around on the plant for a short time, then settle. Female scales molt to an immobile form.

Plants Attacked

Soft scales attack citrus and other fruits, as well as ornamental shrubs, trees, and houseplants.

Organic Controls

Native parasitic wasps and predatory beetles are important controls for scales. Prune and destroy infested branches and twigs. Wash scales from plants with a soft brush or cloth dipped in insecticidal soap solution, then rinse well. Dormant oil sprays on fruit and ornamental trees provide good control. Summer oils may also be used on plants that tolerate it (do not use on citrus after July). To experiment with biological control, release predatory beetles (*Chilocorus nigritus* or *Lindorus lophanthae*). These can eliminate scale on houseplants if fine mesh cloth is used to confine them to the plants. For soft brown scales, experiment with biological control by releasing the parasitic wasp *Metaphycus helvolus*.

Soft scales on camellia leaf

SLUGS AND SNAILS
Class Mollusca

Slugs and snails are land-dwelling relatives of clams and mussels. Snails carry coiled shells on their backs, while slugs have no shells. Common species of slugs and snails are 1/8–1 inch long, while banana slugs found in coastal areas may stretch 4–6 inches long. Slugs and snails are gray, tan, green, or black, and some have darker spots or patterns. They leave a characteristic slimy trail of mucus behind. The eggs are clear, oval, or round, and are laid in jellylike masses under stones or debris in the garden.

Snail

Both slugs and snails feed primarily on decaying plant material. They also eat soft, tender plant tissue and rasp large holes in foliage, stems, and even bulbs. They may completely demolish seedlings and severely damage young shoots and plants. They may also crawl up trees and shrubs to feed. Both are most numerous and damaging in wet years and in high rainfall regions.

The adults lay eggs in moist soil and the eggs hatch in 2–4 weeks. Slugs grow from 5 months to 2 years before reaching maturity.

Plants Attacked

Slugs and snails may attack any tender plants. Slugs in particular will attack vegetables. Snails may be a serious problem on citrus.

Organic Controls

Slugs have many natural enemies in organically managed yards, including birds, garter snakes, toads, and lizards. Ground beetles and fireflies are important predators of slug eggs.

Maintain permanent walkways of clover, sod, or stone mulches to harbor ground beetles and garter snakes. Repel slugs and snails with copper strips fastened around trunks of trees or shrubs. Edge garden beds with copper flashing or screening, first making sure all slugs are removed from the enclosed area. Wrap commercial snail and slug tapes around tree trunks. Where slugs are an occasional problem, spread wide bands of cinders, wood ashes, or diatomaceous earth along rows to protect seedlings (renew frequently). Set out traps such as pots, boards, or grapefruit rinds; check every morning, and destroy slugs. Set out commercial slug traps with yeast bait, or make traps by burying tin cans with the lip flush to the soil surface. Fill traps with beer or other fermenting liquids to attract slugs. Predatory decollate snails are sold for brown snail control in orchards in some counties in California, but do not release these elsewhere.

Research Notes

Researchers at the Agricultural Genetics Co. Ltd., Cambridge, England, have isolated a parasitic nematode (a species of *Phasmarhabditis*) that attacks slugs. They are now working on mass-production methods for the nematode and hope to have a product available on the market in 2–3 years.

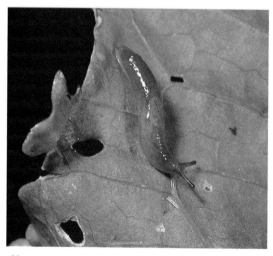

Slug

SOUTHWESTERN CORN BORER

Diatraea grandiosella

Adult females are pale beige moths with 1¼-inch wingspans. The males are darker. The larvae are white caterpillars with brown heads. Larvae in the summer generation are covered with brown spots, while overwintering larvae are solid white. Eggs are cream to reddish brown, laid in overlapping rows on leaves.

The caterpillars bore into leaf whorls, stalks, and roots of corn plants. This weakens stems and causes them to break easily. There are two or more generations per year. The caterpillars overwinter in the roots of corn stubble. They pupate in spring, and moths emerge in early June. The first-generation larvae bore into the leaf whorls and later move down into the stalks, where they pupate. The second-generation adults emerge in early August and lay eggs. These larvae bore into stalks, then down to the roots, where they overwinter.

Plants Attacked

These borers mainly attack corn, but will also feed on sorghum and some grasses.

Organic Controls

Plant corn early in the season to avoid the second-generation larvae. Plant resistant cultivars, which have strong stalks that resist breaking. After harvest, cut off corn stalks at soil level, and remove and shred immediately. Cultivate stubble deeply in the fall to kill all overwintering caterpillars.

SOWBUGS/PILLBUGS

Order Isopoda: Family Asellidae

Adult isopods are dark gray or brown land-dwelling relatives of the lobster. They have numerous segments of jointed armor, seven pairs of short legs, and are ¼–⅝ inch long. The nymphs look like adults, but smaller. Pillbugs curl up into a ball when disturbed.

Both sowbugs and pillbugs feed on decaying organic matter. They usually are not damaging to established plants, but if their numbers are high, they can severely damage seedlings by chewing on leaves and fine roots.

Nymphs and adults must live in moist conditions and cannot survive long in locations where water is scarce. The females carry their eggs and young nymphs in a pouch for several weeks.

*Southwestern corn borer (*Diatraea grandiosella*) larva*

Often in early spring, with warm rains, many sowbugs and pillbugs emerge from their overwintering sites at the same time, so populations seem to explode.

Plants Attacked

When isopods such as sowbugs and pillbugs are numerous, they damage the seedlings of many plants by chewing on the tender leaves and fine roots.

Curled up adult pillbug

Organic Controls

Drain wet areas and remove trash, leaf litter, boards, and other such material from around foundations and garden beds to remove hiding places for isopods. To protect seedlings, allow the soil surface to dry out between waterings, or sprinkle diatomaceous earth around attacked seedlings. Check for isopods under stones or boards every morning and destroy them. Set out traps made from heavy paper painted with sticky glue, then folded tentlike, with the sticky side down.

SPIDER MITES

Order Acarina: Family Tetranychidae

All stages of spider mites are minute and less than $\frac{1}{75}$–$\frac{1}{50}$ inch long. The adults have eight legs, while the youngest nymphs have six legs. They are reddish, pale green or yellow, and have fine hairs on the body. Some have a darker patch on each side. Most species spin

Rose with spider mites

fine webs on leaves and shoots. The eggs are minuscule, pearly spheres found on webbing or on leaf hairs.

Both adults and nymphs feed by sucking the juice from plant cells on undersides of leaves. When numerous, their feeding weakens plants, causes leaves to drop, and results in stunted fruit. Early damage appears as yellow speckled areas on leaves. Extremely fine webbing may be visible on the undersides of leaves (some species do not spin webs). In severe infestations, leaves become bronzed or turn yellow or white with brown edges. The webs may cover both sides of the leaves and eventually cover the tips of branches. Long skeins of webbing carrying hundreds of mites may hang down from the infested tips, allowing the mites to be blown to the next plant. Spider mite outbreaks can be sudden and severe in hot, dry conditions. When humidity is low, spider mites feed more to avoid drying up, which drives them to lay more eggs, thus speeding up their development. Native predatory mites usually suppress spider mites sufficiently in organically managed orchards.

Spider mites have a short life cycle and may reproduce year-round on indoor plants. Outdoors, eggs or adults overwinter in crevices in bark or in garden debris. Overwintering two-spotted spider mites are dark crimson with brown patches and may be mistaken for beneficial predatory mites in the spring. The summer form turns the characteristic pale green. The eggs hatch in 1–8 days, and nymphs develop to adults in 5–10 days.

Plants Attacked

Various species of spider mites attack vegetables, including beans, cucumbers, eggplants, melons, peppers, squash, and tomatoes. Ornamental trees, fruit trees, berries, herbs, annuals, perennials, shrubs, vines, and houseplants are also attacked by spider mites. Fruit trees, ornamentals, and houseplants are also attacked by various species of spider mites, including European red mites, citrus red mites, and spruce spider mites. Controls are the same as for spider mites.

Organic Controls

Maintain high humidity in greenhouse crops and around houseplants. Spray dormant oil on fruit trees to kill overwintering eggs, but minimize the use of pesticides, including sulfur, in orchards during the growing season to protect predatory mites. Release predatory mites *Metaseiulus occidentalis* or *Typhlodromus pyri* on fruit trees, and *Phytoseiulus persimilis* or similar species on vegetables, strawberries, flowers, and houseplants. (Consult suppliers for best species and release rates for local conditions.) Spray neem, insecticidal soap, or pyrethrins. Spray summer oil on woody shrubs and trees that can tolerate it.

SPITTLEBUGS/ FROGHOPPERS

Philaenus spumarius

Adults are called froghoppers because of the frog-faced shape of their head. They are stout, oval, tan, mottled brown, or black bugs, ¼–½ inch long, with sharp spines on their hind legs. The nymphs are yellow to yellowish green, similar to adults, but wingless. They live inside a foamy mass of "spittle" on the stems of plants. The eggs are white to beige, laid in rows on stems or stubble.

The adults and nymphs suck plant juices, and in rare instances cause stunted and weakened plants with reduced yields. Adults may migrate in large numbers from hay fields to nearby crops when the hay is cut. When this

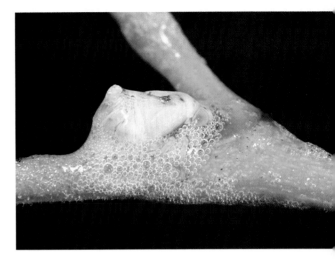

The foamy mass of "spittle," which protects the spittlebug nymphs

happens, nearby gardens may suddenly be infested with froghoppers.

There is one generation per year. The overwintering eggs hatch in mid-April and nymphs feed for 6–7 weeks, protected in the masses of foam they produce. The adult froghoppers feed for the rest of the summer and lay overwintering eggs on field stubble by early September.

Plants Attacked

Spittlebugs attack strawberries, legume forage crops, and nursery plants.

Organic Controls

Native predatory bugs, such as damsel bugs and pirate bugs, attack spittlebugs. Cover susceptible plants with floating row covers before nearby hay fields are cut. Wash the nymphs and spittle masses out of plants with a strong stream of water. If high numbers of nymphs were seen in summer, then plow down the stubble of susceptible crops in fall to kill overwintering eggs.

Spruce budworm larva (Choristoneura fumiferana) on branch

SPRUCE BUDWORM
Choristoneura fumiferana

Adults are grayish brown moths, with ⅞–1¼-inch wingspans. The hindwings are dark brown, fringed with white. The larvae are dark brown caterpillars with lighter sides, up to ¾ inch long. They have dark spines and two rows of white dots along the back. The eggs are green, laid in overlapping masses on undersides of needles.

The caterpillars mine in needles, buds, cones, and twigs of evergreen trees. Conifers often die after 3–5 years of heavy infestations. Surviving trees are weakened and become susceptible to bark beetle attack. Local budworm populations rise and fall over a period of years, with a few peak years followed by low numbers.

There is one generation per year. The moths lay eggs from late June to early August. These hatch in 8–12 days and the young larvae disperse throughout the tree, spin cocoons, and hibernate. The following spring, larvae emerge and mine in old needles, then in young buds. As the new growth expands, they spin webs around the twig tips and feed inside, pupating by late June. Adults emerge from the cocoons in 10 days.

Plants Attacked
This is one of the most damaging forest pests in North America. They primarily attack balsam fir and spruce and occasionally feed on Douglas fir, hemlocks, larches, and pines. Budworms also damage nursery and ornamental trees.

Organic Controls
Avoid using balsam fir in ornamental plantings where budworms are a common problem. To protect attacked trees, spray *Bacillus thuringiensis* var. *kurstaki* (BTK) or neem as soon as the tiny larvae are seen in late summer. Spray again in early spring when they resume feeding. Brush off bud caps on new growth to ensure the spray penetrates.

SQUASH BUG
Anasa tristis

Adults are oval, dark brown to black bugs, ⅝ inch long. Their abdomen is flattened and covered with fine, dark hairs. They give off an unpleasant smell in self-defense. The youngest nymphs are pale green, developing a darker, reddish thorax and abdomen as they mature. The older nymphs are covered with what appears to be a grainy gray powder. The eggs are shiny yellow, turning brick red as they mature, and are laid in groups on undersides of leaves.

Both adults and nymphs suck plant juices, which causes leaves and shoots to blacken and die. The damage may be mistaken for symptoms of a wilt disease. Severely attacked plants may fail to produce fruit. Adult bugs congregate under leaf litter or nearby boards at night. Late in the season, particularly after frost, both adults and nymphs may feed on fruit.

There is one generation per year. Adults overwinter under garden litter, vines, or boards, and the females lay eggs in spring. The eggs hatch in 1–2 weeks, and the nymphs take 4–6 weeks to develop.

Adult squash bug (Anasa tristis) on flower

Plants Attacked
Squash bugs prefer pumpkins and squash, but may also attack other cucurbits.

Organic Controls
Plant resistant squash cultivars (try 'Butternut', 'Early Golden Bush Scallop', 'Early Prolific Straightneck', 'Early Summer Crookneck', 'Improved Green Hubbard', 'Royal Acorn', and 'Table Queen'). Protect young plants from attack with floating row covers (hand-pollinate flowers). Handpick all stages of squash bugs from undersides of leaves. Place boards and shingles on the ground next to plants in early summer and destroy adults found under the boards every morning.

SQUASH VINE BORER
Melittia cucurbitae

Adults are narrow-winged moths, with wingspans of 1–1½ inches. They have olive brown forewings, clear hindwings, and a red abdomen with black rings. There are long, reddish fringes on the hind legs. The larvae are white grubs with a brown head, growing up to 1 inch long.

The larvae bore into squash vines, chewing inner tissue near the base and filling the stem with moist, slimy castings. The attacked vines wilt suddenly and girdled vines rot and die. The larvae may also feed on fruit later in the season. Vine borers prefer squash and are least attracted to muskmelons.

There is usually only one generation of squash vine borers per year, with two in the South. The larvae or pupae overwinter in soil. The adults emerge as squash vines begin to lengthen and then lay their eggs on stems and leaf stalks near the base of plants. The larvae burrow into stems for 4–6 weeks, then pupate in the soil for winter.

Squash vine borer larva (Melittia cucurbitae)

Adult harlequin stink bug

Both adults and nymphs suck sap from leaves, flowers, fruit, and seeds. Leaves may wilt and turn brown or have brown spots. Feeding punctures in fruit cause scarring, yellow or whitish patches under the skin, or dimpling known as "catfacing." Legume pods drop or have deformed seeds. Stink bugs tend to become pests as nearby weedy areas dry out during the summer, driving them into the garden.

There are two or more generations per year. The adults overwinter in garden residues or weeds along fence rows and waste areas. They emerge in the spring and usually start feeding and laying eggs on weeds. Each female can lay 30 clusters of 300–500 eggs each. Eggs hatch in a week, and nymphs develop to adults in 5–6 weeks.

Plants Attacked

These borers prefer squash-family plants with thick stems, such as gourds, pumpkins, and squash (especially Hubbard squash), though they may attack any cucurbits.

Organic Controls

Plant early and promote vigorous growth so vines are able to tolerate attacks. Cover young plants with floating row covers (hand-pollinate flowers or uncover plants later for pollinators). Spray the base of plants with pyrethrins repeatedly to kill larvae before they enter vines.

STINK BUGS

Order Heteroptera: Family Pentatomidae

This group of bugs gets its family name from the adults' five-sided, shield-shaped body. They may be green, tan, brown, or gray and ½–⅝ inch long. One species has bright red and black harlequin markings. Stink bugs emit a foul smell when disturbed. The nymphs are oval, similar to adults, but wingless. Eggs are barrel-shaped, laid in clusters on undersides of leaves.

Plants Attacked

Stink bugs attack a variety of crops, including beans, cabbages, corn, okra, peas, squash, soybeans, and tomatoes, as well as peaches and forage crops.

Organic Controls

Native parasitic wasps and tachinid flies attack stink bugs. Control weeds around the garden. Remove or mow weeds to reduce overwintering sites, and remove crop residues and till the garden in the fall. Handpick all stages and crush egg masses on undersides of leaves or shake plants over a tray of soapy water. Spray insecticidal soap to control nymphs.

STRAWBERRY ROOT WEEVIL
Otiorhynchus ovatus

Adults are shiny, nearly black, hard-shelled snout beetles, ¼ inch long. Their wing covers are fused so they cannot fly. They are all females—there are no males. The larvae are white, C-shaped, legless grubs with brown heads, found in roots.

Adult weevils feed on leaves and fruits, clipping characteristic small half-circles from the edges of leaves and severing flower stems. The larvae cause the worst damage by boring into the crowns and roots of plants. Plants are stunted and may die, often from rots that enter roots through feeding injuries.

There is one generation per year. The larvae and some adults overwinter among plant roots; however, most adults overwinter in nearby weedy or brushy areas. The larvae feed for a short period in the spring, then pupate. New adults emerge in June, feed for 2–3 weeks, then lay eggs near the crowns of plants. The eggs hatch in 10 days and larvae burrow into the root zone for the rest of the season.

The larvae of a similar flightless weevil, the strawberry crown borer, also may be found feeding in the crown and roots of strawberries.

Plants Attacked
Although strawberries are primary hosts, these weevils also attack apples, grapes, peaches, raspberries, coral bells, and camellias, as well as pine and spruce seedlings in nurseries.

Organic Controls
To control larvae, drench the soil with neem or a solution of insect parasitic nematodes in early May, as soon as the soil warms, and again in August to control the next generation of strawberry root weevil larvae.

Damage caused by strawberry root weevil (<u>Otiorhynchus ovatus</u>)

TARNISHED PLANT BUG
Lygus lineolaris

Adults are quick-moving, oval bugs, ¼ inch long. They are a mottled light green to coppery brown and their top wings have a black-tipped yellow triangle on each side. From the side, there is a characteristic downward slant to the rear half of the wings. The nymphs are yellowish green with five black dots on the body, similar to adult bugs, but wingless. The eggs are inserted into stems or leaves.

Both adults and nymphs suck the juice from leaves, buds, and fruits. Their toxic saliva

Adult tarnished plant bug (<u>Lygus lineolaris</u>)

causes buds and pods to drop and distorts leaves and shoots. Parts of plants wilt or are stunted, and branch tips blacken and die back. Feeding on tomatoes and other fruit causes pitted, "catfaced" fruit, while feeding on broccoli and cauliflower leaves dead spots on the florets.

There are up to five overlapping generations per year. Adults overwinter under fallen leaves, debris, and hedgerows and emerge in early spring. They feed on fruit buds and other early foliage, then move to garden plants or weeds, such as clover, chickweed, and dandelion, to lay eggs. The eggs hatch in 10 days. Nymphs feed 3–4 weeks, then molt to adults.

Other plant-feeding true bugs, such as four-lined plant bugs and phlox plant bugs, cause similar damage to plants. Controls for these are the same as for tarnished plant bugs.

Plants Attacked

Tarnished plant bugs feed on a wide variety of plants, including most flowers, fruits, many vegetables, and weeds.

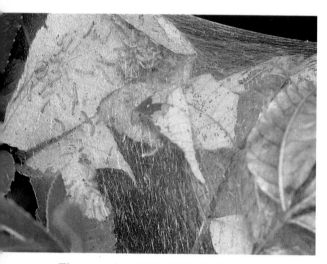

The protective silk tent spun by the tent caterpillar

Organic Controls

Predatory bugs, such as big-eyed bugs, damsel bugs, and minute pirate bugs, feed on nymphs, and several parasitic wasps also attack tarnished plant bugs. Where plant bugs are very numerous, cover small plants with floating row covers. Generally, it is sufficient to keep weeds and crop debris down around gardens and orchards. Where cover crops are used in orchards, avoid most legumes, as these harbor tarnished plant bugs (subterranean clover is an exception). Spray pyrethrins to control nymphs and adults. Summer oil sprays may also be used on plants that tolerate them.

TENT CATERPILLAR
Malacosoma spp.

Adults are yellowish to brown moths with two narrow stripes across the wings and 1–1½-inch wingspans. The larvae are black caterpillars with a white stripe or rows of dots along the back. They also have irregular brownish, blue, and red marks along the sides and are covered with fine hairs. Most species, though not all, spin large "tents" of silk webbing. The egg masses are laid on small twigs under a protective layer that looks like hardened brown foam.

The caterpillars chew on tree leaves. The populations of tent caterpillars rise and fall over a 6–10-year cycle. In low years, they are not particularly damaging. In peak population years, however, they may completely defoliate trees. Such trees usually leaf out again, but growth may be somewhat stunted for several years. Tent caterpillar populations eventually collapse from the combined attack of native predators, parasites, and disease.

There is one generation per year. The moths lay eggs on tree twigs in midsummer. The eggs overwinter and hatch in early spring.

The caterpillars from one egg mass move together to the nearest crotch in a branch and spin a silk tent. They hide in the tent for protection by day, leaving to feed at night. After feeding for 5–8 weeks, they wander down the tree to pupate in leaf litter. The moths emerge in 10 days.

Plants Attacked

Tent caterpillars may attack most deciduous trees and shrubs, especially apples, wild cherries, and aspens.

Organic Controls

In most years, no controls are necessary. Prune branches with tents and burn them, or pluck webs out of foliage (wear gloves). Inspect trees carefully in winter and scrape egg masses from bare branches. When populations are damaging, spray *Bacillus thuringiensis* var. *kurstaki* (BTK) or neem weekly, while caterpillars are small. An application of summer oil may be used on trees that tolerate it. Catch caterpillars in sticky tree bands as they leave the trees to pupate. Do not destroy caterpillars with small white eggs or cocoons attached to their backs because they are hosts for more parasites.

Adult thrips on gardenia petals

THRIPS

Order Thysanoptera: Family Thripidae

Adult thrips are minute, elongate insects, $\frac{1}{50}$–$\frac{1}{25}$ inch long. They are yellowish, brown, or black and have narrow, fringed wings. They move quickly and like to hide in tight crevices in plant stems and flowers. The nymphs are light green or yellow, similar to adults, but smaller.

Both adults and nymphs suck the contents of plant cells, which deposits silvery speckling or streaks on leaves. In severe infestations, plants are stunted and distorted, flowers are damaged, and developing fruit have dry, silvery scars or round, pale spots. Some species spread tomato spotted wilt virus.

There are many generations of thrips per year, and they breed year-round in greenhouses. The adults overwinter in sod, debris, or cracks in bark, becoming active in early spring. They lay eggs in plant tissue. These hatch in 3–5 days, and nymphs feed for 1–3 weeks. They then pass through a quiescent stage (not a true pupa stage), usually in the soil, for 1–2 weeks before molting to the adult stage.

Tomato hornworm caterpillar
(*Manduca quinquemaculata*)

Plants Attacked

Various species attack asparagus, cabbage, lettuce, onions, peas, flowers, privet, and fruit and shade trees. There are also predatory thrip species.

Organic Controls

Native predators attack thrips, including minute pirate bugs, lacewings, and lady beetles. To control thrips on fruit trees, spray dormant oil. Spray neem, insecticidal soap, or pyrethrins. As a last resort, dust undersides of leaves with diatomaceous earth. Use bright blue or yellow sticky traps to catch adults in greenhouses. In greenhouses, for onion or western flower thrips, release predatory mites (*Amblyseius cucumeris*) or minute pirate bugs.

TOMATO HORNWORM

Manduca quinquemaculata

Adults are mottled gray moths with narrow wings and 4–5-inch wingspans. They have plump, furry abdomens with rows of orange dots along the sides. At dusk, the moths sip nectar from flowers. The caterpillars are green, with a single large horn on their tail.

They have diagonal white marks along their sides and grow to 4½ inches long. The eggs are round, yellowish green, and laid singly on undersides of leaves.

The caterpillars chew large holes in leaves, leaving the midribs. They may completely strip young plants. In severe infestations, they also feed on stems and chew large holes in fruit. Native parasitic wasps usually provide sufficient control of hornworms in organic gardens.

There is one generation per year in most areas, two or more in the South. The large, dark brown pupae overwinter in soil and moths emerge in June and July. Eggs are laid on leaves and hatch in a week. Larvae feed for 3–4 weeks, then pupate in soil.

Plants Attacked

In addition to tomatoes, hornworms feed on eggplants, peppers, potatoes, and tobacco.

Organic Controls

Handpick caterpillars from foliage and destroy. Spray *Bacillus thuringiensis* var. *kurstaki* (BTK) or neem while caterpillars are still small. Till the garden in fall or early spring to destroy pupae.

TUSSOCK MOTHS

Orgyia leucostigma **and related species**

Female moths are gray and wingless, with fat, furry bodies. Males are ashy gray, mottled with black and light brown, with 1¼-inch wingspans. The larvae are slender caterpillars with scarlet heads and pale yellow-and-brown striped bodies covered with distinctive large tufts of long black and white hairs. The eggs are white and laid in masses on old cocoons.

The caterpillars feed on leaves of a variety of trees and shrubs, but in most years cause little permanent damage. In peak population years, they can completely defoliate trees. Birds and parasitic and predatory insects are important natural controls.

There are two or more generations per year. The eggs overwinter in the protection of old cocoons and hatch from April to June. The larvae develop for 4–6 weeks, then pupate in rough silken cocoons on bark, branches, or nearby. Moths emerge in 2 weeks.

Plants Attacked

Tussock moths attack deciduous trees and shrubs, including apples, elms, poplars, basswood, roses, maples, sycamores, and willows.

Organic Controls

Inspect dormant trees and scrape egg masses from tree trunks, branches, or nearby objects. When numbers are high, spray *Bacillus thuringiensis* var. *kurstaki* (BTK) or neem to control larvae. Spray dormant oil to control eggs.

Male tussock moth (Orgyia leucostigma)

WEBWORM, FALL

Hyphantria cunea

Adults are pure white moths, with 2–2½-inch wingspans. They have black dots on forewings and yellow abdomens with black spots. The larvae are beige caterpillars, covered by dense yellowish brown hairs, with tufts of long white hairs along their sides. The eggs are laid in masses covered with hairs, on undersides of leaves.

The caterpillars chew on leaves and spin large, conspicuous, dirty white webs over the ends of branches. Sometimes several branch tips are held together by one large web. Native parasitic wasps and predators suppress the populations in most years, but localized outbreaks occur periodically.

There are one or two generations per year. The pupae overwinter in tightly woven cocoons under soil debris or tree bark. The moths emerge in May and June and lay eggs, which hatch in a few days. Groups of larvae feed together inside the web for 4–6 weeks, extending the web as they consume the foliage inside. The mature caterpillars leave the web to wander out of the tree and pupate in soil debris.

Plants Attacked

Fall webworms attack many deciduous trees and shrubs.

Organic Controls

Prune out and destroy branches with webs while caterpillars are still feeding inside. Spray *Bacillus thuringiensis* var. *kurstaki* (BTK)

Web spun by fall webworm caterpillar (<u>Hyphantria cunea</u>)

Garden webworm larva (<u>Achyra rantalis</u>)

or neem on leaves around the fall webworm webs while the larvae are small or when older larvae start wandering outside of webs to feed.

Catch webworm caterpillars in sticky tree bands as they leave to pupate. Spray summer oil to control larvae on trees that can tolerate oil sprays.

WEBWORM, GARDEN
Achyra rantalis

Adults are brown moths, with ¾-inch wingspans and yellowish and gray marks on the wings. The larvae are pale green to nearly black caterpillars, up to ¾ inch long. They have a darker or lighter stripe down the back and three black spots on each segment. When disturbed, they quickly drop from plants on silk threads. The eggs are laid in masses of 5–50 eggs.

The caterpillars spin silk webbing around leaves and feed on undersides of the enclosed leaves, skeletonizing them. Native parasitic wasps are usually sufficient to supress webworms, but when populations are high, the caterpillars cover plants with webs and can cause severe defoliation.

There are up to five generations per year. The caterpillars or pupae overwinter in cocoons in the soil near host plants. The moths emerge by midsummer and lay eggs, which hatch in 3–7 days. The caterpillars feed for 3–4 weeks, then pupate for 7–10 days.

Similar caterpillars, such as the hydrangea leaf tier, attack ornamentals and other plants. Effective control for these is the same as for garden webworms.

Plants Attacked
Garden webworms feed on most vegetables, especially beans, peas, and strawberries, as well as some weeds and field crops.

Organic Controls
Kill webworm caterpillars by knocking them from plants into a pail of soapy water (they drop readily). Spray *Bacillus thuringiensis* var. *kurstaki* (BTK), neem, or pyrethins on leaves when larvae are very small, before webbing protects them from sprays. In fall, till the garden to kill pupae.

WHITEFLIES
Order Homoptera: Family Aleyrodidae

Adult whiteflies are tiny, powdery-white insects, $\frac{1}{20}$ inch long. They are related to aphids and are not flies. Whiteflies rest on undersides of leaves and fly up when disturbed. The nymphs are tiny, flattened, legless, translucent scales $\frac{1}{30}$ inch long, found mostly on undersides of leaves. The eggs are gray or yellow cones the size of a pinpoint.

Both nymphs and adults suck plant juices, weakening plants. They can spread plant viruses through their feeding. They also exude honeydew, which supports the growth of sooty molds on leaves and fruit. The adults tend to be found on the top parts of plants, while developing nymphs are lower down.

There are many overlapping generations per year, continuing all winter in greenhouses and warm climates. The eggs hatch in 2 days into tiny, mobile scales and, after a few days, these become immobile scales. They feed on plant juices until they reach a quiescent stage (not a true pupa) before molting to adults. The complete life cycle takes 20–30 days at room temperature.

Plants Attacked
The most damaging whitefly species attack citrus, ornamentals, annuals, rhododendrons, azaleas, grapes, and vegetables, especially squash- and tomato-family plants outdoors and in greenhouses.

Organic Controls
Native parasitic wasps, lacewings, lady beetles, and pirate bugs attack whitefly nymphs outdoors. Capture adult whiteflies on yellow sticky traps. For a few plants, use a handheld vacuum to remove adults from undersides of leaves. To control greenhouse whiteflies, release *Encarsia formosa* parasitic wasps (indoors). To control nymphs of various species, spray neem, insecticidal soap, kinoprene (Enstar), or summer oil on plants that can tolerate oil sprays. As a last resort, try spraying pyrethrins.

Research Notes
J. E. Wright of the USDA Cotton Research Unit in Weslaco, Texas, has tested a new microbial insecticide containing the insect-attacking fungal disease *Beauveria bassiana* on sweet potato whitefly with excellent results. The fungus acted within a week, infecting all stages of the whitefly to dramatically reduce populations on cucumbers, cantaloupes, broccoli, and other vegetables.

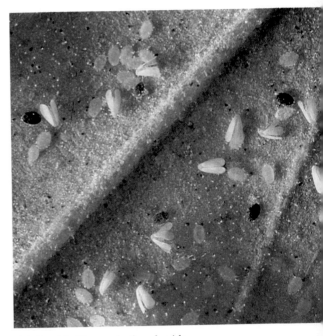

Adult whiteflies on leaf underside

WIREWORMS

Limonius **spp.**

Adults are elongated, brown or black "click" beetles, ⅓–¾ inch long. They have fine, lengthwise grooves on the wing covers. When they are overturned, they produce a sharp click as they flip onto their feet. The larvae ("wireworms") are shiny, brown, leathery, jointed, and wormlike, growing up to 1½ inches long.

The beetles feed on leaves and flowers but cause little damage. It is the larvae boring into seeds, roots, and crowns that are most damaging. Plants may be stunted or killed, and boring in tubers and bulbs ruins them and allows rots to enter. Wireworms are worst in newly turned sod and for a few years thereafter.

One generation may live 2–6 years. The adults lay eggs around plant roots in the early spring. The larvae hatch in 3–10 days and spend 2–6 years feeding on roots. They feed near the soil surface while the soil is cool in spring and fall. They burrow deeper in hot weather and again in late fall to avoid freezing during winter. When finally mature, they pupate in late summer.

Plants Attacked

Wireworms attack most vegetables, particularly potatoes, carrots, and corn, as well as gladiolus, lobelias, and other corms.

Organic Controls

Delay planting tubers and corms until the soil is very warm, and keep the soil bare until planting time. To expose larvae to birds, cultivate the soil for new gardens weekly for 4–6 weeks in the fall, or allow chickens to run on infested ground. Raw potato or carrot pieces buried several inches deep in the soil attract some species; check these traps every few days and destroy wireworms. Applying insect parasitic nematodes to the soil may give some control of larvae.

Research Notes

Researchers at the University of Idaho (Department of Plant, Soil, and Entomological Sciences) have found that decomposing rapeseed (canola) green manure crops plowed into the soil significantly repels wireworms.

*Wireworm larva (*Limonius* sp.)*

ALL ABOUT DISEASES

In this section, you'll find the most common plant diseases in the United States, with their symptoms, prevention, and control, as well as the plants they are most likely to attack. It's a snap to turn to the culprit and solve the problem safely. Start by looking up your plant in "Plants A to Z" beginning on page 8. But if, after checking the most likely diseases, you're still not sure what's plaguing your plants, call your local Extension Service office for a diagnosis.

Plant diseases are caused by bacteria, fungi, viruses, and mycoplasma-like organisms. Most of these organisms are microscopic, although you can see some of them when their populations become enormous or they produce spores. When you suspect a disease problem, you can't search for the perpetrator. Instead, you have to look for symptoms and hope they're characteristic enough that you can identify the problem and step in to prevent or control it.

Bad Bacteria

Bacteria cause three major groups of problems: wilts, unusual growths such as galls, and tissue death. The wilts are caused by bacteria that grow in the plant's water- and nutrient-conducting vessels, eventually reaching populations so large that the vessels become plugged. Galls and other abnormal growths are the plant's response to the presence of some bacteria, while tissue death can range from tiny, almost harmless spots to rotting and death of the entire plant.

Most bacteria are one-celled plants that reproduce through cell division. Wind, rain, insects, animals, and even gardeners carry them from one plant to another. They enter plants through wounds and natural openings such as the pores in leaves and stems. Most bacteria die after a year without a host plant, so it is possible to control their populations by good crop rotation.

Foul Fungi

Fungi cause the majority of plant diseases. They can also cause rotting and death of tissues, the formation of galls, and plugging of water and nutrient-conducting vessels. But unlike bacteria, fungi are multicellular, and most of them can reproduce sexually as well as asexually. Some species, such as those that cause rusts, produce as many as five different spore forms, but most are restricted to only two or three types. Spores are carried by wind, water, insects, and gardeners. Fungi usually enter plants through leaf and stem pores and other natural openings.

Vile Viruses

Viruses and mycoplasma-like organisms are simply little bits of RNA or DNA with protein coating. They do not reproduce in the strict sense of the word; instead, they stimulate their host cell to make more viruses. Generally, they cause growth distortions such as crinkled leaves, galls, or abnormally bushy and numerous root hairs or branches (such as witches'-brooms). Other common symptoms include stunting of the whole plant or a portion of it, and yellowing. They are transmitted by gardeners, insects, and animals, and enter plants through wounds.

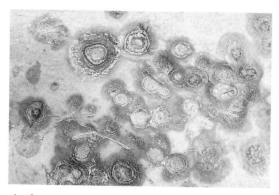

Anthracnose on cucurbits

ANTHRACNOSE

Colletotrichum **spp.,** *Glomerella* **spp.,**
Marssonina **spp.,** *Sphaceloma* **spp.**

Anthracnose fungi cause watery, rotting spots on foliage, stems, flowers, or fruits of many plants. The spots may be yellow, brown, pinkish, or purplish, often with a raised margin. Spots darken and merge as they age, covering the entire leaf in some cases. Infected leaves may drop prematurely, and the entire plant may be defoliated. Spots on stems often enlarge to girdle and kill them. On trees, branch tips may die. Anthracnose spots on fruit are usually sunken and watery, sometimes with tan centers or concentric rings. In humid conditions an ooze or pinkish-colored mold may appear on infected spots.

Anthracnose fungi overwinter as mycelia (fungal threads) in seeds and crop debris. Plants grown from infected seeds often die at the seedling stage. Mycelia in crop debris begin spore formation as soon as the weather warms. Spores are spread by windblown rain or splashing water and require a water film to germinate. Once inside the plant, they reproduce rapidly, forming infective spores through the season.

Plants Affected

Many plants are affected by anthracnose, particularly beans, melons, squash, and tomatoes.

Organic Controls

Preventive tactics include cleaning up garden debris, crop rotation, wide plant spacing to increase air movement, keeping leaves dry while watering, and not working in the garden when plants are wet. Rake up and destroy leaves and twigs from infected trees. On smaller plants, prune off and destroy all infected growth at the first sign of infection. Copper fungicides control these fungi if applied before the disease takes hold, but should be used only as a last resort.

Apple with "corky" spots typical of apple scab

APPLE SCAB

Venturia inaequalis

Apple scab is quite common in all humid areas. It manifests itself as light gray spots on sepals and undersides of early leaves. As spots age, they become a velvety olive green, then chocolate brown, and metallic black. Spots on fruit become corky. Infected fruit may be cracked, deformed, or russetted. Infected leaves drop early.

Scab overwinters on old leaves that were infected the previous season. Spores form in spring and are usually ripe about the time that petals fall. Rain dripping on the old leaves causes spores to shoot into the air, where they are carried by the wind to leaves or fruit. Spores germinate and penetrate tissues that remain continuously wet for a certain number of hours. The time it takes to cause infection depends on air temperatures. For example, at 32–40°F, 48 hours of wetness are required, but at 58–76°F, only 9 hours are required. Pest control suppliers sell Mills Charts listing this information.

Plants Affected
Apples, crabapples, hawthorns, and pears are susceptible.

Organic Controls
Protect against scab by choosing resistant cultivars such as 'Freedom', 'Liberty', 'Prima', 'Redfree', 'Sweet 16', and 'William's Pride'. Space trees widely when planting, and choose locations where air circulation is high. Rake up and dispose of all fallen leaves. Sulfur sprayed on leaves before a rainy period and again just afterward, from the time that buds begin to break until a month after petal fall, will kill most of the spores. If spots appear, continue to use sulfur since scab infects plants through the season.

ARMILLARIA ROOT ROT
Armillaria mellea

This rot, sometimes called shoestring root rot, is not always apparent until the major damage is done. Armillaria root rot causes a gradual dieback on large trees, but more sudden death of seedlings and young trees. White mycelium (fungal thread) mats or fans and dark-colored "shoestrings" grow under the bark, extending many feet up the trunk. On roots, the bark is usually killed all around the mycelial mat. Wood in trunks may or may not be decayed. If decayed, it is spongy or stringy, moist, and pale. As the disease progresses, the trunk is girdled and the roots rot.

This fungus overwinters as mycelia in both living and dead trees. In spring, the mycelia and "shoestrings," or rhizomorphs, grow through the soil to infect healthy trees. In late summer or early fall, honey-colored mushrooms may appear around the base of infected trees. The mushrooms shrivel after producing wind-borne spores. Armillaria can live for many years on dead tissue.

Armillaria root rot mushrooms around the base of an infected tree

Plants Affected

Many trees and ornamental shrubs are vulnerable when they are stressed.

Organic Controls

To prevent attack, control environmental stresses such as flooding or drought, as well as biological stresses such as defoliation from pests and other diseases. There is no cure, but if you provide tender loving care, the tree may live for many years. Cut out all infected tissues on the roots and trunk, leaving roots uncovered until fall. If a tree dies of armillaria, remove the roots and as much soil around

them as possible. Fill the hole with compost and replant with an immune species such as the plum, 'Mariana 2624'.

BACTERIAL SOFT ROT
Erwinia spp., *Pseudomonas* spp.

Anyone who's ever let carrots sit around in a plastic bag in the crisper for too long has seen this disease.

Soft rot bacteria initially create a small, water-soaked spot. As the bacteria feed and reproduce, the spot rapidly enlarges. Infected plant tissues give off a foul odor and the decayed area looks dark and slimy. On cabbage and cauliflower, these bacteria create a dark-colored, moist, rotting area on the head; on celery, the stalks rot. Onions are infected in the field, but as with carrots, the rot doesn't usually show until a few weeks after storage. Peppers develop infected areas just under the skin that quickly rot. On flowering plants such as irises and hyacinths, soft rot infects flower petals. Warm, wet weather favors the spread of these bacteria.

Soft rot bacteria overwinter on plant debris in the soil. In spring, they are carried to new plants by water, insects (such as root maggots), and dirty tools. The bacteria enter plants through wounds, bruises, dead tissue, or when an insect carrier deposits them when it bites into a plant. Soft rot bacteria kill tissues by exuding enzymes that break down the cementing material between cell walls. The bacteria feed and reproduce on the released nutrients.

Plants Affected

Bacterial soft rot creates severe rots on both growing and stored crops, while flowers such as begonias, geraniums, and hyacinths are often damaged.

Bacterial soft rot on celery

Organic Controls

Preventive measures include planting in well-drained soil and keeping air circulation high. Whenever possible, water only the soil, not the foliage. If you must use a sprinkler, water early in the day so foliage can dry before nightfall.

BACTERIAL SPOT

Pseudomonas spp., *Xanthomonas* spp.

Bacterial spot damage can range from mildly annoying to downright life-threatening.

Small, yellowish green, water-soaked spots on young leaves are the first symptoms. Spots are usually round unless the infection is between veins, in which case they are angular. As spots age, they either become dark and greasy-looking or tan and dry. Infected tissue often drops out producing a "shothole" look. Lower leaves of plants often yellow and drop. On cucumbers, squash, peppers, and tomatoes, the first spots are small, translucent, and raised, becoming dark and sunken as they age. The skin covering them is usually wrinkled.

Bacterial spot overwinters in crop debris and infected seed. In spring, warm weather encourages the bacteria to reproduce. Rain, wind, and dirty tools carry them to new plants. Insects can also spread them. The bacteria enter plants through natural openings and wounds. Spots remain small, but the disease is spread easily from one plant part to another, or from one plant to another.

Plants Affected

Bacterial spot attacks the leaves of many plants, including woody plants, as well as the fruit of tomatoes, sweet peppers, squash, and cucumbers. Flowers such as begonias, geraniums and hyacinths are also affected.

Bacterial leaf spot (<u>Xanthomonas pelargonii</u>) on geranium

Organic Controls

Protect plants by choosing resistant cultivars. If you save seed from your own plants, dip it in a solution of 9 parts water and 1 part chlorine bleach before planting. Rotate crops so they don't grow in the same area more than once every three or four years. A streptomycin spray, applied just as the weather warms in early summer, may control the disease. Spray previously infected ornamentals twice a month with copper sulfate.

BACTERIAL WILT

Erwinia spp., *Pseudomonas* spp.

Wilt diseases can be mystifying because the first symptoms may be subtle.

The first wilting usually occurs in the afternoon; by the next morning, plants look like they have recovered. However, this "recovery" is an illusion. The wilt-and-revive cycle will continue during the disease's early stage. Initially, only one branch or one side of the plant may be affected, but as the bacteria reproduce, the whole plant wilts. Infected leaves and branches shrivel, usually without yellowing, and the entire plant eventually dies. When infected stems are cut open, bacterial ooze is usually visible. On cucurbits, it forms a

Bacterial wilt of cucurbit

sticky thread as the two sides of the stem are pulled apart. Stems of infected tomato plants may be hollow and the slime inside corn stems is bright yellow.

Erwinia tracheiphila, the bacteria that causes bacterial wilt in cucurbits, overwinters in the salivary glands of cucumber beetles. *Erwinia* spp. are responsible for many diseases, including bacterial soft rot and bacterial streaks. The beetles transmit the wilt disease as they feed on plants in spring.

Rose leaves infected with black spot

The *Pseudomonas* bacteria that cause bacterial wilt of corn are generally carried on the seed but transmitted by insects such as flea beetles, while the species that infects nightshade crops like tomatoes, peppers, potatoes, and eggplants, can overwinter in the soil without a host. All of these bacteria live and reproduce in the plant's vascular system, clogging it with bacterial ooze as the infection progresses.

Plants Affected

Many plants, including squash-family crops, nightshades, and sweet corn, are affected.

Organic Controls

Prevent infections by planting disease-free corn seed. Choose resistant cultivars when possible (try 'Table Queen Acorn', 'Butternut', or 'Buttercup'). Control insects as much as possible or use barriers such as floating row covers over plants, hand-pollinating early flowers if necessary.

BLACK SPOT
Diplocarpon rosae

Black spot is most common in humid areas. You can tell it apart from the other diseases that cause leaf spotting on roses by the fringed or indistinct margin on the spots. Initial spots can be as small as $\frac{1}{16}$ inch in diameter, but they enlarge quickly and run together to form irregular black patches. Frequently, the spots are surrounded by a yellow halo. If infection is severe, the entire leaf may yellow and drop. The plant can be quickly defoliated by a bad infection. Canes do not show signs of infection, although the fungus does overwinter in them. Nursery stock was once the prime source of infection. Greenhouse propagators used to control red spider mites by frequent misting or syringing, enabling the black rot fungus to spread rapidly on plants. Today, however, that means of transmission is rare, since many growers use predatory mites or, if they are chemical growers, fumigate to control the pests.

The black spot fungus overwinters on infected leaves and canes of rose bushes. In spring, spores form and are carried, primarily by splashing water and rain, to healthy growth. High humidity levels encourage the germination and growth of this fungus.

Plants Affected
Many roses are susceptible to this disease.

Organic Controls
Resistant species and cultivars are available, including rugosa rose and 'Carefree Beauty', 'Simplicity', and 'Bride's Dream'. In humid climates, choose these first. Look for spots on leaves and flowers that are not as vividly colored as is normal. If infection strikes, prune off all infected growth as soon as you see spots. In fall, rake up all dropped leaves. Prune infected canes to just above the graft union. Spray with fungicidal soap or sulfur at 7- to 10-day intervals, beginning in early spring. Baking soda sprayed at 7- to 10-day intervals works for some growers.

BOTRYTIS BLIGHT

Botrytis allii, B. cinerea

Botrytis blight can be devastating, but it's not hard to control once you understand the conditions that favor it. Frequently, this disease starts as a blight on aging blossoms. Succulent flowers such as begonias, peonies, and geraniums are particularly susceptible. Once established on a plant, this fungus rapidly spreads to infect petioles, stems, and entire branches. On leaves, stems, and fruit, the first signs of

Botrytis on primrose

infection are tiny, water-soaked spots. The spots enlarge and become soft and watery. Infected stem and leaf tissues become light brown and crack open, allowing the fuzzy gray spores to emerge. Lower leaves of infected lettuce plants rot first. Botrytis-infected onion leaves develop tiny white spots, then die back from the tip. In storage they develop neck rots.

The botrytis fungus is present in almost all environments. It overwinters on plant debris. In spring, spores form and are carried by wind, water, and dirty tools to new plants. Botrytis enters plants through wounds, bruises, and dying tissue. It reproduces rapidly in humid conditions, forming spores which infect other plants and tissues. A botrytis infection can destroy an entire planting in days.

Plants Affected

Almost all plants are subject to botrytis blight.

Organic Controls

Plant in well-drained soil and keep air circulation high with proper spacing. In greenhouses, increase air circulation and ventilation. Remove faded flowers and destroy infected plant parts to reduce the spread of the disease.

BROWN ROT
Monilinia fructicola

Brown rot is most serious in warm, humid climates. The first symptom of brown rot is flower spotting. Tiny, brown specks cover the flower and its stem. As the spots age, they enlarge, browning the whole bloom. A grayish brown, fuzzy mold may develop. The fungus soon spreads to growing fruit, where it produces small brown spots. Again, the spots enlarge and a grayish brown mold, filled with new spores, grows. The spore masses often form in concentric rings over rotted fruit tissues. Infected fruits eventually rot completely and shrivel, remaining on the twig. Twigs infected with brown rot have sunken brown cankers. These cankers enlarge and may girdle the twig.

Brown rot overwinters on mummified fruit and infected twigs, both on the tree and on the ground below. In spring, warmer temperatures and high moisture levels stimulate the fungus to begin producing spores. The spores are usually carried by the wind to the blossoms as they open.

Plants Affected

Almonds and stone fruits such as peaches, nectarines, and apricots are susceptible.

Organic Controls

Avoid brown rot by planting resistant cultivars whenever possible (try nectarines such as 'Hardired', and 'Mericrest' and peaches such as 'Reliance'). Prune to ensure good air circulation by thinning dense growth and opening up the center of the tree. Don't overfertilize, since high nitrogen levels encourage this fungus. Control insects as much as possible to avoid wounds. In fall, gather and destroy all mummified fruit and fallen leaves and twigs. Sulfur, sprayed twice from when blossoms show pink to petal fall, and again before harvest, helps to control the disease.

Brown rot on lemon

CANE BLIGHT
Botryosphaeria ribis, Leptosphaeria coniothyrium

Cane blight is frequently spread by infected propagating stock. Cane blight diseases can be quite serious. On brambles, brownish purple lesions on the canes are the first symptom. Leaves may yellow and wilt. Infections spread quickly from one cane to another until most of the side branches have been infected. Gooseberries and currants also develop dark-colored stem lesions, which are easy to overlook until other symptoms appear. Leaves on infected canes wilt, yellow, and drop. Canes die back. The disease can spread rapidly from only one or two canes to the entire bush. Both cane blight diseases are most serious in moist conditions.

Cane blight overwinters on infected plant tissue. In spring, warm temperatures and high moisture levels stimulate the fungi to produce spores. Wind and splashing water spread them to new growth.

Plants Affected
Black raspberries, blackberries, currants, gooseberries, and raspberries are the most susceptible species.

Organic Controls
Help to prevent problems by planting in well-drained soil and spacing plants far enough apart to encourage good air circulation. Cane blight of brambles can only enter plants through wounds, so prune early in the day and when the weather is clear and dry to encourage rapid healing. Cut out old canes below the soil surface. On gooseberries, reduce interior crowding by pruning out canes in the center of the bush and those that are four or more years old. Spray with lime-sulfur just before buds open in spring.

CEDAR-APPLE RUST
Gymnosporangium juniperi-virginianae
Cedar-apple rust can be quite difficult to completely eliminate, but with careful control, infections can usually be reduced to more manageable levels.

Cane blight on raspberry

Cedar-apple rust is more destructive on apples than on cedars. The small, yellow spots on the leaves and apples can be quite numerous and, as they age, become brown and sunken, disfiguring the fruit. Raised orange pustules develop, often in concentric circles. Infected cedar trees develop gelatinous orange masses in the branches in spring.

Cedar-apple rust on apple leaf

Citrus scab on lemon

spread the spores for fertilization. After fertilization, the fungus forms fruiting bodies on leaf undersides. Spores from these bodies blow to nearby cedar trees and the cycle is repeated.

Plants Affected

Eastern red cedar and apple trees are alternate hosts for this fungus.

Organic Controls

You can prevent cedar-apple rust if apples and cedars are separated by at least 4 miles. This is sometimes difficult to accomplish, so the best choice for apple growers is choosing rust-resistant cultivars such as 'Empire', 'Redfree', and 'Stayman'. Remove and burn galls on cedars, where the disease spends the bulk of its life.

Citrus Scab
Sphaceloma fawcettii

Citrus scab is as annoying in citrus-growing areas as apple scab is in other regions.

The first signs of citrus scab are small, rounded spots on leaves, raised on the upper surface and depressed on the leaf underside. Brownish, pinkish, or gray scabs form on the raised spots, and spores are formed here, often in time to infect other portions of the tree. On fruit, the scabs are grayish or brown, irregularly shaped, and sometimes warty. Fruit that are infected early often fall prematurely. Twigs may also be infected, and often drop. Lemons on trees with citrus scab are sometimes abnormally large because of the fruit thinning the disease causes. Only the skin of fruit is affected. However, because the disease travels into the twigs, it can severely damage or ruin the tree's structure, drastically cutting yields.

Cedar-apple rust alternates between its two hosts—Eastern red cedar and apple—during its life cycle. The first year that it infects cedars, it creates small, greenish brown swellings on the needle tips. The following year, these swellings grow into hard, brown, dimpled galls up to 2 inches wide. Warm, rainy conditions stimulate bright orange, spore-bearing tendrils to grow from the dimples.

Wind carries the spores to nearby apple trees. Tiny yellow pustules form on the upper surfaces of apple leaves and on developing fruit. These spots form a spore-containing ooze that is attractive to insects. As they move from one spot to another, the insects help to

The fungus that causes citrus scab over-winters on infected leaves, fruit, and twigs. In spring, when cool, damp weather follows a dry spell, spores are formed. They spread by wind-driven rain, air, and insects onto new growth. Citrus trees are susceptible to this fungus for about 2½ months following half-petal fall.

Plants Affected
All citrus trees are susceptible.

Organic Controls
Prevent the spread of scab by pruning off and destroying all infected fruit and leaves, and the twigs on which they are growing. In spring, spray with copper when petals are beginning to fall. Repeat in 10 days.

CROWN GALL
Agrobacterium tumefasciens

Crown gall is difficult to control once it occurs, so monitoring and prevention pay off. You're likely to notice crown gall when canes or branches begin to look unhealthy. Leaves yellow and wilt and branches begin to die back. Look for large, irregularly shaped galls near the soil line. Crown gall bacteria exude acetic acids that promote abnormal and excessive growth of nearby cells. Stressed cell walls eventually break open, releasing more nutrients for the bacteria. Though they look hard, the interiors of galls are soft. A callus sometimes grows over the galled portions, and secondary rotting organisms usually invade.

Crown gall bacteria usually overwinter on infected roots, although they can survive in soil without a host for several years. As infected roots decompose, the bacteria are carried along in the soil water to infect new plants. They usually enter plants through wounds created by nematodes, root aphids, or maggots, but can also enter through a plant's natural openings.

Plants Affected
The most susceptible plants are roses, fruit trees, brambles, grapes, tomatoes, beets, and turnips.

Organic Controls
The most effective preventive measure is close examination of all purchased plants. Soak seeds and roots in a solution containing the beneficial bacteria *Agrobacterium radiobacter* before planting. If plants do contract the disease, dig them out, taking as much surrounding soil as possible. In cases where infection is mild and localized, you can try cutting out only the infected areas, sterilizing tools between cuts.

Roots infected with crown gall

Research Notes

Beets are one of the many plants that host the crown gall (*Agrobacterium tumefasciens*) disease. Researchers are working with this bacterial disease on sugar beets and are beginning to develop an understanding of the way that tumors are initiated in animals as well as in plants.

CURLY TOP OR BEET LEAF CURL VIRUS
Ruga varrucosans

Curly top can be a serious problem in areas where sugar beets are grown. It causes different symptoms on different plants. On beet plants, leaves curl upward and the veins become translucent. Eventually, leaves yellow and die. Hornlike bumps often protrude from the veins on leaf undersides, and the beets may be unusually "hairy." Infected bean plants have downward-curling leaves and clear veins before they die. On tomatoes, the disease is called yellows because of the color of the

Curly top on tomato plant

leaves before the plant dies. Cucurbit leaves also yellow but turn upward at the tips. Curly top-infected plants are often stunted.

The virus that causes curly top replicates only in living tissue. It infects both annual and perennial plants, living in the phloem tissues. It can remain dormant for many years in dead plant debris, but it is usually spread by leafhoppers that hatch and feed on infected perennials before moving to annual plants. Leafhoppers transmit the virus throughout the growing season. The beet leafhopper is capable of flying for hundreds of miles, so the disease can infect plants far away from the initial infection site.

Plants Affected

Beets are particularly susceptible to curly top, but this disease can also infect beans, cucurbits, tomatoes, and other vegetables and ornamental plants.

Organic Controls

The best prevention is good soil care since healthy plants are less attractive to the leafhopper. Cover plants for as long as possible with floating row covers in spring and early summer. For leafhopper control see "Leafhoppers" on page 270. Dig and destroy infected plants.

CYTOSPORA CANKER
Cytospora chrysosperma, C. kunzei

Cytospora canker is easy to spot if you know what the symptoms look like. On deciduous trees, long, sunken cankers form on branches or the trunk. The lesions generally start at a wound or a branch stub. The bark under the canker is often cracked and darkened and may be surrounded by a raised callus. Smaller branches are girdled quickly and then die.

On trunks, girdling will take several years. A gummy material, composed of spores, oozes down the branch or trunk, particularly on fruit trees. On conifers, needles on infected branches have a yellow or purple coloration. They soon drop and the branch dies. The disease generally starts from the bottom of the tree, and is characterised by excessive resin oozing from infected branches.

The fungi that cause cytospora canker overwinter as fruiting bodies on bark and as fungal threads in cankers. In wet spring weather, the fruiting bodies, which look like small black pimples, exude thin threads of spores. Rain and splashing water wash these spores to other branches. Insects, pruning tools, birds, and gardeners can also transmit the spores. The fungus penetrates trees through wounds and bruises.

Plants Affected

Blue spruce, maples, mountain ash, Norway spruce, poplars, willows, and fruit trees are the most common hosts.

Organic Controls

Prevent this disease with good cultural care. Prune only in dry weather and avoid unnecessary wounds. Remove severely infected branches. On trunks and large branches, remove cankers, cutting about 2 inches beyond the infected area. Sterilize all pruning tools between cuts and leave them open to the air. Protect the trunks of young trees from sunscald in winter by covering with tree paint.

DODDER

Cuscuta pentagona

Dodder is a parasitic plant, not a pathogenic microorganism, but it causes damage that looks like a disease. Dodder-infested fields and

Cytospora canker on spruce tree

gardens look as if a huge spider had tried to weave the plants together with orange string. Dodder will parasitize almost any herbaceous plant in your garden, absorbing its nutrients and water. As dodder grows, it twines around its host. Dodder stems grow as tall as 7 feet before frost. If the host plant dies, the dodder stem simply waves around until it finds another plant to attach itself to.

Dodder is a member of the Convolvulaceae, or morning-glory, family. It's an annual plant, reproducing by seeds. Dodders are barely noticeable when they first germinate. The first signs are thin, threadlike stems which emerge from the soil in early spring.

Dodder-infested field

The roots of dodders absorb nutrients and water from the soil, but they have no leaves. The stems wave around in the air until they run into a host plant, and tiny suckers on the dodder stems attach to the host plant. Dodder stems then break off their roots and begin taking all of their nourishment from their host. They produce large numbers of pale, whitish flowers in clusters from July until September.

Plants Affected
Almost all herbaceous plants are vulnerable.

Organic Controls
Dodder seeds usually come in on mulch hay and straw or with cover crop seeds. It's hard to see at first, so sickly looking plants may be your first indication of infection. Look for dodder stems when examining plants for damage. If you see dodder, pull the entire host plant and dispose of it and the dodder.

DOWNY MILDEW
Many fungal species

Downy mildew is most serious in humid regions. Oldest leaves are usually infected first. Upper leaf surfaces have small, yellowing spots; on lower leaf surfaces, a whitish, gray, or purplish mold appears. After spores have been released, the spots turn dark and the leaf withers and dies. When downy mildew infects fruit, the only symptom is the mold on the skin.

Downy mildew fungi produce resting spores late in the season that can overwinter once the plant decomposes and remain viable for several years. In spring, these spores are transmitted to new plants through wind, water, or, in the case of cucurbit downy mildew, by beetles. These fungi require a film of water for germination and enter plants through leaf pores or the cuticle. The characteristic mildew of these fungi is made up of fruiting bodies that release clouds of spores. Most of these fungi take only a week from the first infection until spore production.

Plants Affected
Many vegetables, ornamentals, and fruits are susceptible to downy mildew.

Organic Controls
To prevent outbreaks, space plants to encourage air circulation, and water early in the day. Choose resistant cultivars when possible. Some examples are 'Marketmore 86' and 'Fanfare' for cucumbers; 'Crete' for melons, and 'Green Arrow' for peas. Clean up all debris in fall to remove overwintering spores. In greenhouses and other enclosed spaces, keep ventilation high. Remove and destroy infected tissues. Bordeaux mixture, sprayed at weekly intervals in spring and just before rain, controls some of the causal fungi. To be sure

that the Bordeaux mixture will not harm your plant, test it on a few leaves first. Spray or paint it on a few leaves, some in shade and some in bright sun. Check the appearance of the leaves every day for 5 days. (Generally, if a substance is phytotoxic, the surface of the leaf begins to dry and then the leaf will die, usually within 5 days.)

EARLY BLIGHT
Alternaria solani

Early blight is particularly serious on trellised tomatoes that have been pruned to a single leader. Leaf spots are the first symptom of early blight. The spots are brown with a concentric "target" pattern. They can be as large as ½ inch in diameter and usually appear on oldest leaves first. Spots enlarge and run together. Heavily infected leaves drop. Dark, sunken lesions appear on the stems, often starting near the soil in young plants.

Early blight infections on tomato fruits start at the stem ends and form a dark-colored rot inside the fruit. Potato plants are usually affected just about the time they blossom. Leaf spots look similar to those on tomato leaves, but on the tubers the damage shows as small, dark spots, often with gray to purplish edges. Tuber rot looks brown and dry, but secondary rotting organisms may change its appearance.

The early blight fungus overwinters on seeds and crop debris left in the garden. In spring, spores form as soon as the weather begins to warm. These spores are transmitted by wind, rain, contaminated tools, and sometimes flea beetles. Several generations of early blight spores can grow from the same lesion, so it doesn't take long for early blight to spread.

Downy mildew on rhubarb leaf

The target-like spots of early blight

Plants Affected

All tomato-family crops, particularly tomatoes and potatoes, can get early blight. Zinnias and petunias are susceptible to *Alternaria zinniae*.

Organic Controls

Prevent early blight with good cultural care, since stressed plants are more susceptible. Practice 3- to 4-year rotations and clean up all garden debris in fall. At the first sign of an early blight infection, spray with copper, repeating at 7- to 10-day intervals. Destroy severely infected plants. Mound soil over potato tubers to prevent infection.

FIRE BLIGHT
Erwinia amylovora

Fire blight is unmistakable once you've seen a heavy infection. Sudden wilting of leaves, blossoms, and young shoots occurs in late spring. Infected blossoms look water-soaked, then brown and shriveled. Leaves turn brown or black and curl upward. They remain hanging on the twigs, looking as if they were scorched by fire. Affected shoots bend downward, and young fruit are darkened and remain on the tree. As the disease spreads down the shoots, it creates cankered areas in large branches or the main trunk. The cankers have a distinct margin and the wood under them is first water-soaked and then darkens.

The fire blight bacterium overwinters in a dormant state in infected twigs and at the edges of cankers. Warm spring rains stimulate it to resume growth. The bacterial ooze it produces is attractive to many insects, including flies, ants, bees, aphids, and beetles, which carry the bacteria to susceptible plants. Rain, splashing water, and contaminated tools also transmit it. These bacteria generally become dormant in late summer.

Plants Affected

Apples, pears, raspberries, spireas, hawthorns, and roses are the most common hosts.

Organic Controls

Protect plants by avoiding overfertilization with nitrogen. Look for infections on wild plants and destroy them. Control insects as much as possible. Prune out all infected bramble or rose canes in summer, disinfecting tools between cuts. In late winter, prune out and destroy infected shoots and branches, cutting at least 6–12 inches below the visible infection. Spray with streptomycin during blossoming, at 7- to 10-day intervals. In late winter, spray with copper or Bordeaux mixture.

Fireblight on pyracantha branch

FUSARIUM WILT
Fusarium spp.

Fusarium wilt is most serious in warm regions. Wilting when the soil is moist is usually the first sign of fusarium wilt. Often, only one side or branch of a plant will wilt, but as the disease progresses, more and more of the plant is affected. Older leaves develop yellow patches that later turn brown. Infected leaves drop prematurely. The lower stem often develops a brownish discoloration that sometimes spreads to the roots. Stem interiors are darkened. On tomato seedlings, the first symptom is a downward curling of the leaves. Infected potato tubers develop a soft or dry rot in storage.

Fusarium fungi overwinter on crop debris, producing new spores once the weather is warm. Rain, splashing water, and contaminated tools transmit the disease to new plants. These fungi enter plants through wounds in tissues, particularly those on the roots or on stems and leaves close to the soil surface. This fungus invades the water-carrying xylem vessels, plugging them. Fusarium species produce resting spores that remain viable in the soil for up to 10 years, as well as spores that can infect other plants immediately.

Plants Affected

Many plants, including bulbs, trees, and shrubs, are susceptible. In bulbs, *Fusarium* spp. cause both basal and corm rot.

Organic Controls

Prevent fusarium wilt with good cultural care, planting in well-drained soil. Choose resistant cultivars when possible: try 'Sweet Mama' for winter squash; 'Earlisweet' and 'Crete' for melons; and most contemporary hybrid cultivars such as 'Big Beef' and 'Ultra Girl' for tomatoes.

Carnation showing typical symptoms of fusarium wilt

Warm air and soil temperatures favor this disease, so mulching with light-reflective straw or hay may help in hot climates. Potassium deficiencies and nitrogen excesses also encourage fusarium problems. To reduce root injuries, control nematodes. If plants show infection, remove and destroy them, taking the roots and surrounding soil.

LATE BLIGHT
Phytophthora capsici, P. infestans

Late blight caused the Potato Famine in Ireland in the 1890s. A century later, new strains have developed and the disease is once again a major problem. Other phytophthora species cause root rots and blossom blights.

Late blight damage generally begins just before blossoming on tomatoes and peppers, and just afterward on potatoes. Lower leaves have large, water-soaked, irregularly shaped spots at their tips or margins. Spots are usually a gray color and have a greasy-looking sheen. Within 7–10 days, a whitish mold appears around the spots on undersides of leaves. This mold is particularly noticeable in high-

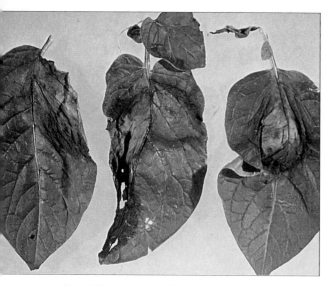

Late blight on potato leaf

humidity conditions. The upper half of tomato fruit has grayish rotting areas, which give off an unpleasant odor. White mold appears in moist conditions. Potato tubers have brown or purplish sunken spots on the skin and develop dry rot or a white mold when kept in storage.

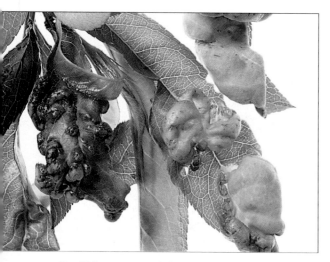

Leaf blister on peach leaf

Late blight fungi overwinter as fungal threads in infected potato tubers or crop refuse. In spring, they produce spores that spread by wind, rain, and contaminated soil. Early blight of peppers can also be seedborne. During the season, the fungus produces swimming spores in cool conditions and spores that float through the air in warm conditions. These spores can form as soon as a week after the initial infection.

Plants Affected
Tomato-family plants host this disease.

Organic Controls
Plant resistant cultivars and disease-free seed potatoes. Some of these are 'Celebrity' and 'Mountain Pride' for tomatoes, and 'Butte' and 'Onaway' for potatoes. Remove all crop residues in fall. If you've had troubles in the past, spray with Bordeaux mixture every 5–7 days when cool, moist nights are followed by warm, muggy days.

LEAF BLISTER
Taphrina spp.

Leaf blisters are common enough that you've probably seen them on trees in your yard. Infected leaves look as if they have blisters or pimples on their surfaces. The raised areas are usually a lighter green color than the rest of the leaf. If you press your fingernail into one of them, you'll see that they don't contain fluids, but are firm and dry. Severely infected leaves often drop in midsummer. Leaf blister is rarely so prevalent that it is life-threatening. However, if infected trees lose so many leaves that you notice the defoliation, control the disease.

Leaf blister fungi overwinter as spores attached to buds on infected trees. In spring, warm weather stimulates spore production. Spores are released just about the time that buds break, and the fungus enters the new leaf through its breathing pores. The fungus releases exudates that cause surrounding tissues to grow more quickly than the rest of the leaf. In fall, the epidermis over these areas splits open and spores are released. Wind and rain carry them to the newly formed buds, where they will spend the winter months.

Plants Affected
Oaks, birches, California buckeyes, elms, maples, pears, poplars, and willows can contract leaf blister.

Organic Controls
To reduce disease incidence, rake up all dropped leaves and burn or destroy them. Do not put them in a slowly decomposing leaf compost since temperatures will be too low to kill the organism. In late spring, just before bud break, spray severely infected trees with lime-sulfur or Bordeaux mix.

LEAF GALL
Exobasidium camelliae, E.vaccinii

Leaf galls are usually so unsightly that you'll want to control them immediately. The first symptom of leaf gall is spotting, most commonly on the leaves at branch tips, but the disease can also occur on blooms and seedpods. The spots can be pale green, yellowish, or reddish. These fungi cause cells near the infection site to grow overly large and divide more than is normal. Leaves, flowers, and seedpods thicken, occasionally becoming bladderlike. Whole leaves may grow abnormally large, curl, or develop a reddish discoloration. In wet weather, white or pinkish spores form on infected areas. Infected flowers and seedpods

grow into waxy, thickened galls that harden and turn brown.

The fungus that causes leaf gall overwinters in infected plant material, producing new spores in spring. Spores spread by wind, rain, and splashing water. These fungi can enter only young, developing tissue.

Plants Affected
Azaleas, camellias, rhododendrons, and blueberries can contract this disease.

Organic Controls
Leaf gall is often transmitted when infected plants are propagated. When buying new plants, check them carefully for symptoms.

Leaf gall on azalea

Melanose on lemon

Some cultivars are more resistant than others; so check with your nursery or garden center before purchasing to choose the most resistant cultivars, particularly when you're buying azaleas. Adequate nutrients, water, and good air circulation can help to prevent this disease from occurring in your garden.

If leaf gall infections appear on plants, prune out and destroy all infected growth as soon as you notice it. Routinely check for signs of infection on developing seedpods. Experiment with copper, which sprayed just before bud break and again 2 weeks later, helps to control outbreaks of leaf gall disease.

MELANOSE
Diaporthe citri

Melanose can be a serious problem if unchecked. Reddish brown to dark brown leaf spots are the first symptoms of melanose. In mild infections, spots may be scattered over the leaf surface. However, in heavy infestations, the whole leaf, or large patches of it, can be so thickly covered that it looks brown from a distance. Rain and dripping dew often wash the spores in rivulets down the surface of the fruit. Long streaks of spots follow these lines.

Light infections do not injure the fruit, but the infection can spread rapidly if unchecked. Moderately infected fruit may be distorted or fail to reach potential size; on heavily infected fruit, the skin cracks open. Some people call this "mudface" because it looks like the dried mud on a riverbed. This disease occurs most frequently on trees older than 10 years, primarily because the fungus has had time to build up populations in old twigs and litter under the tree.

The melanose fungus survives on infected leaves, fruit, twigs, and branches. In warm, moist conditions, it produces spores. Rain, heavy dew, and wind spread these spores onto healthy tissue.

Plants Affected
Citrus trees, especially lemons, are prone to melanose. Some mandarin species and navel oranges are particularly susceptible.

Organic Controls
Control melanose infestations by pruning off and destroying all infected leaves, twigs, and branches in the garden. Rake up and destroy all fallen plant material frequently. One spray of copper at fruit set can help to prevent more serious infections.

MISTLETOES

Arceuthobium **spp.,** *Phoradendron* **spp.,**
Viscum **spp.**

Mistletoes are parasitic plants that extract minerals and water from host trees.

Damage from true mistletoes is rarely life threatening unless the tree is already stressed by environmental conditions, diseases, or insects. Because they have their own leaves true mistletoes depend on their hosts for only water and minerals. Dwarf mistletoes, on the other hand, can be life threatening to their hosts because they lack leaves and do not produce their own sugars. Instead, they absorb them, along with minerals and water, from their hosts. Invaded twigs, branches, and trunk tissue are likely to be swollen or produce "witches'-brooms," a dense, unusually bushy cluster of stems.

The true, or leafy, mistletoes reproduce by seeds coated with a sticky material. The seeds stick to the feet of birds, which carry them to neighboring trees. Dwarf mistletoes also produce sticky seeds, but they also build interior pressure which literally shoots seeds into the surrounding area. The seeds adhere to twigs and branches, where they land and germinate when conditions are correct. Developing mistletoes penetrate their hosts through the bark.

Plants Affected
Hardwoods are attacked by true mistletoes, while conifers host dwarf mistletoes.

Organic Controls
You're likely to notice true mistletoes in fall, when the leaves of hardwoods have fallen but the green leaves of the mistletoe persist. In the case of conifers, you might notice a general decline in the tree's vigor first. Prune out and destroy all the mistletoe you can find. Take down badly infested trees.

MOSAIC
Many viruses

Each virus, including the various mosaics, is slightly different from the others, but the following information is generally applicable to any virus that attacks plants.

Viruses cause many plant problems, including distorted growth, spots on plant tissues, stunting, yellowing, and mottled plant tissue. We call the viruses that cause mottling "mosaics." Mosaic-infected leaves are usually cupped or puckered. The plant grows slowly or is stunted. In some cases, stems are unusually brittle and break easily. Infected flowers

Mistletoe on host tree

Mosaic on rose leaves

also display a mottled coloration. Tomato fruit have yellow, sunken areas on the skin. The stem interiors may be darkened. Cucumber mosaic virus (CMV) affects many other plants, including tomatoes and spinach. Tomatoes infected with the cucumber mosaic virus develop narrow, "shoestring" leaves, while spinach is dwarfed and yellowed.

Most viruses are transmitted to plants by insects, although some are seedborne. They can also enter through bruises and wounds. Viruses are composed of DNA or RNA and a protein coating. Rather than dividing to reproduce, they cause the host cell to replicate them, so they build populations only in living tissues.

However, they can remain in an inactive but viable state in dead tissues for as long as 50 years. They easily survive composting and freezing temperatures.

Plants Affected
Viruses of one sort or another infect almost all garden plants.

Organic Controls
Prevent viruses by keeping plants growing vigorously. Choose resistant cultivars and certified disease-free planting stock. For tomatoes choose contemporary hybrid cultivars, including 'Celebrity' and 'Sweet Gold'. Do not touch wet plants. Try to control sucking insects, and use floating row covers when possible. Remove and destroy virus-infected plants immediately.

NEEDLE CAST
Many fungi

Needle cast kills needles and branch tips, particularly on the lower limbs. Needle cast diseases are usually most severe on young trees. The first symptoms are mottled orange or brown spots, or alternating light and dark bands on new needles. As the disease ages, needles turn dark olive green, yellow, or reddish brown. They die from the tip downward, and plant growth is slowed. In midsummer through early fall, severely infected needles drop and branch tips die. Young trees may be killed. Exotic species are most susceptible since they are likely to be stressed by an environment slightly out of their normal range.

The fungi that cause needle cast diseases overwinter in dropped needles under the tree. In spring, warmer wet weather stimulates them to produce spores. Splashing water and wind carry the spores to the newly emerging needles, and the infection cycle begins again.

Plants Affected

Many evergreen trees, particularly pines, arborvitae, and western red cedars, are affected.

Organic Controls

Avoid problems by planting only native or well-adapted trees. Plant in locations with good air circulation and well-drained soil. Irrigate in drought periods. Wrap young trees growing in an exposed location with burlap for winter, or erect a windscreen. Rake up and destroy fallen needles. Prune off infected growth. If a young tree becomes severely infected, spray with copper or Bordeaux mixture when needles are half-grown, and again 2 weeks later. Test the spray first to check its safety. Spray or paint it on a few leaves, some in shade and some in bright sun. Check the appearance of the leaves every day for 5 days. Generally, if a substance is phytotoxic, the leaf surface begins to dry and then the leaf dies, usually within 5 days.

Rhizosphaera needle cast on spruce tree

NEMATODES, FOLIAR

Aphelenchoides spp.

Nematodes are microscopic, nonsegmented worms. Most of the many nematode species are benign, some are beneficial, but a few are destructive to plants.

Lower leaves are usually the first plant parts damaged by foliar nematodes. These worms feed in the leaf tissues, causing areas to yellow, then brown and die. Affected patches are often almost geometric in shape because the nematodes attack tissues between the veins. Bands, triangles, and other regular shapes are common. These patterns become less distinct as the nematodes attack more of the leaf.

Nematodes can overwinter in moist areas in infected plants or remain in a dormant state on crop debris. When spring comes, they

Foliar nematode on fern

become active again. Rain can splash them onto new plants. Nematodes are mobile in water films, so they travel up a stem or over a leaf, looking for a breathing pore or wound to enter. Reproduction is sexual and females can lay thousands of eggs in their lives.

Plants Affected

Chrysanthemums, strawberries, phlox, dahlias, primroses, asters, and many other plants are affected.

Organic Controls

Protect yourself by examining all nursery stock carefully. If leaves are damaged, hold the plant in a pot and observe it for a month or so before transplanting it into your soil. Once in your soil, nematodes can be difficult to eliminate. If nematodes do become a problem, pick off and destroy all infected tissues, including plant debris that has dropped to the ground. Apply beneficial nematodes as directed on the package. Mulch around mildly infected plants with mature compost. Remove all seriously infected plants.

Root knot nematode galls

NEMATODES, ROOT KNOT
Meloidogyne spp.

Root knot nematodes weaken and kill plants by parasitizing their roots. As they feed, root knot nematodes secrete chemicals that stimulate cells to enlarge abnormally. The first symptom of infection that you're likely to notice is a general stunting, yellowing, and wilting of the plant. If you dig it up, you'll see the enlarged galls (swellings) on the roots or tubers. Most roots have strings of swellings. Root knot nematodes prefer sandy soil types in warmer climates.

Root knot nematodes overwinter in the soil. In spring, they travel into roots through very small openings. Inside, they become sedentary feeders. One female can lay as many as 2,000 eggs. Larvae hatch from the eggs and escape into the soil through cracks in the root. They can travel as far as 2 feet in soil, looking for new roots to inhabit.

Plants Affected

Over 2,000 plant species, including fruit trees and most vegetables and ornamentals, are affected by root knot nematodes.

Organic Controls

To suppress root knot nematodes, grow a cover crop of a nematode-killing marigold, such as 'Nemagold', or dig chitin into the soil. In some soils, turning under green manures while they are soft and green stimulates growth of natural soil fungi that parasitize nematodes. In regions with hot summers, soil solarization can heat the soil enough to kill nematodes in the top 6–8 inches of soil. Drenching soil with neem may give sufficient control during a growing season. Remove and destroy infected plants with their surrounding soil — nematodes may survive composting. Apply beneficial nematodes according to label directions.

PEACH LEAF CURL
Taphrina deformans

Peach leaf curl can be a serious disease if not controlled early.

Curled and puckered leaves early in the season are the first symptom of peach leaf curl disease. Leaves are thicker than usual, and cupping is downward. Affected leaves have a reddish or purplish color initially but turn reddish yellow or gray as the disease ages. When the fungus produces spores, the swollen areas are grayish or whitish. Infected twigs swell and look gray. Leaves, twigs, and small fruit drop. On apricots, symptoms are slightly different in that whole shoots are affected and the downward-cupping leaves are abnormally close together.

This fungus overwinters in bud scales. In spring, it produces spores that germinate on newly emerging blossoms and leaves. The fungus reproduces on this tissue, spreading spores to other new growth, including twigs. Cool, wet spring weather favors this disease.

Plants Affected

Peaches, nectarines, almonds, and apricots can contract this disease.

Organic Controls

Choose resistant cultivars such as 'Elberta' and 'Red Haven'. Prune to allow good air circulation in the center of the tree. If the disease strikes, pick off as much infected growth as possible and destroy it. Rake up fallen twigs, leaves, and small fruit to reduce future infections. Boost plant vigor by applying foliar sprays of liquid seaweed, at 14 to 21-day intervals, through the season. In fall, after leaves have fallen, spray with Bordeaux mixture or copper. Early the following spring, slightly before buds swell, spray plants with lime-sulfur.

Peach leaf curl

POWDERY MILDEW
Many fungal species, including *Erysiphe* spp. and *Sphaerotheca* spp.

These fungal infections are unsightly and also weaken host plants. Powdery white or gray spots are usually the first symptoms you will notice. The spots enlarge quickly, covering the entire leaf, flower, or shoot.

Infected tissues become pale, then turn brown and shrivel. Infected fruit usually develops a soft rot under the coating of white fungal threads and spores. The fungi that cause powdery mildew diseases overwinter on plant debris or buds on ornamental and

Powdery mildew on apple

Powdery mildew on zinnia

weedy perennials. In spring, they produce numerous spores that blow through the air to infect new growth. In extreme northern areas, the first infections of spring are usually caused by spores that travel on wind currents from southern areas. These fungi make new spores rapidly, so wave after wave of infections occur each year. They do not require a water film to germinate and may colonize a plant several days before becoming evident.

Plants Affected

Many plants, particularly beans, squash-family crops, lilacs, roses, delphiniums, and zinnias are affected.

Organic Controls

To prevent or reduce powdery mildew incidence, choose resistant cultivars such as 'Zucchini Select' zucchini; 'Earligold' or 'Crete' cantaloupes; 'Knight' or 'Olympia' peas; and 'David Austin' roses. Plant in well-drained soil, and space widely enough for good air circulation.

Stressed plants are more susceptible to infection by powdery mildew fungi. Keeping plants well-fertilized and watered, especially in drought conditions, helps diminish the severity of powdery mildew infections. Pruning woody plants to improve air circulation around leaves and stems reduces powdery mildew problems, as does thinning susceptible herbaceous plants, such as phlox and zinnias.

Rake up and compost leaves and other plant debris in fall to remove overwintering sites for the fungi. Spraying compost tea on leaves every 2–4 weeks can help prevent attack. Pick off and destroy infected plant tissues. On roses, thoroughly wash off the spores with water on both sides of infected leaves at weekly intervals. Baking soda or baking soda plus oil sprays (see "Oil Sprays" on page 361) are often effective.

PSEUDOMONAS LEAF BLIGHT

Pseudomonas spp.

Pseudomonas leaf blight, also commonly known as bacterial blight, seriously weakens trees and shrubs, eventually killing them if it is not controlled.

Spots on leaves, shoots, and flowers in early spring may be your first alert to this disease. The spots enlarge rapidly and turn dark brown or black. These bacteria spread quickly from leaves to branches, causing dark-colored streaks on the bark of most plants and cankers on willows and many stone fruit trees. Cankers on stone fruit trees usually ooze a dark, gummy material. This disease is most severe in warm, wet springs. Existing cankers on wood are likely to enlarge rapidly just about the time that buds break.

Pseudomonas bacteria overwinter on infected plant tissue. Though they are generally dormant during the winter, they can become active and invade healthy tissue whenever the bark becomes warm. In spring, windblown rain and insects spread the bacteria to new sites. The bacteria enter plants through wounds and natural openings, usually on leaves and shoots.

Plants Affected

Woody plants, particularly almonds, avocados, apples, cherries, citrus, lilacs, peaches, pears, plums, roses, and willows, are affected.

Organic Controls

Excess nitrogen favors this disease, so fertilize moderately. Prune in dry weather. If disease strikes, prune off and destroy infected branches, cutting at least 6 inches below infection sites and sterilizing tools between cuts. Spray with an antibiotic after pruning infected

Pseudomonas leaf blight on pea

growth and again just before buds swell in spring. Copper or lime-sulfur, sprayed when buds swell but before bud break, is sometimes an effective control.

RED STELE

Phytophthora fragariae

Red stele is rampant through many strawberry-growing areas in northern regions of the United States and in southern Canada.

Red stele symptoms on strawberry roots (right) next to healthy plant (left)

You are likely to notice a red stele infection in early spring. Leaves on infected plants take on a gray or purplish cast and plants are stunted and grow slowly. Wilting is common. The first flowers may be as numerous as on a healthy plant, but the resulting berries will be smaller than normal and plants may stop blooming early. If you suspect this disease, dig up an infected plant and slice the major roots in half lengthwise. If plants are infected with red stele, the vascular system will be red and rotted-looking.

Spores of the fungus move into plants' feeder roots in early spring and then travel to the central root tissue. The disease reproduces

Root rot-infected tree with healthy tree in the background

rapidly enough that swimming spores (these have flagella that propel them through the soil water) are released into the surrounding soil while the weather is still cool. This disease cannot start in warm conditions. In early summer, it produces resting spores (sexually formed spores that remain dormant) to carry it through the hot summer months. These spores can remain viable in the soil for up to 10 years without a host.

Plants Affected

Strawberries and loganberries are the only plants susceptible to red stele.

Organic Controls

Prevent red stele by buying certified disease-free plants and resistant cultivars such as 'Earliglow', 'Guardian', and 'Lester'. When propagating your own strawberry plants, be certain they are healthy. Plant in well-drained soil that warms early in the season. If plants contract the disease, till them under or, in the case of loganberries, dig them out. Do not replant contaminated soils with susceptible berries for at least 10 years.

ROOT ROT
Many fungi

Root rot diseases kill many plants in the seedling stage. They also damage and may kill established plants by causing stem and/or crown rots. There are many rot-producing fungi, including *Pythium* spp., *Phytophthora* spp., *Rhizoctonia* spp., *Pellicularia filamentosa*, *Fusarium* spp., *Phoma apiicola*, and *Aphanomyces* spp. The first signs of root rot may be subtle; plants don't look vigorous enough. The next symptoms are much more dramatic. Plants wilt easily, leaves yellow or discolor, and plants grow quite slowly. If seedlings or young plants are attacked, they usually die within a few days or weeks of being infected. Older plants, including trees and shrubs, take much longer to succumb to the disease. If you suspect a root rot, dig into the soil to examine roots. Infected feeder roots will be rotted, or brown and slimy.

Most of the organisms responsible for root rot live as easily on dead as on live material. They overwinter in old organic matter, such as uncomposted crop and weed residue in the soil. Some produce thick-walled, "resting" spores that can survive without a host over the winter or, if necessary, for years. Other fungi produce spores with flagella that enable them to move relatively long distances through the soil water. These diseases are most severe in cool, wet weather, either in spring or fall.

Plants Affected

Most plants are prey to one or another of the root rot organisms.

Organic Control

Since root rot fungi are in all soils, prevention is the best course. When starting seedlings, use a soil-less mix or one containing compost. Do not overwater. Keep air circulation high. Outside, plant in well-drained soil and space plants for good air circulation. Resist the temptation to plant or transplant before the soil warms sufficiently in spring.

RUST

Many fungi, particularly *Puccinia* spp. and *Uromyces* spp.

Rust fungi are among the easiest diseases to notice because of their easily seen, brightly colored spores in hues of yellow, orange, red, and reddish brown. The first symptoms of rust diseases you will notice are general lack of vigor and slow growth. Before long, the fungus produces pustules (yellow, orange, or red bumps), often on leaf undersides, that are immediately recognizable. Plants that are moderately infected are usually stunted; while seriously infected plants die. On asparagus, look for reddish brown streaks or spots on stems and leaves that turn black in fall. The undersides of rose leaves are commonly covered with bright orange spots. In some species, the spots swell into galls.

Fungi that cause rust diseases have quite complicated life cycles. Some produce as many as five different spore forms, while others require two different hosts to complete a life cycle. For example, pines and asters are the alternate hosts for *Coleosporium asterum*, while corn and *Oxalis* species, such as the weed woodsorrel, can be alternate hosts for *Puccinia sorghi*. Spring weather stimulates reproduction and spores blow to new hosts. Rainfall may bring these spores down hundreds of miles from their original site.

Rust on chrysanthemum leaf

Common scab on potatoes

Plants Affected

Most plants, including trees and ornamentals, are susceptible.

Organic Controls

While you can't stop rust fungi from falling out of the sky, you can make plants more resistant. Avoid amendments high in nitrogen, and prune, space, and water carefully to increase air circulation and keep leaves dry. Pick off and destroy infected leaves. Sulfur spray, used when spots first appear, kills new spores.

Scab

Cladosporium cucumerinum, Streptomyces scabies

Scab diseases are widespread in garden soils, causing damage that ranges from cosmetic to devastating. The scab that causes problems for root crops is usually impossible to detect by looking at the leaves of infected plants. Instead, it becomes apparent when you dig the crop and see the characteristic warty "scabs" on the skin surface. These lesions do not usually penetrate far into the root, nor do they affect the flavor. However, they do create a wide entryway for many secondary rotting

organisms. Infected roots and tubers do not store well. Cucumber and melon leaves develop angular spots. Infections on the fruit range from superficial skin scabs on semimature cucumbers to rotting tissues at the stem end of muskmelons and cantaloupes.

Scab organisms overwinter on infected plant debris. *S. scabies* can also live for a number of years in the soil without a host. In spring, both organisms develop spores that spread to new plants. *S. scabies* spores move through the soil, while spores of *C. cucumerinum* are airborne. These organisms reproduce rapidly enough to cause successive infections through the summer season.

Plants Affected

C. cucumerinum infects only cucurbit crops, while *S. scabies* infects beets, cabbages, carrots, eggplants, spinach, onions, parsnips, potatoes, and turnips.

Organic Controls

Choose resistant cultivars such as 'Supersett' cucumbers and 'Butte' potatoes whenever possible, and practice crop rotations of 3–5 years. In the case of *S. scabies*, do not lime soil before planting or apply uncomposted animal manure. Maintain a pH of 5.5 for potatoes and apply an inch of compost to the soil before planting.

Septoria Leaf Spot

Septoria spp.

Septoria fungi cause diseases that range from cosmetically damaging to life threatening, depending on the host.

Plants growing from seeds infected with *Septoria* spp. usually die, sometimes so quickly that you don't know they've germinated. The first symptoms on plants infected with this fungus are leaf spots, usually appearing on the lower leaves first and then moving up the plant. Spots begin as tiny, yellow dots but quickly enlarge and become light brown or gray. Eventually, the spots turn dark brown or reddish brown. They are often surrounded by a yellow halo. Black spores become visible in the center of the spots.

This fungus overwinters on infected seeds and crop debris. In spring it produces spores that spread to new plants, both through splashing water and the air. Spores produced on plants later in the season spread to nearby crops, again by both air and water.

Plants Affected

Septoria leaf spot is the most serious disease of celery. It also causes serious damage to tomato-family crops, cucurbits, and many ornamentals.

Organic Controls

Protect crops by removing crop debris promptly, and practice 3- to 4-year rotations. Treat all self-saved tomato seeds with a hot-water bath of 25 minutes at 122°F to control seedborne fungi. Avoid working in the garden when leaves are wet. Foliar sprays of compost tea, applied before infection, can prevent or reduce infections. (See "Brew a Fungus-Fighting Tea" on page 362) When plants are seriously infected, pull them and compost in a hot pile. As a last resort you can spray plants with copper.

SMUT

Urocystis cepulae, Ustilago maydis

The two smut diseases create disfiguring growths that ruin crop quality. Corn ears are most commonly affected by smut, but other parts may also be affected. White galls form that may not be noticeable until they expand

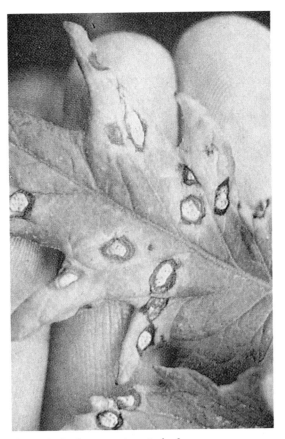

Septoria leaf spot on tomato leaf

out of the husk. The membrane surrounding the gall splits and releases masses of black spores. Onion smut infects only young onion plants. Look for blisters under the skin on first leaves and near the surface of the bulb and roots. A mass of black spores is released when the membrane covering the blister splits open.

Both types of smut fungi overwinter on infected plant debris. Corn smut also overwinters on manure. Both can form resting spores that remain viable without a host for many years. Spring weather stimulates spore formation. Corn smut is wind-borne; onion smut is transmitted by splashing water or by dirty tools. Smut infections remain fairly localized

Smut on corn

in the host, forming new spores that are released to cause successive infections during the season.

Plants Affected

Corn, grasses, and grains are susceptible to *U. maydis*, while *U. cepulae* infects onions.

Organic Controls

Choose resistant corn cultivars such as 'Ambrosia SE', 'Gemini SE', or 'Bodacious EW'. If corn smut has been a problem in your garden, practice 3- to 4-year rotations and monitor plants frequently. If you see a gall, pick it off immediately; do not let the spores mature. Some chefs serve immature corn

smut as a high-priced delicacy, so you might try cultivating this taste if you have problems year after year. Onion smut does not infect plants once the first leaf is mature. To avoid problems, transplant onion seedlings rather than direct-seeding them.

SOOTY MOLD
Several species of fungi

Sooty mold is common on plants in greenhouses, but it also occurs outside. Leaves are covered with a dark gray to black mold. In some cases, the mold forms a papery layer that can be peeled off the leaf, but more often it occurs in discrete patches. Sooty mold does not parasitize plants. It grows in the honeydew deposited on leaves by heavy infestations of insects such as aphids, mealybugs, scales, and whiteflies. However, it does damage plants by blocking their access to light and sometimes clogging stomates.

Sooty mold organisms are in almost all environments. Spores survive in a dormant state until environmental conditions are correct. These spores are airborne and germinate and grow on the sugars in the honeydew excreted by many insects. High humidity and warm temperatures favor sooty mold development.

Plants Affected

Plants with large infestations of aphids or other insects that excrete honeydew are susceptible.

Organic Controls

Sooty mold is sometimes the first sign you have of an existing insect problem. When you see the mold, gently wipe plant leaves with a cloth moistened with warm water. Most of the mold will come off the leaf, but spores will be released into the air. Next, control the aphids (see "Aphids" on page 244) and whiteflies (see "Whiteflies" on page 297). When sooty mold appears on plants in greenhouses, it's also more than likely that humidity levels are too high for optimal plant performance. Controlling the environment is sometimes as important to eliminating this disease as controlling insects is. Once sooty mold has appeared in a planting, both insect presence and environmental conditions must be carefully monitored.

SUMMER DISEASES

Many fungi, including *Gloeodes pomigena* **and** *Microthyriella rubi*

Summer diseases cause a great deal of damage in almost all apple-growing areas, particularly where humidity levels are high.

Common summer diseases include sooty blotch, fly speck, black rot, bitter rot, and white rot. Sooty blotch creates dark, sooty-looking patches on developing fruit, and fly speck makes tiny, dark spots on skins. Frequently these diseases are superficial, although they may allow the entry of other, more serious, rotting organisms. Black rot creates concentric rings of black and brown tissue, bitter rot makes sunken tan spots, and white rot creates watery lesions. Each of these latter diseases can create rots that extend into the flesh.

All of the organisms that cause the problems we call summer diseases overwinter in mummified fruit and cankers on twigs and branches. In warm, humid weather, they produce spores. Wind, rain, and insects can carry these spores to uninfected tissues.

Plants Affected

Apples, pears, and quinces are susceptible to summer diseases.

Sooty mold on leaf

Fly speck, a common summer disease, on apple

Organic Controls

Prevention is the best control of summer diseases. Prune to allow air and light into the center of the tree canopy, removing small branches from the central leader if necessary. Practice excellent fall sanitation, collecting and destroying mummified fruit and fallen twigs and leaves. When pruning, check for cankers on twigs and branches, and remove and destroy this wood. Leave pruning cuts open to the air. Copper can be used once during the season to help control sooty blotch and fly speck, while sulfur, again sprayed only once, controls the other organisms.

VERTICILLIUM WILT
Verticillium spp.

Verticillium wilt is one of the most common diseases of both wild and cultivated plants.

Symptoms vary from host plant to host plant. On fruit trees, for example, wilting leaves on branch tips may be the first symptom of verticillium wilt. On tomatoes, lower leaves, sometimes on only one side of the plant, begin to wilt even when the soil is moist. Leaves turn yellow, then brown, and finally drop off. On chrysanthemums, wilting leaves develop a pinkish color. Stem interiors always show a darkened vascular system. Although symptoms look very much like those of fusarium wilt, this disease is slower acting, so plants do not collapse as quickly. However, infected plants will eventually die.

Verticillium fungi overwinter in crop debris. Resting spores of this fungus are quite long-lived; they can survive on old organic matter in soil for as long as 15 years. In spring, when the weather warms and moisture is present, spores germinate on susceptible tissue. The fungal threads enter plants through wounds and natural openings in the root and travel to the vessels that carry water and nutrients.

Plants Affected

Verticillium wilt attacks many woody and herbaceous plants, especially tomato-family crops, cucurbits, asters, chrysanthemums, small fruits, and ornamental shrubs.

Organic Controls

Choose resistant cultivars such as 'Giant Szegeddii' and 'Northstar' for peppers, and 'Mountain Spring' and 'Celebrity' for tomatoes. Plant in well-drained soil that warms quickly. Remove all crop debris and compost it in piles that reach 150°–160°F for several days. Use 4-year rotations. Cloches, row covers, and other season-extension materials that raise the air temperature around the plants often inhibit spore germination because these fungi prefer temperatures of 70°–75°F.

Verticillium-infected spinach plant on the left and healthy plant on the right

YELLOWS

Mycoplasma-like organism

Although many diseases can be called yellows, the term usually applies to the disease known as aster yellows.

Yellows is characterized by leaves that turn yellow without spotting first. Growth is usually dwarfed, and shoots and internodes (spaces between leaves) may be abnormally short. Flowers are misshapen, sometimes only on one side. Carrot roots are pale and woody and have large numbers of bushy, white side roots. Lettuce is pale and stunted and doesn't form a head. Leaf rolling and stem distortions are common on infected tomatoes and potatoes. Flowering plants are sometimes too erect and internodes are usually short.

The organism that causes aster yellows overwinters in infected plant tissue. When leafhoppers feed on these plants, they suck up the disease organism in the cell sap. Aster yellows disease must live inside the leafhopper for 10–14 days before it can infect a new plant. It can only survive in insects about 100 days before dying, but the disease is prevalent enough that leafhoppers continually pick it up.

Plants Affected

Carrots, celery, cucurbits, lettuce, potatoes, onions, strawberries, tomatoes, some trees such as elms, and many ornamentals are susceptible.

Organic Controls

Floating row covers, used as long as possible into the season, provide a good barrier against leafhoppers. However, once the covers are removed, infections can occur. Remove and destroy infected plants, including trees, to avoid spread. Eliminate weeds such as asters, chicory, dandelions, and thistles.

Ash yellows, one of the many forms of the disease

CONTROLLING DISEASES

Prevention is the best "cure" for plant disease problems. Good garden cleanup, excellent soil nutrition and drainage, plenty of soil organic matter, high microbial populations, wise watering, three- to four-year crop rotations and careful observation go a long way toward preventing most disease problems.

Controls, whether sulfur or copper powders or sprays, refined oils, or baking powder, are the gardener's last resort, to be used only when a disease problem is truly out of hand. Valuable as they are, controls are never as effective when used alone as they are when used as an emergency backup while you're correcting the conditions in the garden that made your plants susceptible to the disease in the first place.

DISORDERS: WHEN IS A DISEASE NOT A DISEASE?

HOW TO RECOGNIZE DISORDERS

In this section you'll find disorders, with their symptoms, prevention, and controls. But what is a disorder?

Disorders look like diseases—but they're not. While diseases are caused by microorganisms, disorders are caused by a problem in the environment. Symptoms of damage caused by frost, cold winter winds, lightning, air or water pollution, and certain nutrient imbalances are all disorders rather then diseases.

The distinction between disorders and diseases can blur when an environmental problem sets the stage for disease attack. For example, in poorly drained soils, roots may not get as much oxygen as they need. Leaves will yellow as a consequence of this disorder. But it isn't long before fungi that thrive in wet soils will attack the roots, rotting them. At this point, what was once a disorder will have become a disease.

Generally, you can tell the difference between a disorder and a disease by the pattern of occurence. For example, if all the plants in a low spot in the garden have yellow leaves, it's safe to assume that soggy soil is the culprit. Similarly, if onions on only one side of a bed are yellowing several days after you cultivated down the pathway, it's likely that roots along that edge were damaged by your hoe or tiller. In contrast, if only two squash plants in a bed show wilting leaves, the problem is likely to be a disease. When trying to decide whether plants have a disease or a disorder, remember that symptoms of disorders are usually fairly uniform and that all of the plants in the same area will be affected. Disease attacks are more spotty. When a disease does infect most of a planting, as can happen with certain fungal diseases such as late blight on tomatoes, it's likely to start in one area and spread in the direction that the prevailing winds blow or water runs.

Finally, just as good gardening habits tend to reduce the incidence of plant diseases, they also reduce the number and severity of plant disorders in your garden. Vigorous, healthy plants, growing in appropriate light, moisture, and fertility conditions, are much less likely to suffer from disorders than are poorly sited plants. Again, prevention is the best possible cure.

Sunscald on tomato

BLOSSOM END ROT
Calcium deficiency

Blossom end rot can occur when sunny days follow a cloudy, wet period. It is a symptom of calcium deficiency in the plant. Calcium moves very slowly in plants, so deficiencies can occur even when soil tests indicate that calcium is adequate. Nutrient balance is imperative. High nitrogen or magnesium levels can interfere with absorption of calcium. Extraordinarily rapid growth can also contribute because the slow-moving calcium can't move into tissues quickly enough. Drought can also contribute to the problem. The blossom end of the fruit develops a dark-colored, watery spot. This area enlarges and the skin sometimes becomes brown and leathery. Often, it dries and wrinkles over the dark, sunken area below it. Secondary rot organisms find an easy entryway through the damaged tissue.

Plants Affected
Blossom end rot is a particular problem for tomatoes and peppers.

Organic Controls
Many cultural techniques prevent blossom end rot from occuring. In areas where summer rain is apt to be variable, water during dry periods to prevent moisture fluctuations. Deep mulches with materials such as straw or rotted hay are useful. Fertilize with finished compost, and do not add extra nitrogen unless absolutely necessary. Foliar sprays with seaweed extract supply some calcium directly to the leaves. Have your soil tested every few years and correct any imbalances. If the problem occurs, work to correct soil moisture fluctuations with mulching or irrigating. If conditions are corrected, subsequent fruit will not suffer from this disorder.

LEAF SCORCH
Drought and heat

Leaf scorch is a drought reaction that usually occurs in response to urban environments or when containerized plants are poorly positioned or inadequately watered. Reflected light and heat from surrounding buildings and pavement can stimulate so much transpiration from a plant that roots, even those in moist soil, cannot supply adequate water.

Leaf scorch can look like a disease, but is easily cured once environmental conditions are improved. The symptoms of leaf scorch

Blossom end rot on tomato

Leaf scorch due to an inadequate water supply

usually shows on leaf margins first. Initially, they turn yellow and wilt in the afternoon. Leaves on some plant species roll inward. Browning of leaves then follows, and first the leaf, then the branch, may die.

Growth is stunted and, if the condition goes unremedied, the entire tree or plant can die.

The potato leaf on the left is suffering from PAN damage

Plants Affected
Leaf scorch is often a problem for moisture-loving plants in containers and for trees growing in pavement cutouts or tree strips on city streets.

Organic Controls
Wise plant selection does much to prevent problems. For example, heat-loving portulacas are a better selection than lobelias in unavoidably hot environments. In urban areas surrounded by buildings and pavement, choose drought-tolerant tree species such as red oak, white spruce, sugar maple, and red maple. For established trees that show symptoms of leaf scorch, increase watering during summer months. Water deeply at weekly intervals to encourage deep rooting. Mulch to shade the soil and increase water retention. If you are growing moisture-loving plants in hanging baskets or other containers, place them where they will receive some shade at midday. Install a small drip irrigation system if you can't be home to keep up with their watering demands.

PAN (PEROXYACYL NITRATE) DAMAGE
Air pollution
PAN (peroxyacyl nitrate) is a pollutant that forms when sunlight hits some of the compounds released in car exhaust. In areas where smog alerts and air inversions are common, PAN levels are apt to be high. PAN damage is becoming increasingly common in almost all industrialized countries.

PAN damage is usually most severe on the youngest and most rapidly growing leaves of a plant. On leaf undersides, white to bronze spots appear that soon turn to a silvery glaze. It's easy to mistake this damage for that caused by thrips, mites, or sunscald. Plants lose vigor and grow more slowly than normal, and yields are reduced.

Plants Affected
Many plants are vulnerable, particularly beans, lettuce, peppers, spinach, swiss chard, tomatoes, as well as dahlias and petunias.

Organic Controls
In areas where PAN injury is common, choose plants that are more tolerant of pollution. Check with neighbors and gardening clubs to learn which species are tolerant in your area. A short list of fairly tolerant plants includes cabbage, cucumber, squash, and ornamentals such as snapdragons, English ivy, and sugar maple. There is no control for this problem.

Salt Injury
High salt levels in soil or windblown salt spray

In organically managed soils in rainy climates, the main source of salt is usually the de-icing material used on roads and sidewalks in the winter. However, in the West, some soils and water are naturally salty. Other causes of high salt content in soils include excessive use of synthetically produced fertilizers or wood ashes, as well as exposure to windblown salt spray in coastal regions. In containers, excessive fertilization and insufficient watering can cause salt to accumulate.

Salt injury is sometimes difficult to diagnose because the first symptoms can look similar to those caused by one of the many wilt diseases. Plant injury from excessive salts occurs because roots are damaged or cannot take in adequate nutrient supplies. Symptoms include wilting when soil is moist, yellowing and dying leaves, and stunting. In coastal areas or near heavily salted roads, vulnerable plants usually

Apple tree with salt injury

show scorching around the leaf margins first. Leaf wilting, yellowing, and dying follow. Severely affected plants usually die within a year or two. In arid regions, undisturbed growing areas show a white crust on the soil surface when salts are high. A white crust at soil level on a pot is a danger signal.

Plants Affected
Almost all plants are susceptible to salt injury.

Organic Controls
To prevent salt damage, choose salt-tolerant species and cultivars in arid and coastal regions as well as runoff areas. Some examples are Austrian pine, birches, quaking aspen, red cedar, red oak, white spruce, and yews. Plant salt-tolerant evergreens as a protecting hedge where possible and fertilize wisely.

Dianthus and verbena with sulfur dioxide injury

Eliminate hardpans by growing a deep-rooted cover crop or double-digging beds. Where salts build up in response to poor drainage, add compost and gypsum to improve the structure of the soil.

Repot container plants and flush the soil with five to six times its volume of clear water once a month.

SULFUR DIOXIDE INJURY
Air pollution

Sulfur dioxide injury is prevalent around industrial facilities. It is also found in areas where air quality is poor as a consequence of air inversions or particular wind patterns, such as those that dump polluted air from industries around the Great Lakes region into northern Vermont and Québec.

Mild injury, caused by sulfur dioxide concentrations as small as 0.3 parts per million, causes many leaves to yellow slightly. At higher concentrations, leaf tissue between the veins turns pale yellow or becomes bleached-looking. Leaf tissue dries and becomes papery. Grasses show light-colored tan or white streaks all down the blade. Needles of susceptible conifers or those in heavily polluted areas become reddish brown, starting at the tips but moving down as injury continues.

Plants Affected
Many plants, including apples, beans, blackberries, cabbages, peas, spinach, tulips, and violets, are prone to sulfur dioxide injury.

Organic Controls
There is no way to control sulfur dioxide concentrations in the air other than to support regulations requiring the reduction of stack emissions and other controls to protect air quality. To prevent damage to your plants, choose tolerant species. Among vegetables, corn, cucumbers, onions, and potatoes are most resistant to damage. Tolerant trees include arborvitae, gingko, juniper, maple, pine, privet, and sycamore.

SUNSCALD
Sudden exposure to sunlight

Sunscald is prevalent in areas with high light levels and temperatures. Sunscald in tree bark is caused by bright light and warm temperatures during the winter months, particularly when a reflective layer of snow is present. Sudden exposure to bright light can injure or kill seedlings. Fruits develop sunscald if sheltering leaves drop or are pruned off the plant.

Splits or cracks may appear in tree bark when warm conditions have caused transpiration to resume, but the soil is still frozen, preventing roots from taking up water. Injured seedlings can lose leaves if the damage is minor. However, in severe cases, the stem withers and dies. Injuries on fruit begin by looking like water-soaked blisters on the skin. These areas age to become dried, brown, and sunken, often surrounded by a grayish white margin. Secondary rotting organisms sometimes invade so quickly that it's hard to determine the first cause of the problem.

Plants Affected
Tree bark, seedlings, and fruits of apples, grapes, peppers, and tomatoes are the most susceptible plants.

Organic Controls
Prevent injury to tree trunks by painting them with a white latex paint or wrapping them with a vented, light-reflective covering. Seedlings should be gradually hardened off over a period of at least a week before being transplanted or exposed to a full day's sunlight. Choose disease-resistant fruit cultivars to avoid summer leaf loss. Also avoid excessive summer pruning. On staked or trellised single-leader tomato plants, be certain to leave enough foliage to cover developing fruit clusters. Tape or clip shade-cloth over developing grape clusters.

WATERLOGGED SOIL
Excess water and/or poor drainage
Heavy rains, poor drainage capabilities, over-watering, and unexpected flooding are all responsible for creating saturated soils.

Saturated soil is responsible for the death of many plants. When soil is saturated, all of the pore spaces are filled with water. The roots do not have access to the oxygen they need to stay alive. If the condition subsides quickly, most plants have a chance of recovery. However, if it persists, roots die and become prey to rot-producing fungi and bacteria. Soils that are consistently soggy, but not saturated, also kill roots of plants such as cucurbits and peas, because these require higher than average soil oxygen levels.

Sunscald on tomato

Plants Affected
Most plants are damaged by prolonged contact with waterlogged soil.

Organic Controls
To protect against waterlogging, do not over-water plants. Water the soil deeply, but only often enough to keep lower soil layers consistently moist. Use a well-aerated soil mix for potted plants: perlite, compost, and sand all

Yellowing juniper in waterlogged soil

increase drainage in container soil mixes. Outside, improve drainage by adding compost and materials such as gypsum and greensand to the growing beds. Build raised beds in areas that tend to flood or dry slowly in spring. If your soil has a hardpan that prevents water from draining well, plant a deep-rooted cover crop, such as alfalfa, and leave it in place for 18 months. For large areas, it's usually cost-effective to hire someone to chisel-plow the area.

WINTER INJURY
Excessive cold; alternate freezing and thawing

Either sudden or abnormally cold winter temperatures can cause plant tissues to die. Alternating freezing and thawing can promote roots to "heave" out of the soil, leaving them vulnerable to freezing temperatures and drying winds.

Winter injury looks different, depending on the plant. Symptoms include large brown patches on broad-leaved evergreens such as rhododendrons, and tip or shoot die-back on woody perennials, including those with needles. You may also notice plants with brown, dry branches on only one side.

Plants Affected

Most plants, particularly those of marginal hardiness for the growing region and those with shallow root systems, are susceptible to winter injury. Strawberries, roses, and rhododendrons are all extremely susceptible to winter heaving.

Organic Controls

To prevent winter injury from occurring in your garden, choose cultivars and species that are reliable in your hardiness zone. Water perennials thoroughly through late summer

Winter injury on yew

and through early fall. Spray evergreens with an antitranspirant to reduce winter water loss from the leaves. Protect tree trunks with a coating of white latex paint. After the top surface of the soil has frozen, mulch perennials with 6 inches of straw or another organic mulch to prevent heaving.

In windy areas, create a windbreak with stakes and burlap, or wrap susceptible bushes in burlap for the winter. In spring, when soils begin to thaw, check perennial roots for heaving, and rebury those that require it. Carefully prune out all injured branches.

The Healthy Garden

A guide to planting and maintaining a healthy garden using organic techniques.

Having a healthy garden is really a lot easier than knowing what to spray to get rid of a fungus or how to dust to deter a caterpillar. It's simply creating the best possible conditions in your garden so your plants will grow vigorously and be naturally less susceptible to problems. It starts with building healthy soil so the plants' roots can find a steady supply of moisture and nutrients for good growth. The next step is buying healthy plants so you don't bring pest and disease problems into your garden.

Once your plants are in the ground, giving them the best care, including regular watering and fertilizing, will help them stay healthy. For extra protection, you may want to try companion planting—combining certain plants to repel insect pests or attract beneficial insects. Traps and barriers are also helpful for keeping pests away from your plants.

But despite your best efforts, some pests and diseases may show up from time to time. When this happens, you can buy and release extra beneficial insects, or use beneficial microorganisms—like *Bacillus thuringiensis* (BT)—that will control the problem without harm to you or your plants. If these techniques fail, then you may choose from a range of effective organic sprays or dusts. In most cases, though, you'll find that your well-tended, vigorous plants will naturally be less prone to common problems, so you can spend more time enjoying your garden and less time dealing with pests and diseases!

In this section, you'll find out how to build healthy soil, buy healthy plants, and prevent pest and disease problems. You'll also find the latest organic pest and disease controls—what they are, how they work, and how to use them effectively.

BUILDING HEALTHY SOIL

To grow healthy plants, start by maintaining healthy soil. Good soil holds water, air, and nutrients in amounts and forms that plants can use. It also supports a healthy population of beneficial organisms both large and small—from earthworms and ground beetles to microscopic bacteria and fungi. These organisms help make nutrients available to your plants, control plant pests and diseases, and improve the structure of the soil. Plants growing in good soil can extend their roots freely to find all the minerals they need to grow. Good soil also provides plants with a steady supply of moisture and contains air spaces that hold the oxygen plant roots need.

Soil consists primarily of rock and mineral particles of varying sizes. Clay particles are the smallest; sand particles are the largest. Most soils are a mixture of clay, sand, and silt (medium-size particles). The percentage of clay, sand, and silt in your soil will determine its texture and affect plants' ability to grow in it. Clay soils, those made up of mostly small rock particles, tend to hold more water than air. Plants that are not adapted to wet conditions can literally drown in waterlogged clay soil. And when clay soils dry out, their fine particles bind tightly together, blocking the growth of all but the most tenacious plants.

Sandy soils, on the other hand, have such large spaces between their particles that water drains through them very quickly. Plants that are not drought-tolerant need frequent watering to survive in sandy sites.

When soil consists of about 20 percent clay, 40 percent sand, and 40 percent silt, it is called loam. Loam soils combine the water-holding qualities of silt and clay with the drainage advantages of sand to provide excellent growing conditions for a wide range of garden plants.

Organic Matter

In addition to rock and mineral particles, all soil contains organic matter—decaying bits of plants, animals, and soil-dwelling organisms. As it decays, organic matter releases nutrients into the soil. Its sponge-like structure also improves the soil's moisture- and air-holding ability. Even after it has decayed to a no-longer-recognizable, dark-colored, and sweet-smelling substance called humus, organic matter continues to improve the soil in your garden.

Humus continues to release nutrients, and it also sticks soil particles together, creating-moisture-holding conglomerates with air-holding spaces between them.

Because of these benefits, one of the best things to do for your soil is to add organic matter to it. Many garden plants, including vegetables, annual flowers, and shade-loving shrubs like rhododendrons, thrive in soil that is high in organic matter, and many others appreciate moderate amounts.

You can add organic matter such as bark, composted leaves, or barnyard manure straight from the bag you buy at the nursery, or you can recycle organic wastes into compost and dig this free amendment into your soil. You can also spread organic amendments or finishedcompost on top of the soil as a mulch around your plants.

When soil contains sufficient organic matter, moisture, and air, it supports not only the life of your garden plants but also many types of helpful soil-dwelling creatures, from beneficial bacteria to earthworms.

In healthy soil, helpful soil creatures tend to be more plentiful than harmful ones. They release nutrients plants can use from the minerals and organic matter in the soil, aerate the soil, fight soil pests, and even live symbiotically with plant roots.

Recycle organic wastes into finished compost like this to enrich your soil.

Organic Fertilizers

In addition to enriching the soil with organic matter, you can also add organic fertilizers. Amendments typically add bulk to soil, while fertilizers tend to be concentrated, and are added either as very small quantities of powder, granules, or pellets, or in a liquid solution. Learn which of your plants need fertile soil, and fertilize them at planting or as they grow. Commonly used organic fertilizers include fish emulsion, blood meal, kelp meal, and rock phosphate. You can also use compost or manure "tea," made by steeping a cheesecloth or burlap bag of compost or manure in water, then straining out the solids and watering plants with the resulting liquid.

Organic fertilizers are gentle on the soil and good for your plants. Use blood meal, cottonseed meal, fish meal, guano, hoof and horn meal, or chicken manure if your plants need nitrogen. Bonemeal, fish meal, guano, colloidal phosphate, rock phosphate, and wood ashes are good sources of phosphorus. If your plants need more potassium, choose granite dust, greensand, langbeinite, seaweed, or wood ashes. Bonemeal, dolomite, gypsum, and wood ashes provide calcium; gypsum, langbeinite, and elemental sulfur are good sulfur sources. For trace minerals, choose materials like granite dust, greensand, guano, colloidal or rock phosphate, seaweed, or wood ashes. Ensure that you don't apply more than the recommended amount of any of these additives; more is definitely not better where fertilizers are concerned.

Soil Testing

A soil analysis can help you determine the availability of plant nutrients in your soil. You can evaluate your soil yourself using a purchased test kit, or send a sample to a soil-testing lab for a professional analysis. Your local Cooperative Extension office can tell you how to collect a soil sample and may also offer soil-testing services. Along with your sample, include a list of the kinds of plants you plan to grow (vegetables, fruit trees, perennials, etc.). Ask the testing facility to recommend organic fertilizers and amendments if test results indicate that your soil needs improving.

Your soil test results will also tell you your soil's pH—its acidity or alkalinity—expressed

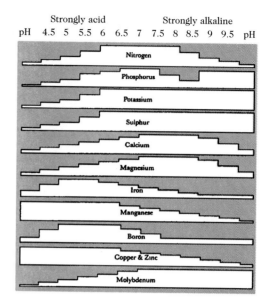

Nutrient availability is lowest at the pH corresponding to the narrowest parts of the band for each element and highest at the widest.

as a number between 1.0 and 14.0. Most soils have a pH of 4.5 (acidic) to 8.0 (alkaline), with 7.0 being neutral. It's helpful to know your soil's pH, since it helps determine whether or not your plants can use nutrients already in the soil. Most plant nutrients are readily available when the soil pH is between 6.0 and 7.5.

MIX YOUR OWN FERTILIZER

If you want to mix your own general-purpose organic fertilizer, try combining individual amendments in the amounts shown here. Just pick one ingredient from each column. Because these amendments may vary in the amount of the nutrients they contain, this method won't give you a mixture with a precise N-P-K Ratio. The ratio will be between 1-2-1 and 4-6-3 approximately, with additional insoluble phosphorus and potash. The blend will provide a balanced supply of nutrients that will be steadily available to plants and encourage soil microorganisms to thrive.

Nitrogen (N)	Phosphorus (P)	Potassium (K)
2 parts blood meal	3 parts bonemeal	1 part kelp meal
3 parts fish meal	6 parts rock phosphate or colloidal phosphate	6 parts greensand

Below a pH of 6.0, major nutrients such as nitrogen, phosphorus, and potassium are less available to your plants. A pH above 7.5 limits plants' ability to take up iron, manganese, and phosphorus. You can gradually change the pH of your soil by amending it with materials such as lime (to raise pH) or sulfur (to lower pH). Adding large quantities of compost to your soil tends to neutralize soil pH, making plant nutrients more readily available and reducing the need to adjust the pH with lime or sulfur or to add fertilizers.

Special Soil Concerns

If your soil drains poorly (see "A Simple Drainage Test"), you'll need to consider your plant selections and planting options carefully. Gardening in wet soil may be as simple as choosing moisture-tolerant plants or building raised beds to put plant roots above the water, or as complex as installing a permanent drainage system.

Compacted or heavily cultivated soil may have an impermeable layer, called a hardpan, lurking beneath its surface. Hardpan reduces water drainage and limits plants' ability to establish deep roots. If a hardpan layer is close to the soil surface, you may be able to break it up by working the soil deeply. A deeper hardpan may need to be punctured with an auger, or you may need to install a drainage system above it.

If your soil is simply compacted, loosen it as deeply as possible and add compost and other bulky organic materials. Soon, earthworms will improve the soil. Rocky soil makes it harder to dig planting holes, but it should be fine for permanent plantings of trees, shrubs, and perennials. On sites where you plan to cultivate more often—vegetable gardens and annual flower beds—you may need to remove the rocks to make the soil workable.

A SIMPLE DRAINAGE TEST

Dig a hole 18 inches deep in the area you want to test. If water fills the hole as you dig it, you have a high water table and need to drain the area. If the hole doesn't fill up, fill it with water yourself, let it drain, then fill it a second time. Measure how quickly the second filling takes to drain. If the water level drops less than ¼ inch per hour, you need to take corrective measures.

Deep digging can break up compacted soil layers, promoting better root growth.

BUYING HEALTHY PLANTS

When you buy new plants for your garden, the choices you make can make a big difference in the amount of pest and disease damage you'll have to deal with later on. Your goal is to choose plants that are healthy when you get them and that are unlikely to develop problems. You want to be sure a new plant is

Strong, vigorous plants (like the one on the left) not only look more attractive—they're also less prone to problems.

not already suffering from a pest, disease, or cultural problem. Certain plants and seeds must be inspected and "certified" free of common diseases or pests before they can be sold. Some examples are raspberries and strawberries, seed potatoes, and, in some areas, seedlings of tomatoes and cabbage-family vegetables. When certified plants are available, choose them over uncertified plants. (Incidentally, don't plant potatoes sold as food—they are uncertified, so they could spread potato diseases in your garden.)

Plants that are in good health when you buy them are more likely to remain healthy. Look each plant over before you bring it home. It should have no visible symptoms of pests or diseases and should look as good as other plants of the same type in terms of size, color, and overall health. Annuals and perennials that are actively growing should have no dead leaves or leaf scars indicating lost leaves. Bedding plants should be under 6 inches tall, with short spaces between leaves on the stem.

CHOOSE RESISTANT CULTIVARS

As you select plants for your garden, keep in mind that some species and cultivars are naturally less problem-prone than others. For example, some tomato cultivars resist many of the most common tomato diseases.

If you can't find a resistant cultivar, you may choose a different plant that has the good characteristics you want without the problems. Japanese zelkova (*Zelkova serrata*), for instance, is a handsome landscape tree that provides the vase-shaped profile of an elm without the susceptibility to Dutch elm disease and elm leaf beetles. Another example is the kousa dogwood (*Cornus kousa*), a small flowering tree that is as beautiful as the frequently diseased flowering dogwood (*Cornus florida*).

In some cases, the kind of resistance you need differs, depending on where you live. For example, beans growing in the dry West rarely get leaf diseases, so western gardeners don't need to look for disease-resistant bean cultivars. Eastern gardeners don't have to contend with curly-top virus, so they don't need tomato cultivars that resist this problem. Learning about which problems are common in your area will help you choose the plants that are best for your needs.

To get the best-quality plants, do your plant shopping in garden centers and nurseries where the plants look well cared for and where there is enough trained staff to answer your questions and make recommendations. Trained staff can help you with all kinds of questions, from choosing the best specimen of a certain type of plant or suggesting care-free substitutes for problem plants to suggesting the best way to care for the plants that you choose.

Plants should be symmetrical and growing straight in the container. Plants that are not currently in bloom are less likely to suffer a setback from transplanting than those that are covered with flowers, though some kinds of plants bloom over a long period and seem to transplant well enough anyway.

Don't forget to lift up the pot to make sure that the roots are not growing out of the bottom of the container. If possible, remove the plant from the pot and check to see that some roots are visible on the surface of the root ball, but that the rootball surface is not matted with roots. Roots should be a healthy color, which, for most plants, is white or light-colored. Reject plants with densely matted roots, dark or discolored roots, or thick roots that circle the rootball.

PREVENTING PESTS AND DISEASES

Healthy plants are less likely to be attacked by pests. To keep each plant healthy, put it in the right spot, give it the best care you can, and inspect it regularly for signs of developing problems. You can also use techniques like companion planting to confuse or repel pests, or encouraging beneficial insects to control the pests for you. Traps and barriers can also help you keep pests off your plants.

Choose the Right Planting Site

Start by learning what you can about your local climate, then study your garden to learn the special conditions offered by each site. From the plants that are adapted to your climate, select those that are best adapted to each area of your garden. For example, you might grow astilbes and hostas in a shady corner, and plant sunflowers and zinnias in a bright, sunny spot. As you select plants, learn any special needs they might have, such as acid soil or protection from winds, and consider how you will meet these needs. While you may be able to make some small-scale changes, it is wise to choose mainly plants that will thrive in the soil and climate that you already have. If you do choose to modify what you have—by creating a more acidic soil, for example, or installing a windbreak—group plants that need this change together in one area so they can all benefit.

Provide the Best Possible Care

Another key part of keeping plants problem-free is giving them good general care. Poor growing conditions can stress your plants and make them more problem-prone. Under- and overwatering, for instance, can both create problems for your plants. Overwatered plants are more likely to develop root diseases; underwatered plants will be stunted and more susceptible to sucking insects and mites. Most plants need to dry out a bit between waterings,

Careful planning cuts down on the time you have to spend on pest control during the season.

but some tolerate or even need a longer drying-out period than others.

Underfertilized plants may show nutrient deficiency symptoms and are likely to be stunted. Overfertilized plants become somewhat more susceptible to predations of sucking pests. To avoid overfertilizing, use restraint when applying concentrated fertilizers like guano and wood ashes, especially to soil in containers, and never apply more than the recommended amount. Before you fertilize, be sure your plants are actively growing and that the soil is moist.

Crowding of plants in the garden can also foster problems. Some diseases thrive in

Cleaning up garden debris regularly helps eliminate pests' hiding places.

humid conditions, which are more pronounced when plants are crowded together or when branches are too close together. Crowded plants must also compete with each other for light, water, and nutrients. Promote good air circulation and discourage diseases by spacing plants properly and thinning out crowded stems. And don't neglect control of weeds. Weeds not only crowd plants, but some are alternative hosts for pests that attack garden plants.

Gardeners sometimes rotate annual plants to different parts of the garden each year to avoid a buildup of pests and diseases. While this tactic is most often used by vegetable gardeners, it is just as effective in growing some flowers. You could, for example, plant snapdragons in a different part of the garden each year to avoid a buildup of rust disease in one part of the garden.

Keeping the garden clean is a critical part of preventing plant problems. To discourage the spread of disease, remove spent flowers and fallen foliage. Compost them or discard them if they are already diseased. Fall cleanup plays a role in preventing outbreaks of many kinds of insect pests that overwinter in specific plants. Even a few overwintering insects can lead to an outbreak the following year. Cleaning up dying asparagus stalks, for instance, removes overwintering asparagus beetles, while turning under corn stalks will destroy European corn borer larvae, which overwinter in the stem.

Keep an Eye Out for Problems

Examine your plants carefully and often. While many plants will be problem-free most of the time, you want to catch problems early, before the pest or disease causes serious damage.

When inspecting, look at the tops of plants, the growing points, and the flower buds.

Examine the stem or trunk at the soil level. Look at the tops and undersides of leaves, at the bark, and into bark crevices. Bring a hand lens into your garden so that you can see tiny pests. Sometimes you can detect small pests by tapping a branch over a piece of white paper, and then looking at the paper.

While this book describes the problems you are most likely to see, there may be times when you can't figure out what's going wrong. If you can't determine what is causing a problem, look for local resources where you can bring samples for identification, such as a botanical garden or your local Cooperative Extension Service office. Whenever possible, bring the actual pest, as well as the plant part showing damage. The more you can see, report, and show, the more likely it is that someone will be able to identify and then help you solve the problem.

Experiment with Companion Planting

For centuries, gardeners have treasured lists of plant companions and plant competitors— those plants that were said to "like" or "dislike" each other. Many combinations were said to protect plants from pests. Researchers have set out to study these plant combinations as well as to seek new possibilities. While the verdict is still out on many companions, so far a few have proven effective, while others have been shown to be frauds.

What is clear is that uncontrollable pest outbreaks are less likely in a mix of plants than in a large planting of any one kind of plant. Many insects and disease organisms seek out specific plants, and when they find a large planting of a favorite plant, they can multiply or spread quickly. A mix of plants growing together in the garden is likely to attract more kinds of pests, but no large outbreak of any one species of pest.

Mixing a variety of plants together makes it harder for pests to find their favorites.

Insects look for food primarily by smell, next by taste, and last by sight. So it is thought that mixed crops probably work mainly by confusing the insects as they seek their favorite foods. Some plants have been thought to repel particular pests by having distinctive odors they dislike. Take advantage of these repellent plants by planting them among your crops.

Plant southernwood with cabbage-family crops to repel imported cabbageworms.

Try catnip to repel squash bugs from zucchini.

Some of the combinations that have proven to have protective value are:

- Southernwood with cabbage-family crops to repel cabbage butterflies (imported cabbageworms)
- Catnip or tansy with zucchini to repel squash bugs
- Catnip or nasturtiums with bell peppers to repel green peach aphids
- Nasturtiums with many plants to repel whiteflies
- Potatoes with beans to repel Mexican bean beetles
- Peanuts with corn to reduce corn borer damage
- Radishes with cucumbers to reduce striped cucumber beetles

MARIGOLDS FOR PEST CONTROL?

Gardeners often mix a few marigolds with their crops, hoping to repel cabbageworms, soil nematodes, or "bugs" in general. But research has shown that, far from repelling cabbageworms, marigolds may actually attract the adult butterflies. And while marigolds can repel Mexican bean beetles and corn earworms from beans, they also seem to release chemicals into the soil that harm bean plants.

Marigolds do reduce nematodes in the soil, but only if you grow certain marigold cultivars (such as 'Nemagold' or 'Queen Sophia') as a cover crop all over a nematode-infested site for an entire season. This treatment will allow you to plant one season of a nematode-susceptible crop the following year.

Encourage Native Beneficial Insects

Even plants that don't repel pests can help your crops by providing food and shelter for naturally occurring beneficial insects. Many of these helpful creatures need plant pollen and nectar as part of their life cycle or can use them as food when pests are in short supply.

Besides providing plants for food and shelter, you'll also want to give beneficial insects a source of water. If your garden is not frequently moistened by rain or morning dew, sprinkle a part of your garden briefly every day, being sure that the plants you are sprinkling are not susceptible to fungal diseases in humid conditions. Or you can make a simple "bug bath." A large pottery saucer with an inch or two of water will suffice. Set some irregularly shaped rocks in the water to make little islands where insects can land and sip without drowning.

In general, the flowers that attract beneficial insects are the small ones, such as those that form on plants in the composite (daisy), mint, carrot, and mustard families. You can purchase seed mixes for some of these flowers or tuck individual transplants into your landscape. The beneficial insects you can attract with these flowers include parasitic wasps, predatory wasps, hover flies, lacewings, tachinid flies, and lady beetles.

Small-flowered plants such as Queen-Anne's-lace tend to attract beneficial insects.

Wasps

Parasitic wasps lay their eggs in other insects. These wasps are so tiny you will rarely see them, and they do not sting. They will help control aphids, corn earworms, cabbageworms, mealybugs, scale, and whiteflies. Plants that will attract them include baby-blue-eyes (*Nemophila menziesii*), caraway (*Carum carvi*), catnip (*Nepeta cataria*), coriander (*Coriandrum sativum*), coreopsis (*Coreopsis* spp.), Queen-Anne's-lace (*Daucus carota*), rose campion

Tiny parasitic wasps develop within pests, leaving empty "mummies" behind when they hatch.

(*Lychnis coronaria*), sunflower (*Helianthus annuus*), sweet alyssum (*Lobularia maritima*), tansy (*Tanacetum vulgare*), and yarrows (*Achillea* spp.).

Various larger wasps hunt and kill aphids and caterpillars, including cabbageworms and tobacco hornworms. While you may not want them to nest too close to your house or patio, try to tolerate wasps in out-of-the-way areas. Flowers that encourage predatory wasps include angelica (*Angelica archangelica*), coyote brush (*Baccharis pilularis*), fennel (*Foeniculum vulgare*), rue (*Ruta graveolens*), sweet alyssum, and white sweet clover (*Melilotus alba*).

Mealybug destroyers are the larvae of Australian lady beetles. They resemble the pest they attack.

Hover Flies

Hover, or syrphid, flies are ½–⅝ inch long flies that hover like tiny helicopters. Some have markings that resemble bees or wasps, but they do not sting. Their gray or greenish larvae eat aphids, beetles, caterpillars, leafhoppers, mealybugs, larval sawflies, and thrips. Hoverflies are attracted by asters, cornflower (*Centaurea cyanus*), black-eyed Susans (*Rudbeckia* spp.), perennial candytuft (*Iberis sempervirens*), chamomile (*Chamaemelum nobile*), coreopsis, coriander, coyote brush, rose campion, fennel, feverfew (*Chrysanthemum parthenium*), Joe-Pye weed (*Eupatorium purpureum*), marigolds, silver lace vine (*Polygonum aubertii*), and yarrow.

Tachinid Flies

Tachinid flies look like large, bristly, dark-colored houseflies, but they parasitize beetles, caterpillars, grasshoppers, sawflies, and true bugs. They are attracted to coriander, fennel, silver lace vine, and white sweet clover.

Lacewings

Lacewings are ½–¾ inch long, green or light brown insects with large, clear wings. Their larvae look like small, mottled brown alligators. Larvae and adults eat aphids, caterpillars, mealybugs, mites, scales, thrips, and whiteflies. Adult lacewings feed on nectar from angelica, coreopsis, cosmos (especially white-flowered kinds), fennel, oleander (*Nerium oleander*), sweet alyssum, and tansy.

Lady Beetles

Lady beetles are ¹⁄₁₆–¼ inch long, with rounded, shiny wing covers that are red, black, or red-and-black spotted. The most common type is the convergent lady beetle, which has two converging white lines on its black thorax (the area behind the head). Look also for lady beetle larvae, little alligator-like creatures that eat even more pests than their parents do. The larvae of the convergent lady beetle are charcoal gray with orange markings. Lady beetles help control aphids, mites, and mealybugs. They are attracted by angelica, coreopsis, cosmos (especially white-flowered kinds), dill (*Anethum graveolens*), fennel, goldenrods (*Solidago* spp.), oleander, tansy, and yarrow.

Other Beetles

Other beetles can also be beneficial in the garden. Ground beetles and rove beetles help control slugs and snails, as well as other soil-dwelling pests. Some ground beetles devour caterpillars that defoliate trees. All of these beetles are attracted to areas with low ground-cover, such as white clover (*Trifolium repens*), or areas with mulch or loose surface stones. Ground beetles are also fond of the pollen of evening primroses (including *Oenothera laciniata* and *O. biennis*).

CONTROLLING PESTS AND DISEASES

Even in the best-kept gardens, pests and diseases may show up now and then. But, by using the first two sections of this book, you'll be ready for them when they appear. Once you've identified the pest or disease, you've got lots of effective control options. You can buy and release extra beneficial insects to keep pests from getting out of control, or use traps and barriers to keep pests away from your crops. Microbial controls—sprays and dusts containing beneficial microorganisms—can work wonders in controlling specific pests and diseases. Other organic controls include insecticidal soap, oil sprays, pyrethrins, neem, and sulfur. Read on for more about all these organic control techniques.

Beneficial Insects You Can Buy

While encouraging native beneficial creatures is cheaper and requires less effort than releasing purchased ones, there may be situations in which you decide to import some pest-eating assistance. When you take this step, be sure to buy the right beneficial. Read catalog information or question your distributor carefully to be sure you are buying the correct insect for the pest you have and the right amount for your situation, and that you understand how and when to release it. The number you are advised to buy may sound excessive to you, but remember that a normal garden population would not provide the rapid control you are seeking when you purchase a beneficial insect.

Sometimes a pest infestation is so severe that you may want to reduce the pest's population with an organic pest control spray before you release the beneficials. You might, for example, use soap spray or pyrethrins to reduce aphid populations before you release aphid predators. Just remember that the spray must either have dissipated by the time the beneficials arrive or be harmless to them, or you will be killing your new helpers as well as the pests. One of the most common reasons for failure of purchased beneficials to thrive is that a gardener has sprayed pesticide in the garden just before they arrived.

A large number of beneficial species are available commercially. Many kinds are most useful in a greenhouse, where they are confined to the area where the pests are, or in large orchards or fields of the same crop, where no matter where they fly, there are more pests to feed on. Only a few kinds of beneficials are an economical solution for a small garden or backyard orchard. These include aphid midges, green lacewings, predatory mites, spined soldier bugs, mealybug destroyers, and parasitic wasps.

BAD BUYS IN GOOD BUGS

Before investing in purchased beneficial insects, make sure that they're going to give you your money's worth. Praying mantids and lady beetles are two predators that you may want to think twice about before buying.

The praying mantid was once a very popular predator to have in the garden, but observation has revealed that it eats a good many beneficials (including other praying mantids) along with the pests. It is now considered more of a novelty that you can enjoy when you find one in your garden, but don't rely on it for pest control.

Convergent lady beetles do eat aphids, but purchased beetles may not stay put long enough to help your garden. They are usually sold as adults that have been wild-collected during their winter hibernation. When released, they won't stick around for a meal, but instead will fly far away to lay eggs.

Some companies sell "preconditioned" lady beetles. These have been allowed to fly around for a period before they are shipped, so they will lay eggs where you release them. They have also been observed in captivity long enough to remove any that are infested with a common lady beetle parasite.

Either kind of lady beetle will be more likely to stay in your garden if you spray your plants with water first, then release the beetles on the ground under the plants in the cool of evening. Still, even preconditioned lady beetles are wild-collected, and there is some question as to whether we should continue to decimate overwintering lady beetles, which, if left alone, would fly to farms and gardens in the spring anyway.

Aphid Midges

If aphids are a problem in your garden, you might consider buying some aphid midge pupae. From these emerge tiny flies, which lay eggs among the aphids. The ⅛ inch long, orange maggots feed on aphids and repeat their life cycle several times a year. For best results, release 200 to 300 pupae in a small garden, repeating every week for 2 to 4 weeks.

Green Lacewings

Green lacewings also help control aphids, as well as scale insects, mealybugs, whiteflies, thrips, mites, and other garden pests. When you buy green lacewings, you will get either eggs or pre-fed larvae. Larvae may be sprinkled on plants directly. If you get eggs, it is probably best to leave them at room temperature until they begin to hatch, then sprinkle the newly hatched larvae onto plants. Make sure the leaves are dry so the tiny insects won't drown in a drop of water. Release these insects once a week for several weeks. You can purchase supplemental lacewing food, a substance that lacewings will eat when pests are few, but it is a lot of extra work for a small return in a home garden. An even better idea is to purchase lacewings only when pests are numerous and to grow flowers that offer the adult lacewings pollen to feed on (as explained in "Encourage Native Beneficial Insects" on page 351).

Predatory Mites

Purchased predatory mites can help to control pest mites and thrips found in small gardens and backyard orchards. Before you buy predatory mites, get professional advice on the best species for your area and for the pest you are trying to combat, as well as the best dates to release predatory mites and the timing of additional releases.

Other Store-Bought Beneficials

Various other purchased predators may help in specific cases. Spined soldier bugs help to combat Mexican bean beetles, and mealybug destroyers can control mealybugs on citrus and grapes. Various parasitic wasps may help with such pests as scale insects, codling moths, or citrus mealybugs, though their tendency to spread out when released makes them most useful in a greenhouse or on a farm.

Try Traps and Barriers

Another way to protect your plants without sprays is to use traps and barriers for pest control. Both controls are easy to use and can be very effective at preventing plant damage.

Best Barriers

One popular barrier is the floating row cover. Placed over plants, this translucent, white, fabric-like material excludes insects but allows water and light to pass through. You can cut the material into small squares for individual plants, or leave it in large pieces to cover a garden bed.

There are two ways to use floating row covers. to keep out pests. One is as a temporary barrier to get plants past a critical stage. This is often the seedling or young transplant stage, but it could be a later period when a pest is active. For this purpose, drape the row cover loosely over the plants and bury the edges of the material on all sides under the soil. Remove the cover when the plants are large enough to withstand damage, or when pests are no longer a problem.

In some cases, you may decide to grow a crop entirely under row covers. On a large scale, you can drape the row cover over PVC or wire arches, burying the edge of the row cover in the soil on one side and weighting the other side with a board pushed against the ground.

Aphid midge larvae attack aphids; the adults feed on pollen and nectar.

Be sure there is plenty of row cover to tuck into the soil at the ends of the hoops. To cover just a few plants or a few square feet, you can make a removable rectangular frame of wood or PVC tubing. Be sure the frame is tall enough to accommodate the mature plants. Cover the sides and top of the frame with row cover, securing the edges with staples or tape. Put the frame over the seedbed or transplants, pushing it firmly into the soil surface. Lift the frame as needed to check on the progress of the crop or to harvest. (If a crop is ordinarily bee-pollinated—as is the case with squash or cucumbers—you will also need to lift the frame to hand-pollinate the flowers.)

Another barrier material that can keep pests off your plants is called diatomaceous earth (DE). This mined material feels like powder to our touch, but it's very abrasive to the bodies of soft-bodied insects (such as aphids), slugs, and snails. Use it as a dust on plants to keep these pests from feeding on foliage, or create a barrier by surrounding plants with a 2- to 3-inch-wide strip of the material. DE works best when it's dry, so always reapply it after rain.

Tar paper barriers prevent root maggot flies from laying their eggs near susceptible plants.

A saucer of beer set flush with the soil surface will trap slugs and snails.

While this material is considered nontoxic, it is dusty, so wear a mask when applying it to avoid inhaling the particles. Buy natural-grade DE (not pool-grade, which has been chemically treated), and apply it only to problem areas to reduce the chances of harming beneficials.

Gardeners are always dreaming up pest barriers, and with a little looking you will locate many other kinds: copper strips to exclude snails and slugs; bird netting to protect strawberries, vegetables, fruit trees, and shrubs; gopher wire baskets under single plants, or sheets of gopher wire under whole beds; or special fences to exclude animal pests. With a little thought, determination, and effort, you can often create your own pest barriers.

Tried-and-True Traps

If you prefer not to cover your plants, or set up barriers you may want to try traps instead. Pheromone traps work by attracting male insects to the scent of breeding female insects, then trapping them. Pheromones are also used to confuse male insects. When pheromone-scented dispensers are attached to many branches in an orchard, the males can no longer locate females in order to breed. Pheromone traps are available for a variety of flying pests, including codling moths, cabbage loopers, cherry fruit flies, leafrollers, oriental fruit moths, peachtree borers, and Japanese beetles. These traps work best in large areas, in orchards, or in neighborhoods where everyone is cooperating in pest control. Follow the directions on the traps for placement and spacing.

Sticky traps catch insects that are attracted to a specific color, or, in the case of red sphere traps, to a specific color and shape. To control pests, you need to make sure that you use enough traps. For example, for yellow sticky traps to be effective in combating an infestation of aphids and whiteflies, they must be spaced 3 to 5 feet apart. Set the traps in direct sun, at the same level as the threatened plants. If you use red sphere traps to control apple maggots, hang one trap in each dwarf tree, two or three traps for every semi-dwarf, and up to six for each full-size tree.

Applying a sticky substance on the trunks of trees and shrubs can trap certain insects that crawl up and down the plants. Tanglefoot, the commonly available material sold for this purpose, consists of nontoxic vegetable-based oils and resins. While it can be applied directly to the trunk, this may encourage fungi to grow on the tree, so it is better to paint the sticky material onto a tree band first. Tree bands have a foam backing that will fill in bark crevices so pests can't crawl behind them.

Another approach to controlling pests that climb up and down trees is to trap them by providing a dark hiding place on the trunk. Corrugated cardboard with one side removed to expose the corrugation is a good choice. Wrap it around the trunk with the corrugation inward. For gypsy moths, gardeners often use large pieces of burlap folded over a string that is tied around t he tree. Remove insects from these traps daily, or pests will congregate there to feed on the plants.

Whether you use a sticky band or a trap, you need to time these methods so that they are ready at the right time of year to interrupt the pest's life cycle. For example, the first gypsy moth larvae climb up the trees in May, and in summer larger larvae climb up and down daily. On the other hand, cankerworms are best trapped as the adult females crawl up trunks to lay eggs in fall.

Mastering Microcontrols

"Microcontrols" are control techniques that use various kinds of beneficial microorganisms to eradicate pests. These may combat insects or disease organisms directly by infecting them with a fatal disease or killing them with a toxin the microorganism carries. In other cases, a harmless micoorganism is used to colonize a plant surface so a disease organism can't get established.

For home gardeners, microcontrols are more useful than many kinds of beneficial insects because microorganisms are far less mobile than insects. This means they will stay where you put them and fight the pests in your garden. They are also a better bet than other sprays and dusts because they are generally quite specific for the target pest insect or the disease, and they are not harmful to humans, pets, or most beneficial insects.

Sprays of BTK (Bacillus thuringiensis var. kurstaki) can control cabbage-family pests.

BT (Bacillus thuringiensis)

Perhaps the most commonly used microcontrol agent is called BT—an abbreviation for the bacterial disease *Bacillus thuringiensis.* When susceptible pests eat a sprayed leaf or treated bait, they stop eating, become abnormally dark in color, and soon die. The strain *B.t.* var. *kurstaki* (BTK) kills a number of caterpillar pests, including cabbageworms, gypsy moth larvae, and tomato hornworms. *B.t.* var. *san diego* (BTSD) controls some pest beetles, including black vine weevils, Colorado potato beetles, and elm leaf beetles.

You can spray BT in a liquid solution on the plants where the pests are feeding, or apply it to plant crevices in baited granules. To reduce cutworm damage, sprinkle bran moistened with BTK on the soil before you plant. (Mix the bran with a dilute solution of BTK and apply it 2 weeks before your planting date.)

To be killed by BT, the pest must eat some of it, and it is most toxic when the pests are still very young. If you first notice the pests when most of them are large, another type of control will be more effective. Also, be aware that BTK will kill all kinds of butterfly caterpillars, so if you have intentionally attracted butterflies to your garden, don't get any BTK on the plants you planted to attract them. In fact, it is best to use BT sparingly—and only on plants you know have susceptible pests—because pest caterpillars have been known to become resistant to it, and they will become resistant even more rapidly if it is overused.

Mix beneficial nematodes with water and spray or drench plants to control pests.

Beneficial Nematodes

A second microcontrol agent that is proving extremely useful to gardeners is beneficial nematodes. These are nematodes that eat insects rather than eating plant roots. Sprayed onto the soil, they parasitize many kinds of slow-moving soil pests, including cabbage maggots, spotted cucumber beetle larvae, root-feeding flea beetle larvae, and onion maggots. You can also apply them to plants to kill above-ground pest insects such as artichoke plume moths and roundheaded appletree borers.

When you buy beneficial nematodes, they will arrive either dehydrated or suspended in a sponge or other moist substance, ready to be mixed with water. Soil applications are most effective when applied to moist soil in the late afternoon or evening. For best results, apply the nematodes just before rain, or irrigate the area to provide ½ to 1 inch of water. Apply them to plants with a sprayer or a watering can.

To inject beneficial nematodes into a borer hole, put the solution into a clean oil can and squeeze it to squirt them in. Always read the label carefully to see if the beneficial nematode species you plan to apply will control the pest you have. Check to find out the proper dilution and the correct timing in the life cycle of the pest. These nematodes do not thrive in cold soil, so apply them during the warmer part of the year. You will probably need to reapply them each year to replace those that die in winter.

Milky Disease

Gardeners whose lawns become infested with Japanese or June beetle grubs can depend on another microcontrol for help—milky disease spores. This microbial insecticide contains two kinds of bacteria, *Bacillus popilliae* and *B. lentimorbus*. Infected grubs die and inoculate the soil with more bacterial spores. In areas with mild to moderate winters, the bacteria live from year to year, so only one treatment is necessary. Bear in mind that although milky disease spores can eliminate Japanese beetle grubs from a lawn, they cannot keep adult beetles from flying in from other yards to eat your garden plants. You'll still need to control the adult beetles.

Other Microcontrols

If grasshoppers annually invade your community, you might try to organize a large-scale application of the protozoan *Nosema locustae*. If sprayed when the grasshoppers are under ¾ inch long, it will kill most of them and remain in the eggs of the survivors to infect more grasshoppers the following year.

Microcontrols have also been developed against some plant diseases. One, *Agrobacterium radiobacter*, is a bacterium that discourages the development of crown gall diseases. It can be

SKIP THESE CONTROLS

Organic gardening books used to recommend potent botanical insecticides, such as nicotine, rotenone, ryania, and sabadilla. In fact, 25 years ago, the only commercial pesticide available to organic gardeners was rotenone. The advantage of using botanicals—insecticides derived from plants—over chemical pesticides is that they break down within a few days after they are applied. This means that beneficial species are at risk for a relatively short period, there is little likelihood of long-term contamination of the environment, and botanicals aren't likely to persist as residues on the food that we grow.

However, before it breaks down, nicotine is one of the most toxic poisons known. Rotenone, ryania, and sabadilla are also very toxic compounds. They can kill bees (and, in the case of rotenone, birds and fish) as well as pests. They are moderately toxic to pets and people. They also pose a risk to the person applying the product, especially because people may not realize that they should wear protective clothing, gloves, and masks when using these products. There are additional concerns that rotenone, for example, may be more persistent on food than previously thought.

Today there are many effective, nontoxic methods of managing all kinds of pest problems. The older botanicals are no longer needed. With the prevention and control techniques recommended in this book, you'll get excellent pest control without having to resort to any of the older botanicals.

Sprayers come in several sizes. Choose one that is suited to the amount of spraying you do.

used to soak seeds, as a dip for bareroot plants, or as a dressing for fresh pruning cuts. Another preparation, containing a mixture of several species of *Trichoderma* fungi, may be used as a replacement for tree wound paint. These harmless fungi become established on your plants and prevent growth of harmful organisms.

The Scoop on Sprays and Dusts

Gardeners who practice active prevention and who understand the role of beneficial creatures in helping to control pests find they rarely need sprays and dusts. In fact, avoiding the use of any pesticides—even organic ones—is one of the gardening practices that is most useful in increasing the population of beneficials. However, there are a few problems that may require these treatments, and you need to choose among them wisely and use them skillfully.

When more than one type of spray or dust will control a pest, begin with the mildest one. For example, if aphids are your problem, you will find that a strong spray of water alone, repeated every few days, will significantly reduce their populations by knocking them off plants. If this does not offer enough control, you may want to try an insecticidal soap spray. For persistent populations, you may choose to use pyrethrins. If a milder treatment will do the trick, you will get rid of pests while causing the least injury to beneficial insects.

Remember that, even though they're organic, the sprays and dusts recommended in this book are still powerful controls. Use sprays and dusts sparingly, only on the plants affected by the pest, only at the time or times during which the directions say you are most likely to kill the pest, and only as often as the label suggests. In some cases, directions will even specify a certain part of a plant that needs to be treated, rather than the whole plant. This kind of selectivity spares beneficial creatures and reduces the chance that pests might develop resistance to overused controls.

Also, for your own safety and the safety of family members and pets, read all of the precautions on spray and dust labels before you buy, mix, apply, or store the products. If protective clothing or eyewear is recommended, be sure to wear it. Never spray or apply dust on windy days. Never put any kind of spray or dust in a container that once held food or pet food or store them near food or pet food. Keep these controls on a high shelf, preferably behind a locked cupboard door.

Insecticidal Soap

One of the mildest sprays is insecticidal soap. It affects only pests that it strikes directly, killing aphids and many other soft-bodied pests by dissolving the membranes around their body cells. Because it has no effect on pests once it has dried on the plant, insecticidal soap must be reapplied every 3 to 7 days, but this also means that beneficials are not harmed by toxic residues. Commercial soap sprays are formulated to contain mainly the fatty acids that are toxic to pests and harmless to plants. Household soaps (and especially detergents) are more likely to injure plants. Even a commercial insecticidal soap may damage some plants, so you should check the label carefully before spraying. If a plant is not listed, apply the soap spray to only a few leaves, then wait 48 hours to see if they are damaged before you spray the whole plant.

Oil Sprays

Gardeners have used oils for a long time to kill disease spores and pest eggs on the bare branches of deciduous trees and shrubs during the dormant season. Now oils have been developed that can be used on some plants during their periods of active growth. These horticultural or "summer" oils have been refined to remove the sulfur compounds that could damage the leaves of growing plants. They are effective in killing or repelling many kinds of aphids, beetles, caterpillars, leafminers, and mealybugs without harming vegetable and ornamental plants.

To avoid damage, don't apply summer oils to plants that are suffering from moisture stress and don't use them on very hot days. Before treating plants not listed on the label, test the spray on a few leaves first. Wait 48 hours, then check to make sure there are no signs of spotting or discoloration before you spray the whole plant. Also, if you treat a plant with an oil spray, wait at least a month before applying any sulfur-containing spray.

One promising line of research is in the use of summer oils combined with baking soda to prevent powdery mildew and black spot. Researchers at Cornell University in Ithaca, New York, found that 1 tablespoon of baking soda and 2½ teaspoons of summer oil mixed into 1 gallon of water, and sprayed once a week, controlled both of these diseases on roses and also controlled powdery mildew on squash plants.

Neem

Neem is a relatively new pest-control product to American gardeners, although it has been used for a long time in India. This extract from the tropical tree *Azadirachta indica* is unique among pest controls in acting in so many ways: as a contact poison, stomach poison, repellent, anti-feedant (causing pests to lose their appetite), growth retardant, and egg-laying deterrent. You can apply this material as a spray or drench. Neem kills at least 75 kinds of pests, yet it is relatively nontoxic to mammals. Preliminary studies suggest that parasitic wasps and predatory mites are also not poisoned by it. Neem is registered for use on a number of fruits, vegetables, and ornamental plants.

Pyrethrins

Pyrethrins are another organic pest-control product to use as a last resort. Pyrethrins are extracted from the flowers of pyrethrum daisy (*Chrysanthemum coccineum*). (Don't confuse pyrethrins with pyrethroids, which are synthetic compounds that resemble pyrethrins but are more toxic and longer-lasting in the environment.) Pyrethrins cause insects to become instantly paralyzed. This may kill them from starvation or leave them vulnerable to predators. Since insects will recover from exposure to pyrethrins, a number of pyrethrin formulations include a substance called piperonyl butoxide (PBO), which makes them more toxic. However, PBO is itself controversial, as there is some indication that it can affect the human nervous system. So, to be on the safe side, choose pyrethrin formulations that do not contain PBO.

BREW A FUNGUS-FIGHTING TEA

Recent research suggests that compost tea, long used as a fertilizer, can also help plants fight off fungal diseases such as powdery mildew and tomato late blight. Microorganisms in the compost apparently either grow more successfully than or actively attack the disease-causing fungus. Make the tea by steeping a burlap or cheesecloth bag containing 1 gallon of well-aged, manure-based compost in a 5-gallon bucket of water. Stir it well and leave it in a warm place for 3 days. Then remove the bag and put the liquid in a sprayer or a watering can. Remove all leaves damaged by disease, then spray or sprinkle the tea over the whole plant. Repeat every 3 to 4 days if the plants still show symptoms. This spray is most effective when applied in the evening so plant leaves will remain moist for a few hours.

Organic Disease Controls

If fungal diseases are attacking your plants, you may need to turn to organic fungicides. Sulfur and copper fungicides have been used for a long time, both alone and in various mixtures. Both are highly irritating to eyes and skin, so wear protective clothing and follow the recommended safety precautions when applying them. These materials can harm plants when temperatures are high, so always follow the application guidelines on the label. Lime-sulfur, a mixture of sulfur and lime, is able to penetrate leaf tissue, where it can kill fungal spores that recently germinated. While this offers more protection, lime-sulfur is more likely to damage plants than sulfur alone, and it is considerably more toxic to humans. It is typically used on dormant plants or at bud break, and should never be used when temperatures exceed 85°F.

Bordeaux mixture, a combination of copper sulfate and hydrated lime, can also burn plants' leaves. It is most safely applied just before buds break in spring. Do not apply it to leaves when temperatures are below 50°F and humidity is high.

Other disease controls that have shown promise in experiments are baking soda (see "Oil Sprays" on page 361 for more on this control) and antitranspirants. Both are used to prevent fungal diseases like powdery mildew. Antitranspirants, sold under brand names like Wilt-Pruf and VaporGard, were originally developed as sprays to keep evergreen trees and shrubs from drying out in winter. However, research has shown that they also create an effective barrier to fungal spores on ornamentals, if applied frequently.

Antibiotics used for human diseases also have some effect on some plant diseases. Streptomycin and Terramycin sprays are both used to control bacterial spot and fireblight.

Where's That Pest or Disease?

A regional guide to the most troublesome pests and diseases.

WHERE'S THAT PEST?

Throughout North America

aphids, p. 244
asparagus beetle, p. 247
cabbage looper, p. 249
cabbage maggot, p. 250
carrot rust fly, p. 251
codling moth, p. 253
corn earworm/tomato
   fruitworm, p. 255
cutworms, p. 259
flatheaded appletree borer, p. 261
flea beetles, p. 262
fruit borers, p. 263
fruit flies, p. 264
fruit tree leafroller, p. 264
imported cabbageworm, p. 266
June/May beetles, p. 269
lace bugs, p. 270
leafhoppers, p. 270
leafminers, p. 271
millipedes, p. 274
peachtree borers, p. 279
rose chafer, p. 281
rust mites, p. 281
scales, soft, p. 283
slugs and snails, p. 283
sowbugs/pillbugs, p. 285
spider mites, p. 286
spittlebugs/froghoppers, p. 287
squash bug, p. 288
stink bugs, p. 290
strawberry root weevil, p. 291
tarnished plant bug, p. 291
tent caterpillar, p. 292
thrips, p. 293
tomato hornworm, p. 294
webworm, fall, p. 295
webworm, garden, p. 296
whiteflies , p. 297
wireworms, p. 298

Northeast

apple maggot, p. 245
bagworm, p. 247
black vine weevil, p. 248
cankerworms, p. 251
chinch bug, p. 252
Colorado potato beetle, p. 254
cucumber beetle, spotted, p. 256
cucumber beetle, striped, p. 257
elm bark beetles, p. 260
gypsy moth, p. 265
iris borer, p. 267
Japanese beetle, p. 268
Mexican bean beetle, p. 273
onion maggot, p. 277
oriental fruit moth, p. 278
plum curculio, p. 280
spruce budworm, p. 288
squash vine borer, p. 289
tussock moths, p. 294

Southeast

apple maggot, p. 245
bagworm, p. 247
cankerworms, p. 251
chinch bug, p. 252
Colorado potato beetle, p. 254
cucumber beetle, spotted, p. 256
cucumber beetle, striped, p. 257
elm bark beetles, p. 260
gypsy moth, p. 265
iris borer, p. 267
Japanese beetle, p. 268
Mexican bean beetle, p. 273
plum curculio, p. 280
spruce budworm, p. 288
squash vine borer, p. 289
tussock moths, p. 294

Deep South

apple maggot, p. 245
bagworm, p. 247
chinch bug, p. 252
Colorado potato beetle, p. 254
cucumber beetle, spotted, p. 256
cucumber beetle, striped, p. 257
elm bark beetles, p. 260
Japanese beetle, p. 268
mealybugs, p. 272
Mexican bean beetle, p. 273
navel orangeworm, p. 275
scales, armored, p. 282
southwestern corn borer, p. 284
squash vine borer, p. 289
tussock moths, p. 294

North Central

apple maggot, p. 245
bagworm, p. 247
black vine weevil, p. 248
cankerworms, p. 251
Colorado potato beetle, p. 254
cucumber beetle, spotted, p. 256
cucumber beetle, striped, p. 257
European corn borer, p. 260
gypsy moth, p. 265
Mexican bean beetle, p. 273
northern corn rootworm, p. 276
onion maggot, p. 277
spruce budworm, p. 288
squash vine borer, p. 289
tussock moths, p. 294

Midwest

apple maggot, p. 245
armyworms, p. 246
bagworm, p. 247
black vine weevil, p. 248
cankerworms, p. 251
Colorado potato beetle, p. 254
cucumber beetle, spotted, p. 256
cucumber beetle, striped, p. 257
elm bark beetles, p. 260
European corn borer, p. 260
Mexican bean beetle, p. 273
navel orangeworm, p. 275
northern corn rootworm, p. 276
onion maggot, p. 277
southwestern corn borer, p. 284
squash vine borer, p. 289
tussock moths, p. 294

Southwest

armyworms, p. 246
cankerworms, p. 251
Colorado potato beetle, p. 254
cucumber beetle, striped, p. 257
elm bark beetles, p. 260
mealybugs, p. 272
navel orangeworm, p. 275
scales, armored, p. 282
southwestern corn borer, p. 284

California

apple maggot, p. 245
cankerworms, p. 251
elm bark beetles, p. 260
Japanese beetle, p. 268
mealybugs, p. 272
navel orangeworm, p. 275
pear psylla, p. 279
scales, armored, p. 282

Northwest Coast

black vine weevil, p. 248
Colorado potato beetle, p. 254
onion maggot, p. 277
oriental fruit moth, p. 278
pear psylla, p. 279

West Coast Canada

black vine weevil, p. 248
onion maggot, p. 277
pear psylla, p. 279

Central Canada

apple maggot, p. 245
black vine weevil, p. 248
cankerworms, p. 251
Colorado potato beetle, p. 254
cucumber beetle, spotted, p. 256
cucumber beetle, striped, p. 257
elm bark beetles, p. 260
European corn borer, p. 260
Mexican bean beetle, p. 273
onion maggot, p. 277
squash vine borer, p. 289
tussock moths, p. 294

Eastern Canada

black vine weevil, p. 248
cankerworms, p. 251
chinch bug, p. 252
Colorado potato beetle, p. 254
cucumber beetle, spotted, p. 256
cucumber beetle, striped, p. 257
elm bark beetles, p. 260
European corn borer, p. 260
gypsy moth, p. 265
iris borer, p. 267
Mexican bean beetle, p. 273
northern corn rootworm, p. 276
onion maggot, p. 277
oriental fruit moth, p. 278
pear psylla, p. 279
plum curculio, p. 280
spruce budworm, p. 288
squash vine borer, p. 289
tussock moths, p. 294

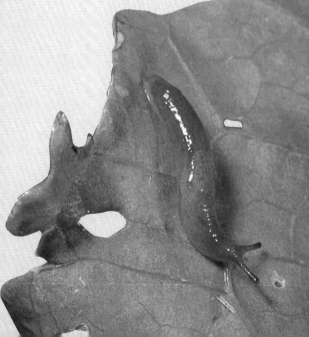

WHERE'S THAT DISEASE?

Throughout North America

anthracnose, p. 300

armillaria root rot, p. 301

bacterial soft rot, p. 302

bacterial spot, p. 303

black spot, p. 304

botrytis blight, p. 305

cane blight, p. 306

crown gall, p. 309

cytospora canker, p. 310

fusarium wilt, p. 315

late blight, p. 315

mosaic, p. 319

nematodes, foliar, p. 321

powdery mildew, p. 323

rust, p. 327

septoria leaf spot, p. 328

sooty mold, p. 330

yellows, p. 333

Northeast

apple scab, p. 300

bacterial wilt, p. 303

cedar-apple rust, p. 307

downy mildew, p. 312

early blight, p. 313

fire blight, p. 314

leaf blister, p. 316

needle cast, p. 320

pseudomonas leaf blight, p. 325

red stele, p. 325

root rot, p. 326

scab, p. 328

smut, onion, p. 329

summer diseases, p. 331

verticillium wilt, p. 332

Southeast

apple scab, p. 300

bacterial wilt, p. 303

brown rot, p. 306

citrus scab, p. 308

dodder, p. 311

downy mildew, p. 312

early blight, p. 313

fire blight, p. 314

leaf blister, p. 316

leaf gall, p. 317

melanose, p. 318

mistletoes, p. 319

nematodes, root knot, p. 322

peach leaf curl, p. 323

pseudomonas leaf blight, p. 325

root rot, p. 326

scab, p. 328

smut, p. 329

Deep South

brown rot, p. 306

citrus scab, p. 308

dodder, p. 311

downy mildew, p. 312

early blight, p. 313

fire blight, p. 314

leaf blister, p. 316

melanose, p. 318

mistletoes, p. 319

nematodes, root knot, p. 322

peach leaf curl, p. 323

pseudomonas leaf blight, p. 325

root rot, p. 326

scab, p. 328

North Central

apple scab, p. 300

bacterial wilt, p. 303

cedar-apple rust, p. 307

downy mildew, p. 312

early blight, p. 313

fire blight, p. 314

leaf blister, p. 316

needle cast, p. 320

pseudomonas leaf blight, p. 325

red stele, p. 325

root rot, p. 326

scab, p. 328

summer diseases, p. 331

verticillium wilt, p. 332

Midwest

apple scab, p. 300

bacterial wilt, p. 303

brown rot, p. 306

cedar-apple rust, p. 307

curly top, p. 310

dodder, p. 311

downy mildew, p. 312

early blight, p. 313

fire blight, p. 314

leaf blister, p. 316

mistletoes, p. 319

nematodes, root knot, p. 322

pseudomonas leaf blight, p. 325

root rot, p. 326

scab, p. 328

smut, corn, p. 329

verticillium wilt, p. 332

Southwest

citrus scab, p. 308

curly top, p. 310

mistletoes, p. 319

nematodes, root knot, p. 322

California

citrus scab, p. 308
curly top, p. 310
downy mildew, p. 312
early blight, p. 313
fire blight, p. 314
leaf blister, p. 316
mistletoes, p. 319
nematodes, root knot, p. 322
pseudomonas leaf blight, p. 325
root rot, p. 326
scab, p. 328

Northwest Coast

apple scab, p. 300
curly top, p. 310
downy mildew, p. 312
early blight, p. 313
fire blight, p. 314
leaf blister, p. 316
mistletoes, p. 319
needle cast, p. 320
nematodes, root knot, p. 322
pseudomonas leaf blight, p. 325
red stele, p. 325
root rot, p. 326
scab, p. 328
smut, onion, p. 329
verticillium wilt, p. 332

West Coast Canada

apple scab, p. 300
downy mildew, p. 312
early blight, p. 313
fire blight, p. 314
leaf blister, p. 316
needle cast, p. 320
nematodes, root knot, p. 322
pseudomonas leaf blight, p. 325
red stele, p. 325
root rot, p. 326
scab, p. 328
smut, onion, p. 329
verticillium wilt, p. 332

Central Canada

apple scab, p. 300
bacterial wilt, p. 303
downy mildew, p. 312
early blight, p. 313
fire blight, p. 314
leaf blister, p. 316
nematodes, root knot, p. 322
pseudomonas leaf blight, p. 325
red stele, p. 325
root rot, p. 326
scab, p. 328
smut, onion, p. 329
verticillium wilt, p. 332

Eastern Canada

apple scab, p. 300
bacterial wilt, p. 303
downy mildew, p. 312
early blight, p. 313
fire blight, p. 314
leaf blister, p. 316
needle cast, p. 320
nematodes, root knot, p. 322
pseudomonas leaf blight, p. 325
red stele, p. 325
root rot, p. 326
scab, p. 328
smut, onion, p. 329
summer diseases, p. 331
verticillium wilt, p. 332

Southern Canada

apple scab, p. 300
bacterial wilt, p. 303
downy mildew, p. 312
early blight, p. 313
fire blight, p. 314
leaf blister, p. 316
needle cast, p. 320
nematodes, root knot, p. 322
pseudomonas leaf blight, p. 325
red stele, p. 325
root rot, p. 326
scab, p. 328
smut, onion, p. 329
summer diseases, p. 331
verticillium wilt, p. 332

USDA PLANT HARDINESS ZONE MAP

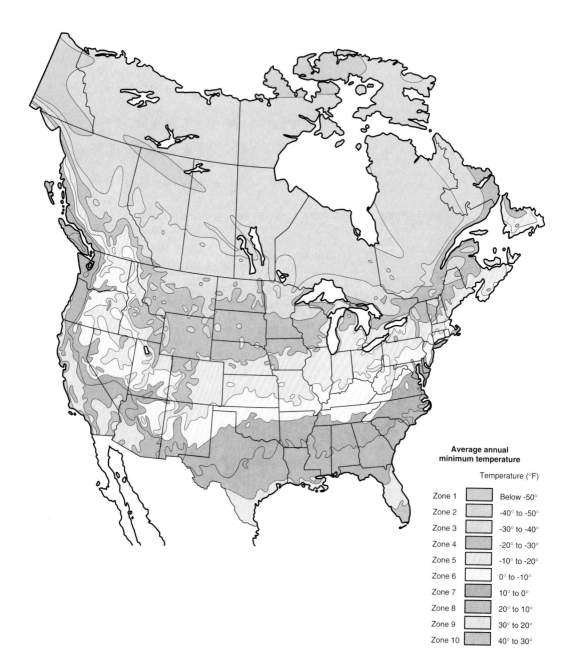

**Average annual
minimum temperature**

Temperature (°F)

Zone 1		Below -50°
Zone 2		-40° to -50°
Zone 3		-30° to -40°
Zone 4		-20° to -30°
Zone 5		-10° to -20°
Zone 6		0° to -10°
Zone 7		10° to 0°
Zone 8		20° to 10°
Zone 9		30° to 20°
Zone 10		40° to 30°

RECOMMENDED READING

Books

Bradley, Fern Marshall, ed. *Rodale's Chemical-Free Yard and Garden.* Emmaus, Pa.: Rodale Press, 1991.

Bradley, Fern Marshall and Barbara W. Ellis, eds. *Rodale's All-New Encyclopedia of Organic Gardening.* Emmaus, Pa.: Rodale Press, 1992.

Campbell, Stu. *Let It Rot: The Gardener's Guide to Composting.* Rev. ed. Charlotte, Vt.: Garden Way Publishing, 1990.

Carr, Anna. *Good Neighbors: Companion Planting for Gardeners.* Emmaus Pa.: Rodale Press, 1985.

Dreistadt, S.H. *Pests of Landscape Trees and Shrubs: An Integrated Pest Management Guide.* Oakland, Calif.: ANR Publications, 1994.

Ellis, Barbara, W. and Fern Marshall Bradley, eds. *The Organic Gardener's Handbook of Natural Insect and Disease Control.* Emmaus, Pa.: Rodale Press, 1992.

Flint, M.L. *Pests of the Garden and Small Farm: A Grower's Guide to Using Less Pesticide.* Oakland, Calif.: ANR Publications, 1990.

Johnson, Warren T. and Howard H. Lyon. *Insects that Feed on Trees and Shrubs.* 2nd. ed. Ithaca, N.Y.: Cornell University Press, 1988.

Martin, Deborah L., and Grace Gershuny, eds. *The Rodale Book of Composting.* Rev. ed. Emmaus, Pa.: Rodale Press, 1992.

Michalak, Patricia S. and Linda A. Gilkeson. *Rodale's Successful Organic Gardening: Controlling Pests and Diseases.* Emmaus, Pa.: Rodale Press, 1994.

Olkowski, William, Sheila Daar, and Helga Olkowski. *Common-Sense Pest Control.* Newtown, Conn.: Taunton Press, 1991.

Peirce, Pam. *Controlling Vegetable Pests.* San Ramon, Calif.: Ortho Books, 1991.

Schultz, Warren. *The Chemical-Free Lawn.* Emmaus, Pa.: Rodale Press, 1989.

Smith, C., ed. *The Ortho Home Gardener's Problem Solver* (adapted from the professional edition of *The Ortho Problem Solver*). San Ramon, Calif.: Ortho Books, 1993.

Smith, Michael D., ed. *The Ortho Problem Solver.* 4th ed. San Ramon, Calif.: Ortho Books, 1994.

Westcott, Cynthia. *The Gardener's Bug Book.* Garden City, N.Y.: Doubleday & Company, 1973.

Westcott's Plant Disease Handbook. 5th ed. rev. by R. Kenneth Horst. New York: Van Nostrand Reinhold Co., 1990.

Periodicals

Common Sense Pest Control Quarterly, Bio-Integral Resource Center (BIRC), P.O. Box 7414, Berkeley, CA 94707.

Organic Gardening, Rodale Press, Inc., 33 E. Minor St., Emmaus, PA 18098.

Hort Ideas, Greg and Patricia Y. Williams, Rt. 1, Box 302, Black Lick Rd., Gravel Switch, KY 40328.

The IPM Practitioner, Bio-Integral Resource Center (BIRC), P.O. Box 7414, Berkeley, CA 94707.

RESOURCES

INFORMATION SOURCES

ATTRA (Appropriate Technology Transfer for Rural Areas)
P.O. Box 3657, Fayetteville AR 72702
(800) 346-9140
Publishes numerous information packages; provides technical assistance on sustainable agriculture.

Bio-Integral Resource Center (BIRC)
Box 7414, Berkeley, CA 94707, (510) 524-2567
A membership organization that offers advice on least-toxic methods of solving pest problems and help locating least-toxic products and services locally. Membership includes a subscription to the IPM Practitioner.

Cooperative Extension Service
Call the Cooperative Extension office in your state, or your local County Extension agent for information about obtaining their publications on pest control. This governmental agency, associated with the land grant university in each state, often offers excellent photo identification guides.

National Pesticide Telecommunications Network (NPTN)
Pesticide Hotline, (800) 858-7378
6:30 a.m. to 4:30 p.m., Pacific Time
Call for help reading a label, for information about the risk, safety, application, and cleanup of pesticides, or for emergency information.

SOURCES OF GARDENING, PEST- AND DISEASE-CONTROL PRODUCTS

Note: Most of these mail-order sources carry beneficial insects, as well as other products needed to carry out the pest-management strategies suggested in this book.

Arbico
Sustainable Environmental Alternatives for Growers
P.O. Box 4247, Tucson, AZ 85378

Gardener's Supply Co.
128 Intervale Road, Burlington, VT 05401

Gardens Alive!
5100 Schenley Place, Lawrenceburg, IN 47025

Harmony Farm Supply
P.O. Box 460, Graton, CA 95444

The Natural Gardening Company
217 San Anselmo Avenue, San Anselmo, CA 94960

Peaceful Valley Farm Supply Company
P.O. Box 2209, Grass Valley, CA 95945

Smith and Hawken
P.O. Box 6900, Florence, KY 41022

Worm's Way Garden Supply and Home Brew Center
3151 South Highway 446, Bloomington, IN 47401

MAIL-ORDER SOURCES FOR BENEFICIAL INSECTS AND MITES

Applied Bionomics Ltd.
11074 West Saanich Road, Sidney, B.C. Canada V8L 5P5

Beneficial Insectary
14751 Oak Run Road, Oak Run, CA 96069

Better Yield Insects
RR#3, Site 4, Box 48, Belle River, Ontario Canada N0R 1A0

Biofac
P.O. Box 87, Mathis, TX 78368

BoBiotrol
54 South Bear Creek Drive, Merced, CA 95340

Buena Biosystems
P.O. Box 4008, Ventura, CA 93007

Foothill Agricultural Research
510½ West Chase Drive, Corona, CA 91720

Growing Naturally
P.O. Box 54, Pineville, PA 18946

Hydro-Gardens, Inc.
P.O. Box 9707, Colorado Springs, CO 80932

IPM Laboratories
Main Street, Locke, NY 13092

Nature's Control
P.O. Box 35, Medford, OR 97501

Rincon-Vitova Insectaries, Inc.
P.O. Box 95, Oak View, CA 93022

Stanley Gardens
P.O. Box 913, Belchertown, MA 01007

PHOTOGRAPHY CREDITS

Max E Badgley Biological Photography
Front cover, p. 246, p. 247a, p. 248, p. 249,
p. 254, p. 257a, p. 257b, p. 260b, p. 262,
p. 264b, p. 266, p. 270a, p. 270b, p. 272,
p. 274a, p. 274b, p. 283b, p. 284, p. 285a,
p. 287, p. 289a, p. 290, p. 292, p. 294, p. 295, p. 319
Back cover (right—stink bug)

James F. Dill
p. 242, p. 245, p. 250, p. 267, p. 269, p. 276,
p. 277, p. 279, p. 280a, p. 280b, p. 281a,
p. 285b, p. 288, p. 289b, p. 291a, p. 304a,
p. 325b, p. 331, p. 336b, p. 337

Entomological Society of America
p. 296a

**Department of Primary Industries, Plant
Protection Unit, Queensland, Australia**
p. 316a

Derek Fell's Horticultural Picture Library
p. 251b

Linda Gilkeson
p. 337, p. 351a, p. 351b, p. 355, p. 356a

Ivy Hansen Photography
Endpapers, p. 8, p. 13, p. 15a, p. 15b, p. 17,
p. 20, p. 21, p. 22, p. 23, p. 29, p. 31a, p. 31b,
p. 33, p. 35, p. 39, p. 42, p. 44, p. 46, p. 47, p. 49, p.
54, p. 55, p. 58, p. 61, p. 62, p. 63, p. 64,
p. 65a, p. 65b, p. 66, p. 67, p. 73, p. 75, p. 76,
p. 78, p. 83, p. 85, p. 86, p. 87, p. 91, p. 93, p. 95, p.
96, p. 99, p. 101, p. 103, p. 106, p. 107, p. 109, p.
110, p. 111, p. 112, p. 113, p. 114, p. 115,
p. 116, p. 117, p. 119a, p. 119b, p. 120, p. 121,
p. 122, p. 124, p. 125, p. 128, p. 129, p. 130,
p. 133, p. 137, p. 140, p. 142, p. 143, p. 144,
p. 146, p. 147, p. 149, p. 151, p. 154,
p. 155, p. 156a, p. 156b, p. 159, p. 161, p. 163,
p. 164, p. 165, p. 167, p. 170, p. 172, p. 175,
p. 177, p. 180, p. 181, p. 182, p. 183, p. 188,
p. 197, p. 198, p. 200, p. 201, p. 202, p. 207,
p. 209, p. 211, p. 213, p. 217, p. 219, p. 221,
p. 223, p. 228, p. 229, p. 231, p. 233, p. 235

**Holt Studios International/
Horizon Photo Library**
p. 11, p. 37, p. 40, p. 71, p. 80, p. 160, p. 206

Lansdowne Publishing
p. 237, p. 239a, p. 239b, p. 240a, p. 240b,
p. 253a, p. 253b, p. 255, p. 259a, p. 263,
p. 264a, p. 271, p. 275, p. 278, p. 281b, p. 282,
p. 283a, p. 293, p. 297, p. 299, p. 300a, p. 300b, p.
301 (Nan Barbour), p. 302, p. 303, p. 304b,
p. 306, p. 308, p. 309, p. 312, p. 313a, p. 313b
(Anthony Healy), p. 315, p. 316b,
p. 317, p. 318, p. 320, p. 321b, p. 322, p. 323,
p. 324a, p. 324b, p. 325a (Department of Primary
Industries, Queensland), p. 326,
p. 327, p. 328 (Department of Primary Industries,
Queensland), p. 331a, p. 332 (F S Sedun, University
of New England), p. 335, p. 336a, p. 344, p. 352, p.
357, p. 360, p. 362, Back cover (center—mosaic)

Charles Mann Photography
p. 3, p. 24, p. 107, p. 131, p. 132, p. 135, p. 139, p.
145, p. 150, p. 158, p. 166, p. 171, p. 196,
p. 204, p. 226

Jerry Pavia
p. 10, p. 16, p. 28, p. 30, p. 50, p. 51, p. 59,
p. 89, p. 97, p. 138, p. 173, p. 179, p. 185, p. 187, p.
189, p. 190, p. 192, p. 193, p. 195, p. 215, p. 236

Pam Peirce
p. 241, p. 251b, p. 259b, p. 286, p. 305

Plant Health Associates Inc.
p. 311, p. 321a, p. 333, p. 339b, p. 340

Lee A. Reich Garden and Orchard Consulting
p. 307a, p. 307b, p. 329, p. 330, p. 334, p. 339a,

Patricia Lynn Seip/Rodale Stock Images
p. 152

USDA/APHIS
p. 244, p. 265a, p. 265b, p. 273a, p. 273b, Back cover
(left—green aphids)

Weldon Russell
p. 341a, p. 341b, p. 343, p. 345, p. 346, p. 347,
p. 348, p. 349, p. 350a, p. 350b, p. 356b, p. 358

Ron West Nature Photography
p. 251a, p. 252, p. 260a, p. 261, p. 268, p. 291,
p. 296b, p. 298, p. 310, p. 314

ABOUT THE AUTHORS

LINDA A. GILKESON

Linda A. Gilkeson, Ph.D., is the Integrated Pest Management Coordinator with the British Columbia Ministry of Environment in Victoria, B.C. She has had 25 years' experience as an organic gardener in a variety of climates, and has conducted research on biological controls for aphids, thrips, spider mites, and other pests. Linda has published numerous popular articles and scientific papers. She is coauthor of *Rodale's Successful Organic Gardening Series: Controlling Pests and Diseases*, and has contributed to *The Organic Gardener's Handbook of Natural Insect and Disease Control* and *Rodale's Chemical-Free Yard and Garden*. Linda lives in Brentwood Bay, British Columbia, Canada.

MIRANDA SMITH

Miranda Smith has been teaching organic gardening and farming since 1971. She currently teaches at the New England Small Farm Institute in Belchertown, Massachusetts, where she also operates a commercial herb garden and bedding plants operation. Miranda is the author of *Backyard Fruits and Berries* and *Greenhouse Gardening*, and coauthor of *Rodale's Insect, Disease & Weed Identification Guide*. Miranda lives in Belchertown, Massachusetts.

PAM PEIRCE

Pam Peirce teaches gardening and horticultural photography at City College of San Francisco. She is the author of *Golden Gate Gardening* and *Environmentally Friendly Gardening: Controlling Vegetable Pests*, and is coauthor of the forthcoming book *Easy Vegetable Gardening Plans*. Pam lives in San Francisco, California.

INDEX

Note:
Boldface references indicate photographs. Page references in *italic* indicate tables and maps.

A

Abelmoschus esculentus, 36–37, **37**

Abies, 189

Abies balsamea, 189

Abies concolor, 189, **189**

Acer, 208–9

Acer palmatum, 208, **209**

Acer rubrum, 208

Acer saccharum, 208

Achillea, 156

Achillia millefolium, **156**

Actinidia, 91

Actinidia arguta, 91

Actinidia deliciosa, 91, **91**

Actinidia kolomikta, 91

Aesculus, 178

Aesculus x *carnea*, 178

Aesculus glabra, 178

Aesculus parviflora, 178, **179**

Ageratum, 106, **106**

Ageratum houstonianum, 106, **106**

Alcea rosea, 145, **145**

Allium, 158, **158**

Allium ampeloprasum, 31, **31**

Allium cepa, 38–39, **39**

Allium giganteum, 158, **158**

Allium moly, 158

Allium sativum, 30, **30**

Allium schoenoprasum, 62, **62**

Almonds, 70, **71**

Alumroot, American, 137

American alumroot, 137

American arborvitae, 170

American beech, 173

American holly, 194, **195**

American linden, 205

American planetree, 229

Anemone x *hybrida*, 149, **149**

Anethum graveolens, 63, **63**

Anglojapanese yew, 236

Annuals, 104–25, **106–25**

Anthracnose, 300, **300**

Antirrhinum majus, 118, **118**

Aphid midges, 354, 355

Aphids, 244–45, **244**

Apium graveolens, 21–22, **22**

Apple maggot, 245–46, **245**

Apples, 71–74, **73**

Apple scab, 300–301, **300**

Appletree borer, flatheaded, 261–62, **261**

Apricots, 74–75, **75**

Aquilegia, 136–37

Aquilegia vulgaris, **137**

Arachis hypogaea, 39–40, **40**

Arborvitaes, 170, **170**

Armillaria root rot, 301–2, **301**

Armyworms, 246, **246**

Artichokes, 10, **10**

Ashes, 171, **171**

Ashes, mountain, 210–11, **211**

Ash yellows, 333

Asparagus, 11–12, **11**

Asparagus beetle, 247, **247**

Asparagus officinalis, 11–12

Aspen, quaking, 216

Aster, 128, **128**

Aster novae-angliae, 128

Astilbe, 129, **129**

Astilbe x *arendsii*, **129**

Azaleas, 220–22

B

Baby's-breath, 130, **130**

Bacillus thuringiensis, 358

Bacteria, 299

Bacterial soft rot, 302–3, **302**

Bacterial spot, 303, **304**

Bacterial wilt, 304

Bagworm, 247–48, **247**

Balsam, garden, 112

Balsam fir, 189

Barberries, 172,
172

Barriers, 355–56

Basil, 61–62, **61**

Basswood, 205

Bean beetle, Mexican,
273–74, **273**

Beans, 12–14, **13**

Bearded iris, 147, **147**

Bee balm, 131, **131**

Beeches, 173–74, **173**

Beet leaf curl virus, 310, **310**

Beetles

beneficial, 353

pests (*See names of
individual beetles*)

Beets, 14–15, **15**

Begonia x *semperflorens -
cultorum*, 123–24, **124**

Bellflowers, 132–33, **132**

Bell peppers, 44

Berberis, 172

Berberis koreana, 172

Berberis thunbergii, 172, **172**

Beta vulgaris, 14–15, **15**, 23,
23

Betula, 174–75

Betula nigra, 174

Betula papyrifera, 174

Betula pendula, 174, **175**

Bigleaf hydrangea, 198,
198

Birches, 174–75, **175**

Bitter rot, 331

Blackberries, 75–77, **76**

Black-eyed Susan, 107, **107**

Black rot, 331

Black spot, 304, **304**

Black vine weevil, 248, **248**

Bleeding hearts, 133, **133**

Blight

botrytis, 305–6, **305**

cane, 306–7, **307**

early, 313–14, **313**

fire, 314, **314**

late, 315–16, **316**

pseudomonas leaf, 325,
325

Blossom end rot, 335, **335**

Blueberries, 77–79, **78**

Bordeaux mixture, 362

Border privet, 218

Borers. *See names of individual
borers*

Botanical insecticides, 359

Botrytis blight, 305–6, **305**

Bottlebrush buckeye, 178, **179**

Boxwoods, 176–77, **177**

Brassica oleracea, 15, **15**,
16–19, **16–17**, 21, **21**,
31, **31**

Brassica rapa, 58, **58**

Bridalwreath spirea, 225, **226**

Broccoli, 15, **15**

Brown rot, 306, **306**

Brussels sprouts, 16, **16**

BT (*Bacillus thuringiensis*), 358

Buckeyes, 178–79, **179**

Bulbs, 157–67, **158–67**

Bumald spirea, 225

Burning bush, 186, **187**

Buttonwood, 229

Buxus, 176–77

Buxus sempervirens, 176, **177**

Buying plants, 345–46

C

Cabbage, 16–19, **17**

Cabbage looper, 249–50, **249**

Cabbage maggot, 250, **250**

Cabbageworm, imported, 266–67, **266**

Camellia, 179–80, **180**

Camellia japonica, 179

Camellia sasanqua, 179, **180**

Campanula, 132–33

Campanula carpatica, 132

Campanula glomerata, 132, **132**

Canada hemlock, 191

Candle larkspur, **142**

Cane blight, 306–7, **307**

Cankerworms, 251, **251**

Canna, 159, **159**

Canna x *generalis*, 159, **159**

Capsicum annuum var. annuum, 42–44, **44**

Care of plants, 347–48

Carolina hemlock, 191, **192**

Carpathian harebell, 132

Carrot rust fly, 251–52, **251**

Carrots, 19–20, **20**

Carya illinoensis, 95–96, **96**

Catnip, **350**

Cauliflower, 21, **21**

Cedar-apple rust, 307–8, **307**

Celery, 21–22, **22**

Chard, 23, **23**

Cherries, 79–81, **80**

Chinch bug, 252–53, **252**

Chinese hibiscus, 193, **193**

Chinese juniper, 200

Chives, 62, **62**

Chrysanthemum, 134–36, **135**

Chrysanthemum x *superbum*, 134, **135**

Citrullus lanatus, 59, **59**

Citrus, 82–83, **83**

Citrus mealybugs, 272

Citrus scab, 308–9, **308**

Citrus sinensis, 83

Cleaning up, 348, **348**

Clematis, 181, **181**

Clematis maximowicziana, 181

Clematis paniculata, 181

Climbing roses, 222

Clustered bellflower, 132, **132**

Cockspur hawthorn, 190

Codling moth, 253–54, **253**

Coleus, 107–8, **107**

Coleus x *hybridus*, 107–8, **107**

Colorado potato beetle, 254–55, **254**

Colorado spruce, 227, **228**

Columbines, 136–37, **137**

Compacted soil, 345

Companion planting, 349–50

Compost, **343**

Compost tea, 362

Coneflower, orange, 151, **151**

Convallaria majalis, 166, **166**

Convergent lady beetles, 354

Coral bells, 137–38, **138**

Coreopsis, 138–39, **139**

Coreopsis lanceolata, 138, **139**

Coreopsis verticillata, 138

Corn, 23–26, **24**

Corn borer
    European, 260–61, **260**
    southwestern, 284–85, **285**

Corn earworm, 255–56, **255**

Corn rootworm, northern, 276–77, **276**

Cornus, 184

Cornus florida, 184, **185**

Cornus kousa, 184

Cornus sericea, 184

Corylus, 87

Corylus maxima, **87**

Cosmos, 108, **109**

Cosmos bipinnatus, **109**

Cotoneaster, 182–83, **182**

Cotoneaster divaricatus, 182

Cotoneaster horizontalis, 182, **182**

Cottonwood, eastern, 216, **217**

Crabapples, 183–84, **183**

Crataegus, 190

Crataegus crus-gallii, 190

Crataegus phaenopyrum, 190, **190**

Creeping juniper, 200, **201**

Crocus, 160, 160

Crocus vernus, 160, **160**

Crookneck squash, **52**

Crowding, 348

Crown gall, 309–10, **309**

Cucumber beetle, spotted, 256–57, **257**

Cucumber beetle, striped, 257–58, **257**

Cucumbers, 27–28, **28**

Cucumis melo, 34–36, **35**

Cucumis sativus, 27–28, **28**

Cucurbita, 51–53

Cucurbita pepo, **52**

Curculio, plum, 280–81, **280**

Curly top, 310, **310**

Currant borer moth, 263

Currants, 84–85, **85**

Cutworms, 258–59, **259**

Cynara scolymus, 10, **10**

Cytospora canker, 310–11, **311**

D

Daffodils, 160–61, **161**

Daucus carota var. sativus, 19–20, **20**

Daylilies, 140, **140**

Delphinium, 141–42, **142**

Delphinium elatum, **142**

Diatomaceous earth, 355–56

Dicentra, 133

Dicentra eximia, **133**

Digitalis purpurea, 143, **143**

Dill, 63, **63**

Diseases, 299–333, **300–333**
   controlling, 353–62
   distribution, 366–67
   preventing, 347–53

Disorders, 334–40, **334–40**

Dodder, 311–12, **312**

Dogwoods, 184–86, **185**

Doublefile viburnum, 230, **231**

Downy mildew, 312–13, **313**

Drainage, 345

Dusts, 360

Dutch crocus, **160**

E

Early blight, 313–14, **313**

Eastern cottonwood, 216, **217**

Eastern red cedar, 200

Eastern white cedar, 170

Eastern white pine, 214

Edging lobelia, 113, **113**

Eggplant, 28–29, **29**

Elm bark beetles, 260, **260**

English ivy, 199, **200**

Euonymus, 186–87, **187**

Euonymus alata, 186, **187**

Euonymus fortunei, 186

European beech, 173, **173**

European corn borer, 260–61, **260**

European cranberrybush viburnum, 230

European larch, **202**

European mountain ash, 210, **211**

European white birch, 174, **175**

F

Fagus, 173–74

Fagus grandifolia, 173

Fagus sylvatica, 173, **173**

Fertilizers, 348

    mixing, 344

    organic, 343–44

Ficus carica, 85–86, **86**

Figs, 85–86, **86**

Filberts, 86, **87**

Fire blight, 314, **314**

Firethorns, 188–89, **188**

Firs, 189–90, **189**

Flatheaded appletree borer, 261–62, **261**

Flea beetles, 262–63, **262**

Floating row covers, 355

Flossflower, 106, **106**

Flowering dogwood, 184, **185**

Flowering tobacco, 109–10, **110**

Flowers

    annuals, 104–25, **106–25**

    bulbs, 157–67, **158–67**

    perennials, 126–56, **128–56**

Fly speck, 331, **331**

Foxglove, 143, **143**

Fragaria x *ananassa*, 100–102, **101**

Fragrant honeysuckle, 197, **197**

Fraxinus, 171

Fraxinus americana, 171

Fraxinus pennsylvanica, 171, **171**

Freezing, 340

Fringed bleeding heart, **133**

Froghoppers, 287, **287**

Fruit borers, 263, **263**

Fruit flies, 264, **264**

Fruits, 68–103, **73–101**

Fruit tree leafroller, 264–65, **264**

Fungi, 299

Fungicides, 362

Fusarium wilt, 315, **315**

G

Garden balsam, 112

Garden mums, 134

Garden phlox, 153

Garlic, 30, **30**

Geranium, 110–11, **111**, 144

Geranium incanum, **144**

Giant onion, 158

Gladiolus, 162–63, **163**

Gladiolus x *hortulanus*, 162–63, **163**

Gleditsia triacanthus, 196

Gleditsia triacanthus var. *inermis*, 196, **196**

Golden oregano, **65**

Gooseberries, 84–85

Grapes, 88–90, **89**

Green ash, 171, **171**

Green lacewings, 354

Gypsophila paniculata, 130

Gypsy moth, 265–66, **265**

H

Hardiness zone map, *368*

Hardy geraniums, 144, **144**

Harebell, Carpathian, 132

Harlequin stink bug, **290**

Hawthorns, 190–91, **190**

Hazelnuts, 86, **87**

Hedera, 199–200

Hedera helix, 199, **200**

Helianthus annuus, 119, **119**

Hemerocallis, 140, **140**

Hemlocks, 191–92, **192**

Herbs, 60–67, **61–67**

Heuchera, 137–38

Heuchera sanguinea, 137, **138**

Hibiscus, 193, **193**

Hibiscus rosa-sinensis, 193

Hibiscus syriacus, 193

Hollies, 194–95, **195**

Hollyhock, 145, **145**

Honeydew melon, 34, **35**

Honeylocust, 196, **196**

Honeysuckles, 197, **197**

Hornworm, tomato, 294, **294**

Horse chestnuts, 178–79

Hostas, 146, **146**

Hover flies, 352

Humus, 343

Hyacinth, 163–64, **164**

Hyacinthus orientalis, 163–64, **164**

Hydrangea, 198, **198**

Hydrangea macrophylla, 198, **198**

Hydrangea paniculata, 198

I

Ilex, 194–95

Ilex crenata, 194

Ilex opaca, 194, **195**

Impatiens, 112, **112**

Impatiens balsamina, 112

Impatiens wallerana, 112, **112**

Imported cabbageworm, 266–67, **266**

Insecticides, 359–62

Insects

beneficial, 351–55, **351–55**

pests (*See* Pests)

Ipomoea batatas, 53–54, **54**

Iris borer, 267–68, **267**

Irises, 147–48, **147**

Iris sibirica, 147

Ivies, 199–200, **200**

J

Japanese anemone, 149, **149**

Japanese barberry, 172, **172**

Japanese beetle, 268, **268**

Japanese holly, 194

Japanese maple, 208, **209**

Japanese privet, 218

Japanese wisteria, 235, **235**

Japanese yew, 236, **236**

Juglans, 102–3

Juglans regia, **103**

June beetles, 269, **269**

Junipers, 200–201, **201**

Juniperus chinensis, 200

Juniperus horizontalis, 200, **201**

Juniperus virginiana, 200

K

Kale, 31, **31**

Kiwis, 91, **91**

Korean barberry, 172

Korean mountain ash, 210

Koreanspice viburnum, 230

Kousa dogwood, 184

L

Lace bugs, 270, **270**

Lacewings, 352, 354

Lactuca sativa, 32–34, **33**

Lady beetles, 352–53, **352**, 354

Lanceleaf coreopsis, 138, **139**

Larches, 202, **202**

Large-flowered clematis, 181

Larix, 202

Larix decidua, **202**

Larkspur, candle, **142**

Late blight, 315–16, **316**

Lawns, 237–40, **237–40**

Leaf blight, pseudomonas, 325, **325**

Leaf blister, 316–17, **316**

Leaf gall, 317–18, **317**

Leafhoppers, 270–71, **270**

Leafminers, 271–72, **271**

Leafroller, fruit tree, 264–65, **264**

Leaf scorch, 335–36

Leaf spot, septoria, 329–30, **329**

Leeks, 31, **31**

Leeks, lily, 158

Lettuce, 32–34, **33**

Leucanthemum x *superbum*, 134, **135**

Ligustrum, 218–19

Ligustrum japonicum, 218

Ligustrum obtusifolium, 218

Ligustrum ovalifolium, **219**

Lilacs, 203–4, **204**

Lilies, 164–65, 165

Lilium, 164–65, **165**

Lily leek, 158

Lily-of-the-valley, 166, **166**

Lindens, 205–6, **206**

Littleleaf linden, 205, **206**

Live oak, 211

Lobelia, 113, **113**

Lobelia erinus, 113, **113**

Lobularia maritima, 120, **120**

London planetree, 229

Lonicera, 197

Lonicera fragrantissima, 197, **197**

Lonicera sempervirens, 197

Lupines, 150, **150**

Lycopersicon esculentum, 55–57, **55**

M

Maggots. *See names of individual maggots*

Magnolia, 206–7, **207**

Magnolia grandiflora, 206

Magnolia x *soulangiana*, 206

Magnolia stellata, 206, **207**

Malus, 71–74, **73**, 183–84

Malus floribunda, **183**

Maples, 208–9, **209**

Marigolds, 114, **114**

    for pest control, 350

May beetles, 269, **269**

Mealybugs, 272–73, **272**

Melanose, 318, **318**

Melons, 34–36, **35**

Mentha, 64

Mentha spicata, **64**

Mexican bean beetle, 273–74, **273**

Meyer lilac, 203

Microcontrols, 357–60

Mildew

    downy, 312–13, **313**

    powdery, 323–24, **324**

Milky disease, 359

Millipedes, 274–75, **274**

Mints, 64, **64**

Mistletoes, 319, **319**

Mites

    pests. *See names of individual mites*

    predatory, 355

Monarda didyma, 131, **131**

Mosaic, 319–20, **320**

Moss pink, 153

Moths. *See names of individual moths*

Mountain ashes, 210–11, **211**

Mugo pine, 214

Muskmelon, 34

N

Narcissus, 160–61, **161**

Nasturtiums, 115, **115**

Navel orangeworm, 274, **275**

Nectarines, 92–93

Needle cast, 320–21, **321**

Neem, 361

Nematodes
    beneficial, 358
    foliar, 321–22, **321**
    pests, 275–76, **275**
    root knot, 322, **322**
New England aster, **128**
Nicotiana alata, 109–10, **110**
Northern corn rootworm,
    276–77, **276**
Norway spruce, 227
Nuts, 68–103, **71–103**

O

Oaks, 211–13, **213**
Ocimum basilicum, 61–62, **61**
Ohio buckeye, 178
Oil sprays, 361
Okra, 36–37, **37**
Onion maggot, 277–78, **277**
Onions, 38–39, **39**
Onions, giant, 158, **158**
Orange, 83
Orange coneflower, 151, **151**
Orangeworm, navel, **274**, 275
Oregano, 65, **65**
Organic matter, 343
Oriental arborvitae, 170, **170**
Oriental fruit moth, 278–79,
    278

Oriental poppy, 155, **155**
Origanum, 65
Origanum vulgare, **65**

P

Paeonia, 152–53
Paeonia lactiflora, **152**
Panicle hydrangea, 198
PAN (*peroxyacyl nitrate*)
    damage, 336–37, **336**
Pansies, 121–22, **122**
Papaver, 155
Papaver orientale, 155, **155**
Paper birch, 174
Parasitic wasps, 351–52
Parsley, 65, **65**
Peaches, 92–93, **93**
Peach leaf curl, 323, **323**
Peachtree borers, 279, **279**
Peanuts, 39–40, **40**
Pear psylla, 279–80, **280**
Pears, 94–95, **95**
Peas, 40–42, **42**
Pecans, 95–96, **96**
Pelargonium, 110–11, **111**
Peonies, 152–53, **152**
Peppers, 42–44, **44**
Perennials, 126–56, **128–56**

Peroxyacyl nitrate (PAN)
    damage, 336–37, **336**
Persian walnut, **103**
Pests, 242–98, **244–98**
    controlling, 353–62
    distribution of, 364–65
    preventing, 347–53
Petroselinum crispum, 65, **65**
Petunia x *hybrida*, 116, **116**
Petunias, 116, **116**
Phaseolus, 12–14
Phaseolus vulgaris, **13**
Pheromone traps, 356
Phlox, 153–54, **154**
Phlox paniculata, 153, **154**
Phlox subulata, 153
pH of soil, *344*
Picea, 227–28
Picea abies, 227
Picea omorika, 227
Picea pungens, 227, **228**
Pillbugs, 285–86, 285
Pines, 214–16, **215**
Pin oak, 211
Pinus, 214–16
Pinus mugo, 214
Pinus strobus, 214
Pinus sylvestris, 214, **215**
Pisum sativum, 40–42, **42**

Planetree, London, 229

Plant hardiness zone map, *368*

Platanus, 229

Platanus x acerifolia, 229

Platanus occidentalis, 229, **229**

Platycladus orientalis, 170, **170**

Plum curculio, 280–81, **280**

Plums, 96–97, **97**

Popcorn, 23

Poplars, 216–18, **217**

Poppies, 155, **155**

Populus, 216–18

Populus alba, 216

Populus deltoides, 216, **217**

Populus tremuloides, 216

Potato beetle, Colorado, 254–55, **254**

Potatoes, 45–47, **46**

Powdery mildew, 323–24, **324**

Praying mantid, 354

Predatory mites, 354

Preventing pests and diseases, 347–53

Privet, **219**

Privets, 218–19

Prunus, 79–81, 96–97, **97**

Prunus amygdalus, 70, **71**

Prunus armeniaca, 74–75, **75**

Prunus avium, **80**

Prunus persica, 92–93, **93**

Pseudomonas leaf blight, 325, **325**

Psylla, pear, 279–80, **280**

Pumpkins, 51–53

Pussy willow, 232

Pyracantha, 188–89

Pyracantha coccinea, 188, **188**

Pyrethrins, 361

Pyrus communis, 94–95, **95**

Q

Quaking aspen, 216

Quercus, 211–13, **213**

Quercus alba, 211

Quercus palustris, 211

Quercus virginiana, 211

R

Radishes, 47–48, **48**

Raphanus sativus, 47–48, **48**

Raspberries, 98–99, **99**

Red horse chestnut, 178

Red maple, 208

Red-osier dogwood, 184

Red stele, 325–26, **325**

Repellent plants, 349

Resistant cultivars, 346

Rheum rhabarbarum, 48–49, **49**

Rhododendron, 220–22, **221**

Rhododendron vireyas, **221**

Rhubarb, 48–49, **49**

Rhubarb chard, **23**

Ribes, 84–85

Ribes fasciculatum, **85**

River birch, 174

Rockspray cotoneaster, 182, **182**

Root knot nematodes, 322, **322**

Root rot, 326–27, **326**

Rosa, 222, **223**

Rosa rugosa, 222

Rose chafer, 281, **281**

Rosemary, 66, **66**

Rose-of-Sharon, 193

Roses, 222–24, **223**

Rosmarinus officinalis, 66, **66**

Rotation of annuals, 348

Rotenone, 359

Row covers, 355

Rubus, 75–77, 98–99

Rubus fruticosus, **76**

Rubus idaeus, **99**

Rudbeckia fulgida, 151, **151**

Rudbeckia hirta, 107, **107**

Rugosa roses, 222

Rust, 327–28, **327**

Rust, cedar-apple, 307–8, **307**

Rust mites, 281–82, **281**

S

Sage, 67, **67**

Sage, scarlet, 117, **117**

Salix, 232–34

Salix alba, 232

Salix babylonica, 232, **233**

Salix caprea, 232

Salt injury, 337–38, **337**

Salvia officinalis, 67, **67**

Salvia splendens, 117, **117**

Sasanqua camellia, 179, **180**

Saucer magnolia, 206

Scab, 328, **328**

Scales

    armored, 282, **282**

    soft, 283, **283**

Scarlet firethorn, 188, **188**

Scarlet sage, 117, **117**

Scotch pine, 214, **215**

Sedums, 156, **156**

Septoria leaf spot, 328–29, **329**

Serbian spruce, 227

Shasta daisy, 134, **135**

Shrubs, 168–232, **172–231**

Siberian iris, 147

Site, planting, 347

Slugs, 283–84, **284**

Smut, 329–30, **330**

Snails, 283–84, **283**

Snapdragon, 118, **118**

Soap, insecticidal, 360–61

Soil, 342–45

    problems, 345

    testing, 344–45

    waterlogged, 339–40, **339**

Solanum melongena var. *esculentum*, 28–29, **29**

Solanum tuberosum, 45–47, **46**

Sooty blotch, 331

Sooty mold, 330–31, **331**

Sorbus, 210–11

Sorbus alniflora, 210

Sorbus aucuparia, 210, **211**

Southern magnolia, 206

Southernwood, **350**

Southwestern corn borer, 284, **285**

Sowbugs, 285–86

Spearmint, **64**

Spider mites, 286–87, **286**

Spinach, 49–50, **50**

Spinacia oleracea, 49–50, **50**

Spiraea x *bumalda*, 225

Spiraea prunifolia, 225, **226**

Spirea, 225–26, **226**

Spirea x *vanhouttei*, 225

Spittlebugs, 287, **287**

Spotted cucumber beetle, 256–57, **257**

Sprays, 360

Spreading cotoneaster, 182

Spruce budworm, 288, **288**

Spruces, 227–28, **228**

Squash, 51–53, **52**

Squash bug, 288–89, **289**

Squash vine borer, 289–90, **289**

Star magnolia, 206, **207**

Stink bugs, 290, **290**

Strawberries, 100–102, **101**

Strawberry root weevil, 291, **291**

Striped cucumber beetle, 257–58, **257**

Sugar maple, 208

Sulfur dioxide injury, 338, **338**

Summer diseases, 331–32

Sunflower, 119, **119**

Sunscald, **334**, 338–39, **339**

Sweet alyssum, 120, **120**

Sweet autumn clematis, 181

Sweet cherry, **80**

Sweet corn, 23

Sweet potatoes, 53–54, **54**

Swiss chard, 23, **23**

Swiss mountain pine, 214

Sycamores, 229–30, **229**

Syringa, 203–4

Syringa meyeri, 203

Syringa vulgaris, 203, **204**

T

Tachinid flies, 352

Tagetes, 114, **114**

Tanglefoot, 357

Tarnished plant bug, 291–92, **291**

Taxus, 236

Taxus cuspidata, 236, **236**

Taxus x *media*, 236

Tent caterpillar, 292, **292**

Thornless honeylocust, 196, **196**

Threadleaf coreopsis, 138

Thrips, 293–94, **293**

Thuja, 170

Thuja occidentalis, 170

Thuja orientalis, 170, **170**

Thyme, 67, **67**

Thymus vulgaris, 67, **67**

Tilia, 205–6

Tilia americana, 205

Tilia cordata, 205, **206**

Tobacco, flowering, 109–10, **110**

Tomatoes, 55–57, **55**

Tomato fruitworm, 255–56, **255**

Tomato hornworm, 294, **294**

Traps, 356–57

Tree bands, 357

Trees, 168–236, **170–236**

Tropaeolum, 115

Tropaeolum majus, **115**

Trumpet honeysuckle, 197

Tsuga, 191–92

Tsuga canadensis, 191

Tsuga caroliniana, 191, **192**

Tulips, 167, **167**

Turnips, 58, **58**

Tussock moths, 294–95, **295**

U

USDA plant hardiness zone map, *368*

V

Vaccinium, 77–79, **78**

Vanhoutte spirea, 225

Vegetables, 8–59, **8–59**

Verbena, 120, **121**

Verbena x *hybrida*, 120, **120**

Verticillium wilt, 332, **332**

Viburnum, 230–32, **231**

Viburnum carlesii, 230

Viburnum opalus, 230

Viburnum plicatum, **231**

Viburnum plicatum var. *tomentosum*, 230

Vines, 168–235, **181–235**

Viola, 121–22

Viola x *wittrockiana*, **122**

Violets, 121–22

Viruses, 299

Vitis, 88–90

Vitis labrusca, **89**

W

Walnuts, 102–3, **103**

Washington hawthorn, 190, **190**

Wasps, 351–52

Waterlogged soil, 339–40, **339**

Watermelon, 59, **59**

Wax begonias, 123–24, **124**

Webworm

    fall, 295, **296**

    garden, 296, **296**

Weeping willow, 232, **233**

Weevils, black vine, 248, **248**

White ash, 171

White fir, 189, **189**

Whiteflies, 297, **297**

White oak, 211

White poplar, 216

White rot, 331

Willows, 233–34, **233**

Wilt

    fusarium, 315, **315**

    verticillium, 332, **332**

Winged euonymus, 186, **187**

Wintercreeper, 186

Winter honeysuckle, 197, **197**

Winter injury, 340, **340**

Wireworms, 298, **298**

Wisteria floribunda, 235, **235**

Wisterias, 235, **235**

Y

Yarrow, 156, **156**

Yellows, 333, **333**

Yews, 236, **236**

Z

Zea mays, 23–26, **24**

Zea mays var. *praecox*, 23

Zea mays var. *rugosa*, 23

Zinnia, 125, **125**

Zinnia elegans, 125, **125**